for Thomas Levenson, Kenneth Manning,
Patrick Riley, and Stephen Smith

IBSEN'S DRAMA

RIGHT ACTION
AND TRAGIC JOY

Theoharis Constantine Theoharis

MACMILLAN

First published by
MACMILLAN PRESS LTD
Houndmills, Basingstoke, Hampshire RG21 6XS
and London
Companies and representatives
throughout the world

ISBN 0-333-68031-6 (hardcover)
ISBN 0-333-77523-6 (softcover)

A catalogue record for this book is available
from the British Library.

10 9 8 7 6 5 4 3 2 1
08 07 06 05 04 03 02 01 00 99

Printed in the United States of America by
Haddon Craftsmen
Bloomsburg, PA

Contents

Acknowledgements vi

Preface vii

Chapter 1. Action in Aristotle 1
   Reality and Change
   Poetics

Chapter 2. Action in Nietzsche 29
   Reality and Change
   Nietzschean *Poetics*

Chapter 3. *Ghosts:* The Sick Will 59

Chapter 4. *Rosmersholm:* Managing the Past 93

Chapter 5. *The Master Builder,* Act 1 135

Chapter 6. *The Master Builder,* Act 2 153

Chapter 7. *The Master Builder,* Act 3 201

Afterword 283

Notes 287

Bibliography 301

Index 307

Acknowledgements

Part of study's recompense is debt, and in this place, as is customary, I ask scholarly forgiveness for mine. This book ranges too far and wide in cultural, intellectual, and literary history for me to make a fair account here of the resources I have inherited. Readers avid to share the Phaeacian bounty heaped on me by the learned should consult the bibliography. Especially pertinent works are recommended in the notes to each chapter. The following deserve special thanks for reading and for improving this, in whole or in part: Louis Galdieri, Rita Goldberg, John Hunt, Barry Jacobs, Alvin Kibel, Thomas Levenson, Geoffrey Pingree, Patrick Riley, Irene Taylor, and Cynthia Griffin Wolff. I am happy to thank John Hunt, of the English Department at the University of Montana, and John Kelly, at St. John's College, Oxford University, for inviting me to develop parts of this book before live audiences. For rich varieties of correction and rescue made by kindness, insight, and laughter, I offer poor tribute in the dedication.

Preface

The joy of life comes differently to different temperaments. Sometimes it appears as blithe, gracious, and unerring talent for making needs pleasures; sometimes it rings out like a summons or alarm that ecstatically moves a mind past all attention to needs. Whatever else Henrik Ibsen was, he was not blithe. From *Brand* (1866) forward all his plays present the joy of life as an imperative that can only be taken up at great cost. The cost in all cases is struggle with duty. Action, throughout the prose cycle Ibsen produced in the second half of his career, discloses that struggle's protean dangers. The ambiguity in Ibsen's subject—the force of joy and the force of duty—also shows up in the design of his plays, especially in their plots. The stories are all Aristotelian sequences in which reversal and recognition reveal controlling causes unknown to deliberating agents. But frequently the revealed cause fails to resolve the conflict between duty and joy. Those balked resolutions indicate that a subversive principle of change is at work in the plots, one that operates against cause-and-effect logic. Beyond all the social radicalism of the plays—their defense of feminism, free thought, and free love; their assault on polluters, dishonest and oppressive employers, whoremongers, and other offenders against the public good—it is their ambiguous defection from cause and effect, the law of common sense, that made Ibsen notorious.

This book explores the ambiguity of Ibsen's dramatic actions and provides a rationale for his defection from the conception of reality and change staged in conventionally organized plots. Ibsen's protagonists suffer the same divided consciousness of moral law that afflicted Saint Paul: the good they would, they do not, but the evil they would not, they do (Rom. 8:19). In their case the stalled good is always some variant of the joy of life, and the evil some compulsive, compromised practice of worldly duty. Separated by many centuries from Aristotle's Athens, Ibsen's Europe nonetheless preserved much of the rational-humanist ethos expressed in that philosopher's works. Its bourgeois culture was, in many ways, a grand elaboration of his substance-based ontology and his ethics, which derived happiness from moderate, purposeful governance of natural and human resources and needs. The dramatic conventions for representing bourgeois life conformed, for the most part, to the analysis made of drama in Aristotle's *Poetics*. When he represented worldly duty, Ibsen did so radically, not only by attacking its contemporary forms, but also by depicting its root conceptions. Since Aristotle provided so many of them, and since he argued that those conceptions were endorsed in the theater, it makes some sense to approach Ibsen's conception of worldly life through Aristotle's. The approach is not source study, or the searching out of influence, but inquiry into Ibsen's ambition to put life's essence onstage. The analysis of Aristotle's view of lived and staged action that constitutes the first chapter of this book is offered to clarify Ibsen's art, to show its radical and historical inquiry into the classical authority preserved in Europe's culture.

The approach Aristotle opens to Ibsen's depiction of worldly duty cannot, except negatively, reveal much about Ibsen's depiction of joy. To take the measure of the other force exerted in Ibsen's ambiguous dramatic actions, this book's second chapter examines Nietzsche's conception of reality and change. A fuller rationale for that procedure can be found at the end of the first section of the second chapter. Here it suffices to say that Nietzsche's departure from substance-based ontology, his repudiation of any ethics that required moderation of impulse, and his view of life's value as ecstasy instead of happiness were all frontal assaults on Europe's Christian and Greek ethical inheritance. In place of that inheritance's corruption of joy Nietzsche offers the world of Dionysus, the celebration of perpetual change and self-affirming impulse.[1] Ibsen presented joy's part in life as radically as he did duty's. When Nietzsche's disengagement from Europe's long-sanctioned understanding of being and doing is brought to bear on the disengagements from stifling worldly duty that Ibsen's heroes and heroines struggle to achieve, the ambiguity of the plots presenting those struggles can be seen for what it is: an assertion of life's undiscovered value.

Chapter 3 opens with a short history of the historical transfigurations of Aristotle's idea of action relevant to Ibsen's plays: Christianity, especially Lutheran Christianity, Cartesian rationalism, the Enlightenment, and the romantic period.[2] The rest of that chapter analyzes the conflict of Aristotelian and Nietzschean action in *Ghosts*. Chapter 4 does the same for *Rosmersholm*. The last three chapters carry the argument forward through *The Master Builder*, which receives unusually lengthy attention for two reasons. First, because Ibsen advanced the compacted thematic and structural ambiguities of *Ghosts* and *Rosmersholm* to a new level of density in *The Master Builder*. Sorting them out takes time. And, second, because *The Master Builder*, more than any other of Ibsen's plays, transfigures and then abandons foundational paradigms in European drama and, by extension, in European culture. Work, love, the family, nature, civilization, and God's dominion over all these fill out one dimension of Solness's story; passion, creativity, and rapture fill out the other. The two dimensions converge and diverge and converge and diverge again repeatedly in the play. That dynamic ambiguity, more than any other in Ibsen's career, rewards philosophical as well as literary analysis and stands as the most important test to the proposition that Aristotle and Nietzsche together give important access to Ibsen's accomplishment.

The philosophical chapters of this book serve a literary-critical purpose; to amplify response to the cultural scope of Ibsen's dramatic experiment. The compact intellectual history they present advances a broader argument: that the world given by rational humanism, while it constitutes the bulk of Ibsen's plays, ultimately claimed none of his allegiance. He depicted worldly life to find the lost life it hides. His allegiance was to joy, and it was to restore that lost name to action that he constructed staged life as he did.

1

Action in Aristotle

The innovative argument of Aristotle's *Poetics* holds that fictions apprehend reality, that they provide a dignified, natural, and intellectually powerful procedure for knowing the substance of human life—action that ends in happiness or unhappiness. Narratives, especially Homer's, had held pride of place as authorities in Greek intellectual life for centuries when Aristotle turned his mind to the problem of what knowledge could be gained in the theater, which produced dramas largely derived from Homeric material. Plato's explicit erasure of Homer's mimetic stories from the realm of knowledge gave Aristotle an occasion and subject for the creation of a new aesthetic in Greek culture. The Trojan epics and the dramas they inspired matter to Aristotle not because *Homer* related them, but because, as supremely well-made *fictions*, they serve as explanations rather than simply as privileged accounts of heroic joy and anguish. Aristotle preserves his civilization's conventional sanction on stories by showing what philosophical principles and activity the convention perpetuates.

By concentrating so intently on the logical integration and unity that plot bestows on the events of a narrative, Aristotle salvaged the theater as a domain in which thinking was not only possible but also essential and excellently accomplished. His frequent insistence that plots are to be judged by standards of necessity and plausibility, the guarantors of scientific and rhetorical validity, and that drama, like any other subject of philosophical inquiry, can be profitably understood by the fourfold analysis of cause—formal, material, efficient, and final—are the most famous and obvious strategies by which *Poetics* promotes the intelligibility of Athens' popular theatrical narratives. This defense also contains a more powerful philosophical case. Narratives are made fictions in Aristotle's treatise, accounts *of* events are transformed into presentations of meaning *in* events, through a philosophical description of the form and content of plays. Actuality, activity, action—the

conceptual names Aristotle gives to plot-structure—are central ideas in the
philosophical analysis of substance and being that Aristotle was engaged in
throughout his career. Aristotle regards knowledge of substantial being as
the preeminent object of philosophy. By importing technical language from
philosophy into advocacy of drama's intellectual value, Aristotle makes his
analysis of aesthetic structure in *Poetics* an instance of his ongoing metaphysical account of reality per se, of substance. Defending drama, Aristotle is not
only rescuing the popular entertainment of Athens from Plato's scorn, but
also arguing for the substantial reality of the phenomenal world that such
entertainment presents.

REALITY AND CHANGE

Reality and *the phenomenal world* are not synonyms in the philosophical systems
Plato and Aristotle articulated but, rather, relational terms. One is discovered
through investigation of the other. For both thinkers reality is always the
object and form of knowledge but not necessarily the content of physical or
mental experience or activity in the world. Change separates the real from
the sensible world; variability distinguishes the knowable from the unknow-
able. Reality is single, unified, invariable, and so the object of rational
investigation, which seeks a stable measure for the maintenance of enduring
intelligence in unenduring circumstances. That the phenomenal world
changes can be known, but what passes away and comes to be in it cannot.
What can be known of the phenomenal world is what endures throughout
the change, and this enduring principle can be known primarily as cause and
substance. Aristotle and Plato split over the meaning of these terms, and over
their relation to the phenomenal world of variability, but not over their
essential place in any explanation of the real. Their ontologies both rely on
relational accounts of what changes to what doesn't; the difference lies in
how each construes the relation, what distance each places between philosophical and worldly reality, and how that distance is closed through
reasoning from one to the other.

For Plato reality exists outside the phenomenal realm and is made up of
permanently enduring intelligible essences called forms. The sensible world
of bodies and motion is an unstable and perpetually agitated collection of
evanescent items and occasions related to forms as muddied grooves are to
wheels that passed over them long ago, or as mono reception is to stereo
broadcasting. In the first metaphorical account physical existence is a distorted replica of an absent prototype; in the second physical experience is a

diminished participation in an operating but not fully accessible source of being. The technical terms for these relations are *mimesis*, imitation in the sense of counterfeit, and *methexis*, or participation. Both relations give the phenomenal world the feel of reality without bringing substantial being, the really real, the forms, out of their transcendent stasis.

The twinned concepts of being and seeming real support a parallel doubling in Plato's understanding of knowledge. The real world of forms is known by pure reason operating on abstractions only; the almost real world of phenomena, in which bodies and motions appear and disappear, in which sense impressions provide matter for mental activity, is never known, but construed as opinion or judgment. Knowledge, technically called *episteme*, is the most valuable and essential rational activity of human beings; opinion and judgment, technically *doxa*, having contingency for their object, can never be more than contingently rational. Plato offers three strategies for moving from the world of phenomena to the world of forms.

The mind approaches substantial being and the objects of knowledge through memory, through longing, or through systematic questioning. If forms are nowhere present in the phenomenal world, knowledge of them must somehow be a departure from examination of phenomena. Plato describes one kind of departure when he argues that the power to reason is inherited from a previous life, during which the reasoning soul apprehended the forms directly, without the corrupting mediation of physical existence. That apprehension, and not sensation or common opinion, provides reason with its proper objects and capacities. Thinking about reality is remembering what you have always known, not developing newly acquired understanding. This approach is called *anamnesis*.

Plato's other two strategic departures from phenomena toward forms do not shun sensation as a source of knowledge but, instead, make it a minimal first condition of thought. Longing, which starts in sexual admiration and appetite, brings the reasoning soul into a progressively disembodied joyful awareness of the formal world, the realm urging on and finally satisfying all longing. This increase of reason's grasp of reality Plato names "eros." Systematic questioning to arrive at definition, identification of knowledge's formal objects and procedures, starts with the information provided by sensation and by common opinions about the reality phenomena present and tests the validity of that information. This testing, technically "dialectic," seeks to discover unchanging reality through identifying unflawed argumentation. The problem calling for perfection of argumentation, the subject of dialectic inquiry, is again a problem of relation: What logical account can be given of the connection between seeming and being, between the changing phenomenal and unchanging formal worlds? What conceptual structure constitutes and accounts for the structure of the forms that together make up or manifest pure knowledge and being? In all three cases, reality is not simply given to people; they must seek it out, and they must seek it out at a very great distance, in the best cases at a limitless remove from the world of phenomenal change.

Sensible bodies and motions, and their relations, display nothing more than their poverty to the trained Platonic eye. Although the changes bringing the seeming world into and out of its seeming existence are systematically accounted for in Plato's philosophy, although he elaborates complex theories of nature's constitutive elements and their susceptibility to variation, the most important thing to be understood in these accounts is the world's inadequacy as an object of thought.[1] Change occurs because nature cannot enact the reality of the forms that have brought it into being. The best attention to nature is attention that reasons from it to the world of forms.

But mimetic narrative, recited or enacted, doesn't move inductively from the world of change to the world of truth; rather, it presents human experience of nature's inadequacy as an object worthy in itself of moral, emotional, and intellectual attention. Fiction convinces people that the world's mutability merits passionate outcry or raucous approbation. Whereas eros and dialectic draw reason to the absent presence of the forms in nature, and so turn people toward the real, fiction counterfeits order in its narrative sequences and other structural devices, damaging the duped by offering them false ideas derived from false facts. In either case, for Plato, stories endanger people already endangered by the almost real. Safety lies in knowing how unworthy the world is in comparison to the transcendent realm flickering in it and summoning the lovers of the real. Drama turns the mind fully to an utterly insufficient object and promises full satisfaction for passionate engagement with nothing. Two millennia later Nietzsche and his contemporaries were to turn this engagement with vacant, changing appearance into the heroic end of consciousness, and so engender much of modern intellectual and artistic life. But for Plato nothing will come of nothing, and drama, presenting nothing in answer to reason's search for knowledge, belongs nowhere in the mental or physical environment of reasonable, which is to say human, beings.[2]

Like Nietzsche, Aristotle opposes Plato's condemnation of worldly experience, his view of it as merely vacant, changing appearance. Nietzsche finds delirium, fatalism, and, most important, self-dramatizing will in the mind's collision with the void around which phenomena veer and collide. Aristotle finds no void as the source of phenomenal change, and no hinting transcendence—in delirium, willing, or cool Platonic reasoning—to the really real in the seeming bodies and motions in nature. Like Plato, he requires that knowledge have stable objects and be invariable, but he finds those objects in nature and sees them organizing the changes of the sensible world. Forms are not absent presence in Aristotle's philosophy, or states of being, as they are in Plato's, but ongoing activities, the manifest energy of reality, the principles of development in nature and human experience. Most significantly, the forms that make nature and humanity real belong to the phenomenal world and are known by observation in that world, not through inductive ascent to any transcendent realm.

Recited or enacted stories present the forms of human happiness and unhappiness, and the passage from one state to the other, to the moral attention of the audience. Because Aristotle holds these forms of life to be the reason for life, drama has special significance in his thinking. Showing life lived well and badly, dramatic structure makes the substance of human reality knowable and, to those with eyes to see and ears to hear it, known. When Aristotle accounts for the continuity and meaning of change in nature, he uses the four-cause argument and an argument relating substance to possible and actual being. He brings elements from both these arguments into play in his analysis of how dramatists portray change. To see why plays do not subvert but, rather, enhance knowledge of the real, some attention must be paid to this philosophical context of Aristotle's *Poetics*.

Change occurs when one opposite replaces another in an enduring subject. When opposites oust each other they bring the enduring subject into some newly organized state. Aristotle's philosophy proliferates categories and taxonomical relations to account for this idea of change, for this concept of the order inherent in the world of becoming: substance, quality, quantity, location, and the genus/species, identity/difference relations, and so on. The whole astonishing array of argumentation and recursive definition articulates what Aristotle understood to be the first experience of philosophy: wonder. The most wondrous experience, the event leading amazed admiration through fear to the curiosity that ends in knowledge, is nature's endurance through change, its stable persistence through incessant mutation and reversal.

Knowing, for Aristotle, means being able to give a systematic rational account, an explanation, of a wonder. This can be done by citing and analyzing the known wonder's cause, or by constructing a syllogism, which, argued validly from premise to conclusion, shows the logical conditions of the wonder's existence. Aristotle generally prefers descriptive explanation by citation of cause and argues that, in the case of change, it is the only available explanation.[3] *Cause* here must be distinguished from the modern sense of the word, the sense that inevitably attaches *effect* to complete the definition. Aristotle's *cause* is not the first half of a logical or physical sequence, not so much *cause* as *because*.[4] More than anything it means "reason," the way a child uses that word when asking about the reason for rain or school or grass. Aristotle gives four reasons for change: formal, material, efficient, and final. They are not four distinct events but, instead, four modes for understanding one event: the emergence or recession of some principle of organization in the phenomenal world.

Aristotle's conceptual name for the phenomenal world considered apart from human deliberation is nature. Nature rests or moves, endures or changes, alone, according to innate principles known through observation. Human deliberation acting to induce motion or change in phenomena for a desired end is artifice, or skill. The Greek term is *techne*. Humans being natural, artifice is a special case of nature's innate principle of self-maintenance. Whereas natural change operates invariably—trees never becoming something other than trees—artifice can combine and transmute innately changing phenomena according to the vast variety of conscious purposes discovered in human reason. Having observed the various properties of trees in various circumstances, skilled people can make trees tables, boats, pipes, gliders. Matching reason's unlimited invention to nature's immutable order, discovering the range and limit of intentional productivity, people become mindful. Simultaneously, the world becomes intelligible. Aristotle presents this striving for balance in many different ways. Ethics, politics, physics, logic, rhetoric, zoology, and poetics, to name some, are all systematic accounts of people placing themselves in nature's changes. These accounts all present change, both natural and skilled, as known through understanding of formal, material, efficient, and final cause.

Phenomenal reality presents itself as composite to Aristotle. Bodies and motions are simultaneously understood as formal and material. Form (*eidos*) is intelligible structure in events or bodies. The essence, the definitive function in and of any object of inquiry, form is primary reality for Aristotle, as for Plato. Shape and ongoing creative activity, form presents substantial reality, "what it is to be" an x, to the understanding. Form acts in and on matter, the substratum out of which forms come to be.

Matter, technically *hyle*, is not directly apprehended by the senses or the intellect; it is not extension or magnitude, but, rather, the capacity to receive and sustain the particular extension or magnitude or direction enacted by some form. There are different kinds of matter for different kinds of change. The matter of motion, not subject to generation or decay, is space, more precisely location; the form of motion is propulsion, falling, circling, and so forth. The matter of bodies and natural artifacts has four abstract conditions: lightness, heaviness, dryness, and moisture. From these qualities Aristotle derives the sensible composites air, earth, fire, and water, the *stoicheia* or elements through which nature makes itself amenable to form. Physical composites change when these elemental qualities activate their innate principles of rest or motion.[5] Aside from development and skill, bodies change through the deprivation or acquisition of some combination of these elements. Form imparts genus and species and further descending orders of universality and generality to phenomena (tables, red tables, Italian red tables); matter imparts particularity and further ascendent orders of individuality (a man's table, Puccini's table, the desk on which Puccini composed *La Bohème* [1896]). The composition of phenomenal reality in Aristotle's thinking is form all the way down and matter all the way up to concrete appearance.

Form and matter exist as mutually cooperative powers, with form as the power to act and matter as the power acted on. Together they make up the self-sustaining dynamism of actuality and potentiality. Actual and potential states can manifest themselves simultaneously, or one item of the pair can be latent while the other is manifest. In natural development matter's potential to display all the forms of an organism acts over time as the organism grows to maturity and declines into death—hair appears and disappears, the timbre of the voice changes at different ages, and so forth. In artificial changes matter's potential to display various invented forms is enacted in production, which adds forms to already existing substances. Production, so conceived, is not development of potentiality, but construction of it, a limitation rather than a fulfillment of matter.

This is the heart of the matter: for Aristotle mental life consists in adjusting intentional control of artifacts and nature to the mutable relations of actual and potential reality. Finding and living according to the mean that brings form out of matter in development, and to it in construction, people find knowledge and happiness. Failing to do so leaves them ignorant and anguished. For Aristotle actual and possible states of being, form and matter, manifest themselves in their greatest complexity and value when they operate in human life. *Poetics* makes so much of the formal dimension of theatrical experience, the plot, because Aristotle conceived of it as the portrayal of humanity's formal, and therefore essential, activity: being alive in a good or bad way in the world of changes.

The forms that come and go in any enduring material condition do not arise from nothing. Plato, correctly deducing their logical distinction from phenomenal reality—forms don't change; the appearing world does nothing

else—concluded, incorrectly in Aristotle's judgment, that the logical separation indicated the absence of forms from the world. Aristotle argues that
forms in natural development are immanent in the changing body or motion
and that forms in skilled transformation of nature are imparted to matter from
the intelligence of the craftsman. The efficient cause is the acting maker of
any change, the imparter or eliminator of form in matter: the hands of the
sculptor in artifice; the immediate source of motion or rest (wheels or nails);
and the physiological and physical systems functioning in nature (teeth for
eating, and the like).[6]

Aristotle calls final form (*telos*) the end or purpose of a change, that for
the sake of which the change occurs. The end of skilled change is some
function in human life: tables are made for writing; plays are written and
performed to move the audience, to enact in them that all-important intellectual and moral change called catharsis. In skilled change the purpose is
completely present as soon as the artifact is completed; the end of the change
is entirely manifest in the artifact. The final cause exists at the beginning and
the end of skilled change, first as an actual form in the craftsman's mind and
a possible form in the material to be changed and, second, after the making,
as a realization of the material's potential, as a functioning table or play.
Actual form governs the transition from start to finish. In this sense final and
formal cause are not different events but, rather, different descriptions of the
same event, namely the knowable emergence of a form functioning in the
phenomenal world. The same holds in natural change, in which the final
cause of all phenomenal activity is formal continuity, the ordered, knowable
replication and development of motion and appearance.

In living creatures final form is not only an achieved state, but also an
activity, a gradual development that provides for a creature's full functioning
in the environment. The purpose of any change in a living creature, the final
cause of all its actions, is attaining and preserving maturity, the full functioning of a creature's form. Thus, the purpose of molting in birds is the
emergence of new feathers, whose purpose is the maintenance of the capacity
for flight, whose purpose is getting food and fleeing predators, all for the
preservation of the bird's form, which is the molting of feathers to achieve
flight to preserve life. Nature's purpose is nothing else but continuing itself,
achieving and preserving its myriad, systematic maturities.

As in artifice, actual forms govern the progress from possibility to
actuality, from youth to maturity in living creatures' changes. The oak is in
the acorn, the adult in the child, imparted through generation and developed
by innately timed transformations. These are not mechanical processes or
random fluctuations caused by matter's imperfect capacity to receive separate

form, as phenomenal changes were to Plato, but knowable actions, whose final cause is nature's regular proliferation of innate form. In the transposition of actual form from parent to child, or motion to motion, and the developing emergence of actual form in living creatures, phenomenal reality makes its substantial being known. Change is by form, according to form, and for form in nature. In the phenomenal realm substance becomes what it is and makes itself known, purposefully, in form.

The opposites replacing each other in change are always forms. This replacement, observed intelligently, makes the substantial being of phenomenal reality knowable. Intelligence, in this case, means understanding how certain actions arise, continue, and cease under certain possible conditions. The crucial idea here is that phenomenal reality exists in constant actions. Knowing the world means knowing how everything is always busy becoming what it already is. Nietzsche will make much of this relation, much that Aristotle would have found bizarre if he granted it was intelligible at all. The conception of reality as substance in action has crucial significance for *Poetics*, and for the dramatic and philosophical traditions that have maintained and transformed Aristotle's thinking about the relation of art to reality, traditions still formative for contemporary thinkers and artists.

The four-cause argument in *Physics* accounts for the existence of change in the phenomenal world. *Metaphysics* seeks to account for existence per se, for the underlying, atomistic order of reality, the being that supports phenomenal change. In this notoriously difficult late work Aristotle presents a philosophical account of what it means to say something *is*. *Is* denotes the irreducible reality of something. Reality being essentially intellectual for Aristotle, something known instead of merely perceived or immediately experienced, the irreducibly real is also the irreducibly true, the independent and basic object of thought. Aristotle calls this foundation of being and thinking "substance," *ousia*.

Substance embodies essence in Aristotle's thought. Because *essence* means definition, or rational formula, substance and form are equivalent. To say most immediately what anything is, is to name its form, the principle of order making and keeping it real. So far we are logically in Plato's world, in which the real is purely and abstractly formal. The difference comes in Aristotle's assertion that essences are not separable from phenomena, not distinct in fact as they are in thought. In one explanation of substance Aristotle identifies essence and existence by examining the logical conditions of predication. In another he shows that substance is in a sense composite—materially formal—by refining the conception of form as actual and matter as possible being. This second argument bears most immediately on Aristotle's topic in

Poetics and on mine in this study: how plays make sense of life's transition from possible to actual happiness or misery.[7]

In Plato's thinking, knowing means looking outside the changes of the phenomenal realm to their imperfectly directed goal: the actively real formal world. Phenomenal experience never exceeds possible, incomplete being in this account. In Aristotle's thinking, knowing means finding out which of the world's changes are ends in themselves, activities, and which are instrumental or incomplete motions, processes. This distinction between *kinesis* (motion, process) and *energeia* (activity, actualization, realization) and between the two different kinds of *dunamies* (possibilities) sustaining each are the crucial arguments by which Aristotle preserves reality's intellectual status without rarifying it into Platonic essence. By arguing that substance is embodied essence, Aristotle shows that, in the irreducible order of reality, actual and possible being occur simultaneously; form and matter happen together. In the ascending hierarchy of composite phenomena this principle of unity holds. In analysis of physics or politics or ethics or biology—or plays—an account of substance shows how in each area of inquiry concrete functioning things make definitions true.

Aristotle separates substance into three types: sensible and eternal (heavenly bodies); sensible and impermanent (bodies in the sublunary phenomenal world); and unchanging activity.[8] In the first and last category all bodies and motions are ends in themselves. The second category, which includes people and their concerns, presents the distinction between process and activity. The sciences of living well—ethics, politics, poetics—study and explain the difference between independent, self-sustaining goods and dependent, contingent ones. Actual and possible being always occur together, form is always matter, in heaven and in the unchanging activity of the mind of God, the first mover, who keeps everything else active. The oscillating emergence and withdrawal of form in natural and artificial substance, the fluctuating disclosure of reality over time in human affairs, lead Aristotle to refine the relation between the twinned pairs defining substance: potency/act and matter/form.

In the world of becoming, being acts in two ways: things change, they acquire and lose formal characteristics and capacities; and things alternately manifest or withhold enduring formal characteristics and capacities, they enact dispositions or hold them in reserve. Potency (*dunameis*) is the power something has to be other than it is either through transformation or through manifesting an innate, enduring function. Act (*energeia*) is the form power takes, the principle at work keeping something busy being what at any and all moments it is. Change is one kind of activity, and manifesting dispositions is another kind of activity. In transformations possibility is directed to an end other than itself and ceases once that end is achieved. In functioning dispositions possibility is its own end and is maintained in that end's achievement.

Examples: the possibility of reaching a destination in any particular act of walking exists only until the destination is reached. Achieving the end of this activity means exchanging one condition for another; the possibility of arrival vanishes upon actual arrival. Physical increase, artificial construction, production of various sorts are all, like going somewhere, activities without an end in themselves, *ateles* in Greek. Such activity is what Aristotle has in mind when he discusses kinesis, (motion or process). Possible seeing or thinking or walking (considered apart from any destination) is not directed to any end outside its own actualization in the functioning seer or thinker or walker and is maintained throughout that functioning. At all the moments one is actively seeing one is also able to see, likewise for thinking or walking or living well or badly.

Being able to see is identical to seeing, not because the disposition is always enacted but because, when it is enacted, the capacity has no other end than itself, no other purpose than its own realization. Potential arrival at *x* destination is never identical to actual arrival: one is not both able to arrive and finished walking at the same time. Rather, the arrival ousts the possibility of coming. The act of seeing or thinking or living well or badly does not oust possible seeing or thinking or living from agents to make room for an actual condition in them, as is the case in kinetic actions, processes, or productions. Nor is seeing or thinking or living well or badly an end approached through a self-canceling sequential unfolding of possibilities preparatory to such actions—the other way possibility vanishes upon actualization in the case of kinesis. The power to think or see or be happy or miserable functions completely and continuously and for its own sake in any thinking or seeing or happiness or misery. Thus action, or energeia, consists in fulfillment or completion rather than consumption of possibility.

This dual sense of possibility allows Aristotle to argue that essence is embodied in substance, that form is mattered or matter formed at the atomistic level of being, that in analysis of substance any "this" is simultaneously some "what." The four-cause analysis of change defines matter as the possibility to receive some form and defines form as the principle imposing sensible and intelligible structure on potency, enacting matter in some particular way. To avoid the Platonic separation of matter and form, and so undo the relational theory of being and knowledge that makes thinking eros or dialectic or *anamnesis*, Aristotle argues that matter and form in substance are not related as possible and actual being are in kinesis but, instead, as they are in energeia. In substance the power that is and the power that can be something exist in the same place at the same time.

In phenomenal change these powers alternate; thus, thinking about phenomenal change is thinking about how what something is came to be and how it might cease, or, to put it another way, thinking about conditions under which the real appears. Thinking about substance per se is not thinking about conditions of the real, but thinking about what the conditions are for, why they exist, what they manifest. Knowledge of substance is knowledge of the irreducible reality of all four causes. The actuality from which these causes take their existence is substance—not as substratum, neither underlying possibility nor underlying essence, but as originating action. Thus, phenomenal change presents reality itself to thought when that change is conceived as a condition of substance, as a species of action. In nature and humanity both incomplete activity, kinesis, and self-fulfillment, energeia, are directed to and by those indwelling forms that make the perishable realm real, to and by a kind of substance that is what it is by acting.

Aristotle has the identity of form and substance in mind when he writes in *Metaphysics* IX, 1048b6-8 "But all things are not said in the *same sense* to exist actually . . . for some are [actual] as movement to potentiality, and the others as substance to some sort of matter."[9] Actual existences that are movement or process extinguish themselves in coming to be, since their goal is outside themselves. Actual existences that are activities enact self-contained ends, they make themselves real, and in this sense are form relative to matter. In substance what a thing is made from (matter) and what it is made by (form) are identical, simultaneous manifestations of reciprocal powers to be. There is no substratum that keeps substance actively what it is; rather, substance is the actuality that makes all further predication, development, or alteration possible. Change is not generation of substance or approximation of a separate unchanging substance but activity in an already real substance, either alteration or enhancement of something busy being what it is. This idea of substance as activity organizes Aristotle's analysis of drama in *Poetics*, in which substance and activity are presented to human intelligence in theatrical action, *praxis*, whose logic is identical to that of substantial activity, energeia.

An example: a person is ensouled matter in Aristotle's thinking. Flesh and blood organically structured by an activity that moves, perceives, desires, self-replicates, and reasons; this is the substance *human being*. The activity does not happen apart from the matter, nor does organic flesh and blood happen apart from soul, the active principle making matter human.

Just as sharpness does not exist apart from a knife blade, so the essence, the form of a person, does not exist apart from the living being. To know what a human is per se, or essentially, is not to know a definition, or an immaterially formal power, but to know a particular case, to know an actual human carrying out self-canceling and self-sustaining actions.[10] Drama makes those actions known in a privileged and valuable way, as far as Aristotle is concerned.

Being itself, the real, in this view, is nothing more or less than instances of substance, occasions of matter and form manifesting themselves simultaneously in irreducible complex unity. The logic governing this unified appearance of matter and form in substance is the same logic governing the simultaneous mutual realization of potency and act in activities such as seeing or thinking or living well or badly. Substance is form as active principle of organization, as knowable structure, and substance is the matter organized by active principle. This unity Aristotle offers against Plato's argument that being and becoming are divided. The knowable is always some actively existing phenomenal substance in Aristotle's thought, and change is not evidence of chaos, not discontinuous flux, but one activity of the real, one function of substance.

Plato's attack on drama charged the theater with a double falsification of being—counterfeiting already counterfeit entities. The people presented in plays, the characters of the drama, are bad copies. Their actions, the changes plays present as meaningful examples of moral conduct, are not simulacra, not counterfeits of the real meaning of change, since change has no real meaning for Plato, but pure deceit, dissimulation with no referential status at all. Pretending to be something that does or could exist isn't bad enough for plays. They also pretend to be something that does not and could not exist, all the while offering themselves as authorities for moral life.

I have undertaken this analysis of substance, the fourfold cause of change, and their relation, to show how Aristotle answers the graver charge that change cannot manifest the real. With a definition of reality as action, as activity established, the argument can now turn to Aristotle's account in *Poetics* of how the action of a play is an instance of the action that reality is. The analysis of action and its imitation in plot is the most important part of Aristotle's theory of drama and constitutes not only another philosophical defense of the substantial reality of phenomenal change, but an answer to the charge of counterfeiting as well. Arguing that imitation, or portrayal of people on the stage, has its origin in our intellectual nature, Aristotle can hold that playmaking and playgoing are crucial strategies for knowing and enacting the possibilities for happiness that phenomenal change presents to

purposeful people. Since well-being is the all-inclusive end of human life—
the highest organization of substance in nature, according to Aristotle, and
some others—strategies for achieving it are of the utmost value. Seeing what
it is to be human in the theater is thus an end in itself, a substantial function
enhancing being itself as it enhances us.

POETICS

Intellectual life divides into arts and sciences in Aristotle's thought: *techne*, craft
or skilled production, and *episteme*, organized bodies of knowledge. Arts are
further divided into practical and productive categories. The skills of building,
healing, and playmaking are productive arts, *poetike*. The arts of behaving well,
prudently discerning the distinction of means and ends in ethical life, and
preserving civilized activity in politics are *praktike*, concerned with deeds, not
products. Though Aristotle at times conceives both these skills as subsets of
knowledge, he normally reserves the term *episteme*, or science, for those subjects
he considers theoretical: mathematics, theology, and physics.[11]

Music, dance, painting, sculpture, and literature—primarily lyric, epic,
and dramatic poetry—all result from *mimesis*, which has various translations,
but in this analytic context means portrayal or representation. Portrayal
involves structuring one substance so that it displays the form of some other
substance, giving a board the shape of a bird, giving melody and dance the
motion of a sentiment, giving the semantic and syntactic organization of
language the causal rhythm of intentional action in phenomenal contingency. This giving of form is construction, a learned and teachable matching
of some matter's potential to some other matter's actual state.

All arts bestow new form on an existing substance through construction
of some kind. Mimetic construction differs from other kinds of creation
primarily because it has an intellectual component that simple making does
not. Portrayal involves resemblance of two different things. The end of this
art lies in the artist and audience matching the made thing against its
prototype. Hence, Aristotle's repeated insistence that the characters in plays
must be recognizably and appropriately matched to people who do or could
exist and his insistence that their deeds must display necessary or plausible
motivation and logical sequence. Such standards are irrelevant to chair-
making, or medicine, in which the result of production needs to be functional
instead of verisimilar or plausible. One isn't concerned to know whether a
chair or mended arm accurately or pleasantly portrays the prototype by
which its maker brought it into being; one sits or plays tennis. The distinction

between creative and productive results bears powerfully on Aristotle's analysis of drama, especially on his argument that plays present a substantial activity of preeminent value—people living well or badly by deliberate pursuit of intelligible ends. His conception of mimesis makes knowledge of essence both the matter and form of theatrical representation and so provides ground for the strong claim that plays make being itself known.

This strong claim is further justified by Aristotle's description of mimesis as humanity's original intellectual activity. Arguing that poetry has natural origins in people's innate miming and in their pleasure in seeing mimesis, Aristotle prepares the ground for treating poetry not only as a productive art but as an organism, one with an evolutionary history and corporeal ontology. His language falls somewhere between analogy and metaphor, with poetry repeatedly positioned as an activity displaying the logic that governs animal, especially human, life. That poetry operates with the logic of life itself matters most when Aristotle defines action as the end of drama, the formal and final cause. In chapter 4 the argument explicitly controls Aristotle's evolutionary history of drama and underlies his observation that mimesis, pretending and portrayal, occurs as a natural propensity in people from childhood onward. Pretending is the first stage of understanding, he writes, the first way children know. Read with the opening statement of *Metaphysics* in mind—that all men desire by nature to understand—this conception of mimesis as the beginning of mental life makes dramatic activity an essential, substantive function not only of humanity, but also of nature. Insofar as people manifest the highest values of nature by displaying phenomenal reality's greatest formal achievement, drama, springing from a natural human function, perfects nature.[12] Enhancing the natural desire for understanding, mimesis, especially drama, also has special access to the most important content of understanding. In chapter 9, when Aristotle compares philosophy, history, and poetry as ways of knowing universal principles governing human action, poetry emerges as preeminent, because it most effectively shows the union of general and particular, idea and fact.

It must be the case then that miming is not only the beginning of knowing, something infants do, but an intellectual function continued through the most serious adulthood. Although Aristotle does not make the case, a clear analogy presents itself linking the evolution of drama into its adult form and the development of miming into thinking in people's intellectual lives. Such a case is implied in Aristotle's second derivation of poetry from natural cause in chapter 4: his observation that people take immediate intellectual pleasure in objects of mimesis throughout their lives. This last fact of mental life explains how people tolerate aesthetic representations of

objects such as corpses that are revolting when presented in life. As Aristotle
sees the matter, mimesis makes thinking that might be repugnant, and so
shunned in life, pleasant and therefore desired in art. An enhancement of
nature, of humanity, a unique access to nature's most desired end—knowledge and knowing as substantive activity—mimesis means much to Aristotle.
An especially pleasant procedure for knowing, portrayal's substantive value
lies in what it makes known: action, the substance of human life and, in a
special sense, of being itself.

The argument of *Poetics* focuses most powerfully on the relation of
action and plot. Defining tragedy in chapter 6, Aristotle writes, "Tragedy,
then, is a representation of an action which is serious, complete, and of a
certain magnitude—in language that is garnished in various forms in its
different parts—in the mode of dramatic enactment, not narrative—and
through the arousal of pity and fear effecting the *katharsis* of such emotions"
(*P*, chap. 6, 37). Seriousness, completeness, and magnitude all apply to the
action, or praxis, and to its representation, the plot (*muthos*). These qualities,
together with the criteria of necessary or probable cause, are the substance
of Aristotle's philosophical claims for drama's value as knowledge. In analysis
of these terms frequent analogical reference is made to concepts from
physics, ethics, psychology, and metaphysics. The previous synoptic analysis of *energeia, kinesis, dunameis, eidos,* and *byle* as elements of Aristotle's
metaphysical account of substance and change should give these references
their full intellectual value and help readers to understand how much more
than aesthetics is at stake in Aristotle's thinking about action and feeling in
the theater.

Serious, *spoudaios*, refers both to an action's social and ethical preemi-
nence and is the least complex of the terms. The action must be performed
by an important person and concern long-term chances and plans bearing
on happiness or anguish. The term belongs more to analysis of character, the
agent of action, and will take a larger place in subsequent analysis of that
dramatic element. Completeness, present in the plot's unity, and magnitude
are the most immediately significant criteria for action, the terms by which
Aristotle most consistently makes drama a highly achieved intellectual
procedure. Clarification of their meaning requires an account of praxis and
its relation to *muthos*, since these are the object and immediate structure of
representation in the theater.

Praxis, action, refers in *Poetics* not to any human behavior, but, rather,
to those deeds that qualify as ethical, those deeds that make men happy or
unhappy. As he puts it in chapter 6: "tragedy is a representation not of people
as such but of actions and life, and both happiness and unhappiness rest on

action. The goal is a certain activity, not a qualitative state; and while men do have certain qualities by virtue of their character, it is in their actions that they achieve, or fail to achieve, happiness" (*P*, chap. 6, 37). Deeds qualify as ethical when they proceed from choice, *proairesis*, which Aristotle defines as "deliberate desire of things in our own power."[13] Reason sees and desires the good; choice discovers means of achieving the good end. Action, in this case, means reasoned choice of means in pursuit of some desired good.

Embedded in this linking of activity and happiness is a rejection of the Socratic position, adopted by Plato, which held happiness to be a matter purely of knowledge. Aristotle's insistence that behavior in worldly circumstance defines happiness, and so defines man's substantial being, makes ethical life and people's achievement of their own nature subject to contingency, the very quality Plato sought to remove from any definition of the good life in the frequent occasions when he has Socrates argue that a good man cannot be made unhappy by the world.[14] Shifting ethics from a separable intellectual realm into the phenomenal world of change, Aristotle gives drama the most substantial object of mimesis it could have: people becoming what they are, acting through and into the unity of reason and nature.

Praxis also has a metaphysical meaning already presented in the previous distinction between *kinesis* and *energeia*, motion and activity. In this context action refers to being at work, the realization of the agent's substance. An *ergon*, a deed, can be either production or activity; when it is production the reality of the act lies in the thing made, when activity in the agent. The distinction is put in the following way in *Metaphysics*: "Where, then, the result is something apart from the exercise, the actuality is in the thing that is being made, e.g. the act of building is in the thing that is being built . . . but when there is no product apart from the actuality, the actuality is in the agents, e.g. the act of seeing is in the seeing subject . . . and the life is in the soul (and therefore well-being [*eudaimonia*, happiness] also; for it is a certain kind of life)" (*M*, 1659). Activity so conceived names an agent's essential function, what an actor does rather than what happens to the actor. Aristotle sees humanity's essential function, happiness, as a complex unity of what is done and what happens in a life, but argues that what happens depends in a crucial way on what is done. Drama presents that relation when it shows how an inadequacy in action, which Aristotle names *hamartia*, recasts the logic of cause and effect and leaves an agent ruined by the contingencies that were to be mastered through enacting some intention.[15]

Happiness being an activity, the best activity of the soul, intentions grounded in it must also be activities. *Nicomachean Ethics* puts the case as follows: "Now if the function of man is an activity of soul in accordance with, or not without, rational principle . . . and we state the function of man to be a certain kind of life, and this to be an activity or actions of the soul implying a rational principle, and the function of a good man to be the good and noble performance of these . . . human good turns out to be activity of soul in conformity with excellence" (*NE*, 1735). The rational principle governing a series of deeds, the cause-and -effect logic that makes sequential events seamless moments in a substantial function, is the action that Aristotle cites as the object of mimesis in a drama. When this principle is intentional organization of the world of circumstance to enact happiness, man's substance is portrayed, the theater presents, as *Nicomachean Ethics* puts the matter, "activity of the soul in conformity with excellence." The soul being humanity's substance, and humanity being phenomenal creation's best being, drama presents the acme of being in its most essential reality when it shows people acting out their well-being.

Substance is always embodied in Aristotle's thinking, and dramatic substance is no exception. The matter of a play and the form, the inseparable unity that is the irreducible reality of a drama, is the realization of an action in deeds, the plot. The deeds organized in a plot are not imperfect images of a separable intellectual reality, faulty indicators of an inaccessible world of being that playwrights ineptly forge, but, rather, the essence of mimesis, both the means and ends of drama. As Aristotle puts it: "the plot structure is the first-principle and, so to speak, the soul of tragedy" (*P*, chap. 6, 38). Reference to first principles brings the language of substance and metaphysics into aesthetics; reference to the soul sets the argument in terms of psychology and natural science. These are not illustrative metaphors as much as they are argumentative enhancements of the philosophical value of the theater. That plots present knowledge when they present causal sequence, that stories are principles in action, and not separable and arbitrary figuring of behavior, is the crucial point here, a point well put by Stephen Halliwell: "In trying to understand Aristotle's position, we must be careful not to think of plot-structure as 'form' divorced from content . . . it can already be seen that his theory requires plot-structure to be both form and substance—or, better, dramatic substance (action) in its formal dimension (unity)."[16]

In energeia possible and actual being are simultaneous; the behavior is not instrumental but its own end. The action of a drama is such an energeia (an activity, not a production), and it is this self-sustaining, substantial completeness that Aristotle ascribes to the praxis, the ethical action organized by a plot. While the intention may have results, it is not qua intention, an incomplete motion, but, rather, a stable activity, an end in itself. A plot's beginning, middle, and end are worldly conditions that bring the unchanging intention into being, that sustain it, and that end it as results. In this way plot substantially embodies action, is drama's first principle, and imitates action not by copying it, but by constructing it, by working its logic into contingency. Thus, Aristotle's criteria for completeness—beginning, middle, and end—apply both to the intention, an end in itself in which possible and actual being are simultaneous, and the deeds that it organizes, which are themselves motions, instrumental changes from possible to actual being.

Bywater's translation of *Poetics* makes the reference to *ousia* and energeia in the term *complete* clearer than Halliwell's: "We have laid it down that a tragedy is an imitation of an action that is complete in itself."[17] The phrase "in itself" refers both to action as an end in itself, a complete and substantial realization of possibility in the agent to plan and pursue the substantial condition of humanity, happiness, and it refers to the completion in time of the cause-and-effect logic that does or does not bring that conception of happiness from possible to actual existence in the world. Beginning, middle, and end are the temporal presentation of the complete, unified being of the logical *praxis*, the organizing intention of an agent. Thus, while change, with its self-canceling, consumptive character of ousting one possible condition to bring in another, does result from dramatic action, it happens not to the action itself and, most significantly, not to the character, the moral disposition, of the agent carrying out the action, but in the circumstances that action brings about, in the fortune—both the luck and the phenomenal conditions governed by that luck—that the agent reasons through and against.

Tragedy shows actuality horribly perfected when it shows an intention ending in an unplanned change of fortune. The completeness of that change has the finality of the self-consuming logic of motion, the annihilation of some possibility for happiness or unhappiness in an agent's life. While the plot of a tragic action does end in transformation, it is not therefore a motion, not less purely substantial a presentation of being at work. The change attached to tragic actions arises not from the separability in them of actual and possible ends, as is the case in instrumental motions, but from some unforeseeable inadequacy, some end concealed in the intention, which Aristotle names hamartia. This concealed inadequacy lends unexpected force to contingency in tragic plots and so brings ruin to the agents by completing their logic in the wrong way. In this sense dramatic action results in change, while keeping its nonchanging status as substantial functioning in a life.

Thus, the reality constructed by a plot is "complete in itself" in two senses. At any point in a dramatic sequence nothing more needs to happen for that sequence to be an action. The intention realizing itself in a plot is at all points in that realization a completed unity of potency and act. This unity at the level of substantial being is reinforced by Aristotle's comparison of wholeness in plot to the organized unity of form and matter, the structural arrangement of parts in "any beautiful object, whether a living creature or any other" (P, chap. 7, 39). An action is complete in itself as the soul of a living creature is, fully functional as embodied principle at all times and places in the living being.

Ends in themselves, actions also end in time and in results. In this sense an action is "complete in itself" when all its causes have become effects, when nothing more can happen in it or because of it. That an action may have results does not make it production, or motion—change that is complete in itself only when it extinguishes itself. That an action embodying happiness gives rise to unhappiness indicates an unmanageable connection of intention to circumstance, not the separability in that intention of actual and possible powers to be. A principled scheme for living well happens perforce in time, but is no less unified, complete in itself, for that reason. The integrity of cause-and- effect relations governing a plot is not broken, but fully manifested by the change of fortune that results from the action and so ends it. When events show that nothing more can happen, we see that nothing more than thinking through planned deeds needs to happen for reality to be presented and known on the stage. This essential and consequential coherence in praxis shows that change, under the proper conditions, can be conceived of as a result of substance at work, an end of reality in action. This dual appearance of completeness, as an ambiguous act and result of substantial form, is the crucial unity of plot in Aristotle's argument, not the spurious requirements of one day and one place invented by the Renaissance Italian humanists and so corrosively influential in the transmission of Aristotle into later theory. This bimodal manifestation of the real in drama is what Aristotle wants to enhance when he compares dramatic coherence to the soul of a living creature, the presentation par excellence of being in action.

This comparison to living beings also introduces the argument for magnitude as a criterion of dramatic action. The scale required must permit, indeed should ensure, that an action's completeness can be apprehended in a single experience of the play. An action is too short if consequences emerge so numerously and rapidly from purposive behavior that they obliterate or overwhelm attention to the intentional logic that brought them about. An action is too long if consequences emerge so distantly or meagerly from the appearance of an intention that they cannot invoke it, do not appear to result from it. Excess or dearth of the causal relation of motive to deed mars knowledge and pleasure in drama. The mean, that proper relation of intentional cause to effective deed, Aristotle describes as follows: "The limit which accords with the true nature of the matter is this: beauty of size favours as large a structure as possible, provided that coherence is maintained. A concise definition is to say that the sufficient limit of a poem's scale is the scope required for a probable or necessary succession of events which produce a transformation either from affliction to prosperity, or the reverse" (*P*, chap. 7, 39-40).

That probable or necessary succession makes the action a plot, embodies the ethical intention. *Result in* is better here than *produce*, since action and plot are not production, or making, but doing. Affliction and prosperity result from action, rest in action, and are action's ends as sight results from, rests in, and is the end and achievement of seeing. Ends in themselves, actions are undertaken for themselves. Their goal is not some product, but, rather, their own realization, their permanent instantiation not as states but as informing principles governing a life.[18] Because moral actions work in contingency, their result is never guaranteed. In fact, tragedy results in distorted living, since its happy ends turn bad. But in Aristotle's account these surprises, which might seem to annul the action's internal coherence, reveal it most powerfully. A duration displaying in full some necessary or probable working out of a distorted goal preserves this coherence and presents it to an audience as terribly beautiful satisfaction. Formal and rhetorical, magnitude clears enough space onstage for ruinous change to make tragically clear sense.

Tragic knowing is no cool analysis of disguised cause-and-effect sequence in an action but, instead, frightened, pitying discovery. The definition of tragedy holds that tragic plots should end in a transfigured goal whose objective is a transfiguring arousal of pity and fear in the audience. That something bad happened to someone enacting some good frightens a spectator at the event, who imagines he or she could suffer the same way. The opposite version of such identification also occurs as the spectator pities the ruined agent, suffering for sorrow that could be, but crucially is not, his or her own. Plato's objection to the arousing of these feelings in drama seems quite sane here. What knowledge of stable being could come from overwrought attention to feigned images of good deeds that end badly? Can seeing virtue defeated make anyone want to be virtuous? This attack on plot's emotional objective moved Aristotle to add the embattled term *catharsis* to the feelings Plato properly attacks as disruptive and corrosive intrusions on virtue and knowledge.

The transfigured goal of a plot transfigures the emotions it arouses. Spectators do not simply weep and howl at some painful wrecking of a life (although there was apparently much more of this in Greek theaters than modern people normally assume).[19] Their expression is *katharsis*, a cleansing, whose ancient medical sense survives in the contemporary pharmaceutical term *cathartic*. Debate over the term's meaning will probably never cease and has not ceased whenever *Poetics* has been thought about. There are two major arguments, one holding that Aristotle means a cleaning *out*, an elimination of pollutants through explosive magnification of irrational response, and one holding that Aristotle means a cleaning *up* of the mind these feelings move in, an alignment of otherwise disordered irrational, imaginative, and logical awareness.[20] Aristotle's psychology, ethics, and metaphysics in general, as well as his insistence on the substantial force of rationality in dramatic experience, weight the second case far more convincingly.

At the end of chapter 9, Aristotle associates fear and pity with wonder, arguing that wonder, knowledge tense with joyous curiosity, enhances katharsis. He writes:

> Since tragic mimesis portrays not just a whole action, but events which are fearful and pitiful, this can best be achieved when things occur contrary to expectation yet still on account of one another. A sense of wonder will be more likely to be aroused in this way than as a result of the arbitrary or fortuitous, since they *appear* to have a purpose (as in the case where Mitys's statue at Argos fell on Mitys's murderer and killed him, while he was looking at it: such things do not *seem* to happen without reason). So then, plot-structures which embody this principle must be superior. (*P*, 42)

Wonder is the intellectual response to surprise endings, the excited discovery of cause in what otherwise seems arbitrary or just accidental. That plots that evoke wonder are superior because they contribute to the effect of pity and fear seems contradictory, if the katharsis that tragedy aims for is pure emotionality. How could discovery of meaning in ruined virtue enhance the fear and pity that the absence of meaning, the contradiction of expectation, provokes?

Critics have puzzled very little over this, if at all, and so missed a crucial factor by which Aristotle makes theatrical emotionality thoughtful. The passage states that wondering perception of reason's force occurs while spectators feel endangered (frightened and sorrowful) by seeing reason absent, or separated, from human volition and that this complex awareness is the goal of the best plots. Since that goal is katharsis, it follows that the cleansing Aristotle required of tragedy is just this mixture of knowledge and feeling. And the mixture cannot be of equally forceful parts, since the elements are contradictory, formally compatible (both are responses), but in content mutually exclusive. Arbitrary or fortuitous distortions of intention would arouse unrestrained emotionality. The surprise that reason governs even ruin arouses mixed feelings, not only pity and fear, but also their alliance, through wonder, with the dominant pleasure of knowledge. Conceived in this way, as the infusion of thought into resistant feeling, katharsis perfectly completes the action of a play, giving spectators a nonfictive experience of reason's informing force, the story in all plays, the substance of life.

All the structures of a successful play will contribute to this emotionally charged discovery of meaning in events that seem to defy explanation. Characters' relation to change of fortune, the direction of that change, the deeds that lead up to the change, the two kinds of plots that can organize those deeds, simple or complex—these components that invoke katharsis do so because they share its mixed status. Each operates by surprise; in each some logic that shouldn't hold does. In chapter 13 of *Poetics* Aristotle shows how this is true of character and the direction change takes in relation to it.

Good men, by which Aristotle means people who are expert in the practical reasoning that brings about virtuous ends, who do not make mistakes about what is valuable or how to enact it, should not be shown ending badly through their deeds. Their ruin would be victimization, and, while this does happen in life, it is repulsive, appalling because arbitrary, and so not conducive to katharsis. Wicked men, moral idiots, should not become happy by their deeds, because that end, while also arbitrary, is not moving or frightening or pitiable. (Some moralists might reasonably demur here, since such an end seems at the least frightening.) Monsters, reprobates, should not end badly, because, while that might be moving, it couldn't be fearful or pitiable, since these identifications are not possible where monsters are concerned. (One thinks of Macbeth, but that was in another country.)

The cathartic combination shows an imperfectly virtuous man, prominent and prosperous, brought to ruin "not because of evil and wickedness, but because of a certain fallibility *(hamartia)*" (*P*, 44). As much argument has passed over the term *hamartia* as over *katharsis*. Here it is sufficient to say that the wrongdoing is clearly not deliberate, since that would make it wicked or evil. Neither is the fault a moral flaw, the result of habitual error in prudent pursuit or knowledge of the good, but a gap in moral reasoning. This gap is filled in at the end of a play, when the change of fortune is seen to result from some cause in the action that the agent didn't or couldn't know or knew incorrectly or enacted insufficiently or excessively. Hamartia makes the fearful ruin of a decent person understandable and so enhances the tense projection of reason over chaos that happens in katharsis.

Fallibility and transfiguring emotional intensity belong to character and plot. How might a character enact the plot, what sort of deeds are most likely to bring fallible purpose to a cathartic end? "What must be sought are cases where suffering befalls bonded relations—when brother kills brother (or is about to, or to do something similar), son kills father, mother kills son, or son kills mother" (P, chap. 14, 46). A story of blood relatives damaging one another offers the best opportunity for tragedy to portray logic's fallibility and cathartic resiliency, because no other action seems less submissible to reason or more in need of such submission. Here, as in hamartia, the cathartic end of a plot is prepared for, enhanced, by surprising combinations in the plot's content.

The best plots display this capacity to surprise in their form as well. Actions that proceed directly to an unexpected but nonetheless necessary or probable result have simple, unilinear plots. Actions that plausibly but unexpectedly shift direction and include surprise revelations have complex plots; they move to their unexpected end by means of reversal and recognition, "tragedy's greatest means of emotional power," as Aristotle asserts in chapter 6 (P, 39). A climactic surprise brought about by climactic surprises gives greater play to reason and feeling in the theater than the blunt balking end of a simple plot does and so intensifies the cathartic achievement of drama, its revelation of meaning in disaster.

Reversal (peripeteia) twists the action by plausibly matching an opposed effect to some pursued cause. For instance, Hamlet wants to kill Claudius and so avenge his father, but kills Polonius instead and consequently delays the vengeance, contrarily strengthening Claudius and endangering himself. So, before the end of the play, wonder, fear, and pity are powerfully invoked. Similarly, in King Lear the transfigured cause transfigures the action's subsequent causal sequence until the agent's intention can only result in what Lear wishes on Goneril, "thwart disnatured torment." [21] Recognition (anagnorisis) twists relations between people by revealing concealed identities and so changing alliances or conflicts through which the protagonist plans to achieve his or her purpose.[22] Casting off beggar's rags, Odysseus switches the relation between himself and the suitors from victim to victimizer. The delay gained through the disguise and the surprise of its vanishing are the crucial means by which he successfully reclaims his patrimony. Like reversal, recognition rehearses the complex of fear, wonder, and pity that the final change of fortune brings into full play. Their rhetorical and intellectual force, their capacity to move an audience to passionate, curious attention, comes from the presentation of knowable cause for apparently incoherent events.

Arguing that reversal and recognition "should arise from the intrinsic structure of the plot" and so display necessity or probability operating in a surprising sequence, Aristotle concludes that "it makes a great difference whether things happen because of one another, or only *after* one another" (*P*, chap. 10, 42). The difference in tragedy separates plays that end in the satisfaction of katharsis from plays that, lacking coherence, result in boredom and frustration. In life the difference separates meaning from chaos, being from nullity. The difference in art matters because it replicates the difference in life. Surprised by cause in the theater, people know life in an especially precious, powerful way.

Cause governs reality under the condition of change, a condition that holds whenever something is said to "happen." Things happen when possible and actual powers to be come together, either in an activity, in which they are simultaneous, or in a process, in which they occur because of, but after, one another, with actual ousting possible existence. The verb *to happen* refers to both relations; an event, what "happens," refers to the result of either combination of actual and possible being. An event that follows a moral activity, such as the action, or praxis, that makes up a play, has a different nature from an event that results from a process or production. The logic and reality of an action continue in an action's end; the logic and reality of a process are subsumed in the product. If the change of fortune ending a play can be thought of as an activity's result, as a continuity of the logic unifying act and potency, the change can be regarded as a portrayal of reality *happening*, and Plato is so answered both on the question of the reality of phenomenal change and on the intelligibility of drama.

David Charles describes the relation of result to action in Aristotle's system as follows: "The result, in the case of some activities [moral ones] is an immanent state . . . which makes the activity the activity it is. In the case of being healthy, the internal good would be health (or health being achieved/maintained); in the case of living well, it would be the good life (or the good life being lived), conceived of as the condition achieved if one lives well." [23] The condition achieved and the achievement of the condition have the same logical relation as possible and actual powers to be in an action: each member of the pair makes the other one real at the same time. Acting according to a virtuous purpose, pursuing an ethically appropriate intention, is one of the ways a good life is lived in Aristotle's ethical system. A drama's action, then, portrays a condition achieved and the achievement of the condition, an energeia in which potency and act happen together.

In tragic actions this simultaneity is distorted and preserved. The logically necessary internal result of some actualization reverses itself; an achievement ends in realization of the immanent state opposed to it. This distortion gives way to the preserving logic of katharsis, reversal, and recognition, all of which reveal that the apparently wrong results are the right ends of a covert action that has been governing the manifest one throughout the play. The immanent state, the indwelling end enacted in killing the man behind the curtain, is not Hamlet's well-being, but his entrapment. Whether or not Hamlet successfully makes possible and actual happiness the same by murdering Claudius is an open question and shows the distance drama has traveled from Aristotle's theater to Shakespeare's. In Aristotle's tragedy there is no such questioning; the agents cannot bring possible and actual happiness together through deeds, but ruin themselves by achieving the disastrous ends indwelling in their disguised purposes. The change of fortune that ends an Aristotelian action is the achievement and maintenance of that action's internal logic and, as such, is an enactment, not a production, of the real. Since substance is irreducibly real, it cannot be produced by already existing things. It follows that the change of fortune, since it is an enacted rather than produced result, is a substantial condition, one that manifests what is most essentially real about the agent—that he has miscreated his life.

Aristotle brings conceptual language from metaphysics, natural science, ethics, and psychology into *Poetics* to explain how dramatic narrative shows us that we are real only through actions, through substantive transmission of purpose to phenomenal circumstance. The changing phenomenal world in which we enact ourselves is likewise a successful enactment of reality in Aristotle's thinking, and not the flickering delusive snare that Plato (or Aristotle's Plato) held it to be. That people belong in the world, that their normative place there is happy, and that their happiness belongs to them but is not guaranteed are the substance of the rational humanism that Aristotle championed and transmitted to European philosophy and art. This conception of reality stayed alive in spirit, while its Aristotelian letter, the technical philosophical and aesthetic terminology, underwent the transformations wrought by medieval scholastics, Renaissance humanists, nineteenth-century German idealists, and Elizabethan, French neoclassical, and nineteenth-century playwrights.

Subsequent chapters pay detailed attention to the problematic relation Ibsen's protagonists bear to rational humanism's modern, bourgeois form. Ibsen presents those problems in dramatic actions that conform closely to Aristotle's standards for construction of plot and character. The question of influence is moot here. Ibsen learned his trade in the theater, not in classrooms or libraries, and the theater he worked in, even in its most formulaic popular forms, barely departed from mimetic plots built around reversals and recognitions through which representative characters found or lost worldly happiness.[24] The more important question concerns Ibsen's career-long ambivalence about the strongly ethical and culturally conservative role

Aristotle assigned theatrical narrative. No less than Aristotle, Ibsen required the theater to present important people encountering substantial reality. But, as his career progressed, Ibsen's view of important people and substantial reality became increasingly incompatible with Aristotle's and with the civilized tradition that had for so long preserved Aristotle's confidence in reason's capacity to bring stability out of change. To measure the distance Ibsen traveled from sanctioned ideas of action, this study now takes up Nietzsche's assault on reason and the world it made.

2

Action in Nietzsche

Nietzsche was, like Ibsen, a disaffected nineteenth-century Lutheran, an independent thinker with an exuberant, prophetic temperament.[1] Both writers found modern, bourgeois Europe's traditional cultural reliance on Christianity and rational humanism repugnant. And, in their different spheres, both laid siege to what they regarded as the tradition's ever-failing bulwark: its conviction that action governed by reason and virtue ended in happiness. Nietzsche excoriates virtue's attachment to Christian thought and feeling unceasingly, most directly in *The Genealogy of Morals* (1887) and *The Anti-Christ* (1895). Reason's long-lived authority in philosophy comes in for similar harsh treatment throughout Nietzsche's writing, most consistently in *The Gay Science* (1882), *Beyond Good and Evil* (1886), and *Twilight of the Idols* (1889). While he has much to say about the political, scientific, and aesthetic failures that produced contemporary Europe, Nietzsche reserves his most scrupulous and damaging condemnation for what he regarded as the controlling failure of his culture: its ontology and ethics. In their various conceptual forms and cultural expressions, virtue and reason promise to establish a correspondence between the fixed order underlying phenomenal change and the fixed order underlying the changing needs and aims of agents. Righteousness, blessedness, sanity, health, happiness, idealism, or realism—in its various names that correspondence makes change intelligible and so manageable. Known and governed thus, change securely locates humanity in the changelessly real and the changelessly real in humanity.

While Nietzsche acknowledged that some reality was at work in phenomenal and conscious change, he presents that reality as unfixed, unintelligible, and unmanageable. And, while he maintains that some correspondence actively locates the real and agents in each other, he presents that correspondence as dangerous rather than secure. Nietzsche's agents create their place in the chaotically real; they do not discover a comfortable

home there. This modernist relation of doing to being appears in all
Nietzsche's writing after the 1870s. Its most extended and subversive presentation comes in *Thus Spoke Zarathustra* (1883-91), a book whose various
rhetorical and intellectual energies invite and frustrate all manner of classifi-
cation. That work, which Nietzsche subtitled "A Book for Everyone and No
One," is a parody of, among other things: wisdom literature, Plato's dramatic
and allegorical presentations of the dialectical ascent to philosophic truth,
and, especially, the Bible as translated by Martin Luther. The most important
concepts in this apocalyptic encyclopedia of Europe's religious and philosophical traditions are "the will to power," the "eternal return of the same,"
and the self-overcoming, self-transfiguring "superman." In those inventions
action changes from deliberate, limited control of natural and human contingency to impulsive, limit-breaking begetting and renewal of ecstatic joy,
that natural force that gives humanity dispositional, not pragmatic, authority
over everything contingent.

This new action requires new agents rather than a reformed world. To
recreate itself present-day consciousness must first recognize and repudiate
the historically accumulated errors to which it has become habituated. When
it has successfully undone itself this way, contemporary awareness faces the
opposite challenge: it must generate from itself that new identity in view of
which it can reclaim its natural disposition to joy. This twofold transformation of humanity calls for a new kind of philosophy, in Nietzsche's view. To
clear away the old problems by taking them up on their own terms, to analyze
their validity and systematic truthfulness, would be merely to extend reason's
damaging authority. Instead of dissecting traditional ontology and ethics
away, Nietzsche discredits the disposition that gave rise to them. He traces
the social and psychological genealogy of moral norms and the appearance-
reality dichotomy back to an original fear of life's persistent, often violent
mutability. Disparaging that fear by exposing it is the first task of Nietzsche's
new philosophy. Its second task is to present life's persistently violent
mutability as the joy sought by self-creating agents, as the intractable reality
they must will in order to become themselves.

Nietzsche's philosophical subversion of philosophy is itself an instance
of the conversion self-creating agents undergo, an apocalyptic undoing and
refashioning of existing modes for consciousness. That irony has generated
much of the controversy in twentieth-century philosophical and scholarly
response to Nietzsche. The intellectual status of Nietzsche's archaeological
investigation into conventional ethics and ontology is at stake in that
controversy, as is the intellectual status of his descriptive exploration of the
new ethics of the superman and the new ontology of the will to power.[2] The

question is what truth content, if any, can be assigned to writing that is and is not philosophical. Unlike many academic quarrels, this one derives immediately from the topic at hand. Nietzsche exposes philosophy as a symptomatic expression of a disposition and, in the process, rejects its claim of independent analytic discovery and conceptual representation of the truth about reality.[3] But he uses analytic discovery to expose philosophy's dispositional base and presents concepts to account truthfully for the new reality a dispositional change will make apparent. The problem is clear enough: What intellectual authority can Nietzsche hope to claim if he uses the tool he destroys, if he rejects and asserts the power of conceptual, analytic discourse, to make and confirm true propositions about the real?[4]

Nietzsche himself takes up the problem, among others, in *Beyond Good and Evil*, a book to which he gave the subtitle *Prelude to a Philosophy of the Future*. His solution to it runs as follows. The long-lived error of philosophy is its refusal to acknowledge that truth, knowledge, wisdom are always willed rather than discovered, are perspectival rather than objective stances. The rational authority of a truth, and of the argument establishing it, derives not from that truth's descriptive or pragmatic function, but from the arational aims and interests—imaginative, impulsive, cowardly, brave, or otherwise subjective—that truth serves. Truth and its object, the real, are then always true and real *for* something or, more accurately, for *someone*. This conviction allows Nietzsche to claim that new philosophy can beget as well as undo a valuable world, can rehabilitate as well as disengage human agency. The intellectual authority of genealogy and the concepts it engenders—the will to power, the eternal return of the same, the superman—is felt by, more accurately *established* by, those who acknowledge and affirm the transformative goal for which the new philosophy's method and concepts are conditional strategies: imminent restoration of life's immanent joy. Argument becomes prophecy here, public proclamation that selectively addresses itself to those who have ears to hear.

Nietzsche hopes that his writing will be understood by, and will help generate, what he calls *The Free Spirit* in part 2 of *Beyond Good and Evil*.[5] In *Nietzsche Life as Literature*, Alexander Nehamas elegantly establishes the link between frankly acknowledged dispositional truth claims and the rejuvenating project of philosophical will to power. Describing the free spirits Nietzsche hoped to address and create, Nehamas writes:

> Anything but disinterested, they no longer see the will to truth as the effort
> to discover, once and for all, the real nature of the world. They now see it,
> in suitably ambiguous terms, as an effort to establish its character . . . The

will to truth turns out to be an effort to establish a world in which one's best impulses and strongest needs find expression, and in which perhaps, at least for a time, they can be satisfied. In other words, it turns out to be the will to power: "'Will to truth,' you who are wisest call that which impels you and fills you with lust? A will to the thinkability of all beings; this *I* call your will. You want to *make* all being thinkable, for you doubt with well-founded suspicion that it is already thinkable . . . That is your whole will, you who are wisest: a will to power" (Z, II, 12). But the will to power is not the arbitrary imposition of order on a world that is in principle chaotic or unstructured. Even the notion of chaos is relative to a particular interpretation: "That is what the will to truth should mean to you: that everything be transformed in what can be thought by human beings, seen by human beings, and felt by human beings . . . And what you have called world, that shall be created only by you: your image, your reason, your will, your love shall thus be realized. And, verily, for your own bliss, you lovers of knowledge . . . You could not have been born either into the incomprehensible or into the irrational." (Z, II, 2)[6]

As the second excerpt from *Thus Spoke Zarathustra* stirringly indicates, Nietzsche transforms philosophy's intellectual authority and cultural value by reversing the traditional relation of reason to the world. Instead of suiting human consciousness to the world, reason now creates the world required by human consciousness.[7] Action, the traditional concept and aesthetic principle that gives humanity a part in the world's changes, takes on a new conceptual and aesthetic shape when reason's relation to the world is inverted. As in Aristotle's thought, action in Nietzsche's is the purposeful transformation an agent undergoes in pursuit of a projected goal. In both cases the result of action is self-realization for the agent, constitutive exertion of that agent's power to become whatever it is. The crucial difference comes in the spheres and modes Aristotle and Nietzsche set out for the agent's transformation.

Coherently ordered natural and social conditions beget and limit agents' projects and pursuits in Aristotle's world. Prudentially, experimentally matching their needs and resources to the needs and resources of those conditions, Aristotelian agents take their self-correcting, contingent places in that world. Taking those places is always the pursued project, the action, for Aristotelian agents. The persistence of their identity derives from the prudence by which they govern their growth and decline in those places. Things happen differently in Nietzsche's world. There agents pursue enhanced projection of their own dispositions; they beget themselves out of themselves for themselves. Phenomenal reality does not control or fulfill self-creation's projects in Nietzschean action. Instead, what traditional philosophy calls the world is variously configured and reconfigured (in that way generated) by those projects, made the subordinate means for whatever dispositional ends agents pursue. To put the matter simply, agents make the world they want. Self-transfiguration is always the pursued project, the action, for Nietzschean agents. Their identity persists as long as they bravely will world-making self-transfiguration to recur eternally.

In the ceaseless coming to be and passing away of environmental conditions and human purposes, Aristotle discerns a stable ratio, an intelligible force binding the conditions and purposes into coherence. Discerning that ratio and forming their projects under its governance, people take the happy place life lawfully provides them. Aristotle presents his philosophical account of that activity as objective and universally valid information. His conceptual terms—*ousia, energeia, praxis, eudaemonia*—are not put forth as provisional descriptions or metaphoric approximations of what is but, rather, as definitions, as transparent, immutable instances of what is immutably real. Nietzsche grants that philosophy's starting point is the ceaseless coming to be and passing away of environmental conditions and human purposes, but that is all he grants. For Aristotle, coming to be and passing away are objective conditions that generate philosophical inquiry; for Nietzsche they are consequences of such inquiry, topics generated by the character and temperament of the wisdom lovers and the truth tellers. Hence, philosophy, for Nietzsche, is not argument about the proper conceptual presentation of the immutably real, but an agon of dispositions from whence such argument ensues. To win that dispositional contest Nietzsche had to get control of the arguments that carried it out. And so he takes up the problem of mutability and presents it in new conceptual terms to assert the new wisdom, love, and truth that belongs to free spirits, the philosophers of the future.

The primary conceptual change Nietzsche works on the old wisdom is to take mutability at face value. For the free spirit mutability is no longer the unreal appearance of the hidden or transcendent real; it is in fact no longer appearance at all.[8] In the new dispensation, mutability is thought to be chaos in action, the self-transforming, unresolved play of force against force. From this field, according to Nietzsche, philosophy has falsely constructed "the world." As he puts it in *The Gay Science:*

> The total character of the world, however, is in all eternity chaos—in the sense not of a lack of necessity but of a lack of order, arrangement, form, beauty, wisdom, and whatever other names there are for our aesthetic

anthropomorphisms . . . None of our aesthetic or moral judgments apply to
it. Nor does it have any instinct for self-preservation or any other instinct;
and it does not observe any laws either. Let us beware of saying that there
are laws in nature. There are only necessities: there is nobody who commands, nobody who obeys, nobody who trespasses. (168)

Given Nietzsche's insistence that thinking is dispositional, his new definition
of "the world" raises an obvious question: what kind of disposition moves free
spirits to celebrate the chaos so long deformed by philosophy's anthropo-
morphic aesthetic and moral judgments?

One version of the answer comes in the summary history of philosophy's
errors that Nietzsche places at the beginning of *Twilight of the Idols*: "How the
'Real World' at Last Became a Myth." At the end of that chapter Nietzsche
writes:

We have abolished the real world: what world is left? the apparent world
perhaps? . . . But no! *with the real world we have also abolished the apparent world!*

(Mid-day; moment of the shortest shadow; end of the longest error;
zenith of mankind; INCIPIT ZARATHUSTRA). (41)

Here begins Zarathustra, or, to put the matter conceptually, here, at the
celebration of mutability's untrammeled power, the spirit of ecstatic, improvised autonomy vanquishes the spirit of benumbed, strategic compliance.
The lawful world proceeds from a timid, obedient, altogether self-abnegating
disposition. The necessary world proceeds from a brave, creative, and joyous
one. In this excerpt from *Twilight of the Idols*, Nietzsche magisterially directs
those who can exchange one temperament for the other to his recent, and
most fervent book, in which they will find more exhortation than doctrine
for their transformation, more encouragement than instruction. Those readers of *Twilight of the Idols* who catch the reference to *Thus Spoke Zarathustra* are
urged by the allusion to remember what the new readers are sent out to
discover: a symbolic biographical account of how autonomous consciousness
emerges from compliant conscience, how the free spirit, at midday, disperses
the mentality of the herd and makes the world what bravery and joy require
it to be: a creative challenge rather than a definitive command.

Throughout his writing in the 1880s Nietzsche makes much of the
ecstatic necessity Zarathustra enacts and affirms. Appropriately, given his
character-based philosophy, the conceptual term he coins to investigate the
necessity at work in "eternal chaos," *will to power*, combines psychology and

physics. *Will to power* works in Nietzsche's ontology as *logos* works in Aristotle's: it provides a rationale for the world's coming to be and passing away, and it establishes humanity's relation to the persistently assembled and disassembled world. The two rationales are distinguished from each other not only by their contradictory accounts of being and doing, but by the incompatible kinds of assent they can lay claim to. Aristotle defines once and for all what is always the case about the world's ordered changes and what is always the case about humanity's orderly or disorderly compliance with those changes. He can lay claim to the impersonal rational assent of anyone who follows his reasoning.

Nietzsche operates very differently. His concepts are not definitions that reveal objective conditions of the world or of humanity or of their relation to each other. Whereas Aristotle's concepts refer to an independent, stable reality, Nietzsche's concepts create the reality they refer to. Nietzsche is calling a disposition into existence when he conceives of the will to power and its subsidiary functions—the eternal return of the same and the self-overcoming and self-transfiguration of the superman. Accordingly, he cannot and does not require impersonal rational assent for his new vision of philosophy's old errors. Nor does he require such assent for his symbolic evocation, especially in the figure of Zarathustra, of the future philosophers of what he calls, in *The Gay Science,* "the great health" (382, 346-47). Instead, he requires what an artist or prophet does: that rapt attention be paid him from his audience's most secret heart. His quicksilver reasoning and, above all, his extraordinary mastery of so many different literary styles and voices display how one learned passion affirms coming to be and passing away. The proper assent to such a temperament is not so much public consent to its views as private cultivation of the joy it now severely, now tenderly, now vatically, announces.

When he turns reason toward passionate affirmation of mutability, Nietzsche transfigures Aristotle's stable world peopled by agents enacting intelligible change. In *Poetics,* Aristotle argues that drama's plots are instructive instances of the stable world's intelligible change. Attending the theater, he concludes, people discern the place they may take up in the order taking place around them. Implicitly, but no less powerfully for that indirection, *Poetics* thus answers Plato's charge that the theater degrades audiences by celebrating chaos. Nietzsche's vision of chaotic change as the necessary occasion for ecstatic self-assertion establishes a new account of being and doing and, in the process, proclaims a new value for drama and the theater. True to his profession—classical philology—and his aristocratic ethos, Nietzsche proclaimed the value only for classical Greek theater. Except for opera, especially Wagner's music dramas and Bizet's *Carmen* (1875)

Nietzsche paid little attention to the contemporary theater of his day. And opera's dramatic, that is narrative, form mattered to Nietzsche only as a subsidiary function of musical design.[9] Indeed, his new account of the value of chaos in ancient Greek tragedy centers on a dramatic structure Aristotle virtually ignores in *Poetics:* the musical resolution of catastrophic action. The visionary affirmation of chaotic necessity Nietzsche expressed in *Thus Spoke Zarathustra, The Gay Science,* and *Twilight of the Idols* lay a decade ahead when he made his subversive debut as a scholar and thinker with *The Birth of Tragedy* in 1872. But the ethos of those works is incipient in the first book, especially in its argument that two interlocked artistic impulses—the Apollonian and Dionysian—together make up tragic form in the ancient Greek theater. More detailed comment on that pair appears later in this argument. At this point it is enough to show in brief how the paired concepts subvert Aristotle's aesthetic theory and its ontological and ethical base.[10] The Apollonian impulse impels consciousness toward unified, formal individuation. The forms of individual beauty it generates are illusions supplied by this impulse to quell the horror chaos evokes. In drama the Apollonian impulse governs dialogue and plot, the formal principles by which agents enact their individuation.

The Dionysian impulse impels consciousness toward ecstatic identification with unindividuated chaos. It arises through intoxicated awareness of impersonal force, especially sexual and other natural force. In drama, the Dionysian impulse governs song and dance, the emotive structures by which the chorus recalls agents to their undifferentiated identity. In Greek tragedy the impulses are raised to their greatest strength: Apollonian dialogue and plot vie with Dionysian song and dance for control over the spectators' response to the destruction of a life. Music asserts that death is a return to primordial chaos; plot makes that annihilating force symbolically intelligible and emotionally sustainable by centering it on a representative individual. Although this synthesis interpenetrates the two impulses, and thus requires spectators to balance contradictory responses, the Dionysian impulse has logical and emotional priority in tragedy. It is the primordial force that generates the world and that reduces itself to Apollonian illusions so that through them it may recall differentiated consciousness back to itself. Whereas Aristotle saw tragic catharsis as Apollonian, as a refining discernment of the intelligible cause of change, Nietzsche saw catharsis as Apollonian and Dionysian, as an intoxicating passage through change's rational shape to change's irrational ground.

Subordinating plot to music, logic to ecstasy, and ethical exemplification to symbolic sacrifice, Nietzsche's theory of tragedy inverts Aristotle's account of the theater's value. In Nietzsche's revised aesthetics tragedy no longer rationally reveals Aristotle's unified world of being and doing. Instead, tragic drama discloses a split universe that Nietzsche accounts for with a subversively Platonic dualism. This particular Nietzschean defection from *Poetics* is especially ironic, given Plato's antagonistic part in Aristotle's thinking about the theater. The Apollo-Dionysus dichotomy reproduces the appearance-reality split that Plato made so much of, and reproduces the dynamic progress through illusion to enlightenment that Plato advocated. The subversion comes, of course, in Nietzsche's transformation of Plato's rationalist dialectic into an irrational confrontation of two aesthetic impulses, and in his transfiguration of Plato's static, transcendently formal reality into the dynamic, immanently formless reality of chaos. Nietzsche's reversal of Plato's thought happens silently in *The Birth of Tragedy*, largely under cover of his complaint that the rationalism of Socrates, Plato's teacher, ruined classical Greek drama and classical Greek life. But the cover is thin enough for Plato's undoing to show through clearly.

By the time he wrote *Thus Spoke Zarathustra*, Nietzsche had abandoned the dualism of *The Birth of Tragedy* and vastly expanded the role of Dionysian impulse in his thinking. From the invention of Zarathustra forward, instead of substituting an alternative dualism for Plato's, and for Christianity's inheritance of Platonic thinking, Nietzsche reforms philosophy by depicting the dynamic that brings powerful dispositions into being. He continues his disparaging analysis of contemporary rational humanism, which is by extension a disparaging of Aristotle's understanding of being and doing, but adds to that historical critique a new account of the Dionysian impulse. The god who earlier bestowed impulsive intuition of the real truth underlying false appearance becomes, in Nietzsche's writing in the 1880s, the god who bestows the simultaneously assertive and affirmative impulse by which "free spirits" of the "great health" will the chaos that brings them into being.

Dionysian impulse no longer takes its origin from mutability's underlying stability, but now posits that lawless mutability is the necessary condition of its own activity. And that switch, from impulse's grounding in the real to impulse's affirmative assertion, its willing of the real, is the culminating transformation of Aristotelian into Nietzschean action. For Aristotle, staged action showed that will, reason, and necessity could be at odds in a life and that, when they were, the contest would be decided by reality's impersonal, rational necessity. When he renounced impersonally rational reality, Nietzsche recast the contest of will, reason, and necessity. Henceforth, reason and necessity would be functions of the will, and action, staged or lived, would display the will resisting and mastering itself instead of resisting

externally mastering conditions. An agent's coming to be would no longer
be a transaction in and with a given world, but an autonomous celebration
and generation of self, a ceremony of impulse that summons the summoning
begetter of joy, Dionysus.

Nietzsche found the contemporary theater's staging of action unworthy
of philosophical comment, but his revision of traditional philosophy's account of being and doing provides a rich source from which to construct a
modernist *Poetics*. Aristotle's structural principles for dramatic construction,
and the worldview they imply, still have considerable sway over the writing,
performance, and interpretation of drama, perhaps permanent sway. But for
the last hundred years intellectually ambitious playwrights have been exceeding the strictures of mimetic realism so consistently and so variously that a
supplementary, if not fully alternative, philosophical account of staged action
seems called for. Pirandello's ontological and ethical relativism, O'Neill's
metaphysically ambitious rendition of psychic paralysis, the persistent vanity
of human wishes in Chekhov's plays, the insatiate reformist heroics of Shaw,
the reduction of agency and world to an exhausted, deliquescent minimum
in Beckett's plays: all these modernist dramatic achievements signal that the
rational humanism that found its first and most influential theatrical rationale
in Aristotle's *Poetics* is somehow an insufficient evaluation of being and doing.

In one way or another these innovations are anticipated in Ibsen's plays,
especially in those he wrote in the last 20 years of the nineteenth century.
More directly and more persistently than these twentieth-century playwrights, Ibsen tested Aristotelian poetics in his dramas, and increasingly
found them wanting. The essential problem for Ibsen's characters is the
struggle to convert their lives from actions of duty to actions of joy. Sooner
or later his protagonists all discover that joy does not belong to the Aristotelian world of moderation, that the world of moderation will not yield to
joy, and that no other world is ready at hand. Some abandon joy; some
adequately will a privately joyous world; others do so inadequately. In all
these cases the fundamental principle of rational humanism—that action
guided by virtue and reason leads to happiness—is disparaged by Ibsen, and
an alternative principle for action is called for. That alternative may be
enacted, as happens in *The Master Builder*, but it is never defined, never
programmatically presented as a rationally assimilable, universally valid
cultural norm.

Ibsen staged his conviction that joy required new agents who willed the
worlds they needed by subversively immersing his radical protagonists in the
old order of duty. Whether they bring new life out or vanish in the old one,
these aspirants to joy discredit the sanction Ibsen's culture placed on lawfully

pragmatic moderation of impulse and will. Ibsen's intellectual and artistic achievement speaks for itself. Attributing it to any other artist's or thinker's influence is at best a vain project. But the achievement does have a philosophical and cultural context, and examining that context makes for clearer perception, and therefore more powerful appreciation, of the dramatic and intellectual values of Ibsen's plays. Although they were not acquainted, worked in different spheres, and had little to say about each other, Ibsen and Nietzsche produced the most focused, sustained, and radical critiques of their epoch's philosophical and religious traditions.[11] And those critiques both returned over and over again to the same topic: the bankruptcy in Europe's thinking about agency's power in the natural and social world.

Ibsen's plays, consequently, clarify Nietzsche's struggle to reject worldly action and invent joy as much as Nietzsche's philosophical works clarify Ibsen's struggle to transform theatrical action from sanctioning mimesis of everyday life into symbolic affirmation of some life to come. Their projects do not stand in need of each other, as those of Sophocles and Aristotle do not, but thinking about them together enhances each of these foundations of modernist culture. Aristotle brought his project directly to bear on Sophocles', and the result was an aesthetic theory that still sets the terms for narrative art and, to a large extent, for civilized life. Nietzsche and Ibsen had both despaired that civilized life could be valuable. Nonetheless, if Nietzsche's project is brought to bear on Ibsen's, the terms that set a large part of the value of twentieth-century narrative and cultural innovation come clear. Constructing a poetics for Ibsen's stage out of Nietzsche's writing, one that will amplify the Aristotelian *Poetics* that so permeate Ibsen's drama, requires that Nietzsche's ideas of action and agency—the will to power, the eternal return of the same, the superman, and the spirit of Dionysus—be accounted for and then brought to bear on Ibsen's plays. The rest of this chapter is an exposition of those Nietzschean concepts relevant to dramatic action, and a preliminary sketch of what a Nietzschean poetics might be. The application of that poetics to Ibsen can be seen in the analyses of *Ghosts*, *Rosmersholm*, and *The Master Builder*.

REALITY AND CHANGE

Will to power is the controlling concept in Nietzsche's new account of being and doing. According to that new account, the world remains blank until it is configured by human disposition. With argument, with rhetoric, Nietzsche asserts again and again that disposition, the figured world it generates, and the figuring transaction itself are all instances of will to power. The term allows him to provide new philosophers, of which he claims to be the first, a cosmology, physics, anthropology, psychology, and aesthetics in which they may affirm and celebrate their ever-arriving, ever-increasing "great health." Salutation and exhortation of the impulse to joy, and analysis of joy's effects, will to power spins the self-creating circle that alone counts as action, as agency, in the philosophy of the future. For all Nietzsche's insistence on its necessity, will to power posits a world that has no positivistic rationale. This parodic, ironic subversion of nineteenth-century dogmatic scientific materialism threatens to escape interpreters of Nietzsche, especially because he is so emphatic about the antimetaphysical nature of his views, and because he grounds those views so consistently in what he proudly regards as iconoclastic attention to physical sensation—and to physiology in general.

For all its centrality to his philosophical project, will to power works in Nietzsche's writing more as a visionary assertion than as a conventional philosophical definition of reality. But it is a reasoned assertion, and, as a principle for ontology, it operates in Nietzsche's project as *logos* does in Aristotle's, with this important distinction: *logos* infuses and sustains all reality uniformly; will to power infuses and sustains only as much reality as one perspective can configure. The double status of *will to power*—its authority as an assertion and its authority as a proposition—requires interpreters to keep their exposition of the term's conceptual meaning balanced by an imaginative grasp of the term's visionary origin and destination. Tracy Strong strikes the balance beautifully in his work on Nietzsche and provides an important reminder from the philosopher himself that concepts must always be brought back to the dispositions that generated them.

> Most people, according to Nietzsche, have "forgotten" that the unity of the world is a double imputation, first from the unity of the knower derived from the act of knowing and then, in turn, by the transfer of the unity of the knower onto the world. "We put value into things," writes Nietzsche in the late summer of 1886, "and this value has an effect on us, after we have forgotten that we were the donors."[12]

In *Beyond Good and Evil*, section 36, Nietzsche presents this double imputation as an instance and an account of the unity it bestows on experience: will to power.

> Granted that nothing is "given" as real except our world of desires and passions, that we can rise or sink to no other "reality" than the reality of our

drives—for thinking is only the relationship of these drives to one another—: is it not permitted to make the experiment and ask the question whether this which is given does not *suffice* for an understanding even of the so-called mechanical (or "material") world? I do not mean as a deception, an "appearance," an "idea" (in the Berkeleyan and Schopenhaueran sense), but as possessing the same degree of reality as our emotions themselves—as a more primitive form of the world of emotions in which everything still lies locked in mighty unity and then branches out and develops in the organic process (also, as is only fair, is made weaker and more sensitive), as a kind of instinctual life in which all organic functions, together with self-regula-tion, assimilation, nourishment, excretion, metabolism, are still synthetically bound together—as an *antecedent form* of life?—In the end, it is not merely permitted to make this experiment: it is commanded by the conscience of *method.* Not to assume several kinds of causality so long as the experiment of getting along with one has not been taken to its ultimate limits (—to the point of nonsense, if I may say so): that is a morality of method which one may not repudiate nowadays—it follows "from its definition," as a mathema-tician would say. In the end, the question is whether we really recognize will as *efficient*, whether we believe in the causality of will: if we do so—and fundamentally belief in *this* is precisely our belief in causality itself—then we *have* to make the experiment of positing causality of will hypothetically as the only one. "Will" can of course operate only on "will"—and not on "matter" (not on "nerves," for example—): enough, one must venture the hypothesis that wherever "effects" are recognized, will is operating upon will —and that all mechanical occurrences, in so far as a force is active in them, are force of will, effects of will. —Granted finally that one succeeded in explaining our entire instinctual life as the development and ramification of *one* basic form of will —as will to power, as is *my* theory—; granted that one could trace all organic functions back to this will to power and could also find in it the solution to the problem of procreation and nourishment—they are *one* problem—one would have acquired the right to define *all* efficient force unequivocally as: *will to power.* The world seen from within, the world described and defined according to its "intelligible character"—it would be "will to power" and nothing else—. (48-49)

Nietzsche's flamboyantly temperamental reasoning takes quite a few rapid, compacted turns in this passage. Analysis of the argument that estab-lishes the proposition here reveals how deeply imbued that proposition is by Nietzsche's disposition. Overcharged with intellectual confidence, Nietzsche gleefully, even archly, toys with logic's hostility, its inadequacy to his vision of the "real." At the same time he presses logic firmly into confirmative service to that vision. This, apparently, is how the new philosophy is done. Indeed, the new philosophy presents itself in the passage's first sentence, which argues that thinking is the relation of drives—passions and desires in consciousness—to one another. From that assertion everything else in the passage follows.

A word is due here about the quotation marks that accent this passage. Nietzsche uses them to disparage logic's conventional claim to neutral discovery of the objective world. Hence, *given, real, material, appearance, idea, from its definition,* and *intelligible character,* all textbook ontological and epistemological terms, appear under the ironic revision of quotation marks, which assert that the terms are place markers rather than names. When he puts his own term under quotation marks, Nietzsche acknowledges that *will to power* is no more neutral a term than *matter.* From his view, however, because the concept proceeds from a passion, it is a name, and not just a place marker, a bestowed identity that supersedes philosophy's indifferently objective designations of "the world."

If relations of drives are the only topic and method of thought, then thought's object can never be anything but relation of drives. Nietzsche puts this assertion forth first as a rude, impatient experiment that begs permission to stand as a philosophical effort. He follows this mocking self-deprecation with an exposition of the project. He is not proposing a new dualism or solipsism, but arguing, rather, that the structure of emotions is the only structure available for thought, and that therefore it must suffice for understanding whatever thought calls the world. His next step is to assert that this principle of sufficient explanation establishes an identical degree of reality for emotions and the world. That assertion is necessary to eliminate the charge that he is merely making the world a solipsistic projection, an unreal appearance cast by a logical circle.

The key term here is *degree,* which bestows some irreducible content on the world and so makes it a fit topic of inquiry. Nietzsche's discharge of Schopenhauer and Berkeley, which brings *degree* into the argument, amounts to a discharge of substance-based ontology. Reality's Nietzschean content is force, not substance. Thus, emotions and the world possess the same degree of force, in this argument, not the same measure of irreducible, static being.

Nietzsche has proposed that understanding the operation of emotions, passions, and drives in consciousness suffices for understanding the operations of the "so-called mechanical world." Having defended the inquiry's method, he now turns to the inquiry's object. For Nietzsche's argument to hold, that object must display the same degree of reality as the mind observing it, and so he silently transforms the "so-called mechanical world" into a vital one. His next step is to show the difference separating the vitality of the observer and the vitality of the world and to show that the difference does not refute his single-degree, drive-based explanation of the mind's reality and of the world's.

The distinction is between conscious and unconscious unity. In the mind, passion dynamically presents itself to itself as passion, much as Aristotle's logos statically presents itself to itself as logos in the divine mind. The world displays passion's more primitive coherence. There the mighty locked unity of emotions bursts forth into unselfconscious organic process. The dissemination weakens passion, makes it more sensitive by dispersing it in so many interdependent, vulnerable forms. But a countervailing strength, what Nietzsche calls "instinctive life," binds these forms into organic synthesis, and passion's primitive nonconscious unity is thereby preserved. The life of the world, in this account, is not an image of the life of the mind, but a primitive, antecedent form of emotional and intellectual self-consciousness, a vestigial counterpart to mental drives rather than a derivation, or aftereffect, of them. This account of the world as vestigially drivebased reconciles the world's vitality and the mind's, and preserves Nietzsche's argument that one passionate measure can account for them both.

Nietzsche has now shown what the world looks like when it is viewed as the dynamic relation of preconscious drives, forces, passions, emotions, and thoughts. He has asserted that understanding those forces' conscious activity is a sufficient way to understand their preconscious activity. But all along he has been ironically asking permission to claim that the mind's operations sufficiently account for the world's. Posing the sufficient explanation as a question, Nietzsche presents his experimental view as a modest request and a sardonic challenge to the old philosophers who cling to a substance-based ontology. Having made the challenge, through mocking submission to the conventional requirement that philosophical propositions be sufficient accounts of the real, Nietzsche now drives the challenge home by asserting that his experimental inquiry is not only a sufficient account of what philosophy calls the world, but also a necessary one. Necessity, of course, is partner to sufficiency in conventional philosophy's test of a proposition's validity. Nietzsche's rhetorical subversion of that test here is one of the finest examples of his temperamental way with argument. Where sufficiency was required, he presented his case with false timidity. Where necessity can be asserted, he seizes the argumentative high ground and undoes substance-based ontology with the logic that has always proposed it.

The subversive turn comes in the sentence: "In the end, it is not merely permitted to make this experiment: it is commanded by the conscience of *method.*" The method he refers to is the procedural rule that explanations should not multiply around a problem. Nietzsche bends the rule to his own purpose, asserting that his experimental account of the world's causality should not yield to any other until it has been taken to its ultimate point, even if that point is nonsense. It is not merely a matter of intellectual custom or efficiency that his experimental account should be shielded from competing conventional ones, but a matter of intellectual conscience and morality. His immunity from contradiction is *commanded* by this conscience. One may no more rightfully repudiate that morality "nowadays" (the implication is that contemporary intellectuals are sorely lacking in the morality Nietzsche holds himself to) than one may repudiate the laws of mathematics. This assertion of aristocratic dignity's abused authority is a hallmark of Nietzsche's intellectual and literary style, an instance of the self-affirming self-creation that counts as action in his philosophy of the future. That he asserts that high rank here, when he is about to define, and so initiate, the future, is rhetorically, if not logically, a masterstroke.

From this self-appointed height Nietzsche now crowns and miters the new world's sovereign causality. He returns now to the opening assertion—that thinking is the relation of drives—and asserts that cause and effect, the primary relation at work in thinking, is a drive, is the primary drive—will. His argument appears in the following sentence: "In the end, the question is whether we really recognize will as *efficient*, whether we believe in the causality of will: if we do so—and fundamentally belief in *this* is precisely our belief in causality itself—then we *have* to make the experiment of positing causality of will hypothetically as the only one." The repetition of "In the end" recalls his very recent arrogation of philosophy's conventional authority, and signals the coming summary point: that nothing else is except will to power. The first statement of that case runs as follows.

The question of whether the given mental world is a suitable structure for analyzing the given physical world is a question about the sufficiency, necessity, and efficiency of cause as it operates in the given mental world. If the will is the efficient cause of drives and their relations in the mind, then it must also be the efficient cause of drives and their relations in the mind's vestigial counterpart, the world. Belief in causality itself is nothing more than belief in the will's efficiency. To put it another way, belief in logical necessity is nothing more than belief in the will's power to command drives' forces. It follows, then, not only that one may hypothetically assert the experimental case that will is the necessary cause of force's activity in the world, but that one must assert that innovative hypothesis and no other.

Inquiry into cause is always inquiry into will. And so inquiry into cause at work in the world or cause at work in the mind is inquiry into will at work in the world or in the mind. Nietzsche's next step is to return to the passage's original object of inquiry—the so-called mechanical world. He eliminates mechanics from will's causal power immediately and keeps will a purely disembodied force by asserting that will can only operate on will and not on inert matter, especially not on "nerves." Nietzsche makes this point to keep will's operation free of any limiting connection to physiology or any other natural science, to keep it from being confused with animal or physical energy. Hence, whatever active force the world's mechanical occurrences may exhibit is nothing but will's force, will's effects.

Nietzsche now makes his final restatement of the passage's opening assertion—that thought and its objects are never more than passions, emotions, desires, and drives in relation. If thought's object is humanity's instinctual life, it will find it to be will to power; if thought's object is organic processes, it will find them to be will to power. Since Nietzsche has excluded all nonliving things from thought's purview, the right to define instinct and organic process as will to power amounts to the right to define all efficient force unequivocally as will to power. "The world seen from within [that is, the world seen from the perspective of the drives at work in it], the world described and defined according to its 'intelligible' character [that is, the world configured by the new "essence," the new conceptual identity bestowed on it by the new philosopher]—it would be 'will to power' and nothing else—." In this passage Nietzsche takes up two questions that are essential concerns of traditional European philosophy: what relation exists between reality and change, and how can that relation be understood? His answers could not be more radical repudiations of the philosophical tradition that generated the questions. No relation exists between reality and change: they are the same thing. Understanding what they are, therefore, is not reasoned discovery of a ratio that brings them into stable functioning. Instead, understanding what they are— will to power—is living them out, willing a powerful change of the changing relation that organizes emotions, passions, drives. In various forms traditional philosophy operates on a substance-based account of being and doing. In that model objective and unified reality remains fixed, and change either enacts that fixity (in monistic theories) or in some way indicates it (in dualistic ones). Agency, in this system, involves deliberate matching of human life to the fixed reality change enacts or indicates.

In Nietzsche's vision reality's fixed substance yields to will to power's conversional dynamic: the always greater impulse to command ceaselessly transfiguring, ordered relations among forces. The change power generates does not enact or indicate any underlying fixed reality. Nor does power reveal force's indwelling coherence when it brings about a changed order in the relation of one force to another. Instead, power acts only to increase, not to develop or recognize, itself. Power's changes, then, are the only "given" condition in Nietzsche's account. Insofar as "reality" is the "given," reality cannot be thought of or experienced, in Nietzsche's world, as anything but self-grounded, endless change.[13] To do something in this world, to act, means to impulsively command a higher degree of ordering tension among forces, among emotions, passions, drives—to speak conceptually, among thoughts. The forces of consciousness already exist at a higher order than the forces at work in mentality's antecedent life, the world, in Nietzsche's view. It follows, then, that Nietzschean action is not a reordering of the world by the mind, but, rather, an internal reordering of the mind, one that carries conscious life ever farther from its antecedent worldly form. This is not transcendence from appearance to transmundane reality, but increase in the scope and degree of power's capacity to command change.

The citation from *Beyond Good and Evil* asserts that will to power must replace all existing conceptual accounts of mentality, the world, and their relation. Because the battleground in that passage is conceptual, Nietzsche presents will to power abstractly there. The excerpt gives will to power authority over cause and effect, logic's conventional account of change; it spends little time describing how change operates when it is thought of as will to power. Such descriptions abound in Nietzsche's work. They range from close analysis of minute transformations in force to panoramic exultations over world-transfiguring renewal. In that range Nietzsche returns again and again to psychology, to affirmation, definition, and exhortation of the new humanity that will to power requires and promises. The ranking of humanity and the world, their relation as higher and lower exertions of will to power, which the excerpt under discussion presents, reappears throughout Nietzsche's writing.[14] Two concepts define that rank most persistently: the eternal return of the same and the superman. True to the hierarchical imperative he pronounces, Nietzsche subsumes these psychological constructions of will to power in his all-embracing term for experience, *the spirit of Dionysus.*

One of the hallmarks of Nietzsche's late writing is its transparent density, its emotionally clear and intellectually compacted presentation of all his themes at once. The following passage from *The Will to Power* is a much cited instance of Nietzsche at his visionary best. It describes what was defined in the previous excerpt and shows the place of Dionysus, the eternal return of the same, and the superman in Nietzsche's world. The passage is long, but it deserves full citation, not only for its rhetorical pleasures, but because its meaning inheres in the grand, oscillating motions, the incremental repetitions by which Nietzsche sought not only to analyze but to enact his fascinated insight into will and power.

> And do you know what "the world" is to me? Shall I show it to you in my mirror? This world: a monster of energy, without beginning, without end; a firm, iron magnitude of force that does not grow bigger or smaller, that does not expend itself but only transforms itself; as a whole, of unalterable size, a household without expenses or losses, but likewise without increase or income; enclosed by "nothingness" as by a boundary; not something blurry or wasted, not something endlessly extended, but set in a definite space as a definite force, and not a space that might be "empty" here or there, but rather as force throughout, as a play of forces and waves of forces, at the same time one and many, increasing here and at the same time decreasing there; a sea of forces flowing and rushing together, eternally changing, eternally flooding back, with tremendous years of recurrence, with an ebb and a flood of its forms; out of the simplest forms striving toward the most complex, out of the stillest, most rigid, coldest forms toward the hottest, most turbulent, most self-contradictory, and then again returning home to the simple out of this abundance, out of the play of contradictions back to the joy of concord, still affirming itself in this uniformity of its courses and its years, blessing itself as that which must return eternally, as a becoming that knows no satiety, no disgust, no weariness: this, my *Dionysian* world of the eternally self-creating, the eternally self-destroying, this mystery world of the twofold voluptuous delight, my "beyond good and evil," without goal, unless the joy of the circle is itself a goal; without will, unless a ring feels good will toward itself—do you want a *name* for this world? A *solution* for all its riddles? A *light* for you, too, you best-concealed, strongest, most intrepid, most midnightly men? —*This world is the will to power—and nothing besides!* And you yourselves are also this will to power—and nothing besides![15]

This is Nietzsche's clearest presentation of reality as nothing but the split moment of transition, the internal change power undergoes as it passes from one degree to another. The impulse to command suspends and exerts itself during every such change. That suspension and exertion make up the "twofold voluptuous delight," the apocalyptically Dionysian joy of self-

affirming self-creation that Nietzsche counts as the ever-present, ever-arriving value of life. The split moment recurs in every new order it asserts. It
recurs because the new order is always the occasion for a new command.
Thus, every self-creation is also self-destruction, a simultaneous ascent and
going under for will to power. The split moment is both the form and content
of all will to power's functions. That distinction allows Nietzsche to present
all those functions as simultaneously development and play; as improvisatio-
nal but not end-driven increase in ordered complexity.

In every stage of every developmental function will to power exhibits,
at all progressive moments in the world's history and the mind's, power
generates a more complex formal organization of already organized forces
in order to undo that organization. Every passage from provisional simplicity
to full complexity passes through the same change that all the stages
advancing it do: it overcomes itself; it goes under to rise up and play out a
new dynamic in power. And power is an oscillating dynamic, not an incarnate, symbolic, or otherwise enacted substance. Hence, Nietzsche can assert
the value of increasingly complex order and not require that the complexity
or order be related to any fixed, substantial reality. His vision has utterly
undone the world given by Plato and Aristotle, by Moses and Jesus, the world
preserved by contemporary European thought, religion, and culture. Being,
along with God, is dead; becoming—confusion from the old perspective, joy
from the new Nietzschean one—is free to make its masterpiece.

Among all Nietzsche's assertions about the world in this passage, the
first counts the most. And, characteristically, the governing claim comes as
a question, not a proposition: "And do you know what 'the world' is to me?
Shall I show it to you in my mirror?" Clearly, Nietzsche does not assert that
the world is per se as he describes it, but that this description is what he
makes of the blank field philosophers have called "the world." That mirror is
more a medium's or sorcerer's glass than a tailor's, a transparency that
summons a spectacle suited to the passion of the viewer, rather than an
impassive reflection of something objectively real that the viewer must take
at face value. Nietzsche's summoned and summoning passion, the form and
content of his vision is ecstasy, that split moment when consciousness stands
rapturously outside itself, when it loses and gains itself. Consequently, when
he turns his mirror to "the world," ecstasy shines forth in both. In Nietzsche's
view the world stands outside itself recurrently, subsumes itself ecstatically,
every time will to power creates and destroys a self-reversing passage from
simple to complex mastery of force.

After seven descriptions of the ecstatically mirrored world, Nietzsche
returns twice to the passage's opening assertion that this world is *his*, with

the phrases "this, my *Dionysian* world" and "my 'beyond good and evil.'" He now addresses the reader again, not to explain himself but this time to include that reader in his vision. The rhetoric here is the same rhetoric Jesus uses in the Gospels. Having displayed his passionate understanding, the visionary identifies those worthy of sharing it by asking them a promising, challenging question. Those who have ears to hear Nietzsche must be, in his view, degraded Europe's "best concealed, strongest, most intrepid most midnightly men." For as many as desire it Nietzsche now offers to give his "world" a *name* by which they can summon and enter it, a *solution* for its riddles. The name and solution will amount to a *light* that will shine, very much as Jesus' light does in the opening of John's gospel, in the un-comprehending darkness that surrounds the midnightly men (John 1:5). Like Jesus, Nietzsche asserts that reception of the name, solution, and light amounts to a new life that can never again be violated by the old darkness. *"This world is the will to power—and nothing besides!* And you yourselves are also this will to power—and nothing besides!"

The address to Europe's midnightly men contains no coercion or proselytizing. It affirms, acknowledges, and celebrates the ecstatic impulse to command without itself commanding anything or anyone. That passion configures the blank world is a constant in Nietzsche's view, but it does not follow from this that every passion configures the blank world identically. Hence, there is no program or system urged in this passage. Will to power gives rise to passion, not dogma, and Nietzsche's address to the midnightly men tells them nothing more than that. When he names those men "will to power—and nothing besides," he celebrates their passion; he does not submit it to his own rule. Indeed, the two symbolic tests Nietzsche devises for those who would be, like him, philosophers of the future guarantee that whatever passion such midnightly men pursue will be theirs alone. The tests are interlocked thoughts that Nietzsche presents as visions, riddles, and strongly hypothetical aspirations: the eternal return and the superman. The thoughts cannot and do not command passion. Instead, they require that passion be already at work in those who take them up. These experimental hypotheses, like Nietzsche's mirroring will to power, select and enhance autonomous dispositions; they do not make them fungible.

Both thoughts require that an individual life stand outside itself and affirm itself. Thus, both promote ecstasy, the twofold Dionysian delight. But they do so from opposite points of view. The eternal return obscures the delighting renewal in ecstatic change by presenting an extreme account of a changing life's constancy. That extreme case calls forth an extreme affirma-tion of change, the joyful willing of the superman, who can ecstatically discern voluptuous renewal in the most constant form change might take in a life. To take up either thought is to take up the other, since both require, and end in, an increase in the power to affirm becoming. Pivotal moments of Dionysian insight into life's apocalyptic self-creation, both thoughts endanger whoever takes them up. Those who survive them become, as Nietzsche puts the matter in *The Gay Science,* "argonauts of the ideal" who can never again be satisfied with "*present-day* man," the civilized European who could not recognize, let alone take up, the eternal return or the superman.[16]

Nietzsche's first presentation of the idea of the eternal return comes in *The Gay Science,* in the following passage at the end of book 4:

> *The greatest weight.* —What, if some day or night a demon were to steal after you into your loneliest loneliness and say to you: "This life as you now live and have lived it, you will have to live once more and innumerable times more; and there will be nothing new in it, but every pain and every joy and every thought and sigh and everything unutterably small or great in your life will have to return to you, all in the same succession and sequence—even this spider and this moonlight between the trees, and even this moment and I myself. The eternal hourglass of existence is turned upside down again and again, and you with it, speck of dust!"
>
> Would you not throw yourself down and gnash your teeth and curse the demon who spoke thus? Or have you once experienced a tremendous moment when you would have answered him: "You are a god and never have I heard anything more divine." If this thought gained possession of you, it would change you as you are or perhaps crush you. The question in each and every thing, "Do you desire this once more and innumerable times more?" would lie upon your actions as the greatest weight. Or how well disposed would you have to become to yourself and to life *to crave nothing more fervently* than this ultimate eternal confirmation and seal? (sec. 341, 273-74)[17]

This challenge immediately precedes the first appearance of Zarathustra in Nietzsche's writing. Section 342 of *The Gay Science,* "Incipit tragodeia" presents Zarathustra's decision to "go down," to create himself by undoing himself and dispensing his wisdom in the world. Nietzsche repeats section 342 virtually verbatim in the opening of *Thus Spoke Zarathustra* and recasts section 341's demonic test of eternal recurrence in part 3 of Zarathustra's tragedy, in the section entitled "Of the Vision and the Riddle."[18] The central conceptual and narrative event in that book is Zarathustra's struggle with the hostile implications the eternal return of the same has for the prophet's vision of humanity as eternally developing, always overcoming itself. If every present condition in every life were to recur, how would the superman come into existence, how would higher organizations of the impulse to command ever take hold in any life or in the world? Zarathustra solves the problem by changing his idea of the superman's self-overcoming. He eliminates any historical aspiration toward permanently ideal humanity from the concept and envisions the superman as someone who affirms the ever recurrent moment of transfiguration instead of someone who thinks of transfiguration as a means to some as yet unrealized, unknown end.[19]

Zarathustra makes that change when he finds himself able to lift the great weight of the demon's provocation to despair, when he sees the sign and seal of the shape-shifting god, Dionysus—unconditional and ever-renewed self-affirmation—in the demon's ambiguous test. The most important words in that test are the ones that introduce it: "What, if . . . " They indicate clearly enough that the proposition is a selective hypothesis.[20] The demon presents a conditional statement that suggests what people must be or become to enjoy life; he does not define what life is and must be.[21] Life's joy, in Nietzsche's view, is increase in impulse's power to command complex organization for emotions, drives, passions, and thoughts. While commanding is definitive, impulse is improvisatory, and that internal distinction in will to power sets up the conflict that anyone affirming joy must resolve. Seen in this light, the demon's question is: could you ceaselessly improvise the same set of definitive commands, recurrently order passion exactly as you have done, and still see your life as impulse's free play?

The demon puts his question at the loneliest hour to the loneliest life. The psychological isolation stands here as a symbol for the groundlessness of becoming, its permanent separation from being. To speak philosophically, this loneliness is nostalgia for a substance-based ontology, dread in the face of dynamic change that has no goal. Such dread is the pivotal transition from old to new philosophy. Those who celebrate joy are the most likely to make that transition. Hence, this dread is their inevitable portion, what they must "go under" before they "go across," to use the terms of "Zarathustra's Prologue" (Z, 39-53). By asking the affirmers of impulse if they could find joy in the most obviously goal-less scenario, one that mocks definitive commanding of passion mercilessly, the demon not only makes people conscious of the internal dynamic of will to power; he allows them to will that dynamic and so enhance its operation in their own lives. The test of the eternal recurrence is a test of the capacity to see free play in fixity. The superman enacts that capacity and no other.

And what future does the superman affirm when he affirms that the past should recur precisely and ceaselessly? Not the redemptive future Christ promised or the evolutionary future that follows from Darwin's biology or the developmental, corrective future variously envisioned by Hegel, Marx, or Freud. Against Christ and these others the superman affirms that life's full value can be enjoyed in full at any moment. In the future, as in the past, will to power at all moments exerts and suspends itself, freely replaces one of life's necessary forms with another, which it will again freely replace. Affirming any instance of that dynamic change, the superman affirms all change's other instances, not as interchangeable, but as concatenated instances of the same dynamic. From this perspective the future, like the past, loses any historical control over consciousness and becomes, instead, an occasion for enhanced willing of what always is: impulse's twofold delight, will to power's commanding play.

Repudiating the chance to revise the past or manage the future amounts to repudiating reason and virtue, which always reject some forms of life. In place of contingent happiness, the end promised by those moderators of impulse, Nietzsche offers the "tremendous moment" of ecstatic affirmation. Action, for the "midnightly man," no longer involves discerning the manageable rationale that integrates worldly and personal change. Instead, action, in a Nietzschean life, assumes the godly prerogative of noncontingent self-assertion. The midnightly man turns consciousness away from pragmatic deliberation, toward strongly hypothetical, ceremonious exertion of will. He unconditionally says to himself and the world "let be," not in acquiescence but in celebrating command, with an all-approving confidence that he and the world are power ecstatically at play. While change, as Nietzsche understands it, may no longer have a rationale, it still has a structure, one he calls necessary. Indeed, Nietzsche highlights that necessity, the commanding aspect of will to power, when he makes the eternal return of the same a demonic shibboleth of constancy that passion must decipher.

When the midnightly men solve the riddle of the eternal return, they affirm a tension between play and fixity. And, while that tension does not amount to a manageable rationale for change, it does present change as something to be known. The knowledge Nietzsche offers is delight instead of skill—faith instead of deeds, to speak in the old style. As becoming has subsumed being in Nietzsche's "world," so willing has subsumed doing. Action is no longer moderate control of contingent events, but dangerous, voluptuous summoning and celebration of absolute change. Life is no longer a ratio that binds interpenetrating, stable orders of cause and effect, but an agitating force that shifts interpenetrating, evanescent orders of power. Life's value no longer rests in cultivating reason, but in worshiping Dionysus. While Nietzsche was working that change, Ibsen was bringing about his own transformation of staged action. Moderate control of contingent events fares no better in Ibsen's plays than it does in Nietzsche's writing, but it receives far more attention from Ibsen than it did from Nietzsche.

That is true largely because the shibboleth Ibsen's women and men have to pass by, especially the women and men in *Ghosts, Rosmersholm,* and *The Master Builder,* is not a hypothesis-whispering demon, but the world of physical necessity, pragmatic affairs, and familial relations, the world made by duty. Dionysus appears in that world, but approaching him requires subverting duty first. And even those who manage that subversion do not always then see the god face to face. That Ibsen subverts duty, and the dramatic forms that present it, has always been clear. That he subverts those moral and aesthetic conventions for Dionysian joy's sake has not always been clear. If Nietzsche's new account of being and doing is experimentally thought of as a poetics, then the quality of that joy Ibsen's characters pursue may come into sharper focus. Helene Alving, Rebecca West, and Halvard Solness are, like Nietzsche's "argonauts of the ideal," "premature births of an as yet uncertain future," and that untimeliness has made understanding the plays these questers move in problematic (*GS*, sec. 382, 386). Some part of the problem may be solved if the transformation these protagonists go through is thought of as a simultaneously Dionysian and Aristotelian change. To that end this chapter closes by sketching a provisional Dionysian poetics, one in which character, plot, reversal, and recognition depict will to power instead of logos. If the new poetics makes sense of Ibsen's plays, it will have disclosed an originating moment in modernist culture, the moment when drama lost the name of action.

NIETZSCHEAN *POETICS*

Some comment is due at the start about why a Nietzschean "poetics" needs to be constructed at all, given the extensive philosophical attention Nietzsche paid to drama in *The Birth of Tragedy*. There are two related reasons for carrying out the project. First, by the 1880s, Nietzsche was not thinking about Dionysian reality and change the way he had been when *The Birth of Tragedy* appeared, in 1872. He had dropped the dualistic view of reality at work in the Apollo-Dionysus dichotomy and had reconceived the Dionysian impulse in terms of will to power, the eternal return, and the superman. Second, while *The Birth of Tragedy* accounts for drama's cultural and philosophical value, it pays very little attention to how drama's narrative structures actually work. The precise way a particular life comes to ruin has little significance in Nietzsche's aesthetic. Instead, he takes ruin as the given end of a great man's life and presents drama more as musical intuition than as narrative discovery of that fact. As a result, reason and the stably changing world of cause and effect it governs are denigrated, and emotion and the primordial stability of chaos it reveals are exalted. Catharsis changes from pity and fear over error's end to joy that illusion has revealed life's inexhaustible ground.

From 1872 forward Nietzsche progressively eliminated grounded being as a category in his thinking, subsuming it in will to power's pure becoming. Will to power, the "monster of energy" bounded by "nothingness," still operates with a twofold dynamic, but the split no longer separates appearance from underlying reality (*WP*, 550) In Dionysus' new reign ordered relations of force are no longer Apollonian illusions, no longer dreams that shield life from chaos, but commands given by power at play, will's and life's constitutive dice throws. This new idea of change calls for a new response. The "twofold, voluptuous delight" of Dionysian willing is no longer nostalgia for primordial unity, but ecstatic assertion and affirmation of every evanescent improvisation by which the impulse to command suspends and exerts itself. In this new "world" nostalgia for reality's underlying unity turns into hypothetical celebration of perfectly fixed improvisation—the eternal return of the same. That transformation, which reciprocally enhances power's creative and destructive functions, is the thought by which Nietzsche finally breaks the ground of being into the wave of force.

Traditional conceptions of action are radically transfigured by that thought and by the ecstasy it induces. Accordingly, a poetics for the new Nietzschean action should center on that ecstasy, should present it as the experience imitated and clarified in a drama's characters and plot. In Aristotle's *Poetics* change in fortune reveals reality's stable, intelligible unity. In Nietzsche's *The Birth of Tragedy* change in fortune reveals reality's unintelligible unity. In the new Dionysian poetics I propose here change in fortune reveals that reality is nothing but change and fortune. No cause-and-effect logic relates them because no substance or ground underlies them. Instead of rationally ordering the forms that enact fixed reality, change and fortune move kaleidoscopically through the moving simple and complex orders by which will to power makes and unmakes the Dionysian world. Fortune ceaselessly fixes shapes for those orders; change ceaselessly undoes those given relations. Change and fortune operate preconsciously in the living world and consciously in human lives. But that consciousness involves purely subjunctive states: willing, affirming, asserting, celebrating. Deliberation plays no part in the Dionysian mind because change and fortune never issue in final results, never generate lingering consequences that limit any of the subjunctive states a passionate disposition can take. Hence, Dionysian willing of change is not a project, not what Aristotle's *Poetics* calls an *agon*, but a ceremony; not a prolonged and then satisfied intention, but an instantaneous ecstasy. In the decades that followed *The Birth of Tragedy*, Nietzsche presented the eternal return of the same and the superman as riddling visionary accounts of that ecstasy. The new poetics proposed here follows the same course.

Two benefits flow from taking up this new poetics. An approach is opened to Nietzsche's idea that will to power is all becoming, and an approach is opened to Ibsen's radical, permanently disruptive artistic achievement. Whatever its ontology and ethics might be, a poetics needs to account for drama's form, the structures by which plays generate and control response in their audience. Nietzsche presents his visionary affirmation of endless change, even at its most bizarre, as a measure of people's willingness to live. His account of experience as Dionysian requires people to will both the sequence and quality of all the moments in which they become what they are. That demand makes his thought especially suitable as a basis for analysis of drama, which requires audiences to respond to characters whose quality is evoked and bestowed by the sequence that makes their moments a life. And Nietzsche's tests for life's quality make his thought a high-powered lens through which to observe the sequences by which quality emerges in the lives Ibsen depicts.

In Ibsen's plots reversals and recognitions move the past into the future. If this pattern is seen in the light of the eternal return of the same, the subversive force ecstasy exerts in Ibsen's pragmatic cause-and-effect sequences comes clear. Ibsen's protagonists are all expert moralists and psychologists struggling with the dangerous enticement of conversion. If this pattern is seen in the light of the superman's ecstatic self-overcoming, the subversive force that private impulse exerts on dutiful, social identity also comes clear. Subsequent analyses of *Ghosts*, *Rosmersholm*, and *The Master Builder* account in detail for the subversive dimension in Ibsen's depiction of change. To make that account possible this chapter closes with an experiment in Nietzschean poetics, a presentation of the eternal return of the same and the superman as plot and character in the modernist drama of ecstatic change.

This new poetics starts with the old idea that theatrical art is mimetic. The idea holds that drama gives hypothetical lives the structure concrete lives have and that this exchange clarifies life's functions and so enhances life's value. This new poetics also preserves the old idea that life is internally ordered sequential change and that hypothetically staged life is as well. This modernist, Dionysian poetics departs from the old, Aristotelian one primarily in its definition of the order displayed by sequential change. Aristotle understood that order to be cause-and-effect logic that gave the sequence of changes an irresistible and unrepeatable beginning, middle, and end. The new poetics presents will to power as the order governing sequential change. In this model the sequence presents change as life's repeating, endless dynamic, not as life's logical progress from intention to deed to result. Will to power's agents invoke and celebrate change's impulsive play with them; they do not plan or carry out strategies to moderate change. The order of their lives is ever-enhanced joy instead of ever-vigilant deliberation.

The plot of this Dionysian joy is the eternal return of the same; its agent is the superman. This new plot reverses Aristotelian action in two important ways. With more or less awareness, characters in conventional drama normally try to bring a new effect out of an old cause. In tragedies they fail; in comedies they succeed. In both cases plot amounts to attempted control of the future through correction of the distant or immediate past. The eternal return of the same is the antiplot. It presents prudential correction of life as a hypothesis instead of a project, and it denigrates the effort altogether. The choice to hypothetically edit a life's accidental sequence or to ceremoniously make that sequence a destiny by affirming it, by willing its precise and perpetual recurrence, is a demonic temptation, as Nietzsche presents it. Choosing to edit their lives, agents yield to the enticing danger of resentment: life could have been this or that had desire's or deliberation's exertions not been balked. Choosing to love their lives enough to regard them as self-imposed fate, indulging what Nietzsche calls *amor fati*, agents yield to the enticing danger of imaginary omnipotence: life is what I make of it.[22] This is hubris from the Greek point of view, pride from the Christian one, and the transfiguration of both those systems from Nietzsche's perspective, the sentiment that ecstatically affirms Dionysus in place of the classical logos that Christianity later deified in the person of Christ. Affirming every change that has happened amounts to affirming every change that can or will happen. Hence, ironically, the demon's riddle, which seems to enhance fixity, actually enhances play. It is in this sense, as an impulsive ordering of change, that the eternal return of the same is the plot of Dionysian joy.

For this plot to infiltrate a conventionally tragic or comic action, the agents of the conventional play must have some characteristics of the superman. Their ambition to overcome particular circumstances must also somehow be a desire to overcome the authority of circumstance over them altogether.

However expert or necessary their maneuvers in the contingent realm may be, Dionysian protagonists will always display some capacity for imaginatively transforming reality's fixed cause and effect into change's willed play. In Aristotle's account of drama an agent's disposition limits his or her capacity to prudently adjust to change. In this new poetics the reverse is true. Devotees of Dionysus take their disposition from change's play with them. Those dispositions are not limiting principles of adjustment to change but, rather, constitutive powers of affirmation, self-creating energies that increase with each improvisation of power they responsively summon. Character, in this Dionysian poetics, displays the same sequentially ordered change that Dionysian plot does. Instead of responding with a persistent limitation to corrective change, Dionysian character ecstatically comes and goes in every moment of serially playful change, enhanced by each toss of the dice.

Ibsen's plays, especially the three examined in this study, all present action as a conflict between this unfamiliar, ecstatic, voluntarist change and the deliberate, pragmatic change presented as life's normative order by the theater, the church, and the philosophy of Europe. His protagonists all have some intuition of joy, some talent for ecstatic willing, but they usually lose sight of joy and turn their wills toward desperate attempts to hide or evade or correct their past. The confusing impediment in all cases is duty. Ibsen scholarship to date has concentrated more on his critique of duty than his endorsement of joy, largely because a poetics for the ecstasy Mrs. Alving, Rebecca West, Hilde Wangel, and Halvard Solness variously glimpse, repudiate, or violently enact has been lacking. This account of modernist Dionysian action is an experimental offering made to move understanding of Ibsen past that gap. Placed against the Aristotelian poetics Ibsen mastered, this Nietzschean account of ecstatic plot and character should give a clearer view of what Ibsen saw as life's value and how he commanded the theater's power to make that value count.

3

Ghosts: *The Sick Will*

Ibsen's plays all show people trying to make their lives happy, usually ruining themselves in the process. His last twelve plays, commonly referred to as the realist, prose cycle, were regarded by Ibsen as a continuous, unified portrayal of the problems of living well. From the historical pageants, folklore romances, and comedies of manners that he wrote in Norway at the beginning of his career through the poetic and theological epics undertaken in exile during the middle period—*Brand* (1866), *Peer Gynt* (1867), and *The Emperor and the Galilean* (1869-73)—Ibsen pursued that radical reorganization of theatrical form and moral life achieved in his last twelve plays, and he wanted the pursuit and achievement to be seen whole. "Only by grasping and comprehending my entire production as a continuous and coherent whole," he wrote, "will the reader be able to receive the precise impression I sought to convey in the individual parts of it."[1] The remark indicates an easily forgotten fact of Ibsen's career, that his fame, and income, rested largely on a reading public. Plays were routinely published before as well as during and after their stagings in nineteenth-century Europe and were regarded as literary events as much as theatrical ones. When, as happened often in Ibsen's career, plays were banned from stages or for other reasons took a long time getting to them, plays were only literary.[2] His status as author, equivalent to a historian or philosopher or serious novelist, guaranteed Ibsen that grave cultural authority that his status as playwright partially jeopardized. Antitheatrical prejudice took no sabbatical in Ibsen's world and controlled his own contempt for the popular dramatic forms whose persuasive force he subversively mastered in his best work. Text or performance, drama had more to do than entertain and endorse conventional understanding, in Ibsen's view. It was to be precisely and coherently understood as the communication of the playwright's awareness. In Ibsen's case that awareness never swayed from prophetic, foundational critique of those actions that middle-class culture promised would end in well-being.

The prose cycle, beginning with *The Pillars of Society* (1877) and ending with *When We Dead Awaken* (1899), shows the consummation of rational humanism as an ethos, the exhaustion, in nineteenth-century Europe, of Aristotle's ancient conviction that, through acting in a certain way, people could know happiness and preserve it as their normative condition. The following chapters take up three definitive points in Ibsen's 22 year summation of civilization's discontent: *Ghosts* (1881), *Rosmersholm* (1886), and *The Master Builder* (1892). The objective is to show what conceptual and structural reworking of action's philosophical and dramatic meaning, what new understanding of cause, makes Ibsen the summary Aristotelian and first Nietzschean dramatist. Attention to action in these three plays amounts to a prolegomenon for further attention to a central issue in modern drama that Ibsen brought into focus more powerfully than any other playwright in the period: what counts as a change or event, what it means to say something happened in a life.

By Ibsen's time Aristotle's conception of action had undergone many philosophical and dramatic transformations. What counted as reasoning, nature, intention, and happiness had been redefined incessantly under the pressure of changing religious, political, social, and technological intervention, so incessantly that it might seem tendentious to talk about any persistent Aristotelian conception of reality at all. A full defense of the claim that Aristotle's fundamental insight persisted through two thousand years cannot be made here. It is accurate to say that the idea that people belong happily in the world by virtue of self-determining, self-correcting awareness of their own substantial powers exercised in the world's substantial order is Aristotelian and also humanistic. This ancient Greek conviction that people act themselves into stable, knowable being in a stable, knowable way governs the intellectual and dramatic history that Ibsen inherited and radically transformed. Drastic telescoping is required to find that the transformed conviction is Aristotle's; the gain is greater knowledge of Ibsen's drastic demands for revisionary and foundational thinking and feeling.

ANCIENT ORDER TO MODERN DEADLOCK

What was Ibsen's immediate inheritance of Aristotle? What were the contemporary problems in thinking about action driving his plays? The Greek conception requires stability throughout: the invariable order of nature presents the constant relation of actual and possible powers to be in which people take their place through selective participation. The participation is accomplished in physical and mental behavior. The selection is accomplished through reason, which organizes physical necessity into civilized life, into the variously constructed sciences and arts that make for human well-being. This well-being, reason's action, is the end, the final cause of nature's substantial unification of actual and possible powers to be. Reason does not create as much as it discovers the conditions of human happiness: thinking acts as a ratio by which people match their indwelling capacities to the conditions in nature that those capacities act in and on.

Although thinking is inseparable from bodies in the phenomenal world, it does not originate in them. The active principle in nature, most capably active as reason in people, is also acting outside nature, in the divinity that is its essence, in which it originates and ends, and in which it acts without material limitation, in which it is perfect. The order of phenomenal reality that reason works in is the order of divine reason existing under the condition of change. The ratio people use to make themselves happy, to manage change, is their participation in that divinity. Success and failure in working with that ratio originate in people's awareness of it, both their knowledge and desire for it.

While this knowledge and desire are both called natural in Aristotle's philosophy, neither is infallible in execution, because both exist under the limiting conditions of people's physical composition. The whole order of action, successes and failures in matching human reason to the world, in making civilization of animal life, manifests how extensively divine mind, perfect action, has permeated limiting matter. Thus, happiness and unhappiness both indicate stability, one the positive, one the negative limit of the permanent order maintaining phenomenal existence. Action will always involve reaction in the natural world; cause and effect will always be played out in variously enhancing or thwarting natural limitations. The surprising structure of dramatic action makes sense of the ambiguity inherent in the ratio binding nature and people: plots show how reasonable action is both separate and cooperatively identical with the divine mind and the world it continually acts into being.

Arguments against this conception of people's place in the world from Aristotle's time until Ibsen's primarily assail the stability keeping all the relationships functional and understandable. The two reconceptions of this stability most relevant to Ibsen's plays were wrought by Christianity and the Cartesian conception of rationality that extended to Ibsen through its eighteenth- and nineteenth-century developments. Christianity introduced the concept of will, which vastly enlarged the authority of desire over reason, and the concept of faith as a kind of loving knowledge that superseded reason and that directed intelligence immediately to the divine order governing phenomena. Accurate observation of the norms of nature and civilization were variously insufficient or distracting in the Christian approach to happiness, which makes faith's loving control of will and reason the access to well-being. Christian faith is never the natural operation that reason was for Aristotle but a capacity for transcendent understanding of reality that may bypass sense data. Essential as this capacity is for happiness, it is inscrutably and unevenly bestowed by God. While the stability of people's place in the created world is maintained in Christianity, the stability of their ability to take that place, or even to discover it, vanishes in the mystery of loving faith.

Eastern Orthodox Christianity rationalized that mystery from the start, especially in Neoplatonic language, but had little influence in European history, especially after the dissolution of the Roman Empire. Medieval Christianity did much to rationalize that mystery, especially in the scholastic, Aristotelian theology of Aquinas, which sought to dignify nature and society as religious objects of reasoned and loving knowledge. The Protestant reformation of the sixteenth century introduced a critique of reason and an alienating concept of religious love powerful enough to compete successfully with Catholicism's humanistic revision of Aristotle straight into the twentieth century. Martin Luther split well-being from deeds when he opposed loving faith against acts. While Luther preached the exaltation of faith as a liberating, cheerful discovery of salvation, of permanent well-being, his severing of that state from any merely human function or capacity introduced a corrosive, systematic anxiety into moral life that Ibsen's characters act out constantly.

In Protestant Christianity neither love nor faith nor deeds nor will nor reason nor nature or society has a stable knowable relation to the divine action. Creaturely or social actions situate an individual ambiguously in relation to God, since they never indicate transparent motivation in faith. Love, the immediate joyous conviction of well-being, can be delusion when it acts separately from faith. That separation cannot always be clearly discerned, since faith itself is no stable function. Because faith is intellectual conviction without sensory evidence, its object can always be readily doubted. Moreover, whether the conviction exists or not is never clear, since the transcendent awareness of faith is not readily distinct from arrogant assumption. Even if faith does apprehend God, its permanence is never guaranteed, since the conviction can be lost or withdrawn easily. And faith's absence can no more readily be discerned through examination of conscience or deeds than its presence. Will, an irrational but self-directing disposal of personal energy, pursues no end naturally or systematically and, even when allied with faith, may oppose or desert faith's ends, if and when those ends are present and known. And reason, "the devil's whore" in Luther's fine phrase, is merely the capacity to conjugate propositions. Thinking has no more necessary connection to truth or reality than wanting or believing. People must strive with all those imperfect means to discover and reach their place in the created order, and that discovery and arrival can only be bestowed on them by God, who does not so reward creatures in any way that has discernible reference to their striving in love, faith, reason, will, or deeds. All that is left of classical humanism here is the conviction that human well-being is provided by divine activity. That happiness is normative, that it belongs to people who belong to the world intelligently and naturally, is not incompatible with Christian thinking about the divine loving action, but the Aquinian and Orthodox humanism that stressed that compatibility was not available in the religion that the people in *Ghosts, Rosmersholm,* and *The Master Builder,* struggle with on Ibsen's stage.

The alienation of mind from action that transformed sixteenth-century Christianity in Europe made a second, equally stark philosophical appearance in the century after Luther. The rationalistic dualism and essentialism that Aristotle had opposed returned in full modern dress in the thought of René Descartes. In *Discourse on Method* (1637) and *Meditations* (1641), Descartes matched Luther's religious fixation on the inner man with a psychological and intellectual one. Doubt led Luther to the spiritual crisis over salvation that he resolved by abolishing moral agency from the good Christian life. Doubt is also Descartes's starting point. Whereas Aristotle argues that knowledge began in wonder, Descartes holds that knowledge begins and proceeds systematically in doubting all received wisdom, indeed all mental experience. When an indubitable content resists skeptical deconstruction, when a disposition to believe something cannot be dislodged upon reflection, but, instead, recommends itself through irresistible conviction, truth and the real have been reached. This method is not technically philosophical, but transformed philosophy nonetheless, largely by making the deductive coherence of scholastic Aristotelianism obsolete. While Descartes retains some scholastic arguments, most conspicuously the relation of cause and effect, the objective referentiality of certain ideas, and the ontological argument for the existence of God, he banishes the grand scholastic conception of humanity's place in hierarchical reality. In place of stably active natural, social, and intellectual orders in which people act themselves into being,

Descartes presents subjectivity as the atomistic, or foundational, reality of human life. Self-consciousness is the substance of life; reality amounts to awareness in any doubt or discovery of certainty that some mental being is doubting or certain. People are not agents in this view but, rather, states of mind. These states of mind are not accomplished through natural or social deeds, but are innate conditions whose content is supplied not by matching the mind to phenomenal reality, but by self-regarding introspection. The subject of mental states comes to be through awareness of itself as subject—in Descartes's Latin phrase *Cogito, ergo sum*.[3]

Descartes's *pense* and *cogito* include all mental states, not just thinking. Subjectivity consists of doubting, believing, knowing, wishing, hoping, wanting, waiting, trusting, fearing, loving, hating, regretting, enjoying, and the like. The truth of any of these states derives not from observation of their origin in any cause external to the subject, but, rather, in the irresistible force they exert in the subject. These states, like any the mind takes, are all called ideas. Three innate ideas recommend themselves most irresistibly to Descartes, and it is from these three unfailing dispositions to believe that he constructs the world. The first is cogito or self-awareness, knowing that one or another mental state presents itself for reflection; the second is the idea of God as a perfect, infinite being who does not deceive the mental beings reflecting upon Him; the third is the existence of the physical world.

Reflecting on the idea of God, mind discerns that God has created two distinct substances: mind and matter. Mind's attribute is subjectivity, and matter's is extension and duration. Their absolute distinction emerges in mind's capacity to doubt the body's existence but not its own. More precisely, the mind doubts not merely the existence of the body attached to it but the identity of itself and that body; it doubts that it *has* a body, that it somehow is constituted in relation to matter. Seen in this light, the doubt does not overcome the irresistible force of the innate idea of matter but enhances the conviction that subjectivity and extension are both real and both different. The undoubted existence of matter is known not through reference to evidence supplied by sensation but through reflective scrutiny of the intellectual principle contained in that idea of matter innate in the mind. Upon reflection the mind knows that matter is extension, that all its properties and qualities, primary and secondary, are modes of extension. The material world is one extended body, infinite, three-dimensional, and isomorphic. This mathematical term belongs essentially to Descartes's conception of physical reality: it is essentially geometric, its operations are mechanical, and there is no final cause in any of those operations. Physical changes are variations in modes of one body's extension, not coming to be and passing away of an infinite number of composite bodies. Knowing physical reality is essentially a matter of elaborating more and more comprehensive mathematical formulas resident in the innate idea of matter irresistibly presented in and to the mind. The physical world, from a Cartesian standpoint, is not so much a thing as it is a meaning, a first-order form with various second-order conditions of quality and quantity.

How is this conception a revision of Aristotelian humanism? The divine action and the human action are preserved, but the natural action is eliminated. People become what they are not by operating in the limiting conditions of nature and culture, not by selectively participating in an action/reaction system that brings actual and possible powers to be into unity, but by contemplating two poles of the absolute: subjectivity and God. People do not belong to a world that belongs to them, in Descartes's view. They do not belong anywhere; they establish themselves; they ground themselves by reflection on themselves as subjects of the cogito sustained by the perfect intellectual activity of God. Their being is given not in behavior but in thought, and achievement of that being is accomplished not in deeds but in states of mind.

And what of nature and society and people's relation to them? The world exists to be appropriated, dominated, made the articulate workshop of the mind. Nature and society, therefore, do not create or enhance human life; they exist primarily to define humanity negatively. Well-being involves intellectual discovery and maintenance of that oppositional distinction. Contingency and the order of phenomenal change, which constitute people substantially in Aristotelian humanism, become in Descartes's thought negative proof that reality is only known through contemplative access to the absolute. People's bodily and social lives pollute or impede subjectivity in the worst case, and are the inert exemplars of it in the best.

The necessity and value of the physical world as a stage for human self-awareness can only be maintained in Descartes's scheme as long as God is maintained as the benevolent, undeceiving creator of the idea of extension. When God lapses from the model, one or another monism develops, in which subjectivity or matter becomes unreal, and the human situation—being placed in both states at once—becomes absurd. This is what happened in the centuries intervening between Descartes and Ibsen, which saw various monisms and unconvincing dualistic ontologies competing for philosophical authority. Materialist philosophies concentrated entirely on matter, idealist ones on the cogito; both did away with the ego, the self that needed to act itself into being in the world. Dualist philosophy tried to reconstruct personal agency as the ground of human reality, usually by having personhood depend on active adjustment of the world to the self or vice versa. The two dualist responses to Cartesian alienation of mind from matter most relevant to Ibsen's dramatic and intellectual achievement are the Enlightenment and romantic redefinitions of nature and mind and their relation in action. The conceptual urgency and social force of these large cultural shifts in eighteenth- and nineteenth-century Europe, their expression in new literary and dramatic forms, and their incomplete restoring of substantive action as the integrated ground of human life culminate in the anguish that Ibsen's characters undergo, and which O'Neill's and Beckett's do as well, when they set out to act in the world and find they cannot.

The Enlightenment exalts reason as the guarantor of knowledge and happiness at the expense of Judaic and Christian conceptions of God and faith. Religion's authority is deemed superstitious, damaging ignorance. Only Aristotle's first-mover account of divinity survives and only in those few rationalists who, as deists, allow that God is a cosmic clockmaker, an artisan, but no sustainer or controller of ordered physical and mental reality. Instead of subjective recourse to absolute, limitless being, seekers of the real look rationally into nature, where they discover a mathematically reliable structure, a principled organization of material limitations displaying all the certainty Descartes required of God. That order belongs to nature in this view and is no projection of the subject. The order emerges in reasoned observation of sensation, not in analytic reflection on the logical structure of innate ideas. The rational faculty exists to make human sense of the phenomenal realm, in the Enlightenment view, to put matter into people's hands as well as their minds. For Voltaire or Franklin or Kant people belong in the physical world, which belongs to them by virtue of their thinking about it.

So far this is Aristotle's humanism revived. The distinction comes in what counts as action in Enlightenment thinking. Aristotle seems to have been confident that human reason and the natural world had reached their optimal conditions in his world, at least in Athens. Anyone with minimally propitious circumstances and well-developed intelligence could perform constitutive deeds, could pursue ends that, when achieved, would unite actual and possible powers to be happy. Eighteenth-century humanism introduced the idea of progress into its revival of classical humanism. The notion is not only positive. Progress in the Enlightenment world means eliminating corruptions that have obscured nature's order, impeded reason's capacity to discover that order, and mangled the relation in people of their rational and bodily, their human and animal, substance. Before the world can belong to the people who belong to it the cankers of religion and various monisms in philosophy that have despotically mangled the fit of mind to matter must be excised and the damage they have done healed. Actual happiness must wait until the possibilities in people to be happy are refurbished through reformation of science, ethics, politics, economics, and philosophy. The mind must correct its own relation to its animal nature, to other minds in nature, and to nature itself all at once before it can make human well-being the normative condition and result of action in and on the phenomenal realm.

Confidence in that correction's inevitable triumph makes the Enlightenment a utopian period; anxiety about the correction's strength makes the period an elitist, stoically skeptical one; in neither case is successful human life thought of as simply provided for by the known orders of nature and society. The skepticism of Alexander Pope and the confidence of Thomas Jefferson indicate the period's negative and positive understanding of what must be done before Aristotle's substantive action can emerge as the norm in human affairs. Neoclassical and conservative or modernist and revolutionary, the Enlightenment conviction holds that the order governing people's successful activity in the realm of phenomenal change, although impassive and invariable, emerges only when people freely pursue reason. Action embodying rationally discovered order is a promise or a regret in this period, at best an incipient achievement, not ever an immediately available option.

From the last quarter of the eighteenth century through the first quarter of the nineteenth the Enlightenment conceptions of mind, nature, and progress were transfigured by romantic thinkers and artists. Rationality and its invariable fit of mind to the invariable order of nature tyrannically ruin life, in the romantic view, as religion did in the Enlightenment one. The new view holds that people's place in the world is given through their unfixed, primarily emotional and imaginative awareness of mutability in themselves and in nature. Two first-order convictions about mutability characterize romanticism: everything is a living part of one everlasting living being, and all change is organic development in that being; nothing exists but appearance, everything emerges from the void into which it collapses, change is always destruction, when it brings an appearance out of the void and when it returns an appearance to the void.

The first view allows that people have some access to the everlasting being that sustains and changes them, some transcendent experience, however limited, of this being's absolute power in human and natural life. The second view holds that partial experience of the absolute amounts to no experience of it; absolute being having no ratio or degree in itself can admit no limited apprehension. Awareness of human dependence on or containment in ineffable change, however transcendent, amounts finally to ignorant alienation from that ineffable, absolute source—hence, the conviction that everything that is emerges from and recedes to the void. The first view revives Aristotle's humanistic conception of action, transforming it by making the constitutive fit between mind and matter an emotional and imaginative response to change, rather than a prudential, pragmatic mastery of it. The second view of mutability transfigures Descartes's conception of people's function and nature's. Here protean subjectivity is seen not so much as feeling overtaking reason to give people and the world to each other but, instead, as Cartesian skepticism unmoored by the absolute.

The Enlightenment preserved a humanistic version of Cartesian absolutism in its concept of nature as a system of principled structures presenting permanently ordered primary qualities for observation and mastery by human reason. Scorning this reasoned pursuit of worldly ends as a condition of happiness, despairing of that alternatively irrational sustaining identification with the spirit of the woods Wordsworth celebrated, the second romantic vision of change gives people no way into their own reality or nature's. When it isn't forthrightly nihilistic, this romanticism presents cosmopolitan ennui or compulsive guilt, usually experienced as damnation, as people's only authentic response to the inaccessible absolute. The idealist struggle toward the absolute is not jettisoned in this view but cast as the obligatory failure ordering human mental life, an effort that always leads to boredom or the torture of self-loathing. Coleridge's "Dejection, an Ode" and most of Byron's poetry present this second romantic conception of reality most clearly.[4]

Where does progress fit in these two romantic visions of life? It has no place in the second view, except as one more necessary expression of people's incapacity to belong to themselves or their world. The Enlightenment's aim at revision of society and mental life is preserved as an objective in romantic ideas of the universe as a living creature, but reasonable restoration of an invariable native order gives way in romantic culture to restoration of feeling, to enlargement of response. The changes romantics hope for are not corrections in thoughtful mastery of nature but joyous affirmation of the organic processes of birth and death that organize mental and natural life. Progress comes not through fitting the world to the mind's rational operations but through enhancement of the felt experience of life, through cultivation of people's subjective awareness of their participation in the everlasting transmutations of birth and death.

Nature's violent irregularity is not the enemy for romantics, as it is in the Enlightenment, but an awesome form of progress. The aim to match human response to nature's paroxysms leads to emphasis on sublimity in romantic aesthetics and metaphysics, to endorsement of apocalyptic revolution in romantic political theory. While nature's violence is generally the preferred experience in romanticism, the intricate, evanescent delicacies of organic development are also a model for progressive enhancement of feeling. Hence, romanticism's emphasis on the exquisite as an aesthetic value, its discovery of childhood as a moral norm, its political antagonism to empire.

Neither in refinement nor magnificence of response do the romantics hope for or pursue a world governed by Aristotelian action, a world in which people's requirements and nature's opportunities are fixed and matched one to the other through intelligent pragmatism and physical necessity. In the romantic view, people become what they are not through deeds, but through feelings; hence, it is not the opportunity to pursue worldly objectives but the opportunity to enhance subjectivity that must be safeguarded or restored. That protection or restoration comes about not through the actions of governments, churches, schools, or any other systematic social force but, rather, through the intimate motions of people toward and back from the everlasting life that they reside in and that resides in them. Familial, erotic, and social life are valuable insofar as they enhance that intimacy, destructive insofar as they impede it.

Whereas priests, politicians, and pedants stifle living response when they regulate it with systems, artists can safeguard and restore the mind's intimate motions by portraying and so enhancing them. Because art is no obligation, for the creator or receiver, its augmentation of subjectivity liberates them both, prepares both to receive life more abundantly. When Shelley claims in *Defense of Poetry* that poets are the legislators of mankind, he is not making an Enlightenment argument that writers objectively articulate the normative formulas that bind people to reality's invariably rational order. Instead, he argues that poets make known the original and most valuable qualities of response that keep people happy, that is affirmative, assenting to their felt experience of living change.[5] Romantic progress hopes for nothing more than such assent.

Ibsen wrote his plays in the aftermath of the romantic rebellion against Enlightenment rationalism. Neither romantic subjectivist nor Enlightenment rationalist by credo, temperament, or conviction, Ibsen did dramatize problems taken up by both cultural movements. Critics and scholars, following the lead of George Bernard Shaw in *The Quintessence of Ibsenism* (1891), have often docketed Ibsen's mentality in the Enlightenment, concentrating on his interest in rationalist social reform. By midcentury a backlash had set in, and Ibsen's continuance of the romantic concentration on subjectivity was held to be the playwright's primary, if not exclusive, subject. H. L. Mencken's introduction to the Modern Library edition of Ibsen's plays is the most powerful and cogent expression of this position and a clear indication of its orthodoxy (few American publishing ventures have been at once so popular and so culturally authoritative as Bennet Cerf's ambition to get the classics what Ezra Pound wanted for them, "a wider circulation").[6] The argument continues today, often most heatedly over the question of Ibsen's feminism. In 1989 Joan Templeton published an article in the January issue of *Publications of the Modern Language Association* entitled "The Doll House Backlash: Criticism, Feminism, and Ibsen." Acknowledging Ibsen's protestations against alignment with any political party and his disavowal of feminism as a restrictive reduction of his spiritual and moral subject, Templeton argues intelligently for the contemporary value of reading Nora's story as a feminist text.

Ibsen's plays make enormous demands on the moral as well as emotional attention of any audience. His jealous guarding and vehement pursuit of the cultural authority of messianic truthteller inevitably infects any sensitive critical account of the plays and often extends to the critic's choice of what truth might be at stake in any given drama. Interpretive advocacy of his Enlightenment or romantic inheritance is always important and fitting when it acknowledges his combination and transmutation of both attitudes, always incomplete and disappointing when it does not. Ibsen made the first 8 of his 12 prose plays exposés of the crimes by which powerful men in finance, politics, the academy, law, industry, and the church wreck not only their own lives, but the chance for happiness in society at large. The Enlightenment struggle to cast off religion and the state and so usher in the decent happiness that native rationalism would give society forms the action of both *Ghosts* and *Rosmersholm* and is thematically important in *The Master Builder*. Those political periodicals calling for progress through free thought, which first emerged in the eighteenth century, move along the plot significantly in *An Enemy of the People* and *Rosmersholm*, and books arguing the free thought case against religion appear on Mrs. Alving's parlor table in *Ghosts*. While theoretical feminism does not organize *A Doll House*, the call for social as well as moral, intellectual, and religious emancipation of women clearly organizes the thematic structure of that play and counts for much in *Ghosts*, *The Lady from the Sea*, *Rosmersholm*, and *Pillars of Society*. In short, Ibsen presents the continuation of the Enlightenment project copiously in his plays and dramatizes that project's control over the material and professional life of nineteenth-century society with buzzing, realistic density.

But he crosscuts the rationalist, social action with a competing psychological one. The characters striving to right a worldly wrong, or suffering as victims of one, also want solutions to private emotional and spiritual conflicts.

They want to make their own lives over in the conviction of sure private possession of an absolute whose logic they hope will reorder worldly affairs once it has healed them. With the exception of Ellida Wangel in *The Lady from the Sea*, Ibsen's romantic searchers strive after an absolute that their guilty requiring makes unavailable. Hedda Gabler, Rebecca West, and John Rosmer kill themselves to reach the absolute. Mrs. Alving's compromised pursuit of absolute value in *Ghosts* ends in an impasse that she can only break if she kills her son. Gregers Werle causes the unavailing suicide of an innocent child in his demand for truth telling in *The Wild Duck*. When no conventional social control checks or modifies it, the pursuit of the absolute in Ibsen's plays ends with death thwarting or ruinously delivering the absolute romantic good: love's joyful assent to life.

These dramatic attempts to reorder life through subjective alignment with absolute value, provoked by the ambiguous anguish of guilty longing for purity and carried forward by the unstable force of weakness longing for strength, all repeat the romantic transmutation of Cartesian and Protestant convictions that some quality of awareness, and not their deeds, makes people what they are. Benedetto Croce identified this conviction in Ibsen's plays in 1921 when he observed: "All of Ibsen's heroes and heroines are strained with expectation, consumed by the yearning for the extraordinary, the sublime, the unattainable, scornful of idyllic happiness in any form and degree and of virtue modest and resigned to its own imperfections."[7] Croce goes on to assume that Ibsen shared this dissatisfaction without criticism, which is a clear mistake, but one that most romantic readers of Ibsen have pursued for a long time.

Close attention to Ibsen's construction of the actions in the prose cycle shows that he integrated Enlightenment and romantic definitions of life and happiness by consigning each to a different dimension of the dramas. The interdependence of these dimensions makes Ibsen modernist. The intrigues his well-made plots dramatize always involve worldly struggles for Enlightenment progress that almost always end in the protagonists' paralysis or death. Their response to that paralysis, their attempt to avoid, disguise, or achieve an absolute vision that would free them utterly, all present the romantic definition of life as a mental condition independent of deeds. Ibsen's reliance on Aristotelian thinking prevails in the intrigue plot that represents rationalism gone bad. His interest in Nietzsche's repudiation of Aristotle's action-based humanism prevails in the mental plot, which shows imagination and feeling ruined. Dramatizing people struggling out of a wrecked worldly action into an equally damaging and unmastered mental action, Ibsen dramatizes the deadlock to which Enlightenment and romantic understanding both lead.

He broke the deadlock in his last four plays by changing the relation between mental and worldly action. Instead of making the psychological plot a repetition and consequence of the impasse in the social one, each of the last plays splits mental action off from deeds. The protagonists' resolution of mental struggles comes only once they have renounced botched aims to control worldly circumstance. The well-made play evaporates from Ibsen's late dramatic structures, giving way to spiritual transformations that occur apart from conventionally dramatic events. Aristotelian drama presents an action that transposes private intention into public deed. The passage, however complex, pleases insofar as it is transparent, plausible, and complete. In his last plays Ibsen departs as far as he can from Aristotelian drama without abandoning it utterly and presents intentions transformed through purely subjective, sometimes mystical, intuition and struggle.

The world of money and family vanishes or fades to a vapor under the superior force of mysterious contests of will in Ibsen's final plots. Telepathy, clairvoyance, and psychokinesis move these plots along more than plausible, transparent pursuit of rational aims. Such mystical forces work powerfully in the realistic world of *Ghosts*, *Rosmersholm*, and *Hedda Gabler*; they completely overtake the action in *The Master Builder*, *Little Eyolf*, (1894) *John Gabriel Borkman*, (1896) and *When We Dead Awaken*. Symbolic events such as the burning of the orphanage in *Ghosts* or the sighting of phantom white horses in *Rosmersholm* display the causal logic binding private and public struggles in those plays.[8] However morally and psychologically evocative, their magical or supranatural status remains ambiguous. The symbols of the last plays, the Rat woman in *Little Eyolf*, the airy castle in *The Master Builder*, minerals in *John Gabriel Borkman*, and mountains in *When We Dead Awaken* are all unambiguously magical and supranatural. While they do bear on the scant public lives of the characters, their most powerful function is to refer these characters subjectively to a transcendent order of cause governed by absolute value.

The first eight plays in the prose cycle show characters failing by living against their worldly situation; the last four show characters achieving some measure of success by living past their world. Will's cooperation with reason makes up the humanistic action of the first set of plays. The failed actions Ibsen constructs in them have two mutually inclusive causes: purposive thinking about social reality has gone wrong, and the will to correct the error, to undo its damage, is inadequate. This structure continues, in broad outline, the Aristotelian model for tragedy. Inadequate willing, while it belongs to the Aristotelian model as a function of character, belongs at the same time to Nietzsche's contradictory account of action and tragedy. Will's failure is guaranteed, in that account, by any and all connection with rational attempts to control phenomenal reality and so satisfy human purposes. This Nietzschean reading sees Aristotelian humanism itself as the error, not any particular application of it. More than an error, prudential rationalism is a disease, for Nietzsche, a nihilistic weakening of people's naturally constitutive action, which is not reasonably adjusting to the world's orderly changes, but ecstatically willing the world's inhospitable chaos. In the Nietzschean reading Mrs. Alving and the rest decline into paralysis not because they make the wrong choices but because they cannot make any right ones as long as they want to change the world that changes them.

Nietzsche analyzes reactive, nihilistic willing to make clear what active, substantive willing is or, more accurately, what it will be when people become strong enough to exert it. Substantive willing makes changing worldly circumstances the occasion for *amor fati* and joyous assent to the eternal return of the same, the two stances that people who overcome all prudential weakness take toward experience. The stances have been examined in chapter 2, so it suffices simply to repeat here that amor fati involves willing the past, and affirming the eternal return of the same means willing that the willed past recur in the future. Neither stance has anything to do with rationality; both make people at home in themselves, not in the world.

Ibsen's final four plays show people taking these stances toward their past and future. They break the deadlock of prudential action not through renunciation of the world but through Nietzschean appropriation of it. Up until these last four dramas Ibsen's prose cycle is a masterful continuation of the liberal tragedy established by Shakespeare as the standard for European drama. In such tragedy people at the height of power and limit of strength challenge an order from which they have been alienated and are defeated by the release of their energy, either because the order is immovable or because the energy released is disorganized by madness or some other anomie that has come about in the period of alienation. The two causes of defeat usually are not exclusive and occur together in the best plays—*Hamlet* is a prime example.

Ibsen develops this structure by making the opposing order, usually society, the source of the challenger's alienation and not only the object, but, indeed, the controlling factor of the challenger's rebellion. In Enlightenment rationalism and romantic subjectivism, social corruption of human potential calls the aspiring reformer into being. Normally in Shakespeare's plays, removing a villain or erring hero will suffice to set society right or make it convalescent. But in Ibsen's plays the stain is general and diffuse: something is wrong with the fact of society itself. This systemic problem extends to the reformers that it creates, trapping them in an endgame deadlock, and this

paradox is the most significant development of the Shakespearean model
Ibsen makes in the beginning and middle of his career.

Nietzsche starts with the Enlightenment and romantic insight that
something is wrong with the way people take their place in the phenomenal
world and argues that the problem is not society but people's hopes for it.
Reality is a matter of the relations among various forces of power, in
Nietzsche's thought. The weakest expression of the frailest force comes in
prudence and sentiment, the mainstays of social life, the reactionary, dissi-
pating source of guilt-inducing philosophy and religion. The strongest
action of which these weak expressions are capable in the struggle to master
the changing force of circumstance is stalemate. It is that action that
dramatic form presents in degenerate periods, according to Nietzsche, and
there can be no doubt that Nietzsche and Ibsen thought of their period as
degenerate.

Greek tragedy, in Nietzsche's view, provides the model for strong
expression of force, for enlargement of power. The affirmation of overmas-
tering change, the human willing of it that Dionysian religion made the basis
of Sophoclean tragedy, shows the way out of the impasse that prudence and
sentiment lead to. Nietzsche's Zarathustra calls people to restore themselves
to that Dionysian force by willing the eternal return of the same, by
extinguishing resentment and regret in amor fati. Ibsen spent 25 years writing
the action of his society. He always presented powerful figures struggling to
find the strongest expression of their life's force. For two-thirds of his career
that force was very rarely stronger than circumstances, and Ibsen dramatized
the stalemate Nietzsche saw as the sick will's only possibility. In the last third
of his career, rewriting Nietzsche's visionary tests of the will's force as
dramatic actions, Ibsen dramatized a possible future for innocent, free
expression of life's force, a way people might become happy. The cost was
abandoning Aristotle's humanistic ethics, metaphysics, and poetics and the
European tradition they inspired. A close look at the opposition of Aristotle's
world view and Nietzsche's in Ghosts should show how Ibsen became willing
to pay that cost.

GHOSTS

With one exception, An Enemy of the People, all the plays in Ibsen's prose cycle
have retrospective actions. The characters are all trying somehow to eliminate the lingering bad effects of a past event, usually a crime or mistake, from
their present circumstances. The past may erupt unexpectedly into the

present after a long absence and redirect the course of a life, as happens in *Hedda Gabler* and *The Master Builder*. Alternatively, attention to it may overtake a life, as is the case in *Ghosts* and *John Gabriel Borkman*. At some point in these plays, and in the remaining seven in which the past makes important but not all-inclusive demands, a crucial and false understanding of the past collapses, with ruinous or liberating consequences. *The Wild Duck* is an ironic travesty of this second pattern but an instance of it nonetheless. Focusing so constantly on the past, Ibsen turns Aristotle's theory of drama into a story and shows that the unity of beginning, middle, and end in human actions is not so much a criterion for modern plays, or for modern life, as a problem. *Ghosts* shows how fully intractable the problem can be.

The action of *Ghosts* has two dimensions. In one a well-made play unfolds, with intrigue that involves, in good melodramatic fashion, blackmail, arson, adultery, illegitimate birth, potential incest, prostitution, the onset of syphilitic lunacy, murder, the impotent protestations of a virtuous mother, and the pious counsel of a minister. These activities, or their effects, all converge in one 24-hour period, beginning early in the morning of the day before an orphanage is to be dedicated to Captain Alving's memory, lasting through the night during which the orphanage is burned, and ending at the dawning of a new day. The crimes and their consequences are all concatenated in a sequence of reversals and recognitions brought about by each of the five characters as they try to fit the creation of the orphanage into their own plans for happiness. Secrets are revealed, new ones are created, and as a result, vice triumphs in worldly ways, and virtue is challenged to exceed itself and triumph against the world.

This challenge to virtue makes up the second dimension of the action, which presents Mrs. Alving's internal struggle: her ambiguous, ambivalent chafing against morality, and her apocalyptic confrontation with joy as the destructive alternative to rectitude. The action here shows reversal and recognition advancing thought and feeling more significantly than deeds. The two dimensions run in tandem, with each new crime in the intrigue plot requiring a new response from Mrs. Alving in the moral one, until the last scene, which occurs after the resolution of the orphanage intrigue. All the crimes of that intrigue, and all her transformative responses to them, result in this last scene's demand that she kill her only son Oswald and that she transform that ultimate crime into exonerating, liberating service of what Oswald has called "the joy of life."

The analogue to Abraham's biblical submission of Isaac for sacrifice is both clear and ironic here. Her love of ultimate value, like Abraham's, is being tested into existence. Ultimately, patriarchal power demands the sacrifice in her case, as in Abraham's. The crucial point of the comparison is that she cannot take the trial up at all, that, unlike him, she cannot bring herself into free, active relation to foundational reality. This foundering of the mental action is a sharp contrast to the satisfying resolution of the social action in *Ghosts*, and that contrast is what makes the play powerful and modernist. In *Fear and Trembling* (1843), Søren Kierkegaard made the sacrifice of Isaac an emblem of modernist striving from lesser to greater authenticity, of transformative passage from ethical to abundant religious life accomplished only through choice made without criteria. Ibsen was certainly not unaware of his contemporary's work, nor have critics ignored how the plays take up nine- teenth- century thought and feeling.[9] In its satire of Pastor Manders the play dismisses religion as access to reality so forthrightly and comically that the last scene's canceling of Kierkegaard's "leap of faith" discredits the philoso- pher as much as it does Mrs. Alving. She fails to answer the demands of joyous life that she has partly embraced, not the demands of religion.

The mental action through which she excludes herself from the joyous life she moves toward has more to do with Nietzsche's analysis of the sick will than Kierkegaard's. In the well-made plot Mrs. Alving's failure to manage the past is presented in an ostentatiously classical dramatic structure. Unity of time, place, and action, structural and thematic references to *Oedipus Rex* and *The Oresteia*, clearly frame that action as an Aristotelian one.[10] In the mental plot her lifelong battle against the moral life, which she calls a haunted one (hence the title), and her failure to leave it, stemming from too weak an intuition of what the good life of joy and freedom might be, clearly and powerfully invoke Nietzsche's ideas of dramatic and lived action. His anti- Aristotelian poetics centered on Dionysian willing and his assertion that well-being comes in amor fati and successful confrontation with the eternal return of the same all turn Mrs. Alving's story into a struggle to the death with classical humanism. Close attention to the sequence of events in both plots shows what large-scale cultural forces are at war in the horrible curtain lines Mrs. Alving stops this play with: "yes" and, more dismally, "no."

First the intrigue plot. Helene Alving has been a widow for ten years. The play begins on the day before the tenth anniversary of her husband's death, which she has chosen as the occasion to dedicate the orphanage she has built as a memorial to him. Helene was an orphan herself when she married; her father had died, and at the advice of her mother and two aunts she accepted a marriage offer from the then wealthy Captain Alving, although she loved Pastor Manders, not Alving. She married and left town to live isolated across a fjord in Alving's country estate, because her female relatives persuaded her that the financial and social benefits of the union were essential to her welfare and, implicitly, to theirs. Orphaned girls in early nineteenth-century provincial Norway were burdens to their remaining relatives, especially if those relatives were a widow and two aunts.

At the end of her first married year she ran away from Alving, who was promiscuous, and sought refuge with Manders, to whom she declared her love and from whom she expected romantic and spiritual salvation. He repudiated her love and sent her back to her husband, with the counsel that her suffering was her duty and that her desired happiness was rebellious aspiration to vanity and pride. She returned. Alving persisted in debauchery, contracted syphilis, and lapsed into a life of sequestered dissolution. In her second year of marriage Helene bore a son to Alving, named Oswald, who was infected with his father's venereal disease either at birth or in a childhood prank in which Alving forced the boy to smoke one of his pipes. The infection is not noticed until Oswald is in his mid-twenties.

After the birth Helene ran the estate and all her dissolute husband's public affairs, maintaining a facade of public activity for him, while confining him to the estate, often by outdrinking him. She did this to preserve an inheritance for her son and to protect him from the scandal his father's life would arouse if it was widely known. When Oswald was seven, his father seduced a maid in the house. Mrs. Alving sent the girl off to town, where an opportunist named Engstrand married her. For 50 pounds, supplied by Mrs. Alving, the maid's daughter, Regina, was made legitimate. Sometime in her teens, after Alving's death and her mother's, Regina returned to his estate as Mrs. Alving's maid, where she still works when the present action begins. Regina's conception had moved Mrs. Alving to send Oswald away from the estate, to which (like Regina) he never returned while his father was alive. He is 27 when the play begins and has returned for the dedication of the orphanage from Paris, where he has been living long enough to have become a celebrated painter.

As the play begins, Mrs. Alving is celebrating the end of 29 years devoted to lying to the world about her husband. For the ten years she has been widowed she has been reading free thinkers' books and has been convinced that people can think and love decently outside the authority of the church and the conventional morality of the wealthy middleclass. The orphanage has been constructed with money she made by managing the estate, and the sum required to build it equals the marriage price Alving paid for her. Hence, whatever the estate is worth when Oswald inherits it will be Mrs. Alving's accomplishment. Nothing done by Alving, she believes, will pass on to Oswald: the orphanage cancels her debt to Alving and ensures that the dead roué's reputation, even if it becomes public knowledge, will have the honor of supererogatory public service as protection against slander.

The action of the play shows Mrs. Alving's dedication of the orphanage destroying her. Pastor Manders, who has handled the legal and financial arrangements for her, arrives to advise that she not insure the orphanage against accidental destruction, for fear of scandal. She agrees, with some hesitation at the imprudence of that temerity and because she cannot make good any loss that such destruction would entail. Engstrand, the adoptive father of Regina, has been supervising the building and has arrived before Manders. In the first scene of the play he obliquely refers to a plot he has set to get money from Manders that he needs to open a "sailor's home" in town. The home is only a barely disguised whorehouse, to which he wants Regina to come. Arguing that she owes him filial obedience, Engstrand also tells Regina that leaving Mrs. Alving's orphanage will allow her to advance her fortunes with rich captains in search of company. Regina has no such desire, having set her cap for Oswald, out of affection, social ambition, and hopes based on casual promises he made two years ago to take her to Paris someday.

Regina's flirtation pays off; Oswald makes advances to her and tells his mother that he wants to marry the girl. Mrs. Alving, having told Manders the truth about her marriage to exonerate herself from his accusations that she abandoned her wifely and motherly duties, decides to tell the truth to Oswald and Regina. If they want to marry in full knowledge of their parentage, she will support them. The first time she tries to tell their story to them, she is interrupted by the second-act curtain news that the orphanage is burning. The third act reveals that Engstrand brought Manders to the orphanage for a prededication prayer service, set fire to the building at the end of the service, and has convinced the gullible pastor that he, Manders, accidentally caused the fire by tossing a smoldering candlewick into sawdust and shavings. Engstrand then courteously blackmails the pastor, suggesting that he will take the blame on himself, if Manders can find a way to help him build that spiritual haven for sailors they have discussed recently. Manders, of course, agrees.

Losing the orphanage means nothing to Mrs. Alving, who by this point has set her mind on liberty and the joy of truth-telling. She informs Regina and Oswald of their relation, and Regina rejects Oswald. Having discovered that Oswald is seriously ill, as well as her half-brother, Regina accuses Mrs. Alving of having wrongly patronized her for years and leaves, saying that she can seek her fortune with Manders or, if that fails, in her father's house. At this point the orphanage intrigue has finished. But Oswald launches the play into a more horrible finale.

Having previously elicited his mother's promise to do anything he required of her and making her repeat it, Oswald tells Helene that his syphilis is terminal, has ruined his mind for good, and can break out into the tertiary stage of idiocy and paralysis at any moment, indeed has already manifested itself in a transient attack in the last year in Paris. He tells her that his real reason for returning was fear of death and a longing for her care, not to see the orphanage opened. He blames her for driving Regina away with the truth and says that this deprivation obligates her even more to keep her promise to do anything he asks to help him. He has enough morphine to bring about his death and forces Helene to promise she will administer the 12 pills if he lapses. She promises. The sun rises, and, while she assures him he will not lapse, he lapses. She must, yet cannot do what she has promised; he twice dribbles out a mechanical repetition of his last conscious request for "the sun," and the curtain falls.

The intrigue plot moves along with a major reversal spinning the ending of one act into the new problems that occupy the next. At the end of act 1 Mrs. Alving declares: "now this long, loathsome comedy is over. From the day after tomorrow, it will be as if the dead had never lived in this house. There will be no one here but my boy and his mother."[11] Precisely the opposite occurs in the rest of the play, and Mrs. Alving starts to recognize the inevitably wrong outcome of her plan immediately after this remark, when she sees Oswald kiss Regina and says, hoarsely, "Ghosts" (G, 56). The father, who was to be finally laid to rest in the orphanage's community service, has returned in his son's lust, returned at the moment Mrs. Alving pronounced his final banishment. At the end of the play his ghost takes full command of the house and offers her son to her in a solitude she never anticipated.

At the end of act 2 when Mrs. Alving tries for the second time to rid the house and family of Alving's influence by telling the truth of his life to his children, she is interrupted by the news that the orphanage is burning. Again, Alving interferes from beyond the grave, this time in the person of his surrogate, Engstrand, who took up his place as Regina's father and who ironically converts the orphanage, which is an ameliorative response to Alving's debauchery, into a whorehouse where Alving's own orphan will work. Helene's plan to turn the wages of sin into charity only converts those wages into profit reaped from baser practice of the same sin. Alving's final return, and his worst, is in the last moment of the play, when the disease he gave his son overtakes the young man and overtakes Helene's long-term protection of her son. Building the orphanage to complete the project of delivering herself and Oswald from Alving, Helene has unwittingly delivered them both disastrously to the ruinous effects of Alving's miserable philandering.

The English translation of Ibsen's *Gengangere* as *Ghosts* will probably not be improved on, but it does miss one importantly nuanced description of the plot that the Norwegian includes. Ibsen's title means "those who return" and is better represented by the French title, *Les Revenants*. English does have the word *revenant* which means "one that returns after death or a long absence," and that word precisely describes Alving's absent and perversely controlling presence in each forward-moving reversal of this action. Helene's life has been a series of Herculean labors by which she contains the original damage of marrying Alving: the play's action shows her culminating labor unleashing the worst damage that marriage could do. That her apparent success vanishes in the final reversal and recognition of Oswald's death demand, that her 29-year-long prudential mitigation of Alving's power results in her terrible deliverance to that power, makes the action a classically tragic one. She is victimized by Manders and Engstrand, the respectable and criminal agents of Alving's male authority during and after his life, but the failure belongs primarily to her. What *hamartia* in Helene brings about the preeminently Greek change of fortune? How does she become an accomplice in parental destruction of children?

The Aristotelian analysis looks to an inadequacy in her thinking or feeling, a gap in understanding that let misery into a life directed by the pursuit of happiness. Ibsen's masterstroke in *Ghosts* was making Aristotelian prudence and pragmatism the inadequacy driving the well-made plot. Wanting to manage the past ruins Helene, not managing it badly. Mrs. Alving dimly acknowledges this herself in act 2 when she tells Manders: "I can't stand being bound by all these conventions. I can't! I must find my own way to freedom." (G, 60) She continues, tapping on the window frame: "I should never have concealed the truth about Alving's life. But I dared not do otherwise—and it wasn't only for Oswald's sake. I was such a coward." (G, 60)

That tapping is a nice example of Ibsen's symbolic realism: with the gesture Helene accuses and identifies her fear—the confining, external world of conventional opinion that she sees watching her. Tapping the transparent boundary, she tests, confirms, and threatens conventional morality's power, but does not exceed it. Her reading has ended in firm intellectual conviction that conventional morality has death as its objective and authority and rules by making ghosts of those who carry out its nihilistic ends. But reading is not living, in Mrs. Alving's case, and, disgusted as she is by the moral life of her culture, she knows it has corrupted her will. All that is left of her innocence is fear, the strong weakness that forces her to pretend that one lie will oust another.

Oswald's "joy of life" is the alternative Helene has been struggling toward in her decade of widowed reading and contemplation, not a morality but a standard of value for happiness, for well-being. Her hamartia, as she sees it, is being inadequate to that standard of action. Nietzsche's thinking about the will is invoked in her distinguishing the moral from the good life and in her consciousness of morality as deathly. It is this filling in of the Aristotelian dramatic category with Nietzsche's thinking that makes *Ghosts* so challenging, so painful, and so urgent. The recognitions that the melodramatic reversals bring about allow for Mrs. Alving's incremental awareness of the Nietzschean view of her life. The moral ghosts of Alving's patriarchal culture and the real ghost of Alving himself force that awareness on Helene and prevent her from accomplishing its ends. This thematic reversal is what the English word *ghosts* captures so well; this enervating haunting is the corruption of the will Nietzsche cites as rational humanism's contribution to happiness; this living death is what Helene confronts in Oswald and herself in the last cathartic moment of the play.

As is true in the intrigue plot, most of Mrs. Alving's moral action has gone on in the past. The change she has lived through emerges quickly in the first act, as Manders reproves her for reading reformist books that undermine the authority of religion in moral life. Oswald's appearance and the argument between him and Manders over free love—not promiscuity but unmarried family life in artistic circles—bring the matter of Mrs. Alving's conscience up again and results in the long exposition scene that forms the bulk of act 1. The pastor's accusation that Helene has willfully abandoned her familial responsibilities as wife and mother provokes Mrs. Alving's long retrospective defense, in which she tells Manders the true story of her marriage and explains her motives for building the orphanage. Far from abandoning familial life, she carried it out fraudulently, protecting Alving's reputation successfully for 19 years, at the cost of separation from her son and division against herself. Guilt over that fraud, and fear that it would be revealed, have led her to the ultimate fraudulence, the commemoration of the orphanage in memory of the adulterer. The irony of this plan is lost on her. All she hopes for is the permanent suppression of Alving's real life, which Manders agrees the memorial will accomplish.

Guilt is the first prize in nihilism's contest against life, and repression the strategy for winning it. Mrs. Alving will learn that from Oswald as the play continues. His part in her moral progress is signaled by the second motive she gives for erecting the memorial: canceling the bride price Alving paid for her by using funds she earned managing his affairs to build the orphanage, she will insure that Oswald inherits nothing from his father. The reversal of that expectation forms the Nietzschean plot of *Ghosts* and closes the prudential one, in a doubly ambiguous way.

Bringing Oswald home, Helene discovers that her son has inherited all of his life and his death from Alving and that her sending him away did not remove him from his father's influence, but delivered him to that influence. Further, she discovers from the banished son that the value she has been searching for to free her from confinement was in Alving himself from the start, that she damaged that value in him and damaged herself and her son when she entrapped them all in conventional suppression of the Captain. It is not only syphilis that Oswald inherited from Alving but joy in life—joy enhanced by art in Oswald's case, not etiolated by the service to duty that has ruined Helene's.

Oswald's return, and the final annihilating, liberating demand it makes on Mrs. Alving, certainly dramatizes Freud's psychoanalytic conception that the repressed returns until it is either confronted or destroys consciousness. The analogy of Freud's theory of mental economy to Aristotle's description of revelation of suppressed cause in the catharsis that ends a play is worth noting, if only as a modern instance of prudential managing of the past gone wrong. The retrospective analysis Oswald's return forces Helene to make of her life brings her repeatedly to think about joy as the superior force of familial life, as the action she spurned for the reactive scheming by which she sought to placate and subvert duty's force over family life. Nietzsche's conception of reality is all about force subverted or directly experienced, and the importance of life's joy in *Ghosts* is in large measure Ibsen's presentation of Nietzsche's conclusions about healthy and sick experiences of force in life.

The Aristotelian, Freudian account of Helene's action is subsumed under the play's Nietzschean analysis of will to power in its sick state. Her struggle to act finally from the joy she was forced to abandon by Manders and forced to acknowledge by Oswald shows what measure of Nietzschean health is left in her—not enough. The Aristotelian dimension of her tragedy belongs to the world of duty, of prudential, social morality; the Nietzschean dimension belongs to the world of joy and will to power. They overlap in Oswald, the ruined product of her ruined struggle to become herself through negative, reactive force, through denial. That overlapping has an Aristotelian explanation, Oswald presents the error of her prudential action to her, and a Nietzschean one, Oswald's return is the eternal return of the same in her life, the challenge to joyous affirmation of her past. The previous analysis of the intrigue plot presents the Aristotelian action; what remains is consideration of the Nietzschean project, her attempt to free Oswald and herself from ghostly social obligation, an attempt that the social intrigue of the Aristotelian orphanage plot makes possible.

Helene's relation to Oswald is dominated by the strife that has grown in her life between joy and duty as motives for familial and public life, as the wellsprings of love and work. These last two names for action are the traditional subjects of drama and the constant concerns of Ibsen's prose cycle. *Ghosts* is Ibsen's most ferocious reworking of the domestic melodrama, his century's conventional presentation of well-reasoned pursuit of duty as the force ensuring that love and work will end happily. Every encounter Mrs. Alving has with Manders and with Oswald and Regina subverts that convention, attacks its moral and dramatic authority. The strife of joy and duty first erupted into Helene's life when she left her husband for Manders, who rebuffed her with the priestly advice that she pursue her marriage dutifully and think of joy as wicked rebellion. Cowardice forced her back to Alving but never eradicated her abhorrence of duty, an abhorrence that led her to examine Manders's logic closely enough to find it mechanistic cant instead of wisdom.

In act 2, afraid that cowardice is keeping her from helping Oswald love Regina as wife or consort, Helene explains her fear to Manders in the signature speech of the play:

> When I heard Regina and Oswald in there, it was as if I saw ghosts. I almost
> think we are all ghosts—all of us, Pastor Manders. It isn't just what we have
> inherited from our father and mother that walks in us. It is all kinds of dead
> ideas and all sorts of old and obsolete beliefs. They are not alive in us; but
> they remain in us none the less, and we can never rid ourselves of them. I
> only have to take a newspaper and read it, and I see ghosts between the lines.
> There must be ghosts all over the country. They lie as thick as grains of sand.
> And we're all so horribly afraid of the light. (G, 63)

Manders blames this thinking on her reading, and she tells him that his rejection of her led her to these convictions, not her reading. Manders's and Oswald's convergence in her life for the dedication of Alving's orphanage bring her fatally old submission and the origin of her quest for freedom back to her again, this time with a stronger possibility for liberty than her youthful longing for Manders had offered. Now she has the example of youthful, enlightened courage apparently offered by Oswald. Having succumbed once to duty, Helene is determined to break out and hopes that, by helping Oswald and Regina to love in full knowledge of their lives, she will cancel her own criminal abandonment of love and the harm it has done her. If she can will their love's freedom, she will have done the same for herself.

After she gives this speech she learns how fearfully apposite it is to her life. Oswald tells her, later in act 2 that a doctor in Paris has told him that he has inherited syphilis from his father. Letters Helene has sent him praising his father's dutiful life of virtue are enough for Oswald to refute the doctor's etiology. Telling Helene that his painting career is over because of the illness, Oswald blames that joyous work itself, and the comradeship that went with it, for the disease: "If it had been something I'd inherited. Something I wasn't myself to blame for. But this! To have thrown away in this shameful, thoughtless, light-hearted way one's whole happiness and health, everything in the world—one's future, one's life—" (G, 76). One plot detail rarely mentioned in analysis of *Ghosts*, but crucial to the play's meanings, is that Oswald is certain he hasn't contracted the disease through his own sexual activity. It seems, in fact, that he is a virgin, at the age of 27. "I've never lived intemperately," he tells her. "Not in any way. You must believe me, mother. I've never done that" (G, 74). The unmerited guilt he feels for his career leads to this summary outburst: "Oh, if only I could start my life over again, and undo it all!" (G, 76).

Willingness to suffer and err through life exactly the same way is the hypothetical test that imagining the eternal return presents to Nietzsche's active person. Oswald's feeling of guilt, more than anything else, proves that the joy of life has departed from him, that he has lapsed into the rule of duty, which is the rule of resentment and negation. The desire to know what secret cause might subvert prudential action and the longing to undo that cause in the retrospective fantasy "If only I could live again" are the hallmarks of regret that emerge in the catharsis of Aristotelian tragedy. Nietzsche's fantasy of living again aims at purging this humanistic desire for managing the past. And, most important, Nietzsche associates the capacity for willing the past joyously with aesthetic creativity. That Oswald should will not to be an artist, that he should take up Manders's moral negation of the power of aesthetic life, makes his utterance here one of the most powerful of many places in *Ghosts* in which Nietzsche's idea of action converges in ironic opposition with Aristotle's.

Mrs. Alving, who is trying to undo her life by living it over again through her son, has to remove his guilt, for her own sake as much as his. She must preserve his belief in joy to come to it herself, and to that end she needs to tell him the truth about Alving, the truth that will give the meaning of his art back to him, the truth that will give future joy with Regina to him, if he still wants her once it is known. The problem here is that, for all her impulse to joy, she still thinks nullifying her past life is the means to a positive future. The same ambiguous willing, the same strong weakness that governs her prudential action in the marriage/orphanage plot governs this Nietzschean action, which centers on her responsibility to Alving's orphans, the victimized results of that marriage. The nihilistic basis of her hope will make for the final reversal of the play, in which the unstable logic of simultaneous, compromised service to life and death reaches its hideous conclusion. But before that moment, through the rest of act 2 and most of act 3 Ibsen has her hope vainly, in Oedipal delusion, for release.

After the Nietzschean disclosure Oswald continues, explaining to his mother that he came home hoping his mother would help him bear the remorse of self-destruction. Finding Regina there, Oswald discovers that his mother's comfort is insufficient; it cannot still a fear attached to his remorse. When Helene asks what the fear is and why Regina can save him by banishing it, Oswald withholds the answer to the first question and answers that Regina's saving power is her healthy, happy, amorous attention to him, all signs that she is "full of the joy of life" (G, 81). Mrs. Alving's first response to Oswald's hope is to prohibit him from pursuing the union. But she overcomes this ghostly submission to duty's obsolete voice, calls Regina back to the room, and invites her to drink with Oswald, from whom she requires an explanation of "the joy of life" to help her understand what he hopes for in the girl.

In act 1, Manders had responded as follows to Mrs. Alving's remark that unhappiness led her to leave Alving: "Yes, that is the sign of the rebellious spirit, to demand happiness from this earthly life. What right have we to happiness? No, Mrs. Alving, we must do our duty!" (G, 49) His continued accusation offers a negative definition of duty: "All your days you have been ruled by a fatal spirit of wilfulness. You have always longed for a life unconstrained by duties and principles. You have never been willing to suffer the curb of discipline. Everything that has been troublesome in your life you have cast off ruthlessly and callously, as if it were a burden which you had the right to reject." (G, 50)

Now Oswald begins his description of the joy of life by telling his mother that it doesn't exist in her house. Reversing Manders's accusation, Oswald says she knows nothing about happiness and cares only about duty. He begins his naive, perfervid sermonette with the traditional linking of joy in life to love of work. Oswald continues his reversal of Manders's harangue against Helene by citing the standard Calvinist doctrine that Manders preaches—that work is a curse, a punishment, that life is a long misery best escaped quickly—as the belief of his mother's world of duty and contrasting that world to his lost life in Paris: "But out there, people don't feel like that. No one there believes in that kind of teaching any longer. They feel it's

wonderful and glorious just to be alive. Mother, have you noticed how
everything I've painted is concerned with the joy of life? Always, always,
the joy of life. Light and sunshine and holiday—and shining, contented
faces." (G, 82) When Oswald finishes the explanation by telling his mother
that joyous life would degenerate to ugliness in her sphere, Helene answers:
"Now I understand for the first time. And now I can speak" (G, 83). Her
elucidating speech has to wait because news that the orphanage is burning
interrupts it.

By act 3, Helene has turned that interruption from the balking of her
liberation into its efficient cause. With her duty to convention eliminated
by the purgative fire, Helene believes she is utterly free to relieve Oswald
of his remorse and herself of her guilt by telling him the truth about his
father and about her dutiful, corrupt sacrifice of the family to that convention. That belief is short-lived. The events of act 3 show that her first free
endorsement of the joy of life, made for Oswald's sake, under his tutelage,
is the beginning of her hardest struggle with duty, not the triumphant
dismissal of it. His delayed confession of the reason for his fear forces her
to a second endorsement of the joy of life, made again to gain her deliverance through his. But this return of the same lesson comes with exponentially increased complexity, as Oswald makes death, not love, the test case
between duty and joy.

Act 3 opens with Engstrand closing the orphanage plot, offering himself
as scapegoat for Manders, as he once did unwittingly for Alving in the case
of Regina. The pastor is too witless and self-interested to see the blackmail
as anything but Christian self-sacrifice and rewards Engstrand with a promise
to transfer funds from the ruined orphanage for the creation of Engstrand's
more salacious memorial to the Captain, the Alving Sailor's Rest. Engstrand's
opportunistic subversion of respectability and duty ironically duplicates Mrs.
Alving's strategy for self-liberation that brought the orphanage into being.
Her noble but guilty lie is transposed downward, socially and ethically, with
the appearance of public benefit and private respectability. This change of
fortune in the prudential action, made in precise and blatant contradiction
of the theatrical convention of poetic justice, is the first of this act's strong
subversions of Aristotelian thinking about ethical and dramatic action. Mrs.
Alving has no interest in the orphanage once it is ruined and dismisses the
matter quickly so that she can return to removing Oswald's remorse, an action
interrupted by the fire at the end of the second act.

Oswald enters as Manders and Engstrand leave. He complains to
Regina, who has been onstage from the beginning of the act, of the fear
he mentioned in the previous act and asks her to deliver him from it. She

disappoints him, mistaking his fear for remorse over an ill-spent youth. Provoked by his choice of savior, Mrs. Alving invites Regina to stay, while she tells Oswald the truth about his father. Alving was filled, she says, with the joy of life Oswald spoke of and lost it to the invincible ugliness of provincial life that Oswald sees everywhere in his mother's world. Society offered no commensurate passion for Oswald's love of work and companionship, and she had no sexual love or even cheerful affection to offer him, only thoughts of duty. Alving's public and private disappointment transfigured vitality into depravity, which resulted in Oswald's syphilis and Regina's birth.

Oswald responds by mumbling to himself, "I think it was wrong, all this" (*G*, 94), referring to his hope that Helene or Regina could save him. Regina repudiates Helene and Oswald, claiming that the joy of life she has will be better served, if it comes to that, in Engstrand's establishment than in Mrs. Alving's home, where she can hope only to be patronized by a distant and ungenerous stepmother or waste away serving an invalid. She exits, having now become the true daughter of both her false fathers, another corrupted corrupter of life's joy. The French world of champagne and fashion, which she has practiced inhabiting in aspiring French phrases and awkward drinking with the Alvings throughout the play, and which she has been encouraged to hope for by careless, merely courteous promises from Oswald two years ago, is all Regina grasps of Oswald's magnanimous, abstemiously joyful Parisian life. Mrs. Alving's revelation does convince Oswald that he did not destroy himself in that life, but the conviction, as it turns out, does not matter to him or free her. This same sad irrelevance of the truth occurs once more in Mrs. Alving's warning that Regina will destroy herself if she seeks a route to Paris through Engstrand's memorial to Alving. A great deal of Ibsen's dramatic genius sounds in Regina's flippant, vain, and hopelessly resentful, foolish dismissal of the warning: "Oh, rubbish. *Adieu!*" (*G*, 94). The truth does not set anyone free in this last act, at least not as Mrs. Alving hoped it would. Once more prudential Aristotelian action fails.

Mrs. Alving, seeing Oswald's continued anxiety, now mistakes it for shock at knowing that his idealized father was debauched. He dismisses family feeling as the source of his anguish peremptorily, and, when his mother reprovingly, pleadingly, invokes such feeling as a duty, Oswald forces her to acknowledge how spiritually inauthentic such feeling is, how meagerly conventional. Ibsen's ironies overrun one another here, as the play moves to its horrible ending. Having acknowledged that the presumption of love as a duty to family members is a "ghost," Helene promises to help Oswald in the following utterance: "Oh, I could almost bless your sickness for bringing you home to me. I realize it now. You aren't mine. I must win you" (G, 95). That remark moves Helene's experiment in free willing, and the play's Nietzschean action, to its climax.

Oswald immediately takes up the advantage Helene has offered. Reminding her of her all-inclusive promise to help him, forcing her to renew it, Oswald tells his mother that what he fears is the livingdeath of lunatic, syphilitic paralysis that is incipient in him and likely to overtake him at any moment. He's already suffered a promissory spell of the disease's tertiary stage and learned from his doctor that the next stage of the disease will not abate. He's come back with enough morphine to kill him when the onset comes and tells Helene that since she has driven Regina away, she herself must do what he is certain Regina would have done—administer the drug when he needs it. She protests, invoking the standard of duty and natural feeling, which he rejects: "I didn't ask you for life. And what kind of a life have you given me? I don't want it. Take it back" (G, 99).

At this most radical challenge to motherlove Ibsen clears the stage and thus gives ocular proof that Mrs. Alving still wants to evade or subvert duty rather than move positively against it. She has run off to get a doctor. Oswald follows, forbidding her, and locks the door, telling her that she cannot leave and that no one will be allowed to enter. The empty stage receives them newly isolated, with Helene calling Oswald her child. Seizing the opportunity in that word, he invokes duty again, seeing that she will not help him if she cannot act from it. "If you have a mother's love for me, how can you see me suffer like this?" (G, 99). The reversal is not an opportunistic hypocrisy on his part but a transposition of duty. Oswald shifts it here from conventional impersonal commitment to religion, ethics, and the law, which forbids taking life, into the rebellious, personal dimension of joyous action, in which love obliterates suffering instead of bearing it. Oswald's second demand redefines motherhood for Helene, precisely in the terms of freedom and action she has never been able to take for her own, but has always wanted to live by. Silent, temperate, she finally takes them up and promises to do as he asked. Living death has been her portion and her fear for 29 years, and the creation of the orphanage was supposed to free her from it and restore her son to her. The reversal of that prudential plot launches her into the Nietzschean conflict with Oswald, and it is in delivering him from fear of living death that she ends hers. Aristotelian prudence seems finally to have given way to Nietzschean willing.

But the habit of evasion, the ghostly spirit of compromise asserts its dominion in her immediately, as she tells him that it will never be necessary for her to keep the promise, that he will never lapse, never require the morphine. The penultimate moments of the play show her playing out this fantasy, comforting him with talk of a happy future. This last act starts in the darkest hour, just before dawn. At this cathartic point, having willed joy and hoping never to enact its terrible form, Mrs. Alving moves away from Oswald to a side table, where she puts out the lamp that has lit her transformation. The rain, which has been incessant onstage from the first act until now, from the morning before until this one, finally stops; the sun breaks through for the first time, revealing the glacier and snowy peaks that frame the scene. The sun has, of course, all its traditional symbolic value—life's grandeur and eternal renewal preeminent among them here. But a special meaning attaches to it now, a meaning Oswald had first stated in act 2 when he explained the joy of life to Helene: "Mother, have you noticed how everything I've painted is concerned with the joy of life? Always, always, the joy of life. Light and sunshine and holiday—and shining, contented faces." (G, 82) In the passage Oswald had continued that he had been afraid to come to his mother's house because that light never shines there. Now it seems at this final moment that Ibsen has given Oswald and his mother that shining light as a reward for their final flight from the dark, dutiful service of life-in-death, for their hard-won freedom from ghosts.

And then comes Oswald's transformative invocation of the symbol's apocalyptic creativity: "Mother, give me the sun" (G, 100). Overcome by the disease, he drops the word *mother* and repeats twice more the catatonic imperative "the sun, the sun." He cannot know, but Mrs. Alving must, that he is asking for the death that joy demands she accomplish. Screaming, shocked, panicked, on her knees, Helene asks if he knows her and gets no recognition, only the demand. The stage directions Ibsen wrote for her final moment bear the full weight of her response and should be examined closely.

> Mrs. Alving (*jumps to her feet in despair, tears her hair with both hands and screams*): I
> can't bear this! (*Whispers as though numbed.*) I can't bear it! No! (*Suddenly.*)
> Where did he put them? (*Fumbles quickly across his breast.*) Here! (*Shrinks
> a few steps away from him with her hands twisted in her hair, speechless, and stares
> at him in horror.*)
> Oswald (*still motionless*): The sun. The sun.

Her jumping up, her motion to and away from him, her screaming, her whispering, are all physical indications of the vacillation in her will between commitment to Aristotelian duty and Nietzschean will to power. Her fumbling discovery of the morphine on his body and her immediate but slight retreat from him without retrieving the dosage show what her repeated *no's* and her singular and abandoned *yes* say—that once again she faces living death without the power to act against it.

Ibsen poses her at the end in the conventional melodramatic stances of the sexual criminal and the lunatic at the moment of revelation, when, through some drastic reversal, they have recovered just enough innocence or sanity to know that they have created the doom that will quickly overcome them. Tearing her hair, she also presents the virginal or chaste heroine of the melodrama at the moment of ultimate crisis, the victimized moment past all reasonable hope, which brings the strong hero rushing onstage as avenging savior. These postures invoke the cathartic resolution of poetic justice from the well-made play only to deny it. Halting Aristotle's action, Ibsen ends Helene's story with the definitive Nietzschean action: the chance to will the past through confronting its recurrence in the eternal return of the same.

Oswald's bodily life-in-death repeats Helene's spiritual entrapment, in one sense results from it, and represents to her the disastrous consequence of that original compromise with the world of duty Manders forced her to live under. His request that she kill him makes her both the guilty sexual sinner and the chaste avenger of the melodrama. Freeing him from inane suffering, she will finally kill the guilt of sinning against her own joy and transform her part in fatally transmitting the sexual ruin of Alving's joy to him from witless harm into willed power. This logic belongs to Nietzsche's twofold analysis of how force moves against itself in the sick will to the ultimate weakness of guilty paralysis or, in the case of the will's recovery, to the joy in power that the supremely powerful spirit achieves in apocalyptic destruction of any present state of affirmation to achieve an even greater one.

To care for him in his invalid state would be to maintain the Aristotelian action of duty, in which force denies itself. In such duty power annihilates itself in the abyss of restriction. No renewed force comes from that abyss; only grim, criminal exhaustion. To kill him would be to redefine duty, to become the avenger of joy against duty, to make the sun's appearance a provocation to the transvaluation of all values, that supreme willing of the past that Nietzsche argues supremely powerful spirits accomplish when they affirm the eternal return of the same. In the Aristotelian reading of the last scene, Mrs. Alving suffers poetic justice for having sought good ends by bad means, having lied to be honored by people she doesn't honor. Oswald gives her a way to enact the second, healing end presented in Nietzsche's refutation of Aristotelian thinking about action, the apocalyptic destruction of prudential duty that she might accomplish by transforming crime into noble power. If she kills her son, she wills that her initial succumbing to duty, the error of so many years ago that his illness repeats, should become the first instance of her discovery of joy. Oswald, in the dutiful plan, was the hoped-for surcease of sorrow. He fulfills that role ironically once the intrigue plot fails. Killing him, Helene subverts the poetic justice of the Aristotelian action, and converts the return of the repressed, the power of fraud and failure, into the willed return of life's constant joyous option for sublime, apocalyptic self-fashioning. Not killing him, she becomes a proof of that poetic justice, a proof not of Aristotle's dramatic and ethical values but of Nietzsche's conviction that they nullify life. She does not kill Oswald onstage.

Aristotle observed that fatal strife between relatives made for the most cathartic tragedy, and, according to that standard, *Ghosts* is preeminently a classical, Aristotelian work. In chapter 14 of *Poetics* Aristotle argues that the most cathartic action comes when an agent is about to commit an irreparable deed in ignorance and refrains at the last moment because of a recognition. He gives as an example Merope, who would have killed her son in *Cresphontes* had she not recognized him in time.[12] At no point in *Ghosts* does Ibsen simultaneously observe and repudiate Aristotle's action theory more powerfully than in Mrs. Alving's parodic duplication of Merope's failure to do the tragic deed. It is Nietzsche's logic that makes the comparison an ironic disavowal of the conventional theory of moral and dramatic action.

According to the standard of joy, Helene's irreparable deed would be caring for Oswald, not killing him. Her recognition of the heretofore disguised cost and power of Oswald's joy, and of her recent commitment to that joy as their mutual salvation, should exalt her will enough so that she can transform the crime of murder into an affirmation of life's value, her life's and his. At the same time that Helene recognizes the defeated artist in Oswald, who summons her to joy, she also recognizes the sick child, the summons in extremis to familial duty. That conflict should, in Nietzschean logic, provide enough resistance to provoke Helene to a powerful affirmation of the artistic life and to an apocalyptic transformation of her maternal duty.

The ambiguous revelation that Oswald's call for the sun brings about in Helene contracts her 29 years of life-in-death into one moment. She cannot manage the past presented to her in that moment, but willing it is an option. Knowing that she cannot take that option is the final recognition Oswald's paralysis brings about in Helene. Merope's hesitation pleases because it is willed; she acts by submitting her aim to the substantial governance of reason and natural feeling. Mrs. Alving's hesitation disappoints because it shows that she cannot will. Merope's hesitation pleases especially because it averts death, which is always a calamity in Aristotle's reading of tragedy. In Nietzsche's poetics, and his conception of life, death can be an occasion for sublime exaltation, for Dionysian joy and apocalyptic self-fashioning, and Mrs. Alving's hesitation hurts primarily because she abandons that conclusion.

   Ghosts horrified its first audiences not so much because it put an Enlightenment rationalist light on sexual life or even on merely conventional familial morality and its basis in religion. The horror of *Ghosts* lies in its frustrating arousal and cruel canceling of exalted romantic expansion of feeling. In Mrs. Alving's case the spirit is willing, but the spirit is weak, not at all fatally willful, as Manders proclaimed with such ignorant rectitude early in the play. Fatal willing is the normal action in Ibsen's plays, and its absence in this one signals a crucial advance in his thinking about the matter. In *Rosmersholm*, for instance, Ibsen portrays two spirits struggling into more strength than Mrs. Alving can find and willing death, as she cannot. But their action is no less haunted than her paralysis, since it confirms the murderous force of duty and conventional morality they have struggled to transform. Nietzsche's apocalyptic action cannot take hold of life in either play. Instead, his analysis of the sickness of prudential reasoning insinuates itself into the retrospective intrigues of both plays, indicating that the moral and dramatic logic of Aristotelian action theory is, as Mrs. Alving said of Manders's authoritarian moral vesture, abominable and "machine-sewn" (G. 63). Ibsen does not show the hand- or spirit-sewn robes of the new kingdom until *Master Builder*, and they are not lightly worn even there.

4

Rosmersholm: *Managing the Past*

Ibsen finished *Ghosts* in 1881; he finished *Rosmersholm* five years later, in 1886. In the intervening plays, *An Enemy of the People* (1882) and *The Wild Duck* (1884), Ibsen continued subverting conventional plots—stories of financial and political scandal, domestic crises arising from sexual crime or suspicion of it—convinced that, by appropriating familiar and approved forms of entertainment and supplying them with ambushing revolutionary content, he could give the theater irresistible moral authority. His project was nothing less than the creation of a new conscience for modern Europe, one that would replace what he saw as the dry-rot authority of church and state. *Pillars of Society* (1875-77) and *A Doll House* (1878-79) confidently make scandalous rebels the occasion for potent, detailed criticism of inadequate and ruinous cultural authority. Rebel confidence and power fail in *Ghosts* in which the cultural authority has become an internalized, psychological tyranny. Written after this inward gazing, *An Enemy of the People* and *The Wild Duck* show Ibsen becoming more complex and anxious about his messianic project. The first play makes some criticism of Thomas Stockman's exposure of a dangerous criminal secret, of the cost in isolation and danger to his family that he pays for the exposure, of his explicitly messianic expectations to create a new society starting with 12 schoolboys whom he can make "free-spirited and accomplished men."[1] The next play does much more to discredit its self-styled messianic scourge, Gregers Werle. His messianic exposure of past crimes is shown to stem from oedipal hatred of his father as much as from love of justice, and his hopes for an innocent, morally heroic future are based on vain nostalgic misjudgment of the feeble moral capacities of a former teenage idol. In *The Wild Duck* the project by which Werle seeks to reform life brings about only the unnecessary and morally ineffectual death of an innocent, confused adolescent girl. Opposed to Werle's naive, ruinous, utopian truthtelling in that play is nothing better than Doctor Relling's cynical, indulgent endorsement of "the life-lie," the fraudulent anodyne of eccentric fantasy that keeps murderous reality unknown.

Ibsen did not resolve his ambiguous judgment of messianic moral aspiration in *The Wild Duck* but carried it over into the subsequent drama, *Rosmersholm*. This play is Ibsen's first explicitly analytic treatment of the tragic entanglement of utopian rational humanism, corrosive sexual compulsion, and the implacable force of occulted guilt. More than ever before, *Rosmersholm* attenuates the propulsive, extravagant emotionality of melodramatic presentation of outlaw saviors. Now the emotional force of received, mastered conventions is not only subverted onstage, but transformed into newly determined intellectual daring. The dangers and impediments of messianic living become identified with action itself in *Rosmersholm*, and, as a result, the story of Rebecca West and John Rosmer becomes Ibsen's first explicitly ideational treatment of the connection Aristotle's *Poetics* makes between dramatic and ethical action, between virtual and real experience of substantial change.

Rosmersholm continues the structural division of *Ghosts*, in which Aristotelian humanistic praxis and Nietzschean will to power converge in a plot that sets the past's force against longing for a transformed future life. The familiar struggle of Enlightenment and romantic social reform dominates the cultural story, in which Rebecca West, Ulrik Brendel, and John Rosmer try to make emancipated, noble, utopian innocence a social force strong enough to defeat the prevailing pessimistic middle-class respectability and punishing religiosity of schoolmaster Kroll and his party. And a moral, psychological plot, an intimate and criminal love story, is once again inextricably bound to political struggle for cultural authority. Kroll's implacable probing into the cause of the recent suicide of his sister Beata, Rosmer's former wife, forces Rebecca West and Rosmer to confront the unmanageable, corrosive sexual hamartia that has secretly driven their cultural rebellion. In this sardonic transformation of the Magdalen play and the remarriage comedy, Nietzsche's thinking about will and morality partially overtake Aristotle's ideas of praxis, as was the case in *Ghosts*. Sex, familial love, and murder all converge in the personal dimension of *Rosmersholm*, as they did in *Ghosts*. Their relation to the Aristotelian aspect of the play, its narrative reversals and recognitions, its concern for ethical organization of social life, has changed, though. And that change signals a new intensity, range, and anguish in Ibsen's Nietzschean project, his aspiration toward artistic transvaluation of all value.

Rosmersholm's political and erotic stories unfold in illusionistic realism. Once more a professional, wealthy household occupies the stage, dialogue is conversational, and the political intrigue and psychosexual events unfold in the midst of domestic rituals—walks, meals, arrivals and departures of friends and relatives, and instructions to the servant, Mrs. Helseth. The three acts cover three consecutive days. The scenes in each act are continuous in time and place and so make the technical construction of Rosmer and Rebecca's ruin feel intensely and unavoidably real. Exposition, reversal, and recognition, the mainstays of the melodrama, are tamped down in *Rosmersholm's* intensely analytic plot, transposed into ideological struggle.

Forging the drama so powerfully out of ruined salvational aspirations, focusing the sexual story on repression and sublimation emerging from unwitting sexual crimes inside families, Ibsen gave this potentially lurid shocker the aesthetic dignity and moral authority of Greek tragedy. The ideational and imaginative power of symbolism, which counted for so much in *Ghosts*, is refined here. The supranatural element in the play that those symbols invoke appears with more precise intellectual force than it did in *Ghosts*, primarily in references to *Faust*, the New Testament, folkloric association of white horses with death, and the legend that children do not cry or laugh at Rosmersholm. And the suspense and thrill of intrigue, which counted for so much in his previous plays and would count for as much again in *Hedda Gabler*, recedes almost to the vanishing point in this play. The political issues are never precisely stated, the machinations of the struggle between Kroll and Mortensgaard for Rosmer's editorial service at one or the other rival newspaper never heat up. The obligatory incriminating letter figures in the play, but it is only mentioned and plays a diminished role in the political and sexual story, corroborating rather than revealing crucial information. More than ever in Ibsen's plays, or in nineteenth-century theater, emotion and ethics submit their rhetorical force to moral analysis in *Rosmersholm*.

This is not apparent as the play begins. The first act is mostly exposition of circumstances that have led to a political and cultural conflict that Kroll seeks to resolve with Rosmer's help. Rebecca West's status in Rosmersholm and the mysterious suicide of Beata are only incidentally associated with that conflict in the first act. Disclosure of these women's lives will progressively eclipse the political action of the remaining three acts and transpose the struggle for social reformation into a spiritual quest for radical innocence. The first two scenes of the play focus very briefly on the lingering effects at Rosmersholm of Beata's suicide, an event that occurred 18 months before the present action begins. In the first scene Rebecca West and Mrs. Helseth, servant at Rosmersholm, appear alone onstage. Rebecca watches John Rosmer walk the grounds, avoiding the bridge that was the site of his first wife's suicide. She comments that the living cling to their dead at Rosmersholm,

and Mrs. Helseth counters with the opposite opinion that the dead haunt
Rosmersholm, offering as proof an oblique reference to a legendary white
horse that has been rumored to be haunting the grounds.

Ibsen originally called this play *White Horses,* and Mrs. Helseth's introduction of what will become an important motif brings a number of
ambiguities forward that will complicate the characters' struggles to take
action. Chief among these are the relation of ethical and natural, especially
sexual, agency in human action; the relation of traditional moral values to
innovative ones; the struggle of atonement against liberation; and, controlling all the rest, the visionary ambition of making new effects emerge from
old causes, of making the future annul the past. When he changed the title,
Ibsen demoted the supernatural status of these issues, constraining the
impulse to treat them poetically and mystically, as he had in *Brand* and *Peer
Gynt,* to some extent in *Ghosts.* While the prosaic realism of psychosexual
and cultural conflict remains the primary mode of *Rosmersholm,* the mystical
topic remains potent in this play, as does the question of super- or supranatural control on action.[2]

Indeed, the distance between mundane experience and *Rosmersholm's*
action increases exponentially as the play progresses, but starts off quite
small. Rosmer, who will be defeated by the ambiguities of the white horse,
fears the bridge his wife leapt from and avoids it, as Rebecca notices. Kroll,
as the scandalized Mrs. Helseth notices in the same scene, has no such
sentiment and walks straight across it to pay his first visit in a long time to
Rosmersholm. Here realistic detail suggests one part of the psychological
dimension at work in the political struggle between Kroll and Rosmer: the
husband evades the scene of a decisive action in his past, frightened, pained
by it; the brother-in-law has a strictly pragmatic regard for the scene of that
action, trampling its past associations as he acts to contain a present danger
and pursue a future political and cultural safety. In the second and third acts
Kroll will focus all his attention on discovering and revealing what happened
at that bridge. In doing so, he will shift the play away from political intrigue
into what is for him a moral detective action, for Rosmer and Rebecca a
challenge to move beyond good and evil. That ambiguous transformation of
the plot transforms the opposed psychological meanings of action for the
ruined priest and the threatened schoolmaster into a full-scale critique of
Christian and humanistic ontology, ethics, and aesthetics. And the focus of
that critique will be Rebecca, in whom the Nietzschean opposition to
Europe's Aristotelian and Christian inheritance works most painfully.

Ibsen signals this transformation of the play mutely in the next scene,
in which Kroll enters the house before Rosmer and visits with Rebecca. As

a result of the political reversal that Kroll suffers in act 1, this schoolmaster comes to view Rosmer's intellectual consort as the incarnation of the licentiousness that threatens to wreck his family and civilization. What will become a successful drive to extirpate her later on starts here as friendly, courteous encouragement that she secure her place in Rosmer's life by marrying him. Praising her for noble self- sacrifice, a virtue he associates with his traditional opposition to libertines who slanderously oppose his authority, Kroll suggests that, having cared for her difficult father and Rosmer's difficult wife, Rebecca should now take the reward of her humble service and marry the master of the house. Adding the satiric role of matchmaker to the austere authority of paterfamilias, Kroll asks Rebecca's age and deems that she is "highly suitable" at nearly 30 to marry the 43-year-old Rosmer.[3] Rebecca politely tables the matter with a noncommittal repetition of the judgment that such a union would be suitable, invites Kroll to tea, and Rosmer enters. Innocently, Kroll sets in motion the central thematic and narrative organization of the play in this short exchange. The reward of noble self-sacrifice will be union for Rebecca and Rosmer, that Kroll's insistence will help bring about, but the union will be a negative action, one that culminates in a recognition scene that ironically affirms Kroll's conservative Christianity and tragically affirms Rebecca's messianic failure to create new values. His conversation with Rosmer in the next three scenes sets Kroll on a much less innocent intimacy with Rebecca than he initially desires. After Rosmer enters, he and Kroll affirm their renewed intimacy, banish the notion that Kroll's absence implied disapproval of Rebecca or suspicion of the circumstances of his sister's death, and plan more frequent contact on the strength of Rosmer's declaration "We have nothing with which to reproach ourselves. Our memory of Beata is purely a happy one" (R, 233). Ibsen, with Kroll's action as efficient cause and Rebecca's as final one, will reverse everything in that declaration, but for now Kroll accepts it as the occasion to bring up the political purpose of his visit. Announcing that the "decadent, cantankerous, and demoralizing heresies" of radicals in the county of Rosmersholm have invaded his household and gained the allegiance of his wife and children, Kroll confides to Rosmer that he and his conservative allies have purchased the *County Telegraph* to do journalistic battle against their enemies, who publish under Peter Morgenstaard's editorial leadership in the *Morning Star* (R, 235). Kroll wants Rosmer to join him as editor. Rebecca's interjections that John reveal his committed resistance to Kroll's position and John's evasive demurs go unheard until Kroll corners Rosmer with this full-scale invocation of the authority of Rosmer's past and present position.

Kroll: Your goodness and incorruptibility, your sensitivity and intellect, your
   unimpeachable integrity, are known and prized by everyone throughout the county. To say nothing of the honour and respect which you
   command as a former man of God! And, last but by no means least,
   there's your family name.

Rosmer: Oh, my family name—

Kroll: (points to the portraits): The Rosmers of Rosmersholm. Men of God and
   men of war. Respected servants of their country. Every one of them a
   man of honour who knew his duty. A family that for nigh on two
   hundred years has been venerated and looked up to as the first in the
   county. (Puts a hand on Rosmer's shoulder.) Rosmer—you owe it to yourself
   and to the traditions of your family to defend and protect everything
   that has hitherto been held sacred in our society. (Turns.) Well, what
   do you say, Miss West?

Rebecca: (with a soft, quiet laugh): Dear Dr. Kroll! I find all this unspeakably
   funny. (R, 238)

In a good production of Rosmersholm Kroll's speech will not be satirically
pompous or wheedling, and Rebecca's response will not be an instruction to
the audience to laugh at him, but, instead, an incisive reversal in the action,
the opening gesture by which she assumes the "highly suitable" authority
Kroll wants her to have in Rosmersholm.

   Kroll's speech displays much of the logic that led Ibsen to name this
story of failed messianic effort for a place instead of a person. All the virtues
Kroll enjoins on Rosmer propagate stability—domestic, social, and cultural.
Rosmersholm the estate operates as fulcrum for the time-honored actions of
Christian domestic life and respectable bourgeois commerce and govern-
ment, and it is those actions, their accumulated authority and sanctity, that
Kroll is calling Rosmer to preserve. Making for stable transitions from one
generation to the next, requiring economic matching of evolving human
needs and resources to nature's ordered changes, a house gives history human
dimension and gives humanity its basic and most functional strategy and
model for pursuing whatever value history has to offer. Focusing on threats
to the continuance of a great house and a noble and powerful family, Kroll
seeks to make Rosmer conceive of himself not only as an agent of Aristotelian
eudaemonia, but, more grandly, as an agent of history. The various and opposed
consequences of antagonists forcing this domesticated "great man" view of
historical development onto Rosmer's inadequate life make up the action of
the play. Kroll discovers, in two masterful reversals, that his tutelage of
Rosmer has been superseded. The change in action starts when Rebecca

laughs at his assumption that she will corroborate his opinions, continues with the entrance of Brendel, and doesn't finish until the last scene of act 4.

The conjunction of Rebecca's comic deflation and the appearance of the clownish Brendel is a masterstroke on Ibsen's part, at once announcing the competing claims for Rosmer's supposed power and showing their weak points. The foolishness of Brendel and the indecorous fleering Rebecca indulges in here incite the implacably vindictive action by which Kroll finally destroys the ally he hoped to preserve. To Rebecca first. John is the last of the Rosmers, and he is a childless widower. When Kroll asks Miss West's opinion of his view that Rosmer has an obligation to propagate the sacred values of bourgeois respectability, he reveals the serious purpose in what earlier seemed to be only comically effeminate matchmaking. Convinced that her self-sacrifice indicates an extraordinarily strong measure of conventional female virtue, as well as chaste, submissive love of Rosmer, and that she is prudent enough to know the benefits of becoming Mrs. Rosmer, Kroll assumes that Rebecca will support his view of John's familial inheritance and the necessity of continuing it. Having encouraged the marriage socially only moments before, now having approved—more, having required it morally—Kroll is of course thunderstruck when Rebecca quietly, calmly finds him and his plan ridiculous. She is set to explain in detail her serious reasons for mocking his convictions about sex, marriage, and social life but stops, interrupted by the entrance of Brendel.

Ulrick Brendel is one of Ibsen's great comic creations. Rosmer's boyhood teacher, evicted at least 30 years ago from Rosmersholm with a horsewhip by John's father for teaching his son what Kroll calls "radical nonsense," Brendel has since been a traveling actor, resided in a workhouse, and wandered about as an itinerant tramp in service to utopian idealism. Equally a canny opportunist, an innocently delusional self-aggrandizer, and an uncannily accurate moralist and judge of character, Brendel recalls Dickens's Mr. Micawber and prefigures Shaw's knockabout resourceful vulgar prophets—Mr. Doolittle from *Pygmalion* (1913) comes to mind—as well as the pipe-dreaming wrecks in O'Neill's *Iceman Cometh* (1939) and, at a greater distance, the poetic philosophical tramps in Yeats's poetry and Beckett's *Waiting for Godot* (1952). He comes from and fathers a long line of wise fools, and Ibsen works that pedigree beautifully in *Rosmersholm*, adding to it a dark power to instigate fatal resolutions to barely hidden sexual dilemmas. This last talent, which works most powerfully on Rebecca in the final act, first appears comically. On his entrance into the play Brendel mistakes Rebecca for Rosmer's wife at the moment that Miss West has rudely confuted Kroll's plan to bring about that union.

Brendel has come back to Rosmer's county to change his life, to become, as he puts it "a new man" (R, 242). Having spent his adult life indulging solitary fantasies, dreams, and visions of liberation, having lifted himself to heavenly rapture in unwritten poems that gain him imaginary fame and authority, Brendel now plans to risk profanation of his joy, to make his inner man "a sacrifice upon the altar of liberation" by delivering "a sequence of closely argued lectures—throughout the country" (R, 243). Moved by Brendel's enthusiastic plan to act through self-sacrifice, Rebecca insinuates that Rosmer should do the same. With a distant reference to Lady Macbeth, an extremely popular nineteenth-century tragic heroine, Rebecca asks how many men would have the courage to take Brendel's course. Rosmer takes the point but answers with the enigmatic question "Who knows?" (R, 243). The sacrifice will require new clothes, which Rebecca leaves to fetch, and money, which Brendel asks for in the presence of Kroll and Rosmer before he exits.

Having lent his clothes to utopian liberation, touched in his self-esteem by Rebecca's instructive praise of the tramp's promised praxis, Rosmer makes the break with Kroll in the absence of the schoolteacher's opponents. He tells Kroll that he is on the side of the emancipators. Not committed to their antagonistic party efforts, Rosmer declares his purpose: "I want to devote my life and all my strength to this one end, of creating a responsible public opinion in our country." He hopes to unify the warring factions and make the populace noble by "emancipating their minds and purifying their wills" (R, 247). He does not hope to purify or emancipate anyone directly himself, only to persuade them of their need of such transformation and to rouse their strength, which he cites as the only cause of such salvation. This last idea explicitly contradicts Lutheran fideistic Christianity. Enunciating it, Rosmer not only proves that he has abandoned the clerical cloth but also provokes Kroll into an interrogation in which he confesses that he has left Christianity altogether. His description of the sway liberty holds over him is strangely passive and reveals a sexual power that Kroll will search out for the rest of the play: "When I saw things clearly—when I knew for sure that it was not a passing temptation, but something that I never could nor would escape from—then I left" (R, 249).

The die, it appears, is now cast. Kroll declares war on Rosmer, at which point Rebecca returns, flinging the door wide open with the following surprising remark about Brendel: "There! Now he's off to his sacrificial orgy. And now we can go and eat" (R, 249). Why has she taken on Kroll's mockery of the liberator? Having manipulated Rosmer with praise of Brendel, is she now trying to ingratiate Kroll, to beguile him out of his antagonism? Is she brandishing her own resources by showing that she can trump Kroll's worldly assessment of vain political ambition? Whatever the gambit is, Rebecca abandons it immediately when Kroll announces his alienation from Rosmersholm. She remains silent while Kroll predicts that Rosmer will not be able to bear the solitude of his rebellion against the conservatives, silent while Rosmer boldly proclaims that Rebecca stands by him in that solitude, silent while Kroll reveals that Beata disclosed her fear of that solidarity just before her suicide. Kroll perceives an antagonism between the women for the first time when he hears Rosmer cite Rebecca as an authority for his rebellion, but he dismisses the suspicion that the antagonism figured in the suicide as vile and unthinkable. He will not respond when Rosmer asks to have the reference to Beata clarified, except to urge that the matter be forgotten and that he be forgiven for raising doubts. All this recanting, of course, sets the murder mystery plot going as powerfully as the ejaculated insight does. Unnerved by his involuntary accusation, Kroll is nonetheless unwilling to leave off his fury at Rosmer's apostasy and prohibits Rosmer's planned visit to him as he exits. When Rebecca asks what Rosmer thought Kroll meant by calling his suspicion of her "unthinkable," she is met with Rosmer's palliative observation that Kroll couldn't believe ill of her and that he will be brought about tomorrow. Rosmer exits, declaring himself at peace with his declaration, urging her to take his emergence into action calmly.

The unthinkable thought is, of course, that there has been sexually criminal collusion between Rosmer and Rebecca in the political intrigue and, more direly, that the collusion exacerbated Beata's anguish and may have led to her death. Kroll will pursue that thought, and Ibsen signals as much clearly to the audience. But he keeps Rebecca and Rosmer ignorant for now of Kroll's fledgling intent, using that dramatic irony to foreground anxiously an instability threatening their union and their messianic aspiration. Rebecca's status as sexually enticing instigator of fatal action, presented in this scene as a distant kinship with Lady Macbeth, will eventually dominate the play's inquiry into messianic action. But at this point Ibsen merely suggests her power. He ends the act with another enigmatic remark from Rebecca, one that takes the play back to its opening concern with guilt's power to make past cause overtake unstable plans for the future. Disguising Kroll's angry departure from Mrs. Helseth's curiosity as worry about an oncoming storm, Rebecca dismisses the servant's deftly impertinent obser- vation that the sky is clear with the following nonsequitur: "As long as he doesn't see the white horse. I'm afraid we may soon be hearing from one of these ghosts of yours." (R, 251). To calm, and confuse, the maid's supersti- tious fear that her mistress believes a death is imminent at Rosmersholm,

Rebecca observes, as she exits, that "there are many kinds of white horses in this world, Mrs. Helseth," to which the maid responds: "Blessed Jesus! That Miss West. The way she talks sometimes" (R, 251). The way she talks, what that talk hides when it discloses her, what Aristotelian and Nietzschean action it makes and breaks, will take up the rest of the play. The chiasmic structure of this first act, ending by return to an initiating symbol of an ever-encroaching past, is a particularly elegant technical presentation of the tragic order binding the characters and of the most ambitious intellectual order governing this play, and Ibsen's career—prophetic revision of modernity's dramatic and philosophical inheritance.

Inquiry into Rebecca's past takes up all of acts 2 and 3. The form and content of *Rosmersholm* merge with increasing intensity in these two acts, as each stage of the melodramatic, Aristotelian action by which Kroll, Mortensgaard, and eventually Rosmer pursue Rebecca's hidden influence at Rosmersholm becomes a defeating and provoking challenge to the messianic action that Rosmer ever more confidentially aspires to. Each assault on Rebecca leads Rosmer to increased reliance on her for the accomplishment of their Nietzschean transvaluation of all values, and each assault leaves Rebecca more urgent to accomplish that project and more unwilling to do so as Rosmer requires, by marrying him and becoming a second Beata. The constant and ever more confining association of Rebecca and Beata as authorities for Rosmer's potentially liberating action in these middle acts comes under many thematic and technical descriptions. That developing conjunction displays the return of the repressed that Freud found so fascinating in the play; it drives the reversal/recognition logic that makes this lurid detective story almost a classical tragedy; it makes an ironic critique of the nineteenth century's conviction that love of virtuous women initiates and guarantees the salvational acts of otherwise aimless or destructive men; and, most significantly, it dramatizes the Nietzschean challenge of the eternal return of the same, bringing the action of amor fati, the happy expression of will to power, into direct conflict with the Aristotelian, humanistic and Lutheran convictions that the past must be managed by punishment or justification.[4] A brief précis of the action in these acts shows how Ibsen made drama out of this cultural and intellectual conflict.

Act 2 presents three impediments to Rosmer taking up his messianic project. Each time the impediment is some newly revealed aspect of Rebecca's past influence on him and on Beata. The opening scene is Rosmer's study, the morning after his break with Kroll. Rebecca begins the act by telling Rosmer she has sent Brendel to the radical party leader, Mortensgaard, with a letter of introduction from Rosmer. He disapproves of the maneuver, wishing to stay aloof from the political fray, but she justifies it, saying he will need friends now that Kroll opposes him. Innocently, Rosmer protests that as a gentleman Kroll can be brought around through reasonable conversation that very evening. This opposition of Rebecca's independent action on Rosmer's behalf and his naive hope of avoiding an already real conflict over which Rebecca's action seeks control presents their history in miniature. This act, and the following one, reveal that history to Rosmer and make it both more necessary than ever and finally impossible for Rebecca to hide her past authority in his life or claim the present position that this authority has gained her.

Immediately after Rosmer calls him pliable, Kroll enters and proves the pastor wrong. After driving Rebecca offstage with a direct insinuation that she is criminally licentious, Kroll reveals that Brendel has disgraced himself and that Rebecca has aligned Rosmer with the radicals. When Rosmer defends Rebecca, Kroll calls him her dupe for the first time in the play and launches into the more weighty topic of Beata's suicide and its relation to her knowledge of Rosmer's life with Rebecca. Kroll starts by casting doubts on Beata's insanity. To Rosmer's defense that his wife's frightening, uncontrollable fits of sensuality—which he could not reciprocate—and her extravagant anguish over barrenness proved her mad, Kroll opposes the view that Beata's anguish was not primarily caused by rejection or childlessness, but by her knowledge of Rosmer's apostasy and Rebecca's part in it.

Kroll delivers the two causes separately, linking them by reporting Beata's final conversation with him, in which she said, "Soon now they can expect to see the white horse at Rosmersholm," and justified the prediction by telling her brother: "I haven't much time left. John must marry Rebecca now—at once" (R, 259). Acknowledging his apostasy, baffled that Beata knew it, Rosmer ignores the sexual accusation until Kroll forces him to confront it. When the platonic lover indignantly, but accurately, pleads high-minded chastity and liberal aspiration as defense, Kroll sounds the depth of bourgeois conservatism, telling Rosmer that no great gulf separates free love and free thought. Now the accusation is complete. Rebecca brought radical convictions that value could exist outside the church, that love could exist outside marriage, into Rosmersholm, perverted John with them, and in the process drove Beata to suicide so that she could take her place.

True to the brutality and hypocrisy attending the unassailable prerogative of male desire in the double standard governing bourgeois sexual ethics, Kroll has some sympathy, wasted as it turns out, for Rosmer's sexual weakness. He has not come to separate him from Rebecca, or even to blame him for the presumed sexual liaison, but to prevail upon him to keep his apostasy from the church, and its source in Rebecca, a private secret. Invoking again the social power and responsibility of Rosmersholm's traditional cultural authority, Kroll tells Rosmer he will unleash fatal confusion on the community if he publicly pursues his reformer's goals of secular enlightenment. To Rosmer's protestation that duty lies in canceling that authority, replacing its misery with happiness, Kroll contemptuously replies that Rosmer is by temperament and ability too weak to engage in the battle his sense of duty requires. At this point Mortensgaard enters, and Kroll exits, promising that the code of gentlemanly conduct will not restrain him from assaulting Rosmer if he emerges from his study to act on his beliefs. When Rosmer invokes noble standards for conflict, Kroll counters that Rosmer lost all claim to nobility when his allegiance to Rebecca drove Beata to suicide at the millrace. Rosmer takes the point and closes this act by trying to recoup his nobility. Pursuit of that goal ultimately drives the play's resolution in act 4.

Mortensgaard has come to evaluate Rosmer's potential service to the radical cause and, ironically, balks Rosmer's urge to act on the same grounds that Kroll did. For opposite reasons the editor will not have a public apostate on his side. Years ago, before his reformation, Rosmer was instrumental in ousting Mortensgaard from his position as a teacher after a passionate indiscretion, and that history reverberates in this scene. The echo begins in the cause of Mortensgaard's visit, Rebecca's letter of introduction sent with Brendel. When Mortensgaard learns of Rosmer's plans to declare his apostasy in the *Morning Star*, he politely but firmly rejects Rosmer's allegiance, instructing him in the political necessity of maintaining allegiance to respectable authority while bringing about change. With icily pleased resentment, Mortensgaard observes that the pastor helped teach him the power public disapproval has to nullify the influence of offenders against community standards of decency. At this point the play switches over powerfully into melodramatic intrigue as Mortensgaard reveals his receipt of Beata's incriminating letter just before her suicide 18 months ago. Eager to protect her husband, she had written to his political victim. Confessing her fear that Rosmer's enemies were eager to harm the pastor by spreading false stories of marital offenses against her at Rosmersholm, Beata urged the editor not to revenge himself on the pastor by publishing the stories. Rosmer again pleads her insanity as a defense against the scandal, but the editor, like Kroll, replies that Beata seemed more sane than not in the period leading to her death.

Mortensgaard explains that he has revealed the story of the letter to warn Rosmer that his conduct is ripe for society's reproof and the dangerous consequences that follow. Apostasy is not the only offense endangering the parson if he acts for the liberal cause. But, as he leaves, urging Rosmer to keep silent, the editor only hints at the potential scandal that could erupt over Rosmer's presumed sexual liaison with Rebecca. In this regard he cuts a more sympathetic figure than the respectable, sexist Kroll. Such oblique delicacy, coming from a condemned offender against the culture's sexual decorum, goes a long way toward mitigating the bad impression Mortensgaard's cynical political worldliness makes. Without any of the vanity or naïveté of Rosmer's self-involved ruminations about purity or innocence, Mortensgaard demonstrates here an honest and effective commitment to sexual liberation and an admirable, politically canny solidarity with free-minded women. By showing this aggrieved party boss strategically subduing an opportunistic impulse to make politics personal, Ibsen shows how liberating action might finally annul the historical oppression to which Rosmer opposes only un-moored spiritual struggle. Rosmer's tutor, Brendel, will praise Mortensgaard's talent for praxis at a crucial dramatic point in the last act, with an ugly thematic spin, but at this point Rosmer has no ear for this editor's wisdom about speaking to the public and continues to urge him to make full disclosure of the apostasy at Rosmersholm. Mortensgaard leaves with the cool, winning irony "I'll print everything that our good readers need to know" (R, 270).

The exit line announces the play's subsequent Aristotelian action: strategic revelation from different sources to different characters for different reasons at different times in different measures of everything readers, watch-ers, and characters, some of them only indifferently good, need to know. Everything turns out to be Rebecca's past, and the second act closes with Rosmer ironically, innocently, making that past an impediment to his or her action. Rebecca enters after Mortensgaard's exit and reveals to Rosmer that she remained in the bedroom adjoining his study after Kroll's arrival and has overheard both his and most of Mortensgaard's remarks. Rosmer makes no protest or complaint about her eavesdropping, in fact exonerates it, and asks for her counsel, claiming he has greater need of it now than he ever has before. As he guiltily searches for some cause in his behavior for Beata's knowledge of his changed life, and for the suicidal sacrifice that that knowledge ended in, Rebecca constantly urges him, six times in five minutes of dialogue, to forget Beata and concentrate on their future noble work of liberation. After the dismissals fail to stop his recriminating brood, Rebecca challenges his commitment to the future by asking if he would bring Beata back. Irresolute about future deeds, Rosmer is equally irresolute about willing the all-important Nietzschean return of the past, confined by remorse to "think of nothing but this one thing—that can never be undone" (R, 273).

Rebecca finally does rouse the pastor from this paralysis by invoking his past commitment to creating happy, noble lives. When he falters in his confidence by insisting that he cannot pursue that angelic service unless he can reclaim his serene innocence, she promises that serene innocence will return when he starts a new life of work and action. Rosmer takes the point, invoking once more her inspirational authority over that life of action. Asserting that he needs her to give him the courage to fight Kroll and the rest, he asks her to be his second wife. She responds with three incomplete, irresolute joyful exclamations, until he repeats the proposal with this revision: "I will not go through life with a corpse on my back. Help me to throw it off, Rebecca. And then let us lay all memories to rest in freedom, and joy, and love. You shall be my wife—the only wife I ever had" (R, 276). Something in this urge to repudiate the past kills her joy, stills her trembling, and leads her to reject the offer and forbid his mentioning it again. He repeatedly asks her to explain the astonishing rebuff; she refuses, alternately composed and terrified but throughout resolute, promising that his insistent inquiry into her refusal will exile her from Rosmersholm and finish their union.

Rosmer now makes his most resolute stand in the action so far, telling her their union will never be finished, that she will never leave Rosmersholm. Now perversely willing Nietzsche's eternal return of the same, Freud's return of the repressed, and the tragic logic of doom that governs classical drama and melodrama, Rebecca exits, after promising to answer his insistence that she supplant Beata by following the first wife's example:

> *Rebecca:* But if you ever ask me that again—it will be finished none the less, John.
> *John:* Finished none the less? How?
> *Rebecca:* Because then I shall go the way Beata went. Now you know, John.
> *Rosmer:* Rebecca!
> *Rebecca (in the doorway, nods slowly)* Now you know. *(Goes.) Rosmer (stares as though lost at the closed door):* Rebecca! (R, 277)

Aristotelian praxis and Nietzschean will to power, competing throughout this act for authority over the play's action, converge with their greatest tension so far in this propulsive standoff. The closed door and the repeated antiphonal struggle between Rosmer and Rebecca to continue, end, or know the action unifying their lives are wonderfully deployed devices of the well-made play and, as such, emphatic theatrical renditions of praxis. The ambiguities in these devices, especially the repeated, opaque disclosure in Rebecca's "Now you know" and her promise to repeat Beata's suicide, balance the suspense of ethical intrigue against the turmoil of conscience beautifully. The psychological struggle of wills fought over Rosmer's plans for messianic action in act 1 shifts decisively in this second act to an antecedent, correlative ground—Rosmer's guilt. That topic itself has an antecedent in Rebecca's guilt, which she has progressively hinted at from the start in enigmatic remarks about the white horse and evasive palliation of Beata's death. Act 3 will focus on finally exposing that guilt; act 4 will display its ultimate power to govern action.

Driving one kind of action and stalling another, ceaselessly bringing the present and future under the authority of the past, guilt coordinates the dramatic orders of *Rosmersholm* with pitiful and terrifying efficiency. Focusing the play's resolution on the struggle bad conscience induces between atonement and self-transcendence, Ibsen advances his career-long analysis of Nietzsche's repudiating critique of modern life as recalcitrant, delusionary, and murderous submission to the anachronistic moral systems of Aristotelian and Christian humanism. Until Rebecca's suicide threat the will to power has been subordinated to pragmatic, ethical logic in the action. From that point forward the will's Nietzschean goal of powerful expansion through explicitly antimoral self-transcendence will come progressively into play, opposing apocalyptic, liberating joy to praxis, and making the double suicide that resolves this remarriage plot a horrible instance of modern culture's defining ills.

In act 3 Rosmer, Kroll, and Rebecca all compete explicitly for control over the power innocent and guilty love, Platonic and sexual, has to cause or impede the ethical action of cultural reformation. In five scenes Beata's love of Rosmer is compared to Rebecca's, and battle is done to make one or the other primary. In the process of reversals and recognitions that drive forward the ethical intrigue, Ibsen brings the power struggle of nature and convention explicitly forward for the first time and so establishes the ontological argument, the contest over defining reality and change, that will end the union of Rosmer and Rebecca in act 4. Identifying sex and guilt with a natural will to power, Ibsen puts Nietzsche at the center of this play's struggle to find the meaning and value of reality and change. The act, set again in the living room of Rosmersholm, opens on the morning of the third day. Once more Rebecca and Mrs. Helseth start the action by discussing Beata's death, but this time the discussion provides melodramatic exposition, as Mrs. Helseth informs Rebecca of the sexual scandal surrounding Mortensgaard. The maid goes on from that topic to reveal her part in delivering Beata's letter to Mortensgaard and quickly exonerates her present mistress of the sexual accusation against her that the letter contained.

Because she is a servant and operating in the traditional theatrical role of the inside outsider in domestic affairs, the witness whose diminished social status often includes diminished consciousness of the action's full value, Mrs. Helseth gets the question of Rebecca's guilt right and wrong. But everyone else in the play, and the audience, also has been in the dark on this subject from the start, and so the representative example of Mrs. Helseth's error at the start of this act makes her a modern tragic chorus whose partial knowledge proclaims the act's direction: revelation of that guilt. And her servant's understanding also introduces an important new part of the play's thinking in this first scene—namely, the relation of nature, specifically sex and childbirth, to conventional morality and cultural authority at Rosmersholm.

Marriage is, of course, the time-honored order that humanistic civilization in Europe has established for sexual life, bringing the natural will for powerful, joyous, and multiplying gratification under the rule of economic and historical planning. So much is made of the remarriage plot in *Rosmersholm* because Rosmer's possible new marriage has immediate consequences for the maintenance or destruction of civilization, in his view, and in Kroll's and Rebecca's.[5] That struggle over civilization also involves a personal struggle to be happy, and in that struggle for happiness marriage is redefined by Rebecca and Rosmer as a spiritual elevation of natural force, instead of an economic, social order for continuing the species. Mrs. Helseth unwittingly weakens the revolutionary argument of Rosmer and Rebecca about marriage when she takes up the topic of Beata's barrenness.

To Rebecca's observation that being childless suits Rosmer, who was not made to occupy himself with crying children, Mrs. Helseth replies that children do not cry at Rosmersholm, nor, what is equally strange, do they laugh once they have grown up. To Rebecca's observation that people in the region do not laugh much, Mrs. Helseth makes the following assent: "That they don't. It started at Rosmersholm, people say. And then it spread around like a kind of plague, I shouldn't wonder" (R, 281). When Rebecca admires the profundity of this observation, Mrs. Helseth invokes her servant status to abort further inquiry into the matter. Taking umbrage poised between pert irony and comic humility, she exits, enigmatically admonishing her mistress not to mock her with praise for that generalized insight into Rosmersholm's blighting cultural authority.

In addition to displaying Ibsen's dramatic skill at writing deft psychological and social realism into melodramatic exposition (Rebecca is, after all, a kind of servant, a servant whose work has gained her a marriage proposal, hence the friendly envy of the subordinate servant, Mrs. Helseth), this exchange over the superstition attached to emotional development at Rosmersholm establishes an important element in the play's opposition of nature to culture. That traditional civilization has maimed human nature instead of ennobling it is essential to the liberating concept of love and cultural authority that Rosmer and Rebecca want to promote. Rosmer's aversion to sex, and Rebecca's guilty evasion of its authority in her life with Rosmer, severely compromise their messianic commitment to freeing natural sentiment from bourgeois convention and that ambiguity will loom very large in the play's resolution. Rebecca's aversion to children, her constant reference to Beata's barrenness, Rosmer's unnatural emotional development, his naive idealism, are all implicated in the maid's observation that childhood is magically suppressed at Rosmersholm, and that the evil force oppressing that house, elsewhere symbolized as the haunting white horse, has spread from there by means of the family's social authority into the culture at large as a biblical punishment, a plague.

Delivering this superstition through a servant, Ibsen not only corroborates Kroll's earlier observations about the extensive cultural authority of Rosmersholm in the community, but, more significantly, signals a distorted, weakened nature in the heart of the two imperfectly noble lovers opposing that authority. Assailing that weakness, Kroll becomes more than a vengeful tyrant; he takes on some of the authority of the biblical prophet who announces and enacts that divine retribution that the term *plague* blends into Mrs. Helseth's folklore. Bringing that natural weakness under the irrational authority of superstition in this scene, Ibsen also establishes the ground for the play's final association of thwarted sex and ruined liberty with Nietzsche's opposition of irrational action to humanistic praxis.

The rest of this act discloses Rebecca's natural liabilities, revealing how her sexual history made, and continues to make, action possible and impossible for her and for Rosmer. When Mrs. Helseth exits, Rosmer enters, and he and Rebecca discuss Kroll's slanderous assault on his apostasy and her licentiousness, which has appeared that morning in the *Country Telegraph*. Rosmer responds to the attack with a renewed zeal to bring liberation to his people, fully dressing it out in the religious language of shame, repentance, love, and transcendent striving toward light, happiness, and universal brotherhood along individually predestined paths. He falters, as he did earlier, when he realizes that he lacks the innocence to inspire the emulation such transcendence would require. He goes on to explain to Rebecca that he now believes his guilt toward Beata consisted in his carrying out not merely a friendship, but a spiritual marriage with Rebecca while Beata lived. That adultery prompted the spurned, still-loving Beata to sacrificial suicide, which she hoped would free Rosmer to pursue a happy life. Tragically, her sacrifice has delivered him to guilt instead of freedom, to paralyzing guilt that Rebecca knows, even as Rosmer confesses it, belongs more justly to her than him. He once more promises that he could find joy in his life and bring others to it if he were freed of guilt, but he stops short of asking her to make marriage his liberating discovery. Rebecca asks him whether joy can count for so much to a man who never laughs, and, when he answers yes, unaware of her reference to the superstition about thwarted joy being a curse in the Rosmer line, Rebecca seems convinced that she might somehow, without marrying him, deliver him from the guilt about Beata that stops his liberating action. She sends him off so that she can receive Kroll, whose impending arrival she has hidden from Rosmer.

Kroll has come not only to uncover Rebecca's guilt, but to explain its origin to her and to require that she marry Rosmer not to free him for liberating action, but to prevent him from being destroyed by its ravages, to allow him, instead, to retreat to tarnished respectability under the cover of a "legalized" relationship with a less than perfectly presentable consort. Kroll starts by accusing Rebecca of cold-bloodedly scheming to take Beata's place and have Rosmer in her power. She ruthlessly bewitched Beata to gain entry to Rosmersholm and now has worked the same desperate infatuation on Rosmer, at the cost of ruining his chances for happiness. When Rebecca counters that Kroll introduced guilt about Beata into Rosmer's life, the schoolmaster approves of Rosmer's remorse. He next makes her concurring observation that Rosmer is still deeply committed to his family traditions the occasion for a masterfully exonerating accusation and tells her that she couldn't ever have appreciated that loyalty because the circumstances of her birth corrupted her moral faculty.

Here the argument connecting moral nobility and nature gets its full conservative exposition. In the process Kroll provokes a revelation in Rebecca that no one else in the play ever receives and which holds the key to the final opposition of messianic idealism against guilty commitment to tradition that makes up the harrowing fourth act. He begins by reciting Rebecca's genealogy to demonstrate that she is the illegitimate daughter of a prostitute and Dr. West, the radical freethinker who extended to her the harsh haven of his home when she was orphaned, whose old age she nursed, whose last disease first brought her to Rosmersholm. Kroll proves that paternity, which Rebecca vehemently denies, by recounting the dates of West's presence in the northern province where Rebecca was born and by arguing that only unconscious filial piety could account for her loyalty to this abusive, renegade stranger. After some playing with dates, Kroll convinces Rebecca that he is right about the paternity, and she responds with extravagant, distracted anguish, tersely repeated ejaculatory denials, and hand-wringing. This is the standard histrionic code on the melodramatic stage for remorse over sexual sin or violation, the conventional, definitive set of gestures given to the unmasked adulteress or the nearly ruined or innocently spoiled virgin.

When Kroll asks why Rebecca is enacting them, she passes her anguish off as humiliation over illegitimacy, which he doesn't believe but will accept so that he can continue pressing his case. What neither will say, what Rebecca has just discovered, and Kroll might suspect, is that West was not only the free-loving father of Rebecca, but also her free-loving seducer and common-law-husband for the five years they were together. The stage directions announce the tragic violation; Rebecca's fourth-act confession that another man has bequeathed her indelible sexual remorse confirms it.[6] Kroll now takes advantage of the inconsistency that Rebecca's concern for social convention displays to make the most powerful conservative argument, that traditional norms belong to nature, that enlightenment ideas are vain, doomed attempts to change reality.

> *Kroll:* You've read books that have given you a whole lot of new ideas and
>   opinions. You've picked up a smattering of new-fangled theories about
>   this and that—theories that seem to upset much of what has hitherto
>   been regarded as gospel and unchallengeable. But you've only accepted
>   all this intellectually, Miss West. You don't really feel it in your blood.
> *Rebecca (thoughtfully):* You may be right about that. (R, 292)

The appeal to irrational (blood) knowledge of one's sexual guilt, and guilty natural origin, invokes Christian humanism and Nietzsche's opposition to it, but neither Kroll nor Rebecca take up the argument. He is convinced he has already won it, that she is an irretrievable reprobate who can only be restrained by shame not only for her origin but, more important, for her adulterous violation of Rosmer's marriage and moral integrity. A powerful irony undermines Kroll's conservative denunciation: Rebecca has not slept with Rosmer, has in fact been prevented from that offense partly by the noble enlightenment morality that Kroll believes has no authority over nature. The other impediment to her gratification *is* blood guilt, however, that only she knows, and it is the struggle in her of these two moralities that this act has progressively revealed and that the final one will consummate. She hints at the struggle in their final exchange over the need for her to marry Rosmer. To her argument that the time has passed for Rosmer to avoid the dangers attending his commitment to a changed future, Kroll responds that their marriage will neutralize the scandal his apostasy and its origin in their affair have caused. Wounded, frightened, she wonders aloud that he is so convinced their life together is sexual, and he offers as

proof the observation that sexual feeling makes it easy to overcome traditional cultural authority, that corrupt natures habitually and deem morality
readily evaded prejudice. Her response: *"(wanders across the room and looks out
through the window)*: It was on the tip of my tongue to say—I wish you were
right, Dr. Kroll" (R, 293).

Rebecca's motion and remark, like the anguished hand-wringing, involuntarily, partially disclose guilt. The strangeness Kroll observes in her
behavior displays irresolute longing to accede to his plan for her atonement
and Rosmer's. Contrarily, the strangeness gleams with a sardonic urge to have
boldly seduced Rosmer, as Kroll believes she has, to not be languishing in
guilt for an incomplete crime, but to have actively mastered the natural joy
that, under her authority and Rosmer's, could bring a future into being that
would destroy Kroll. Both desires aim at changing the past to make a future
change possible, and Ibsen embodies that aim by having Rebecca wander
across the room where she is accused and deliver her line to Kroll facing away
from him, looking through the window that opens onto the site of Beata's
suicide. Deliverance from the past lies in controlling the meaning of that
suicide, finally ending Beata's life. Looking through the window, Rebecca
discovers a way to annul the effects Beata continues to cause at Rosmersholm.
At Rosmer's entrance she takes action to stop Kroll's punitive plan for shoring
up respectability, to restore Rosmer's zeal for messianic deliverance, and to
free herself from both men's marital designs on her. The action is justification
through confession of her part in Beata's death. That action, inspired by
gazing at the millrace, only summons the white horse that Rebecca has been
drawn to from her initial sighting of the millrace through that same living-
room window in the first scene of the play, but it takes one more act for this
eternal return of the same to become clear. At this point she thinks she can
draw a new and consummate effect from refined imitation of the old cause
of sacrificial love that she initiated and imperfectly governed in Beata.

She begins by telling Rosmer explicitly that she wants to restore that
joyful innocence that he has clamored for, which he needs to live actively.
Initially, it appears that her tactic will be to reveal how desire eclipsed her
naive devotion to enlightenment. She came to Rosmersholm tutored by West
in free-thinking ethics, eager to continue the departed Brendel's tutelage of
Rosmer in those ethics, "but then," she says, and is at the point of revealing
the disruptive force of attraction to Rosmer when he bluntly interrupts to tell
her he knows all about what he presumes will be a description of her ideas
at the time. Having her painful feelings covered over by Rosmer's obtuse,
self-regarding attempt to encourage her—she had lapsed into strained whis-
pers on the words *but then*—Rebecca realizes she doesn't have to tell the

emotional truth to Rosmer. Judging that he will accept a purely ideological account of her actions, that he perhaps cannot understand her emotions or does not want to, she suppresses them once more and takes the expedient route, presenting herself as the inspired handmaid to his pursuit of a new world. It turns out this expediency hurts more than helps her and adds one more instance to the play's ongoing indictment of men erasing female authenticity, this time an offense from the liberal power base. Rebecca's feminist dilemma, the doublebind women experience when they try to harmonize the discontinuity by which priests and generals keep nature and culture in conflict, is muted here, and throughout the play, but is potent and will become even stronger in the last act, when Rebecca once again takes Brendel as her authority where self-sacrifice is concerned. Ironically savoring a purely private, sadly self-defeating victory, Rebecca concedes here, with the same mocking "right" she used to deflect Kroll's earlier conservative gambit. Composed again after a fearful approach to disclosure, as she was so recently with Kroll, she responds to Rosmer: "Yes, yes—you're right really. I suppose you do know all this" (R, 295).

She proceeds to say what she wants to in the terms he accepts, only partly freeing herself and bringing him to recrimination and desertion instead of joyous innocence. Like all other reversals and recognitions so far, this third-act crisis is masterfully crafted so that relief also enhances suspense. There is a cultural argument and a metaphysics in that propulsive balance, but Ibsen reserves full treatment of those larger concerns for the final act. Here we are at the play's most Aristotelian turn, what Ibsen's contemporaries would have called the *scène à faire*, that moment when all forces in the action finally converge and balance. That Rebecca's Nietzschean self-transcendence yields to the managerial logic of the well-made play at this point gives brilliant theatrical expression to the plight of the sick will. Crushed, the sick will resists more or less powerfully, ambiguously appropriating and submitting to the terms of the oppressor, and this yielding prepares for the final resurgent battle Rebecca will fight against Rosmer alone in act 4. The sick will does not always accurately discern the difference between appropriation and submission where power is concerned, and that error accounts for Rebecca's conviction in this scene that she can finish the action before it finishes her. Generous and self-protective, she tells Rosmer that she saw how marriage to Beata was impeding his messianic advance and decided to free him by revealing his apostasy to Beata. To ensure Beata's separation from Rosmer, Rebecca explains, she suggested that Rosmer's apostasy might soon lead to adultery and on that ground begged Beata's permission to leave Rosmersholm. Kroll forces her to confess that she in fact made Beata believe that adultery had already supplanted the marriage and criminally provided the child Beata's barrenness could not. These prevarications are the labyrinth Rebecca acknowledges she built for Beata, and treacherously led her through, until the deluded wife believed she could love Rosmer only by destroying herself for his sake.

When Rosmer asks for her motivation in all this, Rebecca responds with a contradictory analysis, first asserting that she saw herself choosing between two possible lives for Rosmer and her. To Kroll's accusation that she had no right to make such a choice, Rebecca answers not with a defense of the liberal cause, or her commitment to it, but with an account of herself as possessed, confused, alienated at the time from the ideological clarity she has just been rehearsing. Dismissing Kroll's view that she acted cold-bloodedly, Rebecca reveals the shape but not the content of her sexual motive to the two men. Eager to be understood, if not exonerated, she tells them how she operated almost mechanically under a split compulsion, choosing each turn through the labyrinth, but also vainly opposed at each point by her forbidding conscience and by pragmatic doubt about the plan's ultimate success. She describes herself as acting under two wills, neither of which was entirely rational: one commanded action; one prohibited it. She finishes her account with a remark that makes her description of ambiguously rational struggle between morally opposed forces one of the play's most important definitions of dramatic and messianic change: "And then it happened. That's how such things do happen" (R, 298). At this point Rosmer abandons her, exiting with Kroll, who, having accomplished his mission at Rosmersholm, never appears in the play again. Rebecca's attempt to restore John's innocence by removing his guilt has, instead, restored him to the traditional oppression of the Rosmer line, now more as judge than victim. His concession to Kroll is visually emphasized in Rosmer's imitative donning of his hat after Kroll's and in their shunning Rebecca as they leave. But the alliance doesn't signal complete transformation in Rosmer. At the window Rebecca notices that he and Kroll avoid the millrace as they leave the estate and concludes that, even after her confession, even aligned with the respectable Kroll, Rosmer is still guilty, will never not be. Her comment on their aversion to Beata's death site signals the final invocation of the white horses in this act. Arranging for her departure from Rosmersholm with Mrs. Helseth, Rebecca makes no mention of the evening's confession, but says she is leaving because a glimpse of the white horses of Rosmersholm, who, she says, never sleep, has frightened her that day. Remorse has frightened her, but not remorse over Beata. The white horses in her case are shame and guilt over her origin, over the corruption of her nature and her cultural project, which the cause of both, her father, bequeathed to her. Challenged by Kroll's accidental revelation to annul that remorse, to will her tragic past affirmatively and so become free, she has lapsed into confining, rearguard action against the claims of respectability. Seeing the temporizing exculpation fail, Rebecca has no chance for freedom except flight from all claims, and that is prevented by Rosmer, who intercepts her departure when he returns to Rosmersholm late that night. At the point when all strategies of deliverance have become snares, when no action seems possible, Ibsen drives the play forward to its most definitive event: the double suicide in which Rosmer and Rebecca at once change everything and nothing.

Act 4 takes place late on the night of the third day, in the living room of Rosmersholm. Now that the past has been discovered the action shifts from revelation of guilt as cause to struggle with guilt's effects. Hoping to bring new effect from an old cause, to make a guilty past yield an innocent, joyous future, Rebecca and Rosmer transform the Magdalen convention that has governed their story by adding to the last scene of this remarriage play an operatic finale from Wagner's stage, the *liebestod*. Gladly consummating their spiritual marriage in a loving death leap from the millrace, Ibsen's defeated messiahs do more than conflate theatrical actions. They also bring together opposed ideas of agency, change, and cultural authority and, in doing so, transmute Aristotelian, Christian humanism and Nietzsche's modernist critique of power. The issue most at stake in this last act is not whether or not the new spouses will kill themselves, not even whether one is responsible for the other's decision, but which concept of agency and change governs their behavior. Rosmer, Rebecca, and Brendel all discuss action explicitly and at length in this last act. That discussion, together with Mrs. Helseth's curtain line, indicates that Aristotelian praxis, spurned as moribund suspicion haunting Rosmer's line, has more to do with the apparently transcendent suicide that ends that line than either of the finally enraptured lovers knows.

The act opens with Mrs. Helseth sadly helping Rebecca prepare to leave Rosmersholm. The maid blames Rosmer for abandoning Rebecca when he should be marrying her and so rescuing mother and child. Rebecca responds to this female solidarity by asking how Mrs. Helseth could believe the gossip about Rosmer or find her capable of adultery. Ignoring her mistress's self-presentation as noble seeker after freedom, the maid answers that Rebecca is single, female, and human and therefore triply weak where sex is concerned. In her denial of Rebecca's special status as vestal virgin of enlightenment—"I mean, we're all human, Miss West" (R, 301)— Mrs. Helseth expresses some faint disapproval of what she regards as Rebecca's fraudulently fancy ideas, but, more significantly, she extends to Rebecca the only disinterested kindness that unhappy woman ever receives in the play. Miss West's response, an enigmatic approval of the truism that everyone is human, can be played as icy, dismissive assertion of superiority, assured defense of the liberal cause, or sad concession to the compassionate but servile view that humanity cannot be improved. It should suggest all without settling for one and thus indicate that Ibsen is beginning the play's final argument about nature, culture, and humanity's power to enact change in the relation of these orders.

Power to act concerns both Rebecca and Rosmer throughout the next scene. Rosmer enters and Rebecca tells him she is leaving. They converse formally about pragmatic matters until Rebecca makes Rosmer "suddenly alert," as the stage directions indicate, by disclosing that Rosmersholm has broken her. To his one-word query "What?" she responds: "Broken me completely. When I first came here, I was so alive and fearless. Now I am a slave to a strange and foreign law. After today I don't think I shall ever dare attempt anything again" (R, 302). When she asks about his meeting with Kroll and his plans for the future, Rosmer answers that he too has been broken. The members of Kroll's party, gathered en masse that afternoon, have convinced him that he is unfit to ennoble humanity. When he adds his own view that the goal is hopeless in any case, Rebecca assents. He calls her assent a lie, complains that she never believed in his moral strength but merely flattered him to advance her own station. In what she believes is her final attempt to restore his confidence in himself, in the liberal cause, and in her honest love of both, Rebecca answers that accusation with a confession of what she calls "the most important thing . . . The thing you've never guessed. The thing that both excuses and condemns all the rest" (R, 303). That thing is sexual passion, and Rebecca proceeds to explain to John how this natural force and the cultural project of enlightenment converged in her life at Rosmersholm, how "this most important thing" first made action possible and then impossible.

Ambitious, energetic, free, Rebecca felt omnipotent when she started life at Rosmersholm. Her fearless commitment to making life noble was broken and turned to fright when sexual passion ousted cultural ideology with the force of a northern sea storm in winter. Acted on, Rebecca acted on Beata in what she calls a fight for survival. When Rosmer asks why she will not take the prize of her natural victory, marry him and resume the cultural project that the victory has made possible again, she answers: "Because Rosmersholm has drained my strength. It has broken my courage and paralyzed my will. The time is past when I was afraid of nothing. I have lost the power to take action, John." He requires further explanation, and she answers that the platonic companionship they shared after Beata's death silenced the fury and torment of passion. She accounts for her new chaste calm with another natural simile: "A calm came over me—the kind of calm you find on a bird-cliff up in the far north, under the midnight sun" (R, 305-06).

But that calm is not innocent release of moral agency; it is an anodyne that stills the anguish of animal force—hence, the frigid, paradoxically lit stillness of the bird in her metaphor. Rolfe Fjelde's translation of this passage brings the dormancy into sharp focus: "A profound inner peace settled on me—a tranquility, like an island of sleeping birds, up north, under the midnight sun."[7] The noble humanism of Rosmer's messianic aspiration works on her like the midnight sun, shining when exhaustion makes any activity impossible. Platonic ethics, maintained in the rationalism of Rosmer's enlightenment project, holds that knowing the good means doing it. Ibsen contradicts that morality by associating the knowledge that came to Rebecca under the midnight sun of chastity with remorse. When Rosmer asks again why she cannot marry him, Rebecca answers that Rosmer's view of life has infected, poisoned, and enslaved her will, has ennobled her, and in the process killed happiness. That murderous salvation comes when the animal force of sexual joy is ousted by the idealistic willing of innocent love. To his third appeal for marriage, Rebecca answers that a previous sexual experience, more terrible than her passion for him, also stands in the way of her accepting him. Rosmer declines her offer to be informed of the past corruption, arguing that she and he can forget it and so nullify it. At this point Ibsen brings the central idea of the play, the problem that will resolve its action and argument, forward in absolute clarity. Rebecca can't forget the past. "Yes, John. That's what's so dreadful—that now, when all life's happiness is offered to me with open hands—now I've become the kind of person whose conscience about the past makes it impossible for me to accept it" (R, 306).

Rebecca's early role as vestal virgin of enlightenment, falsely maintained while she acted under the ferocious authority of unconsummated lust, dismissed by Mrs. Helseth, who inaccurately detects the role's sexual component, dismantled by Kroll, who also inaccurately detects a sexual corruption in it, is finally authentically restored to Rebecca when she can no longer enact it. Rebecca's unconsummated lust murdered Beata. That passionate action ironically banished passion from Rebecca's life, and that banishing has murdered Rebecca's power to act. Presenting and absenting itself as the origin and end of praxis, sex only occurs by not occurring, repeatedly, in Rebecca's story with Rosmer. The eternal return of the same, which Nietzsche's aesthetic people hypothetically invoke as a continuous occasion for that powerful willing that increasingly lets them become what they are, is not invoked or contemplated by an aesthetically transcendent Rebecca. Instead, in a terrible reversal the eternal return of sexual frustration is visited upon her, first as lust transmuted into murder from a distance, next as platonic love, finally as the alien transformation of that love into the nihilistic assault of conscience. Internalized via guilt, the invading force of conscience displays the same double logic displayed by appetite. Under accusation she both must and cannot view herself as both virgin and whore. Her aesthetic willing to become what she is consists of compulsively punishing the falsely accused whore with the alien moral code of the innocently ruined, falsely esteemed, ineffectual virgin.

All Rosmer understands of this is that her newfound conscience should enable her to see herself as delivered to a happy future with him. "Your past is dead, Rebecca. It no longer has any hold on you. It has nothing to do with you. All that happened to someone else" (R, 307). He is not only obtuse and egocentric. He invokes here a secular version of the theory of justification by which his formative Lutheran faith brings new effects from old causes. Human nature is de facto evil, but not unalterably so, in this thinking, which originates in Augustine. Faith in Christ, whose sacrifice annulled universal condemnation, justifies believers, makes them newly capable of innocent love and action. Secular transpositions of this model for regeneration normally substitute saving faith in native human goodness for faith in Christ. In Ibsen's century the most famous literary instance of this secular justification is Charles Dickens's A Christmas Carol, in which Ebenezer Scrooge, confronting the eternal return of the same in a supernatural tour through his past, discovers salvational love. The climax of Scrooge's conversion comes when he pleads with the ghost of Christmas yet to come to be saved from the future he has made for himself in the past. "I'm not the man I was, spirit," he argues, "I'm not the man I was."[8] Aristotelian humanism, which underlies so much of Rosmer's Enlightenment convictions, also provides for correction of moral errors and for rational moderation of future effects stemming from old causes—hence, the readiness of justification, religious or secular, in the fallen pastor's courting consolation of Rebecca.

Ibsen will have none of it and will not let Rebecca free that way either. Rosmerholm's foreign law of conscience rests more heavily on the concept paired with Luther's fideistic theory of justification, the one that required it: the incapacity of sinners to be justified by their own efforts of conscience or by any works. This concept makes for paralysis after knowledge of the past, and that condition is what Rebecca suffers. "Oh, my dearest, those are just words. What about that sense of innocence you spoke about? Where shall I find that innocence?" (R, 307). Rosmer, who cared so much about innocence when his was at stake, at first fends Rebecca off when she talks about finding hers, arguing that people cannot be ennobled, as he once thought, from without, through the effect of a noble example or messianic instruction. She counters with a second secular version of justification, the more popular and conventional one in fiction and on the stage, when she asks whether being loved cannot ennoble people and make them innocent.

Rebecca invokes the fundamental ethos and plot logic of the Magdalen play here (love changes everything),[9] and Rosmer seizes on the deliverance that logic might offer in his response to her question: "(*thoughtfully*): Ah, that would be the thing! The greatest thing that life would have to offer. If it were true. (*Restlessly*): But how can I find the answer to that question? The real answer?" (*R*, 307-8). And so the play goes back, in an eternal return of the same, to the action of act 2 and act 3—the search for a sure way to manage the past, to bring innocent effects out of a guilty cause. The Magdalen play lives up to its religious origin by presenting a heroine in whom innocence and guilt are sorted out through love of some compassionate redeemer. Ibsen's turn on the convention in *Rosmersholm* is to redistribute the roles of redeemer and sexual offender. Neither Rosmer nor Rebecca has actually sinned sexually; both have sublimated that natural power under the authority of conscience, what Rebecca calls the "foreign law" of Rosmersholm. In that sublimation both she and John have become sinners and redeemers simultaneously. Rebecca's acknowledgment of passion stains them both sexually and brings that foreign law into question—hence, their doubt about whether either can compassionately redeem themselves or each other.

The action that brings the sinner into contact with redemptive authority in Magdalen plays normally includes tests of the sinner's contrition and the redeeming authority's validity. Ibsen reverses the normal pattern here and puts the redemptive authority under more probing test than the contrite sinner. In addition to doubling the roles of sinner and redeemer, Ibsen subverts the Magdalen convention even more powerfully by conflating them. Rosmer's request that Rebecca restore his innocence so that he can once again pursue his redemptive mission is a perfect instance. Ironically making Magdalen Christ this way, Ibsen focuses once more on the double bind surrounding Rebecca's struggle to become, in the personal and political, ideological senses of the phrase, a new woman. Taking up the male role of public reformer or guardian of ethics, the new woman not only forfeits the chance to fulfill her role as wife or mother, but invokes the retroactive judgment that she has all along been naturally unfit to fulfill it and for that reason has sought out the inappropriate male role.

This logic drives Kroll's investigation of Rebecca's moral past and Rosmer's doubts about the saving power of Rebecca's love, but doesn't stop either man from requiring that Rebecca take on the natural role of wife. Kroll wants Rebecca to save moral appearances; Rosmer wants her to save his mission to exceed them. But neither believes her action could be authentic or free in either case. At different times, for opposite reasons, both require her to be sinner and redeemer at once. And Rebecca cannot find her way out of that commanding, imploring accusation and plea. She cannot bring power to bear; she lost it when conscience killed her passion. She cannot take up any praxis; her passion has retroactively annulled the effect of any ethical pursuit. Ibsen will continue his critique of the double bind that the action of justification entails in the fourth scene, which adds conflicting Aristotelian and Nietzschean accounts of retro-active guilt and innocence to the play's argument. Here he shows Rebecca trying once more to loosen the bind. In a reversal that preserves both roles Rebecca presents herself as Christ to Rosmer by emphasizing her relation to him as Magdalen: she offers the ennobling change his chaste companionship has wrought in her as redemptive proof of love's power to justify the past. Rosmer cruelly annuls that action, telling her he doesn't believe in his ability to change anyone. Lost without faith in himself, which he blames her for, which he will not let her restore, Rosmer bullies her with anguished repeated demands for proof of love, without any idea of what might satisfy that demand. Enter Ulrick Brendel, Rosmer's first tutor in free thought, to provide the answer.

Brendel has stopped at Rosmersholm on his way out of town to say good-bye to John. With the same grandiloquent vanity he used to proclaim his coming oratorical deliverance of the people in act 1, Brendel tells Rebecca and Rosmer that he went dry when the time came to speak, and that Mortensgaard subsequently convinced him that he had nothing left to offer the liberal cause. Brendel does not tell them what Kroll related in act 2, that he began his reformation of the masses drunk in a tavern, whose denizens, after he had jeeringly branded them as unfit to receive the light, tossed him out. Nor does Brendel reveal that Mortensgaard gave him back Rosmer's coat, after redeeming it from the pawnshop where Brendel had exchanged it for the stipend that supported his sermon at the bar. What he does say about Mortensgaard, though, is crucial to the play's argument about action: "Peter Mortensgaard is the lord and master of the future! . . . Peter Mortensgaard possesses the secret of omnipotence. He can do anything he sets his mind to . . . Because Peter Mortensgaard never wants to do more than lies within his power. Peter Mortensgaard knows how to live life without ideals. And *that* you see—*that* is precisely the secret of action and of victory. It is the sum of all the world's wisdom. *Basta!*" (R, 310).

Mortensgaard, in this account, is the perfect Aristotelian agent, who matches final cause to the formal, material, and efficient causes he has power to command. Idealists such as Brendel and Rosmer invent final causes without inventing the corresponding power to enact them, or else they go astray by enlisting weak or fraudulent power that corrupts their invented goal. Brendel's attitude toward the editor, ironically named after Christ's messianic sergeant and worldly deputy Peter, mixes the buffoon's resentment, contempt, and admiration with the sage's insight and the Tempter's cynical, corrupting lie. The unstable combination of voices that Ibsen has given him here makes Brendel a very unholy fool. His sinister, grasping show of loyalty, balanced with his long-standing love and noble poverty suggest Judas and Christ at once, and recall Ibsen's earlier use of the same ambiguously magnifying references for the ruined messiah of *The Wild Duck*, Gregers Werle. The impulse to fraud is nothing worse than comic vanity when it causes Brendel to suppress the truth about his failure to preach and so be a new delivering son of man. The same impulse takes on a much more sinister force when the ruined tutor magnifies his disappointment into prophetic insight and teaches freedom through nihilism. Quoting Christ when he teaches Rosmer the new lesson that he hopes will expunge all his previous tutelage, Brendel ceases to be merely a fool and displays treachery akin to Judas' and corruption akin to Satan's.

Be like Mortensgaard in your pursuit of the ennobling action, he tells Rosmer; "Build not on shifting sand" (*R*, 310). The reference is to Matthew 8: 26-27: "And every one that heareth these sayings of mine, and doeth them not, shall be likened unto a foolish man, which built his house upon the sand: And the rain descended, and the floods came, and the winds blew, and beat upon that house; and it fell: and great was the fall of it." In Christ's parable denial of the ideal life is exemplified by ruinously impractical building of that all-important harmonizer of nature and culture, the house. Brendel has reversed the parable and matched avowal of the ideal life with foolish carpentry. He may only be making a drunken (or sober) gaffe or blasphemy; in either case he is playing a very false Jesus, indeed, to this modern instance of Christ's most loved disciple, John.

All this biblical language belongs to the scene for an immediately realistic reason: Rosmer is a species of spoiled minister (although the sexual taint, ironically, never quite amounts to lust in this thin-skinned lover) who has throughout the play been confusedly seeking a role as justifier of his people. While it suits and displays the play's realistic dimension, the biblical language also carries out the play's argumentative probing of the ambiguities and ambivalences surrounding messianic aspiration and advances the play's critique of Christianity's anachronistic commitment to humanistic ideas of praxis that are so easily and constantly appropriated by cynical forces more interested in coercion than in happiness. Brendel's unmoored citation of the carpenter Jesus' parable, in which house building analogically represents the stable relation between contemplation and action in the virtuous life, resonates everywhere in this play, named after a house whose master is unavailingly seeking to know how to do the good.

Common wisdom asserts that the devil can quote Scripture to his own purpose, and Ibsen makes dramatic use of that notion by explicitly adding Satan and his vicar, Judas Iscariot, to Brendel's repertoire of New Testament mugging in the tutor's final revisionist encouragement of his former pupil. The remark about shifting sand, which cautions Rosmer to pursue messianic action pragmatically, retroactively diminishes the idealistic force of humanistic justification for messianic action that Rosmer has embraced and despaired of throughout the play. Brendel also has something damaging to say about the alternative amatory justification of messianic action that Rebecca and John were struggling over at the moment of his entrance. Alluding to Rebecca, whom he calls a charming creature, Brendel urges Rosmer to be cautious about the effects of love on his project. At his entrance in act 1 Brendel, in an ominous piece of social comedy, mistook Rebecca for Rosmer's wife. He clearly is aware in this scene that they are not married and presumes, quite offensively from Rebecca's point of view, they are lovers. When she forces him to name her directly as a sexual threat to Rosmer's mission, Brendel does so, calling her "bewitching lady from the sea" in Meyer's translation and, more suggestively, "my seductive mermaid" in Fjelde's (R. 310, I. 579).

With this reference to Rebecca as undine, Ibsen adds to her symbolic status as Magdalen a long-standing association of women with the cyclical forces of creation and destruction in nature that starts as science in Paracelsus and by Ibsen's time has become both superstition and literary cliché.[10] As she has repeatedly, Rebecca repudiates the sexual innuendo immediately and questions why it has been introduced to disqualify her from suitably supporting and stabilizing Rosmer's active life. Like Kroll, Brendel has a plan for turning the sexual disqualification into suitable service, but, unlike Kroll's, his is murderous. He instigates the final resolution of the play's action and its argument about action, when he tells Rebecca the plan. So much of the play's ending starts here that it is worth citing the exchange in full.

> Brendel (takes a step closer): I gather that my former pupil has a cause which he
>   wishes to carry to victory.
> Rebecca: Well?

Brendel: His victory is assured. But—mark this well—on one inescapable
    condition.

Rebecca: What is that?

Brendel (takes her gently by the wrist): That the woman who loves him shall, with
    a light heart, go out into the kitchen and chop off her delicate
    rosy-white finger— *here*— just *here* at the middle of the joint. *Item,* that
    the aforesaid adoring woman—equally gladly—shall snip off her in-
    comparably formed left ear. *(Lets go of her and turns to Rosmer.)* Farewell,
    Johannes! My victorious disciple!

Rosmer: Are you going now? It's such a dark night.

Brendel: Night and darkness are best. Peace be with you. *(He goes.)*

There is a moment's silence in the room. (R. 311)

In Magdalen plays the fallen woman must undergo tests of her contrition
that normally involve sacrificial mortification of sexuality. The sacrifice both
atones for the sexual offense and purifies fallen nature, thus ensuring that no
sexual offense can recur. The "inescapable condition" Brendel presents for
Rebecca's atonement, which is vicariously Rosmer's, transforms this conventional theatrical test of moral fortitude into a Mephistopheles bargain that
promises salvation but can only deliver doom. The mechanical legalism of
Brendel's plan, icily displayed in his language of "inescapable condition," "Item,"
and "aforesaid adoring woman," together with the cool, intimate yet impersonal
sadism of Brendel's highly specific and technical instructions for Rebecca's
dismemberment and disfiguring, all indicate that the sacrifice enjoined on this
sexual penitent is not sanctifying or justifying mortification but, rather, a
deluding magic formula, a scheming spell cast to damn her soul and her
beloved's. That Brendel holds Rebecca's wrist while he presents the plan to her
gives his recitation the physical appearance and force of an infecting, supranatural possession that instills a demonic curse. And when all this happens, we
are, of course, approaching midnight, the natural time of greatest vulnerability
to Satanic devices in religious and superstitious tradition.

Ibsen switches back from Goethe's *Faust* and associated folklore identifications of Satan as deluding rationalist and trickster to the New Testament
when Brendel drops Rebecca's hand and addresses Rosmer as "victorious
disciple" and "Johannes." Assuming the role of Christ, Brendel gives Rosmer
the formal biblical name of the beloved apostle to whom Christian tradition
also assigns authorship of the fourth gospel. In John's concern that Brendel
is leaving Rosmersholm on the way to nowhere in the middle of the night,
in the portentous, extravagant dismissal of that concern that comes in the

tutor's exit line "Night and darkness are best. Peace be with you," Ibsen brings
the tutor's complex association with Jesus and Judas forth in an elegant,
sophisticated reference to the last supper scene in John's gospel. The allusion,
capping Brendel's theorizing about action, brings Christ's self-willed betrayal
and subsequent self-sacrifice, his announcement of ethical reformation, and
his promise to sustain those who carry out that reformation into the resolution of Rebecca's and John's struggle over the justifying action of love.

In John's account of the last supper Christ reveals to all his disciples that
one of them will betray him, but lets only John know, through a coded gesture
at the table involving wine-soaked bread, that the traitor is Judas. John
explicitly identifies Judas and Satan and enigmatically presents Christ as
commanding both, in the verse "And after the sop Satan entered into him,
then said Jesus unto him, That thou doest do quickly" (John 13: 27). Brendel's
exit invokes these lines from the same scene in John: "He having received
the sop went immediately out: and it was night. Therefore, when he was gone
out, Jesus said, Now is the Son of man glorified, and God is glorified in him
. . . A new commandment I give unto you, That ye love one another; as I
have loved you, that ye also love one another. By this shall all men know that
ye are my disciples, if ye have love one to another" (John 13:30-31, 34-35).
After repeating and explaining the new commandment and requiring his
disciples to preserve it after his impending death—the first, paradigmatic
instance of deliverance through self-sacrificing love—Jesus encourages them
by promising that God the Father will send God the Holy Spirit to preserve
and enliven in them the reformation preached and enacted by God the Son.
In addition to the promise of a divine Comforter, Jesus provides them a
present strength to help them begin the work of reform: "Peace I leave with
you, my peace I give unto you: not as the world giveth, give I unto you. Let
not your heart be troubled, neither let it be afraid" (John 14: 27). Brendel's
last words, "Peace be with you," echo the closing words of the Latin mass,
"Pax vobiscum," in which the celebrant quotes John's gospel to reenact and
so reaffirm Christ's closing promise, comfort, and exhortation at the last
supper, the initiating sacrament of Christian life, spiritually reenacted and
reaffirmed in the Mass. With theological and liturgical variation, the sacrament and exhortation to peace are preserved in Rosmer's now abandoned
Lutheran ministry.

Rosmer has carried over idealist aspiration toward innocent, dignified
happiness from that ministry into his now failed project to enlighten the
people. In place of reliance on God's saving grace, Rosmer has substituted,
as his authority for idealism, trust in unaided human power to know and do
good. Now, searching for confidence to resume belief in merely human moral

force, Rosmer receives distorted New Testament encouragement in a surprise visit from a destitute, discredited prophet of humanism. And the Christian logic comes in radically unstable ambiguity, in language that makes its speaker Judas, Satan, and Christ at once. And that speaker advances humanist justification primarily by marring the competing theory of justification in this scene, by making sacrificial love gruesomely subsidiary to ethics. Rebecca's eagerness to prove that human love justifies human ethical striving puts nature and culture in a balance that Brendel wrecks by urging that she literally mortify her flesh in order to convince Rosmer that she is chastely devoted to him and will not seduce him into sensual gratification when she should be inspiring him to messianic deliverance of humanity.

The travesty Brendel makes of loving self-sacrifice, his perverted guarantee that hideous cruelty will advance ethical reformation, rests on such bizarre logic and displays such unstable motivation that the scene takes *Rosmersholm* momentarily out of the realm of theatrical realism. Elements from all the conventions Ibsen has transmuted so far—the Magdalen play, the remarriage comedy, the adultery tragedy, the murder mystery, the problem play—converge in Brendel's horrible performance and are submerged in it. The aggrandizing allusions to metaphysical and supernatural sources of action that references to *Faust* and the Gospel of John ironically present as guidance for Rosmer and Rebecca shift the play powerfully out of pragmatic moral analysis into a delirium of confused spiritual striving. Something inhuman has intruded on the lover's struggle with ethical and amatory praxis; the power of eternity has momentarily touched on these vulnerable agents of temporal change, and the incursion is not at all to their benefit. They are delivered back to their moral difficulties when Brendel leaves, but his nihilistic conversion of love's action to mutilation, and his linking of that destruction to successful promulgation of an ethical reformation that has no ideals as goal or source, ensures that the resolution of Rebecca's problems, and John's, will be disaster.

Like his descendent Hickey in Eugene O'Neill's *The Iceman Cometh*, Brendel preaches a sparkling, cynical, transcendence in which desolation converts ennobling self-sacrifice to guilty self-destruction. Hickey's sales pitch mangles both Nietzsche's delivering concept of power and Aristotle's rationalist ideas of ordered cause and effect, and the mangling results in a suicide. The same is true in Brendel's case, with this difference. Hickey distorts Nietzsche's ideas of will and self-overcoming to persuade people that deliverance from guilt lies in banishing all ideals and thereby eliminating any variety of Aristotelian praxis, any reason and all power to act purposefully. When Brendel recommends that Rosmer discard ideals and that Rebecca destroy her beauty, his aim is to guarantee successful pursuit of purposeful action. Aristotelian and Nietzschean logic both shatter when O'Neill examines the doomed action by which people seek to bring new effects out of old cause. These logics are not broken, but reconfigured when Ibsen's characters take up the same action. The polemical force these intellectual orders exert on each other displays nothing more than illness in O'Neill's play. In *Rosmersholm* the polemic involves real possibilities of health, personal and cultural. Making those possibilities actual requires an unambiguous commitment to one or another of the opposed sides, or magnanimity and genius sufficiently inventive to make a harmonious balance of them. Brendel's most important function in this act, signaled and enhanced by the play's most aggrandizing and complex allusive frame, is to drive Rebecca and Rosmer into enacting what they see as a harmonious balance of praxis and power. That his pusillanimous idiocy evokes what the lovers regard as magnanimous, delivering genius is Ibsen's masterstroke in this play, a dramatic and intellectual transition whose full value can only be accounted for once the lovers' final conversation is understood.

After Brendel's departure Ibsen keeps the stage silent for the first and only time in the play to indicate the strangeness and magnitude of the tutor's effect on Rebecca and Rosmer. As if to exorcise that effect, Rebecca ends the silence with a deep breath and opens the window through which she has watched Beata's death site so often, complaining that the room has become suffocating. Brendel has frightened Rosmer into wanting Rebecca to leave, requiring her to, and, when she agrees, apparently frightened in the same way, Rosmer tells her that wherever she goes she will be provided for when he dies. When she responds that her death will proceed his, he hints very broadly that the humiliating defeat of his messianic project will very likely soon result in his suicide. To dissuade him and encourage his resumption of the cause, Rebecca again begins the argument that love justifies. When she senses that his fear to engage her harbors a secret conviction that some horrible justifying proof of her love exists, she demands, for the sake of her innocence as well as his future, that he reveal the test, however fearsome. He answers, in Ibsen's stage direction "as though forced to speak against his will," that, if she will courageously, gladly, and willfully, as Ulrick Brendel suggested, freely reenact Beata's suicide for his sake that night, he will believe in her love and the future of his ennobling mission.

She agrees to the deed, and he stops doubting that she has the requisite courage for it when she tells him that, being newly subject to the law of Rosmersholm, she seeks atonement for her offense against Beata. Rebecca's avowal here blends Nietzschean self-overcoming and the Aristotelian order of justice embedded in the Magdalen play in exactly the combination Brendel has just proposed. As Rosmer affirms Rebecca's plan, Ibsen ironically starts closing the play's argument about the relative strengths praxis and power have in the lovers' messianic ambition to change reality.

> *Rosmer (with decision):* Very well. Then I kneel to our emancipated view of life, Rebecca. We acknowledge no judge over us. Therefore we must pass judgement upon ourselves.
>
> *Rebecca (misunderstanding him):* Yes, John, yes. If I go, it will save what is best in you. (R, 314)

There are many misunderstandings here, but the primary one is that she misses his decision to kill himself with her. She tells him that, if she stayed, she would be a "troll" on the ship of his advancing deliverance, and the characterization reinforces Brendel's authority over her decision and Rosmer's urging of it, recalling the maiming Brendel advised. Maiming is both initiation into and identification with the demonic troll world in Scandinavian superstition and a symbol of supranatural menace Ibsen treated extensively in act 2, scene 6 of *Peer Gynt*, in which Peer's entry into the troll world, a result of sexual seduction, is greeted in the scene's second line as follows: "*Troll Child:* Can I cut off his fingers?"[11]

Rebecca continues to misunderstand John's suicidal intentions. To his promise to join her, she responds that he will have courage enough to witness her leap from Beata's bridge into the millrace but not enough to come onto the bridge with her. She then informs him that his unwillingness to confront the past, which she saw enacted every time he avoided the bridge, convinced her that he could never love her. Sad and broken, according to Ibsen's stage directions, Rebecca unwittingly reverses the remarriage plot in this confession of erotic hopelessness. The marriage, which she resisted when John professed love she believed in, occurs as an immediate result of her expressed conviction that he can never love her. He marries to garner courage for the suicide she doesn't yet know he has decided on; she accepts the previously scorned status of "lawful wife" as a sign that he has repudiated Beata and garners strength from that repudiation for her own suicidal resolve. Freedom, devotion, and courage are all horribly disfigured in their mutual misapprehensions. The murderous sexual allure that gained her comparison to Lady Macbeth in act 1 is transmuted here into exemplary sacrificial sublimation, a murderous project that they both regard as deliverance to innocence. This reversal ironically closes the play's thematic association of will to power, the eternal return of the same, and liberating joy with forbidden, unconsummated love.

> *Rosmer:* Rebecca, now I place my hand on your head. *(He does as he says.)* And
>   take you in marriage as my lawful wife.
> *Rebecca (clasps both his hands and bows her head against his breast):* Thank you, John.
>   *(Lets go of him.)* And now I go gladly. (R, 315)

When Rosmer finally makes her understand that he is going to his death with her, Rebecca lapses into doubt over whether his decision to die is transcendent independence or merely oppressive remorse illusively inspired by the white horses of Rosmersholm. John answers that he may be under the illusive spell of remorse, but that his destiny as scion of the house, and hers as new mistress, is to submit to that spell. She tells him to stay, and he rebuffs her with a minister's liturgical admonition that the husband and wife shall go their way together. All talk of resuming the cause of public enlightenment has vanished now; joyous ennobling has been replaced by exonerating atonement, innocence belongs only to the backward glance. When she wants to know who leads the way, Rosmer answers that they are finally unified, that they go forward together. She agrees in serene endorsement of their delivering action: "Yes. Now we are one. Come! Let us go gladly!" (R, 316).

To assure the audience that these equivocators actually do the deed, Ibsen has Mrs. Helseth return to the stage they leave empty. Looking for them through the window when she can't find them in the house, Mrs. Helseth invokes Jesus' name (for the first and last time in the play) when she sees something white near the millrace, something she fears but will not name as the fatal white horse. The superstition and religious invocation are elided immediately with the servant's conventionally licentious moralism. Ibsen puts a magnifying comic grace note, after the manner of Shakespeare, into the terror and pity of the scene when he has Mrs. Helseth spy the couple on the bridge and conclude that they have gone to that eerie spot for a salty embrace. When she sees their embrace become a descent into the millrace, Mrs. Helseth makes her most telling mistake of all: "Ah! They've fallen—both of them! . . . Help! Help!" And, finally, the errors that have so far put a noble catastrophe into the skewed frame of inadequately common wisdom culminate in a superstitious interpretation that retroactively commands the whole argument this play has carried out over idealistic action's capacity to manage the past. Realizing that her calls for help are futile, trembling, as befits the witness of a melodramatic disaster, which is what the deaths are for her, the maid finds enough presence of mind for this final oracular utterance: "No. No help. The dead mistress has taken them" (R, 316).

When Mrs. Helseth mistakes the leaping embrace for a fall she unwittingly focuses a crucial ambiguity at the center of the lovers' action: did they indeed finally act, or were they once more acted on? The servant sees no enigma, of course, only the compelling force of supranatural vengeance. Invoking the authority of her first "dead mistress" over that vengeance, Mrs. Helseth's curtain line ends the play by returning it to the topic of its first scene, as indeed the offstage suicide does. This retrospective invocation of Beata also consummates the most consistent motion forward in *Rosmersholm*: Rebecca's gradual submission, explicitly presented at the close of all three previous acts, to the fearsome comfort of remorse mysteriously promised by the other-worldly white horses. Mrs. Helseth's line also returns the play's finale to Rebecca's act 2 promise to follow Beata's suicidal lead if Rosmer insists on proposing marriage. This final retrospective arrangement is the play's most ironic reversal. What was a repudiating will to freedom as a plan becomes a consummating will to nullity when moralistic delirium makes it a deed. Retroactive logic is, of course, the engine of Aristotelian tragedy. Reversals and recognitions, while they drive erring agents forward, simulta-neously, and more significantly, draw them back to destructive confrontation with an originating cause of their action that they have ignored or not known. The goal of tragedy, catharsis, should be illumination of the agents and the audience through necessary but surprising final confrontation of heretofore hidden cause. The errors, ambiguities, and compulsions surrounding the double suicide that ends *Rosmersholm* do not make for cathartic reversal or disclosure of this kind.

Retroactive logic also governs Nietzsche's concepts of dramatic and real world action, but neither the will to power nor innocent affirmation of the eternal return of the same nor delivering self-transcendence have prevailed in *Rosmersholm*, although all have been invoked throughout the action. With-holding the satisfaction of catharsis or the exhilaration of becoming what one is, Ibsen delivers a challenge, instead, at the end of this play. Aristotelian praxis has gone wrong dramatically; has its ethical value also failed in the story? Nietzschean will to power and its continuous occasion, the eternal return of the same, have ended in moralistic atonement rather than affirma-tive, aesthetically joyful self-overcoming. In the absence of catharsis the natural conclusion that Nietzsche's voluntarism has been overtaken in the play's thinking by some species of Aristotelian humanism does not hold. Instead of catharsis, the challenge Ibsen forces on the audience is understand-ing what the lovers do not, perhaps cannot, know. In the last scenes of act 4 Rebecca and Rosmer seem as deluded in their Nietzschean joy as Mrs. Helseth is in her choric, Aristotelian gravity. Leaving Aristotle and Nietzsche aside for a moment, the question to ask at the end of *Rosmersholm* is: "Did they jump, or were they pushed?"

The answer, which in its largest scope does involve the thinking of Aristotle and Nietzsche about action in plays and in life, is, "They jumped at the chance to be pushed." To find deliverance in sacrificing themselves, Rosmer and Rebecca allied Nietzschean voluntarism to perverted humanistic ideas. Brendel gave them the intellectual model, and they transformed its sexual dynamic from enabling chastity guaranteed by physical damage to ennobling chastity guaranteed by death. Rosmer's kneeling to acknowledge emancipation is the physical image of the ideological confusion displayed in his belief that their self-judgment has no external model. The model is clear enough, and, although they have fought off the model's authority throughout the play, it is finally not at all external to Rosmer or Rebecca. Their self-judgment is a willed introjection of humanistic praxis, specifically of the principle that agents can do nothing but match effect to cause with logic supplied by nature and codified in culture. Guilt is the infallible messenger of error in this order, signaling that agents have mismatched cause and effect, have ruined their actions by miring them in distant past causes when they think they have directed them to future *telos*. The unstable relation guilt makes between conscious and unconscious willing is the governing cause of the lovers' ideological confusion. Far from transcending the traditionally rational order of well-being in his delivering love-death, Rosmer in fact submits himself to it, however irrational and deluded his awareness may be.

Nietzsche's repudiation of guilt is a radical repudiation of the whole system of cause-and-effect logic to which guilt belongs. To overcome themselves in Nietzsche's order of value Rosmer and Rebecca would have to affirmatively will that their unchosen past occurred, not try to justify it through atonement. Agency in this thinking is not matching cause and effect but overcoming the impulse to experience the world with those categories. Certainly, neither Rosmer nor Rebecca has overcome the categories; in fact, both think of nothing but how to control them, and while their impulse to power and joyful liberation is Nietzschean, the submission of that power to rationalist pragmatism of any species clearly is not. The longing to invent an order of value higher than any existing one is Nietzschean, inventing it through willed death can be Nietzschean, but inventing it through exonerating atoning death certainly is not. That variety of changing the past is Christian, and Rosmer and Rebecca, who have both explicitly repudiated Christianity, end their lives more compelled by it than either knows. Brendel, again, is the final and most forceful agent of that compulsion.

The church makes its fatal incursion into secular reformation in Brendel's demonic elision of Christ's martyrdom, Rebecca's love, and Rosmer's messianic ambition. Awash in the guilt they want to annul, the lovers are poised to transcend that defining torment through some retroactively affirmative action when Brendel appears. From the Nietzschean point of view, which underlies their messianic aspirations, deliverance requires that the imbalance between conscious and unconscious willing induced by guilt be stabilized. To overcome themselves they have to discover in themselves an integrating action derived from and directed to values outside the humanistic order of good and evil that has trapped them. The New Testament presents Christ's delivering self-sacrifice as an action that cancels guilt, that retroactively affirms and restores innocent agency by redirecting previously unstable willing toward ends outside the world's inadequate orders of value. It is no wonder, then, that Rosmer and Rebecca latch on to Brendel's perverse advice that messianic transformation of values requires martyrdom inspired by love.

From Nietzsche's point of view Christ's deliverance does not annul guilt or the law of cause and effect that authorizes guilt. Instead, the Crucifixion perversely aggrandizes both guilt and its derivation from the supposedly natural order of cause and effect. The humiliating anguish of Jesus' execution does not free humanity to pursue a higher order of happiness, but, rather, condemns it to deluded, self-destructive misery—slave morality— by presenting the interlocked actions of conscience and natural law as psychological and cosmological paradigms of absolute power. Put comically, Brendel's advice that Rebecca make love effective through sacrifice amounts to the injunction "hang yourself before it's too late." Retroactive logic governs the hanging joke, the Crucifixion, and Nietzschean and Aristotelian poetics. It also governs the Magdalen play and, most significantly, the experience of guilt that is the psychological sine qua non for all these actions. The task that *Rosmersholm's* resolution sets is distinguishing between these logics, discovering whether any one of them banishes guilt in a way that enhances well-being.

Erotically charged reenactment of the Crucifixion is what Rosmer and Rebecca settle on, and, while they are for the most part glad with the choice, few witnesses could be. Neither is Christian; both have explicitly rejected Christian praxis—hence, the double fallacy of their conviction that they invent a new order of value, one that delivers them from tradition to free-thought, when they pursue atoning death urged by love. The leap to inundation is a perfect physical symbol for the confusion of deliverance and condemnation that their death displays and for the confusion between guilt's power and the will toward freedom that Nietzsche found at the heart of humanistic Christianity and its definitive action, the Crucifixion. And, of course, the same confusion governs Brendel's urging of the loving sacrifice to begin with. Whatever Nietzsche might have to say about the Crucifixion, he never doubts its authentically idealistic logic. In fact, he hates it most vehemently for its perverse achievement as paradigm for idealistic praxis. Brendel's sacrificial plan is explicitly anti-idealistic. Rebecca's idealistic adoption of it is a horrible example of guilt's power to simultaneously require and confound the pursuit of innocence.

The infinite regress in guilt's simultaneous inducement and baffling of joy, cut loose from any possible resolution by divine or natural law, makes *Rosmersholm* modernist. The ambiguity of guilty action, how remorse conjoins and destabilizes praxis and the will to power, defined modern experience for Ibsen. His constant artistic ambition was to redeem civilization by presenting exemplary actions onstage. To be exemplary and redeeming those actions had to at once portray the ambiguity corrupting well-being and offer some deliverance from it. In *Rosmersholm* the deliverance comes in what Ibsen offers instead of catharsis, in his challenge to the audience to evaluate Rebecca's and Rosmer's final joy and Mrs. Helseth's conventional pity and fear. As has been true throughout the play, in the last act Rebecca has keener interest in and awareness of reality than Rosmer, is less purely subject to oppressive persuasion. However corrupted the will to power in her suicide may be, she still has enough freedom to ask if Rosmer is dying under the authority of illusion and remorse instead of enacting his own self-transcendence. His indifference to the problem, his easy yielding to conventionally aggrandizing notions of destiny, make his death unambiguously inauthentic. Rebecca's final action is harder to evaluate, since her self-transcendence seems to have authentic and free love as its origin and end. That Rosmer never seems as worthy of that love to the audience as he does to Rebecca vexes any attempt to understand her deed, but that is a trivial irritation compared with the larger issue their liaison presents: is her love of him ever free? Is it not from the start submission to the very ambiguity her final loving sacrifice is meant to banish from his life and hers?

Rebecca understands that her willingness to submit to Rosmer's chaste companionship, her eagerness to die in service to chastity, originates in guilt over her incestuous past. Acts 2 and 3 bring her to that realization. What eludes her is not psychoanalytic understanding but a happy strategy for restoring any of the life-sustaining harmonies changed to corrosive conflicts by her discovery and acknowledgment of guilt. Kroll and Rosmer impose resolutions that confine her to guilt, and until this last act she has managed to evade those oppressions. The dangerous difference in Brendel's perversion of Christian self-sacrifice is that his plan, unlike remarriage, puts a secure and irreversible end to guilt.

Exhausted by conscience, alienated from the saving energy of sexual consummation, unable to discover in herself or her culture any value that she could use to will her past, she settles for the one womanly prerogative that her culture does allow, and which she has successfully carried out already: martyrdom. Beata's sacrifice, under Rebecca's mesmerizing tutelage, was false and true at once; Rebecca's, under the uncanny tutelage of Brendel, is also false and true at once. The one advantage Rebecca has is that she, unlike Beata, is in a position to know the true and false elements of her action. But prudential secrecy has failed her from the start in this play, and it returns to do so again in the fourth act, this time turned against Rebecca herself in a painful inversion of Nietzschean self-overcoming.

Her tragedy is that she takes no advantage of her knowledge. Action seems possible to her for the first time, and that precious chance to change has more force over her than her will to truth does, for all its probing of the motives or authority by which Rosmer cooperates in that change. From the point of view of Aristotelian praxis Rebecca's suicide is a botched action, a tragic mistake that ends a tragic mistake. From the point of view of Nietzschean voluntarism the suicide is a horrible example of noble power bedeviled and finally vitiated by too long a resistance to the traditional forces of cultural authority. That truth and joy are separated by her action is the final evaluation Ibsen leads an audience to make. The play's final victor is neither praxis nor power but guilt, which both systems center on, which both were created to annul.

Rosmersholm has never been a popular play because it never presents the action, messianic or otherwise, that its characters strive for so passionately. Instead, it presents an unstable resolution of the ideological, psychological, and spiritual ambiguities by which guilt at once calls for and defers radical change. In *Ghosts* Mrs. Alving is called on so hideously by guilt that she doesn't have the force even to defer change. She ends stymied, saying no to any action, as her son, who initiated the demand that has paralyzed her, mindlessly invokes the ironically renewing sun. Praxis and power are not confounded in that play, but so antagonistically compounded that they reach a stalemate. *Rosmersholm* is an advance, insofar as it shows an attempt to act and insofar as it shows that failure of messianic action stems not from the impossibility of radical change but from insufficient confrontation of what role compulsion, naïveté, and confusion have in the desire for and enactment of such change. Praxis and power are confounded in *Rosmersholm*, but Ibsen has not compounded them this time as much as he has shown their mutual resistance. In the shifting struggle over action, anachronistic humanism carries the day, but only in its decadent form as oppression, a form that makes the failure of Nietzschean liberation a potent critique of tradition rather than a repudiation of the radical stance.

In *The Master Builder* Ibsen continues the struggle against pragmatic humanism and again resolves the play ambiguously, this time with a powerful insinuation that Nietzschean poetics can substitute for Aristotelian action where success in drama and in life are concerned. The story of Solness's building a castle in the air to deliver himself from humanism, especially from building houses and churches, closes the long argument Ibsen carried out over the relative dramatic and experiential value of praxis and power. As in *Ghosts* and *Rosmersholm*, the call to change comes to Solness by way of familial and sexual guilt, but this time idealism and supernatural power are successfully allied with artistic aspiration, and the result is a startling, antirealist transformation of dramatic action.

5

The Master Builder, Act 1:
"Have it your own way—say I did it!"

The Master Builder, unlike Ghosts or Rosmersholm, does not present the problem of finding or accomplishing an action, but, rather, scrutinizes in anguished detail the difficulties of transcending an ongoing one. The play is famously autobiographical, especially for its transformed depiction of a late love affair in Ibsen's life.[1] To a great extent the love affair had to do with Ibsen's anxiety over continuing his career, and that anxiety—how and why to end the action of his life—gives the play many metatheatrical resonances, not the least of which is its invocation of Shakespeare's similarly anxious departure from the stage, The Tempest. Halvard Solness's story, like Prospero's in The Tempest, involves an artist's renunciation of supranatural authority to command victimizing service from others for the achievement of his work. In both plays the maestro's magical will yields to a young girl's commanding sexual vitality, and that yielding is the salvation of both men. The plays' differences lie primarily in the relation of the male and female sexual forces in each and in the different metaphysical and natural orders those sexual stories display. Prospero's renunciation restores political, familial, and natural orders, aligning them all with divine ontology. Punitive death, which normally accompanies such restoration by eliminating offenders, is magically simulated by Prospero in his restoration. Eliminating offense, magic death offers the chance for justification to the offenders and so shows how new effects might be brought out of old causes. Death is real in The Master Builder, and its punitive status is ambiguous, and therein lies the essential distinction between the metaphysical orders of the two plays and the place sexual vitality has in those orders.

Sex, magic, art, and death all emanate from Solness's will to power in Ibsen's play, and all, in various ways, struggle there to overcome a theistic ontology. The play also indicates that these forces all also emanate from nature conceived according to Aristotelian and Christian humanism. That ambiguous location of action in two opposed ontologies makes Solness's story paradigmatically modern. Prospero's consonance with divinity guarantees his salvation in *The Tempest*; Solness's spiritual rebellion guarantees guilt. Whether the challenge to transcend his artistic accomplishment that Hilde Wangel presents to Solness is a means for overcoming that guilt and successfully defying the divine architect or whether the challenge is a seduction by which Solness guiltily undoes himself, submitting to the hangman god, is one of many questions posed by *The Master Builder*. The play's action presents Hilde's challenge as an ambiguous conjoining of Aristotelian humanism and Nietzschean voluntarism. The change Solness undergoes as he reconfigures that ambiguous union signals an important change in Ibsen's career, one that had powerful formal and ideational consequences in drama for the century that followed.

The Master Builder takes place over one 24-hour period, from evening to evening, in the house Solness is about to vacate. Act 1 takes place in the builder's office, located in his dwelling, after the sun has set, act 2 in early morning in the sitting room, and act 3 on the veranda while the sun vanishes. Progress through the natural cycle of change runs in tandem with progress through the sites of Solness's building. First, the office (significantly situated in his dwelling) in which Solness planned the new house to which he will move and in which he carried out his rise to prominence; then the sitting room, the social setting of domestic and social life in that house; and, finally, the veranda, where nature makes a bridge from the old house to the new one, whose tower is glimpsed, surrounded by scaffolding, at the extreme verge of stage right. Hilde Wangel appears in all three locales, and her challenge to Solness unfolds with progressively antirealistic force in all three. The appearance of the other characters in each setting is governed primarily by their function in the Aristotelian or Nietzschean dimension of that challenge.

The play begins in misleading illusionistic realism. The action unfolds through sequentially interrupted and overlapping conversations, instead of discrete scenes (an innovation for realistic stage narrative that Ibsen introduced in this play), and at first seems to be an adultery plot embedded in a story of professional rivalry. Crosscutting the conversations with sequential suppression and revelation, Ibsen perfects a new strategy for overcoming the tedium of exposition with suspense (a persistent technical challenge in the well-made play) and establishes a tense form of narrative ambiguity that will support the ideational complexity that this play's action, like that of *Ghosts* and *Rosmersholm*, displays. The issue throughout the first conversation is whether Solness will free his young draftsman to work and to marry his fiancée. The conjoined actions of love and work, which Freud cited as the praxis of a healthy life, are transposed into an ideal, magical realm by the appearance of Hilde Wangel, whose entrance in the middle of the act temporarily halts the intrigue of Solness's oppression of youth. Will to power, the eternal return of the same, willing the past, and the end of all these— self-transcendence—all explicitly emerge in act 1 as organizing concerns for Solness. But they do so only as forces opposing his action in the humanistic dimension of the play, in which Aristotelian orientation of self-correcting rational agency toward changing means and ends is at stake.

Solness's action in the first act is preventing action, maintaining and extending the devices by which he keeps his guilty dominance of the building trade alive. Preserving his professional station is preeminently a means of preserving his personal identity. In both realms the means Solness adopts for avoiding change only barely contain it, in fact enhance the likelihood of change occurring. This ambiguity displays at once the reversal/recognition logic of Aristotelian tragedy and the strategic perversion of power scrutinized in Nietzsche's analysis of the sick will. The first line of the play, spoken by Brovik, a dying architect, whose career Solness ruined and who has been contained in Solness's employ for many years, together with his talented son, is "No, I can't go on with this much longer" (*MB*, 284). That situation applies to everyone in the play; indeed, the action consists in showing how everyone's strategies of containment collapse under the urgent call for change in Solness that Hilde Wangel demands, unable herself to go on waiting for him to deliver her long-ago promised kingdom.

In the first confrontation of the play Brovik asks Solness to let Ragnar take over the building of a new house for a young couple that the master builder has stalled. Solness refuses, touched but unmoved by the dying man's plea to see his son established in life as a professional and a married man (the commission would provide the financial stability for marriage to Kaja Fosli, Solness's secretary and Ragnar's betrothed). Solness presents the refusal as self-preserving opposition to youthful competition. Brovik's response that the community could support multiple builders shows the irrationality and disingenuousness of Solness's defense. Solness brusquely, although indirectly, acknowledges the charge, but nonetheless will not relent, suggesting, in the closing lines of this exchange, a deeply and mysteriously personal need to constrain the humane, natural, and easy change Brovik asks for: "*Solness* (. . . *almost desperately*): I can't do otherwise, don't you understand? I am what I am. And I can't create myself anew" (*MB*, 289).

As in *Rosmersholm*, much of the play will consist in unkenneling the guilty secret that keeps Solness eager and unwilling to create himself anew. And, as in *Rosmersholm*, the guilty secret has a sexual lock on it, but not a sexual origin, and it is that difference that allows for change to emerge from Solness's struggle. Sublimation of sexual vitality wrecked the happy transformation of lives and culture in *Ghosts* and *Rosmersholm*. The same sublimation wrecks lives in *The Master Builder*, but, in a mystical way, restores creative happiness to Solness and professional and domestic opportunity to the next generation of builders. Solness's sexual power over Ragnar's fiancée, Kaja, displayed in the next scene, starts the thematic association the play progressively elaborates between suppressed desire, joy, creativity, will to power, and transcendent, aesthetic self-creation.

In its first appearance sexual force is all oppression and denial, a strategy for preventing rather than generating vital change. Solness keeps Kaja in the office after her fiancee and his father leave. All commands and accusation, he demands to know if her desire to marry Ragnar is behind Brovik's request that the young man be granted independence. She convinces Solness that she is merely dutifully submitting to Brovik and Ragnar's desire that her five-year engagement end in marriage very soon. When Solness asks about her feeling for Ragnar she answers that it was long ago superseded by a permanent and all-encompassing passion for Solness, one she can't possibly live without. At that confession Solness urges Kaja to marry Ragnar if she likes then immediately switches the directive, explaining that she should persuade Ragnar to stay in his present position so that she can stay in hers. Kissing her, Solness makes no protestation of love but convinces her nonetheless that she stands to him as indispensable beloved consort, muse to an aging artist. Her hopelessly naive appreciation of what she calls his kindness is quickly answered with Solness's rebuke of the embrace that he initiated and his sharp command that she rise up from her knees because he hears someone coming. True to adultery plot and sexfarce conventions, that someone is his wife.

Aline's first entrance identifies her structurally as the cast-off wife who nonetheless retains enough power to curtail, if not prevent outright, Solness's sexual shoring up of his professional position. Aline has come to tell Solness that their doctor is waiting to see him, and, after delivering the message and casting cold glances and remarks at Kaja, she leaves. The young girl acts out her role in the adultery plot for the rest of the scene, frightened of the offended wife, but Solness doesn't take up his place in that convention. Instead, he ironically takes up the role of *senex* from the Roman comedy, indicating clearly to the audience (not her) that his sexual power over her is an old man's ruse, worked to prevent youth from supplanting his authority. Solness demands that by the next day Kaja persuade Ragnar to stay in the office, and Kaja responds by promising to end her engagement with Ragnar if that will enable her to stay with Solness. Frustrated that the sexual device might annul the advantage it gains him and the power it provides him if it becomes more than imaginary, Solness almost blurts out what everyone in the audience knows by now, that Ragnar's presence is what Kaja's romantic attachment guarantees. He recovers from the gaffe, persuades Kaja that Ragnar must stay so that she can, and sends the easily deluded girl away, after requiring her to bring Ragnar's plans for the new house to him for inspection, craftily promising to consider how he can make Ragnar's professional advancement a way to keep them both with him.

The action of the play appears in miniature in this opening set of scenes. Solness can no longer take his place in worldly affairs with the same energy or ambition that once located him firmly there, and he cannot withdraw from that place. He staves off change with fraud and stratagems, thus setting in motion an Aristotelian action in which reversal and recognition will make those stratagems devices of successful or ruinous orientation toward the changing means and ends of his life. That his main stratagem is sexual and antisexual makes the Aristotelian structure of the play ambiguous as far as its outcome is concerned and, more significantly, introduces the Nietzschean action of divided, and therefore sick, will to power. Ibsen presents the twin possibilities of comic or tragic outcome in the Aristotelian dimension of this play by having Solness enact, in transformed but recognizable shapes, conventional roles of the adultery tragedy, the sexfarce, and the professional problem play, all familiar theatrical forms for depicting the definitive real-life actions of love and work in his culture. The sexual stratagem that collects all those realistic conventions also begins the antirealistic Nietzschean action, the inversion of power in the sick will, which cannot assent to worldly cause-and-effect logic, but cannot exceed it either and so confounds itself in neurotic compromises that reinforce the authority they are constructed to defeat. The next two scenes elaborate this Nietzschean, psychological action and explicitly present will to power and the challenge of the eternal return of the same as the primary modes of change defining Solness's struggle.

Solness's scene with Dr. Herdal combines exposition and character analysis to uncover the nature and source of the master builder's personal and professional power. Solness starts the scene wanting to discuss something troubling in Aline's attitude toward him. Unwittingly, the doctor presumes Solness is thinking about his sexual indiscretion with Kaja and steers the conversation toward Solness's confessing the true nature of that relation.

Solness dismisses the topic brusquely, eager to talk about something more intimately troublesome in his marriage, until the doctor's insistence on the subject provides Solness a way to make analysis of his power over Kaja analysis of his trouble with Aline and with his career. Announcing that it is a strange story, Solness describes the telepathic communication by which he compelled Kaja to remain with him and so keep Ragnar employed in his office.

On one of her visits Solness understood that he might exploit the infatuation between Ragnar and Kaja to keep that architect working for him. Initially, he hoped for Kaja to come to work so that Ragnar would stay without mentioning this deeply willed outcome to the girl, who nonetheless responded to it as if he had clearly enunciated it and came to work for him immediately after their first brief meeting. He confesses none of his present active seduction of the girl to the doctor, casting that as a nuisance all of her making. He wants to know if the doctor has any explanation for the appearance of his wish as a fact in the world without any action on his part: "But what about this other business—that she thought I'd told her what I'd only wished for? Silently, inwardly, secretly. What do you make of that? Can you explain such a thing to me, Dr. Herdal?" (*MB*, 298).

The doctor has no explanation. That neither doctor nor builder offers any commonsense account of sexual communication occurring here through innuendo or intuition should be enough to reinforce an audience's conviction that Solness is right to regard his psychic power to command others merely by private willing as mysterious. This action at a distance, accomplished by all-powerful hypothetical willing, has no explanation in the Aristotelian realm of cause and effect the doctor moves in, but it has a central place in Nietzsche's understanding of aesthetic self-transcendence. That the spiritual exercise of self-transcendence from Nietzsche's thinking comes alive as worldly cause and effect in Solness's story is an important transformation, one that shows that Ibsen did not merely inherit the ambiguous resources and requirements of humanism and voluntarism, but reworked the elements of both systems, as well as their relation, in his theater. The instantiation of Nietzschean power in Aristotelian praxis will become the central struggle of this play once Hilde Wangel appears. For now magical objectification of Solness's subjective power is merely raised as a question.

That question is immediately wrapped into familiar humanistic psychology and ethics as Solness subdues the transcendental possibilities of his will to power by submitting his magic thinking to the victimizing terms of justice, debt, and their controlling authority, guilt. When Herdal asks why Solness has not explained the circumstances of Kaja's employment to Aline, the following exchange ensues:

Solness: Because somehow I feel it does me good to suffer Aline to do me an
    injustice.   •

Herdal (shakes his head): I'm damned if I understand a word of that.

Solness: Oh, yes. You see it's like paying a minute installment on a great
    debt—a debt so vast it can never be settled.

Herdal: A debt to your wife?

Solness: Yes. And that—eases my mind a little. I can breathe more freely—for
    a while, you understand. (*MB*, 298).

Hilde's appearance eventually will require Solness to explain this debt and
its relation to the magic thinking by which he advanced his life, but at this
point the audience is in Herdal's place, damned if they understand a word of
Solness's sexually charged punishing isolation from Aline. It is enough here
to say that Solness relieves guilt about his career, and reinforces guilty
protection of that career, by preserving pragmatic and magic thinking in the
guilty sexual compromise with Kaja. To speak in realistic ethical terms,
Solness's false seduction secures irresponsible power over one victimized but
enabling woman and makes him answerable, at a self-imposed and self-
governing distance, to his previously aggrieved wife. The isolation, hubris,
and solipsism by which Solness converts intimate cooperation with women
into instrumental alienation of them makes his situation ripe for Aristotelian
reversal and recognition and for Nietzschean self-overcoming and for the
clash of both.

    Having touched the nerve where these forces pulse when he outlines the
shape of his compromise with Kaja to Herdal, Solness momentarily submits to
the violent incoherence of his inner world and accuses the doctor of being an
agent working to confirm Aline's suspicion that he is mad.[2] When Herdal
convinces Solness, at least momentarily, that neither he nor Aline believes the
builder is mad, Solness says that he just might be and continues to observe that,
if his success in professional life doesn't seem to the doctor to have come about
through the inspired genius of lunacy, then it must illusively appear to Herdal
as an achievement brought about by luck. While Solness ironically disparages
the enviability of his professional prominence, Herdal agrees that luck does
appear to have played a large part in that prominence, citing the burning down
of Aline's ancestral home 13 (not, one might say, an extremely fortunate
number) years ago (which indirectly cost the lives of her two children) as the
lucky break that catapulted Solness's career. Solness confesses that this luck
has made him afraid that his career will end when fortune changes under the
demand of youth for its own advancement. He uses the image of youth banging
on the door to signal the end of his career, and immediately the door stage left

is pounded on by, as it turns out, Hilde Wangel, the youth who will lead him out of the paralysis by which he maintains his life. Not only a symbol, the event is another instance of Solness making something happen by wishing for it. In this case the wishing is inversely presented as guilty fear of being superseded. Hilde's role will in large part consist in uncovering and transforming the builder's longing for punitive, exonerating release from the power of his magic thinking.

The opposition in this scene of madness and luck as competing sources for Solness's self-creation operates in many dimensions at once. In terms of dramatic structure the opposition displays the oscillating formal relations of character and plot that Aristotelian poetics, especially in its various nineteenth-century generic guises, resolves by having plot cause, reveal, and enact character. Action brings substance into real existence in this ontology; hence, whatever Solness has become has been ordered by the changing means and ends of the world that requires his services. Luck in this system does not mean absurd relation of Solness's power to the world's, but, rather, a successful relation of those forces, an alignment not created or ordered by Solness's will or nature, but nonetheless generatively appropriate to both.[3] An order of cause unavailable to procedural or instrumental rationality, luck nonetheless is meaningful in the realistic theater that presents humanistic praxis.

The questions about meaning that luck raises by exceeding rational cause-and-effect logic are normally questions about agency, specifically speculation about whether agents can invoke or create the secret fortune governing their affairs. In Christian thinking this mysterious relation between an agent's nature and his power to change the order of cause and effect governing his place in the world is accounted for by the theology of grace. In Nietzschean thinking the relation of agents to luck is reconfigured in the concept of self-overcoming through willfully creating and repeating the past aesthetically, a mental action that exhibits transcendent amor fati. Both systems, for all their stark differences, focus on how an incomplete power to act might complete itself by meriting the assistance of a superior force available but not automatically present to aspiring agents. The inclusion of merit opposes both systems to the Aristotelian ontology in which immutable cause-and-effect logic creates an agent's volition without ever being effected or in any way invoked by the agent's merit or nature. Christianity and Nietzschean voluntarism, focused on the power of the agent's nature to effect the actions reality presents as conditions for self-creation, are both governing concepts in the possibilities for transformation that Hilde presents to Solness and are repeatedly and explicitly discussed in their dialogues. The madness that Solness believes has governed his life undergoes Nietzschean elaboration as will to power once Hilde comes on the scene, and in this Nietzschean guise that "madness" is progressively opposed to the Christian analogue of merit, which Solness guiltily uses to understand his life, and the Aristotelian analogue of luck, which the worldly Herdal offers as a plausible account of the extraordinary success Solness cannot live with or without.

Hilde recognizes Solness as soon as she enters his house, but it takes her conversation with Herdal, in which her last name is revealed, for Solness to remember that she is the daughter of the country physician in Lysanger, where Solness traveled to build a church years ago. Hilde reminds him that his visit occurred exactly ten years ago and reveals that she also met his wife in Lysanger at a time when Aline had traveled there apart from Solness. Coquettishly, she tells Solness that his wife had extended an invitation to her to visit them in town, one that was supererogatory, since she already had a compelling desire to come and visit Solness. He takes up the sexual tease only enough to wonder why Aline never mentioned the girl to him. At the mention of Aline, Herdal exits to look after her, telling Solness as he goes that youth has indeed banged on his door. Solness takes up the sexual innuendo comically—he was expecting male competition and received a female flirt. The comic connection of sex and artistic, worldly self-creation will be overtaken by the Nietzschean dimension of the play, in which other-worldly willing becomes the action, but for now the theme is established as a piece of social comedy, embedded in the Aristotelian logic of realistic presentation of sexual and professional machinations.

Solness calls Aline onstage briefly and asks her to arrange for Hilde to stay with them. Aline dutifully agrees, and, when Solness suggests that Hilde should stay in one of the nurseries, the builder's wife cryptically emphasizes how available those rooms are for visitors and exits. Hilde takes the mystery up quickly and, upon inquiry into the matter, is told by Solness that there are no children to fill up any of the three nurseries but that she can be surrogate child for the duration of her visit. She teasingly agrees to the role for that night, looks forward to sleeping not to rest but to dream, and suggestively indicates to him that sometime in the future she might tell him her dreams. Boldly, but without arrogance, she inspects the office, and, when her tour brings her to the ledger, Solness returns the flirtation, offering the suggestion that she might wish to replace the woman who now keeps his accounts for him, but who will soon abandon him to marry.

Hilde rejects the offer scornfully but continues the flirtation, telling him she has a more important project to pursue during her visit. After dismissing conventional causes for the visit—a shopping trip, entry at university—Hilde indicates that her stay has an indefinite length and sits silently rocking, while she waits for Solness to discover the secret reason for her arrival. Finally, she has to bring the subject up herself. For the remainder of the scene she controls the action, moving it forward by returning Solness to his past, which she plans to make his future. Once again Aristotle's reversal and recognition pattern and Nietzsche's affirmative willing of the eternal return of the same converge, this time with Nietzsche's ideas emerging as the dominant, explicit order of the plot.

Throughout her exposition Hilde forces Solness to concede to her construction of his behavior in the past. In a progressively strange and intimate series of revelations she tells him she has come to make him finish an action he began and abandoned when he came to Lysanger to build a church there. She brings back Solness's ascent to the top of the church spire to crown it with a wreath first, concentrating on the dangerous thrill she felt thinking he might get dizzy and fall from the height. He remembers feeling giddy when one girl in a crowd of girls with flags waved hers about calling out his name. She tells him she was that girl, that his bravery made her giddy, and, when he asks how she knew he wasn't giddy himself, she answers that she heard him singing at the apex. When he protests that he never sang anytime in his life, she insists that he sang then, adding that his voice sounded like harps in the air. She trumps his thoughtful surprise over this by telling him that the "real thing" happened after his singing.

He urges her to lead his memory of this event, and she obliges, telling him that they were alone together that night in a room at the town club, where a banquet was held in his honor. In a series of questions by which she reconstructs the event against his feeble dismissive or diminutive protests, she tells him that he called her a princess and, like a troll, promised to carry her off to a foreign land, where he would build her a kingdom when she grew up, in ten years' time. Disputation over his intention and attitude and the failure of her coaxing his memory lead her to reveal the deed by which he proved and initiated the reality of his plan.

> *Solness:* Well, give me a hint, and perhaps—Well?
> *Hilde:* You took me in your arms and kissed me, Mr. Solness.
> *Solness (gets up from his chair, his mouth open):* I did?
> *Hilde:* Yes, you did. You took me in both your arms and bent me backwards
> and kissed me. Many, many times.   .
> *Solness:* Oh, but my dear, good Miss Wangel—
> *Hilde (gets up):* You're not going to deny it?
> *Solness:* I certainly am!
> *Hilde (looks at him scornfully):* Oh. I see. (*MB*, 309)

His guilty denial stems from a refusal to acknowledge transgression against the mundane order of sexual psychology and familial ethics—married men may not embrace 13 year-old girls that way on business trips. More significantly, as their next exchange shows, the denial masks his fear of her transgression against the more intimate, inviolate law by which he maintains his identity: willed self-creation. Her scorn dismisses his submission to worldly ethics and his reliance on self-determination and shows her confident sense of superiority to humanistic praxis and her willful dominance of his supposedly independent voluntarism and self-creation.

That scorn, coupled with her walking away from him and her final standing with her back toward him, holding her hands behind her in a masterful impatience, propels him to diffident, ambivalent acknowledgment of the seduction. He crosses to Hilde and tries to get her attention, telling her she must have dreamed the event. When her silent rejection of this provokes him to touch her, for the first time in the play, she makes an impatient gesture that puts him off and drives him to a new account of the event. Emphatically, softly, Solness thinks aloud that he must have thought and hoped for the event and then asks Hilde if that can't be the explanation for her memory of it. He drops the crucial causal element from this explanation—that he could telepathically will her to participate, imaginatively at least, in his wishes—relying on her powers of inference or intuition to discover or recognize the secret power he is unwilling to declare.

Startled by what may be a second appearance of the power he has acknowledged for the first time ever a few minutes ago, to his doctor, Solness may think the connection of his magic thinking to sexual feeling declares itself to Hilde. Or he elides it to hint at it, to discover whether she knows about his strange power and whether or not he needs to endanger his chance secretly to wield that power over her in the future by revealing its occurrence in the past. Protectively scheming, naively startled, or merely absentminded, Solness in any case wants a confirmation from her of his partial explanation, and, when she doesn't provide one, he impatiently bursts out, frustrated by the isolation she has imposed: "Oh, damn it. Have it your own way— say I *did* it! (*MB*, 310). At this point Hilde turns her head without looking at him and, in a series of questions, requires him to confess explicitly and repeatedly to the actuality of the seduction. When he concedes utterly to her, telling her he kissed her as many times as she might say, she finally turns to him, glowing with excitement, crowing about her success in forcing him to remember and confess the event.

At this crucial point Ibsen has Solness smile wryly as he delivers the insouciant line "Yes, just fancy—that I could forget a thing like that!" (*MB*,

310). She picks up his mocking insinuation of sexual mastery and complains that she must be only one of many conquests, which Solness, with no mockery at all, denies, saying he is not that sort. At this point the audience and Solness, but not Hilde, know that he is lying. The lie now is not exonerating but strategic: Solness tells it to gain her confidence so that he can learn if the seduction passed the oral phase. When she tells him it did not because they were interrupted by the arrival of the guests at the banquet, Solness again plays the dashing seducer, archly astonished at forgetting about them, and Hilde unmasks the posture, telling him his feigned memory lapses cover shame.

She then reminds him that the seduction occurred on 19 September ten years ago. When Solness realizes that she has returned to him on 19 September ten years later, he tries again to dismiss the reality of the unkept promise that her anniversary visit has restored to him. She will not accept his account of the promise as a frightening prank, tease, or joke and forces him to repeat the promise of magic flight to a new kingdom. He parries by accusing her of returning to make a joke of the promise and asks how long she has known of his marriage, hoping to learn that her motive might be sexual competition instead of longing. She dismisses adultery as a motive, saying she knew from the start that he was married. Solness will not answer when Hilde asks why he thought his wife mattered to her, casually dismissing the matter, unwilling to disclose the obvious psychosexual significance their association holds for him. When he presses Hilde again on the purpose of her visit, she finally declares it forthrightly: she wants her kingdom, immediately, in one shape or another. The stage direction is crucial here. As Solness laughs at her demand that the time has come for him to deliver on his promise, Hilde responds: "(merrily): Stump up my kingdom, master builder! (Taps with her finger.) On the table! (MB, 313).

Sex, creativity, professional accomplishment, marriage, the ethics binding all these, and the generative change brought about by willing the past all converge in that tapping. Ibsen will sort them all out for the rest of the play and signals as much by having Solness earnestly approach Hilde at this moment and ask again for the purpose and plan of her visit. She starts by saying she wants to see everything he's built in town. When Solness responds to her desire to see the spires he's built by saying that he has stopped building churches and now builds homes instead, Hilde asks if he has put spires on the homes, spires with giddying weathercocks perched at top. Solness takes the question as clairvoyant insight on her part into his own most secret and frustrated hope. He doesn't comment explicitly on what he thinks might be a further instance of magic willing on his part, but says, instead, that he doesn't build spires on churches because people don't want them. He does tell her that he has built such a spire for his own new home, one he fears will gain him public opprobrium, and she responds by promising to see it immediately in the morning.

His crowning that spire with a wreath will turn out to be the building of Hilde's magic kingdom, but at this point Solness doesn't yet know that. He unconsciously approaches that understanding of her visit when the subject of his memory comes up again. He asks her to remind him of her first name. When she does, and he then asks to be reminded what Princess Hilde's kingdom was to be called, she changes her plan. Suppressing any mention of the original childish kingdom's name—Orangia—she tells him: "Ugh! I don't want any of that stupid kingdom. I want a quite different kind of kingdom" (*MB*, 314). That suppression frees him to make the challenge of her visit part of his self-creation. She's already told him the kingdom's name. He strategically forgets it, and she strategically doesn't remind him, so that he can remember another facet of the seduction scene, a facet somehow connected to the distinction between building churches and houses. That distinction, vital to his present work, somehow involves his singing accomplishment on the church spire at Lysanger ten years ago.

Hilde has returned to restore that accomplishment to him and to magnify it. All this groping, inconstant recognition occurs inchoately here, as Ibsen portrays Hilde and Solness tilting for control of his memory. As the scene ends, Solness tries to master memory's power over his identity. He tells Hilde that her visit has made him aware that he has been torturously trying to remember a signal event from his past for many years. He never concedes that he has been trying to recover the ebullient joy of the seduction she has compelled him to confess and the transcendent power it expressed. But everyone watching the play knows that the torture that has accumulated in him over the years, the guilty anguish that has culminated in the false seduction/adultery scheme with Kaja by which he maintains his current prominence, has been suppression of the ecstatic event at Lysanger, whatever it was. From this point forward the play's action will be his gradual confrontation with the consequences of that decade-long betrayal and his gradual undoing of the compromise by which he ambivalently keeps joyous self-creation at bay.

In a perfect example of Nietzsche's sick will and Aristotle's recurring hamartia, Solness transforms Hilde's challenge to create a kingdom into a device for continued oppression of himself and all those close to him. He transforms the challenge unconsciously, believing he frees himself as he does so, as the following exchange shows.

Solness (gets up slowly): I'm glad you've come to me just at this time.

Hilde: (looks into his eyes): Are you glad?

Solness: I've been so alone. Staring at it all. So helpless. *(Lowers his voice.)* You
    see—I've begun to be so afraid—so terribly afraid—of youth.

Hilde (scornfully): Youth? Is youth something to be afraid of?

Solness: Yes, it is. That's why I've shut myself up here. *(Secretively.)* Someday,
    youth will come here and thunder on my door, and force its way in to
    me.

Hilde: Then I think you ought to go out and open the door.

Solness: Open the door?

Hilde: Yes. And let youth in. As a friend.

Solness: No, no! Youth means retribution. It marches at the head of a rebel
    army. Under a new banner.

Hilde (gets up, looks at him and says, her mouth trembling): Can you use me, master
    builder?

Solness: Yes! Yes, now I can use you! For you, too, march under a new banner.
    Youth against youth! *(MB, 314-315)*

Ibsen dissolves the real-world action of the play in delirious abstraction
at this point. This paradoxical plot construction, which sets a crucial reversal,
the protagonist's confession of a changed purpose, in almost impenetrably
lyric imprecision, displays that ideational and aesthetic ambiguity that Ibsen's
detractors have always called nonsensical and that his advocates still praise
as genius. The controlling concepts of this play all bear on Solness's strangely
concealing honesty here. But at this point the best approach to them is
through minimal unpacking of his immediate intention. While this exchange
with Hilde depends for its value on the unnerving effect of dark brightness
in the speech of both characters, it nonetheless contains intelligible psychology. Indeed, the obscurity of his outburst compels understanding of Solness's
pragmatic strategy here.

In the realm of Aristotelian praxis, the professional intrigue plot, Hilde's
arrival allows Solness to continue the false seduction/adultery plot that Kaja's
imminent defection and her newly insistent, imprudent desire have jeopardized. The unconsummated sexual fascination he exerts over Kaja keeps an idle
Solness preeminent professionally by keeping the next generation of builders
under his control. Now that Hilde has come to admire and challenge his talent,
to sustain it through unconsummated sexual submission and adoration, Kaja,
whose longing has become awkwardly demonstrative, can be cast off, and,
consequently, Ragnar can be let loose into the open market. Motivated once

more to build, Solness has little to fear from Ragnar's competitive entrance into a market in which most contracts are already pledged to the master builder.

In the plot driven by worldly cause and effect, Solness's joy displays his discovery of a means for resurgent activity, purposeful behavior that will subdue the next generation through powerful accomplishment instead of inciting its members to dangerous rebellion through the more vulnerable, negating, and self-damaging strategy of defensive containment that his paralysis urged. The oppressive element in his relation to Hilde, her control of him and his of her, and his instrumental use of her to continue the ambiguously penitential, sham adultery by which Solness repays a marital debt to Aline in painfully false coin promise that the new plan will not go smoothly. But Solness has no sense of that danger when he announces the gladness through which her arrival has enabled him to rise above the fear and helplessness with which he formerly confronted youth.

What Solness will build to deliver Hilde's promised kingdom remains an urgent but unanswered question in the Aristotelian intrigue. The intense focus on Hilde's restoration of Solness's *will* to act at the close of act 1 excludes any detailed consideration of a positive, real-world goal for his action. That exclusion strategically discloses the play's Nietzschean dimension. Here the action occurs not in an agent's changing place in the ongoing, rational orders of cause and effect in nature and society that harmoniously require and answer his purposeful deeds, but, instead, in the will's transcendent, or degraded, presentation of the self to itself for itself. In the Nietzschean order of value, Solness's plan for self-creation, gladly governed by guilty, compromising appropriation of devotion from two women whom he sets against each other, displays the ugliest sickness of the will: resentful inversion of power. The master builder's motto for deliverance, "Youth against youth!" makes that inversion ferociously clear.

Clear, that is, to the audience. At the end of act 1 Solness and Hilde, in opposite ways, both mistake the self-canceling call to arms for self-transcendence. The error occurs easily in the Nietzschean action, which calls for inversion of the divided will's ambivalent commitments to anachronistic repression and dangerous self-creation. The successful inversion, according to Nietzsche, is inversion upward, away from rational, pragmatic managing of worldly cause and effect toward endlessly aesthetic self-transformation accomplished through continuous, apocalyptic self-presentation. From this point forward the play shows Hilde and Solness struggling to accomplish an ascendent inversion of the masterbuilder's will, always against the degrading force of one or another mistake.

Throughout, their errors stem partly from the vagueness of the action that has brought them together. What happened between Solness and Hilde at Lysanger is not clear; her purpose in reporting the event to him ten years later is not clear; his purpose in ambiguously assenting to her report is not clear. This imprecision allows Ibsen to put the Aristotelian and Nietzschean actions of this play in shifting relation to one another. At times regressive or stalled opposition of pragmatic humanism and aesthetic voluntarism, at times liberating alignment of the two, Solness's story is always governed by how he and Hilde, at any given moment, remember Lysanger. That the governing action of his life cannot be known but must, under various personal and worldly pressures, be constantly reinterpreted, by two unequally matched interpreters, makes Solness's story fundamentally different from Mrs. Alving's in *Ghosts* or Rebecca West's in *Rosmersholm* and that difference signals an important development in Ibsen's thinking about reality and change. A fuller account of that development will come once Solness has finished his interpretations. At this point the particular errors by which Solness and Hilde drive forward the action call for elucidation.

Hilde's questioning repetition of Solness's observations that her arrival has made him glad, that he has been afraid of youth, have analogous functions in the realist and antirealist dimensions of this scene. They present a struggle to control his will. In the realistic dimension that struggle displays their different motivations and pragmatic purposes; in the Nietzschean dimension that struggle displays the sick will twisting against itself, moving at once toward new health and more fatal illness. The references to her clairvoyant intuitions of his desire, his growing conviction that she can be the new subject of his magic willing, all indicate that Hilde is not only a distinct person in this play, but also an incarnation of Solness's will. That she has a naturalistic identity as a vivacious young woman and a supranatural identity as an instantiation of his unrealized power to act, and that neither identity reduces to the other, demands doublevision from Solness and from the audience, hence Ibsen's constant association of her power over Solness with giddiness.

Aristotelian tragedy delivers cathartic gravity as knowledge of change; Nietzschean tragedy delivers vertiginous rapture. That vertigo appears in this scene in her trembling question "Can you use me, master builder?" and in his dazzled vision of her as his Joan of Arc. At this point Ibsen cuts Aristotelian hamartia into the rapture and shows both characters mistaking the intention of the other. As the play progresses, the question of which tragic order governs Solness's story will recur, in progressive complexity and resonance. Here the orders run in tandem: a recognition prompts a reversal, and an inversion from an old plan to a new one occurs; and the reversal introduces an error that will repeatedly govern the attempted transition, in both orders, from paralysis to action. Hilde correctly understands that Solness discloses the first principle of his unhappy self-creation when he tells her that he has fought off youth to protect himself from retribution. Her question "Can you use me, master builder?" challenges him at precisely the right moment but contains an ambiguity that her exuberance keeps hidden from her. She clearly imagines that he will use her to free himself from retribution and the order of value sustained by guilt. Her searching gaze and trembling mouth sublimate sexual passion and allure and present her youthful energy as a spiritual promise and challenge.

He takes the offer in exactly the opposite way, appropriating her ascendent will to refurbish the repressive project in which guilt remains the defining element of his magic will. Instead of his former rearguard defense against retribution, Solness now plans an attack. The military metaphor he uses for his struggle with retribution is itself ambiguous, suggesting action, but, in fact, disguising a species of resentment and evasion. When Hilde suggests that Solness regard youth as a friend to be let in the door, he characterizes it as a rebel army pounding at his gates, marching there under a new banner. She makes the term *new* an opportunity for transforming affirmation of whatever past event has made him fear retribution. The new banner she wants Solness to see youth carrying reads, "my future promises an eternal return of the same chance for accomplishment which I mastered in the past." The rebel army changes to an honoring parade in her mind.

The word *new* to Solness means a different martial plan for exploiting, not eliminating, the guilt that sustains his magical artistic self-creation. In that plan Hilde will betray herself and her kind, delivering the formerly rebel force of youth to his continued repression of it. In the Aristotelian dimension of pragmatic affairs that repression involves him switching to competitive elimination of Ragnar and the next generation of builders and abandoning tyrannical suppression of them. In the Nietzschean dimension of self-creation and self-presentation Hilde's submission will allow him to stay guilty about the domination he magically exerts over nature and people. The treachery assigned to her in the military metaphor presents the bad faith by which Solness deals with himself and his loved ones, the weakness by which he seeks to remain strong, his devious, damaging submission of will to power to the defrauding, managerial logic of cause and effect. He fears retribution for having transgressed against that managerial logic and cannot yet transform that fear into affirmative willing of the continually recurring, constitutive past transgression.

Hilde's error is believing he wants to make that transformation, or believing that she can spark that desire in him; Solness's is believing that he does not need to make that transformation to regain an active life, that he can devise a compromise that will make him happy and guilty at the same time. Ibsen highlights the ambiguity and error floating in the pair's giddy hope for a "new" action at the very end of the act, when Hilde and Solness, left alone onstage, repeat their erotically charged aspiration. Repeating the ambiguous term *use*, which means instrumental exploitation as much as participatory creation, Hilde requires Solness to confirm his need and desire for her, and when he does she declares that she has her kingdom, immediately qualifying the ejaculation in the curtain line "*(her mouth trembling again): Almost*—I was going to say" (*MB*, 316). The ambiguity of saying and unsaying the accomplishment of her project, the end of the action that began at Lysanger, presents once again the instability of Solness's will struggling against its self-destruction and the instability of Solness's instrumental rationality, which situates the master builder in a professional world he continues to make precarious. In both orders, Nietzschean and Aristotelian, the curtain line both stops and propels Solness's self-creation. The journeyman suspense that the line creates wraps melodramatic intrigue into the larger scope of existential struggle. *Almost* signals that retribution and the old order of naturalistic cause and effect that sustains it have not yet given way to joyful self-creation.

6

The Master Builder, *Act* 2:
"I should have done it."

Act 2 reveals what force retribution still has in Solness's life, how it impedes affirmative willing of the past. The act consists of Solness talking to his wife and Hilde and, briefly, to Kaja, and Ragnar, all of whom he has made, and continues to make, servants to his sick will's mixed project. His relation to each person shifts in this act, toward liberating disengagement with Kaja, Ragnar, and Aline, toward liberating engagement with Hilde. In the professional intrigue plot he finally releases Ragnar and Kaja, after a lapse into his old plan to suppress them, which Hilde forces him to abandon. In the Nietzschean plot he gradually returns to a full-scale confrontation of the past, accounts for its dominance in his present, glimpses what mental force affirming that past requires from him, and appropriates that force from Hilde. In both the realist and voluntarist orders of this act, how and what Solness can change in his life and world occupy him constantly.

Ibsen puts ontology, ethics, and art on an imaginative and conceptual continuum in this act's analytic representation of the problem of change. Moving through that continuum, trying to master it, Solness seeks commanding understanding of the cause-and-effect logic that ambiguously binds natural and supranatural force to human will—as delivering, creative potency and as captivating, incriminating doom. While the search makes Solness a classical tragic hero, one who struggles in innocent error to make the cosmological wrong of his life go right, Ibsen builds the confrontation with more resonant reference to Nietzsche's concepts of will, power, and creativity than ever before. The play's power comes from this radical relation of classical and modern ideas of change.

Solness remains onstage for the whole act, and the overlapping scenes are structured primarily by the interlinked appearances of the women who

sustain him, especially by two long scenes in which he and Hilde appear
alone together. The play moves now from Solness's office to a sitting room
in his house, signaling a move to the interior, to the domestic and psychological dimension of his professional intrigue. Solness appears with his wife
as the act opens. While he examines Ragnar's drawings, she, dressed in black,
silently waters flowers. Neither speaks, and she does not acknowledge or
notice his occasional glances toward her. Without a word the setting declares
that their alienation has a direct connection to his repressive career. The brief
opening dialogue, in which Kaja enters to inform Solness that Ragnar will be
late because he's tending to his dying father, expands the connection between
the builder's marriage and career. Revealing that Solness has not yet decided
to approve Ragnar's drawings, that dialogue displays once more the profes-
sional/sexual imbroglio guilty will has made for him.

Having ended the first act with a plan to transform Solness's life, Ibsen
opens act 2 with a masterfully condensed stage picture of Solness's stubborn
continuance of what he hoped to change the night before. The rest of the
act will show how Solness got to the state the opening tableau presents, and
what he needs to do to change the picture. The Aristotelian exposition,
which also presents a forward-moving Nietzschean retrieval of the past, has
three progressively revelatory phases, all disclosing Solness's relation to
Aline. The first phase includes Solness's only scene alone with his wife and
ends when Hilde appears. The next two phases show Solness and Hilde
unpacking the guilty secret that cannot be undone or even fully mentioned
in Solness's conversation with Aline. Ragnar's brief appearance with Kaja
separates these phases, highlighting yet another dimension of the relation to
Aline, allowing Hilde to force Solness into the action that will finally
transform the force of that relation in the builder's life and work.

Once her rival, Kaja, has left the scene Aline clears the air, and asserts
the prerogatives of matrimony with morbid talk of Brovik's impending death,
in which she fashions him one of a long sequence of people who die near the
master builder. Solness suggests that his wife leave the parlor for some fresh
air. The barely suppressed subtext indicates clearly that he wants her gone
for his welfare as much as for hers. With studied indifference he asks after
Hilde, and, when he learns she's been up a long time, he takes the occasion
to make her staying in the empty nursery a promising symbol of good things
to come, of an easing of Aline's burden. When Aline inquires how her life
has been gladdened by Hilde's arrival, Solness has to suppress rancor at
Aline's suspicion that he wants to make his secret cause of happiness a false,
convenient cause for hers. He deflects Aline's aggrieved marital insight by
claiming that the promised ease he refers to is their impending move to the

new house he has built for her. In the final event Hilde will control the happiness of that move, and all for Solness's benefit and her own. Aline, as it turns out, rightly doubts that Solness's new building could ever benefit her, but at this moment her skepticism appears to be at least as much a symptom of depression as foreknowledge.

The weight of failed married love, the release of vital, nascently adulterous love, and their connection to Solness's professional advancement of human happiness through building family dwellings all converge here and subsequently emerge as the primary topics in his confrontation with the past in this act. The first move in that confrontation comes as Solness and Aline painfully lunge at and evade discussion of the traumatic effect that the destruction by fire of her ancestral home had on Aline. When Solness promises that she will be happy in a new home that will be free of memories of her old one, Aline repudiates his goodwill with the unanswerable line, which should be delivered with an almost indifferent gloom: "You can build as much as you like, Halvard—you'll never be able to build a real home for me again" (*MB*, 320).

The line contains an ambiguity that is crucial for the play as a whole, and which Ibsen exploits immediately: does the impossibility of his making her happy in his craft derive from him or her? Solness responds to her dismissal of his capacity with a testy command that she drop the subject. Aline defends herself against his anger by reminding him that they don't normally discuss the blow she suffered because he avoids the subject. Startled and frightened by what he takes to be her implication that he might have something to hide where the fire is concerned, Solness asks why she believes he avoids mentioning it. Her answer, offered as a resolution of his anxiety, compounds it, and intensifies the accusatory undercurrent of her despairing remark that set them arguing.

> *Mrs. Solness:* Oh, I understand you so well, Halvard. You want to spare me.
> And stop me feeling guilty. As far as you can.
> *Solness (stares amazed):* Stop *you* feeling guilty! Are you—are you talking about
> yourself, Aline?
> *Mrs. Solness:* Yes, who else would I be talking about?
> *Solness (involuntarily, to himself):* That too! (*MB*, 320)

That she claims to understand him intimately and misses entirely his guilt over the fire's effect on her ironically settles the ambiguity in her accusation. Blaming herself for being too guilty to take up the new chance for happiness he has built her, she adds the burden of her guilt to his, as far as he's concerned ("That too"), all the while as confidently oblivious of his remorse as he, until now, has been of hers.

In this reversal, hamartia mars any potential redemptive action that might issue from the partial recognition. Disclosing her guilt, Aline represses Solness's urge to reveal his, obviating and annulling his involuntary unburdening. Preoccupied with his own hidden, unnamed crime against Aline, Solness not only has failed to see his wife's guilt, but, when she naively discloses it to exonerate him from failure to please her, Solness first thinks not of the pain that guilt causes Aline, but of the added suffering his feeling of responsibility for her guilt brings him. The interchange shows Ibsen's skill at psychological portraiture beautifully and displays how that device of Aristotelian realism also advances the play's Nietzschean action. That guilt ruinously binds two egos in the marriage plot reminds the audience of the delivering merging of wills in the telepathic voluntarism by which Hilde and Solness unite to overcome guilt in the Nietzschean action. What appears as ineluctable hamartia in his marriage appears as the spur to self-overcoming in his imagined seduction of Hilde. Aline's innocent suppression of her husband's capacity for such transcendence, caused by his invocation of the symbolic promise Hilde offers for new joy, at once shows the value of Hilde in his life and the power of guilt to cancel that value.

At this point Ibsen details Aline's guilt and Solness's response to it. His will resurface at the end of the scene and invoke the delivering Hilde. Having ironically made her guilt an absurd, unwitting function of his, Solness tries to control her thinking to protect himself and to alleviate her suffering. When she minimizes the loss of the house, consigning that pain to accident, Solness quickly approves, hoping that he can get her to put all her grief under that blameless cause. Displaying the omnivorous self-maintenance of guilt, she immediately transforms the blameless accident into a moral challenge that she failed. After the fire grief or fear over loss of the house made her negligently responsible for a nameless catastrophe she cannot forget, and which no loving solicitude from Solness can put out of her mind. When, together, they acknowledge the hopelessness of their future and the vanity of searching for happiness in the new house, Solness violently asks her, in despair, why they built it, and she answers that she cannot tell him, that he must answer for himself.

Solness takes that instruction, which she makes partly as protective retreat from his violence, as an accusatory disavowal of his efforts to make her happy and suspiciously demands that she disclose the blameworthy motive she has assigned to his creation of the new house. When she protests, disingenuously, that her words contain no implication of blame and asks why he thinks they do, he projects his guilty self-estimation onto her feeling for him, telling her that she finds devious secrecy in his idle remarks. Confounded, eager to exonerate herself and to discover if in fact she acts suspiciously, she twice asks if she so hectors him, and he bursts out in full paranoia. Instead of confirming that she does or doesn't so interpret him, Solness sardonically invents and justifies a motive for her suspicion, saying that skeptical scrutiny understandably accompanies any dealing with a lunatic.[1] Aghast at the accusation, which violently masks an anxious confession, and which she obviously hears for the first time, Aline sinks into a chair. Solness switches now from sarcasm to offended repudiation of Aline's alleged view that he is mad, mixed with indignant accusation that she has secretly enlisted the doctor to prove him mad: "But you're wrong, both of you. You and your doctor. There's nothing the matter with me" (*MB*, 322).

Having approached self-revelation through neurotic inversions, in which ambiguity turns every exit from suffering into firmer confinement, Solness now turns the assaultive pronouncement of sanity that culminates the paranoid episode into an occasion for loving openness. Now eager to ease her fears, and his, about his sanity, Solness repeats that there is nothing the matter with him and tells her that worry about a boundless debt to her crushes him. What might be relief in the tender marital intimacy turns to another confinement, one maintained by conscience—a graver force, in Solness, than paranoia.

> *Solness (quietly):* I owe a boundless debt to you. To you, Aline.
> *Mrs. Solness (rises slowly):* What is behind all this?
> *Solness:* There's nothing behind it. I've never done you any harm. Not wittingly, anyway. And yet—it feels as though a huge stone of guilt lay on me, weighing me down, crushing me.
> *Mrs. Solness:* Guilt? Towards me, you mean?
> *Solness:* Towards you, most of all.
> *Mrs. Solness:* Then you really are—sick, Halvard.
> *Solness:* I suppose I must be. Sick—or something. (*MB*, 322)

Taking his words at face value, Aline can make no other conclusion except that Halvard's guilt, which he says has no cause in any deliberate malfeasance toward her, must have sickness for its cause. When he shuns her request that he disclose "what's behind" his oppressive remorse, when she ignores his broad hint that an *unwitting* offense troubles him, and forgoes the relieving inquiry into his past that the hint covertly invites her to make, their best and only chance for happiness vanishes. Aline and Solness never appear

alone onstage after this disastrous conversation. In its various manifestations—as paranoia, resentment, and doomed, conscientious solicitude in
him; as morbidity, torpor, and unconsciously vindictive, martyred despair in
her—guilt has locked them into a Sisyphean dynamic that ceaselessly
requires and cancels reconciliation. Thinking too precisely on tormenting
events that neither will allow the other to interpret, both have lost any chance
to make their marriage an action aimed at happiness. At this point Solness's
building appears as nothing more than a deflection into the public sphere of
his private Sisyphean vanity.

In the Aristotelian dimension the resurgence of his conscience would
normally prepare the way for some species of tragic recognition. Hilde
diverts Solness's lapse into conscience, entering precisely at the point when
the builder has forestalled the effective retribution that full recognition would
bring about and chosen, instead, to dissipate his will in temporizing,
rearguard defensiveness. Solness's line "Ah! Now it grows lighter!" displays
the builder's relief at a chance to evade the evasive revelatory conversation
with Aline and his less-conscious hope that the twilight world of negative
willing might turn to the sun of joyful self-assertion that Hilde represents to
him (MB, 322). Again, Ibsen pivots into the Nietzschean order at an intense
moment in the humanist order, making the paralysis that emerges in rever-
sal/recognition logic an occasion for aesthetic willing, implying in the
structure of the play that, if Solness is ever to recover an action, he will have
to make the same switch himself from moralized orientation to the orders
governing nature and culture to voluntarist creation of reality and change.
The pivot also continues the Aristotelian plot, since Hilde's candidacy for
adulterous sustainer of Solness's craft is not lost on Aline, Solness, or Hilde.

Ibsen reinforces the correlation of the two orders by having Aline and
Hilde remain onstage together for a brief time. Aline learns that Hilde and
Solness share a common dream of falling (one more reinforcement of the
telepathic sympathy binding them). Immediately after hearing the shared
dream, Aline decides to leave, without any comment on it, explicitly
distancing herself from her husband's new intimate by telling her that the
kindness she does her by bringing her suitable clothes from town displays
duty alone and not the affection Hilde thanks her for. When Hilde naively
resists Aline's advice to civilize her appearance by saying that social disapproval of her eccentricity will be fun, Solness brings the subject of his
madness back into play. He warns her that the town already contains one
madman —him— and that she might come under the contagion of his
reputation. Banter about his sanity ensues, in which Solness embarrasses
Aline, and Hilde refuses to acknowledge any signs of madness in the builder,

except "one little thing" that comes to her as an afterthought and that she teasingly refuses to disclose. Aline, with acid scorn and bitter acceptance of her husband's flirtation with Hilde, leaves after announcing that her absence might loosen the tongue of this new favorite, whose seduction dates—and this detail carries all the opprobrium of the wounded wife—from her childhood meeting with Solness.

Throughout this realistic dialogue Ibsen details the marital intrigue to reconfigure the dynamic struggle of the sickwill against itself that makes up the Nietzschean self-creation plot. Forward motion in this play occurs much more in recurrent and incremental shifts from classical to modernist accounts of change than it does in the linear concatenation and unraveling of conflicting purposes governing professional or domestic aims in the realistic plot. Representing Solness's stalled compromises, the realistic plot repetitiously reenacts them in different domestic and professional configurations, which unravel, finally, anticlimactically. The repetition's mimetic value in the intrigue plot has more force in the voluntarist order, in which it indicates the will's incessant struggle to reverse the dynamic of Solness's self-creation.

For the rest of this scene with Hilde, and the second one that follows Ragnar's appearance, the topics of Solness's crime against Aline and the relation of that crime to his willed professional success and his present anxiety and paralysis recur. Both scenes with Hilde repeat the dynamic of the first one with Aline: a chance for a change to happiness presents itself in Solness's career; he partially discloses fear that his career advanced through a crime against Aline; he examines what personal power led him to commit the crime and assesses the effect of that power on his chances to bring a change to happiness about. The three exposition scenes progressively reveal the past and challenge Solness to change his relation to it: in the first two he ends in guilty retreat from the challenge; in the last he makes an artistic assertion to be free. And so act 2 ends as act 1 did, with an assertion instead of a pragmatic change. In the realistic dimension of this play the repetition of elements and structure in the actions of scenes and acts operates under the logic of variation, an aesthetic analogue for the incessant shifting realignment of stalemated forces in the sick will; in the Nietzschean dimension repetition constantly invokes the chance for development, for some difference to emerge from the eternal return of the same conflict. The tension holding variation and development together in the play is Solness's guilt, and that tension increases in the two conversations with Hilde that make up the bulk of this act and of the play.

Throughout the scene Hilde makes judgments and suggestions that she requires Solness to assent to. She begins by complaining that Aline's explicit citation of duty over affection as the cause of benevolence displays violent hostility. When she asks Solness if he doesn't feel that duty damages people, he evasively answers that he hasn't thought about that much and turns the question back on her, asking what she would have preferred as Aline's cited motive. When Hilde says she would have preferred affectionate volition, Solness forces her, interrogatively this time, to say directly that she wants to be wanted. The opposition of duty and desire Hilde makes here and Solness's refusal to acknowledge their conflicting force recapitulate the domestic conflict represented in the first scene with Aline, and set the topic for the ensuing confrontations that Hilde will stage throughout the act to force Solness into a liberating action. His evasive containment of that conflict has brought him to a crisis in his career, and Hilde turns to that topic next.

Wandering through the parlor, she stops at the bookcase, where a conversation occurs in which she and Solness disclose that they have abandoned reading as meaningless. Writing's preservation of the past and its illumination of the present and future normally inspires the heroic struggles for transcendence in Ibsen's plays—recall Mrs. Alving's transformative reading and Rebecca West's. Dismissing it here, Solness and Hilde separate themselves from those protagonists, suggesting that their quest for happiness will take them beyond any traditional or contemporary public instruction in good and evil. The active alternative to reading is doing, and Hilde turns immediately to the architectural drawings she sees, thus bringing Solness's professional control of the past, present, and future into play. Archly, she criticizes him for endangering his exclusive prerogative to build by letting young men learn his professional secrets. Stunned, Solness unwillingly reveals that in his isolation he has silently, unceasingly, thought exactly that. His surprise, his unwillingness to acknowledge her telepathic empathy, is a psychologically realistic presentation of the play's antirealist, Nietzschean depiction of the sick will's self-presentation. In that dimension Hilde enacts power's positive self-assertion, and he enacts the resistance that calls that transcendent action forth.

The brief telepathic revelation immediately provokes Solness's anxiety about the power governing his self-creation, which the builder expresses by asking if Hilde's reference to signs of madness in him was reference to this ruinous teaching of young builders. She playfully tells him no and withholds the meaning of her taunt. Solness responds to her refusal by pointing out the product of his alleged madness to her—the new house he has built for Aline—and now Hilde reveals what provoked her teasing by asking why he includes nurseries in a new house that will not have children. Observing that she slept in the existing empty nursery, Hilde explicitly presents the thematic link of will to power, guilt, and ruined action in the builder's life to him. Placed in the empty nursery by Aline and Solness, probing the vanity of building future empty ones, Hilde introduces transforming content into the vacancy of Solness's self-creation: she challenges him to enact the difference that her presence in that room symbolizes, to bring a new effect out of his continuing old crime against generation.

Solness takes the challenge up immediately, quietly telling her that his twins are dead and then exclaiming, with explosive relief, his happiness that someone has come to whom he can talk about their death. When Hilde learns that Solness cannot talk to Aline about this, or much else, as he wants to, she asks if the use that he happily wanted to put her to last night was not, as she thought, professional advance but domestic lamentation. Solness evasively accedes to her mistaken reinterpretation and then confounds that equivocation by telling her he isn't sure this morning what he meant last night. Solness's confusion over Hilde's domestic or professional use to him indicates that conscience, aroused in his conversation with Aline, has turned the builder's great enterprising hope in Hilde awry.

This reversal in the realistic dimension once again presents the central dynamic in the Nietzschean one: power facing resistance in submission instead of mastery. Submission can transform itself into a strategy for mastery in Nietzsche's scheme, when the aesthetic soul wills the resistant, repeating past, and Hilde, the spur to Solness's happy aesthetic self-creation, gives him that chance for transformation by agreeing to hear the story that traces the ambiguous success of his career to the empty nursery. Solness's narration also invokes the aesthetic logic of Aristotelian tragedy, in which gradual disclosure of an originating crime, brought about by apparently successful action, ends not in the chance to bring a new effect from an old cause, but in complete submission to a hitherto suppressed doom. To a great extent the second act of *The Master Builder* pits Hilde and Solness against each other in a struggle to make inherited humanism or insurgent voluntarism the end of the builder's story, and of his life.

Solness begins by pointing out the new house to Hilde and telling her it stands on the site of Aline's ancestral home. Hilde asks if Solness tore the house down, and he answers that a fire destroyed it. She now asks if the fire killed his children, and Solness answers that an infection, contracted from Aline, who dutifully nursed them during an illness brought about by her anguish over the fire, killed them. Through most of the narration in the two exposition scenes Solness relates his past under Hilde's questioning. This interrogatory mode of dialogue clearly presents Solness's guilty will, which the Aristotelian dimension plays out as the struggle of conscience against condemnation in the pragmatic order and which the Nietzschean order presents as a struggle between transcendent and submissive self-creation. Both orders enact Hilde's telepathic identity with Solness: in the pragmatic one she represents his destructive introjection of morality; in the voluntarist one she displays his longing to transcend such guilty confinement in humanist cause and effect logic. At those moments when Solness questions her the struggle shifts, now to his debasing enactment of judgment, now to rehearsal of his imminent transcendence.

The first shift comes when Solness tells her that his response to the children's death was to question the very possibility of its occurrence. That question launched him on a theodicy, which he answered by abandoning God and building homes instead of churches. He puts the initial abandonment weakly, calling it a loss of interest in building churches, but states his present conviction more strongly, saying he will never build churches again, only homes for families. Hilde tests his assertion of liberation with a leading question about whether he took pleasure in the church project at Lysanger, where their union began, and elicits a repeated assertion of freedom when he says he was glad and relieved to finish that project. His confidence persists, as he explains how the fire launched his career. Ibsen sketches this professional intrigue vaguely, but the gist of it is that Solness's poverty prevented him from studying architecture in any formal way. Self-taught, lacking the license that institute study would have provided, he could not advance in the open market. The fire cleared ground on property he owned, which he parceled out as lots for sale. Building as he pleased on these, he circumvented the legal impediments to his career incurred by his irregular, solitary training. Hilde takes the initiative at this point, asserting that Solness must be happy with the success that fire initiated, and when he demurs, she brings the question of his anguish over the children's death to the fore, asking if they still obstruct the satisfaction he should rightly take in his accomplishment.

Solness takes the initiative away from her with his own question when he asks if she didn't notice any detail in his narration of the fire that might reveal how unhappiness mars his bootstrapped success. She yields with the observation that she can think of none, thus allowing and challenging him to disclose himself to himself (and to that part of himself she enacts) by himself. Solness takes up the chance, presenting a Faustian account of his professional advance that suggests and conceals an originating crime, which he does not disclose until their conversation resumes after Ragnar's interruption. He tells her that the fire enabled him to bestow peace, comfort, and joy on people, enabled him to make life self-evidently good for those who enacted familial love in the houses he built. When she repeatedly questions his conviction that he can never experience such joy for himself, he answers: "to be able to build homes for other people, I had to renounce forever all hope of having a home of my own. I mean a home with children. And for their father and mother." When she asks whether the cost was "absolutely necessary," Solness nods slowly and answers: "That was the price I had to pay for this 'happiness' people talk so much about. *(Takes a deep breath.)* That happiness—hm—that happiness wasn't to be had at a lesser price, Hilde" (*MB*, 331).

Solness reveals the pragmatic origin of this cost when he tells Hilde that, as a result of her illness after the fire, Aline can never have children again. This realistic disclosure launches the play into its most explicitly anti-Aristotelian expostulation, presented in the following interrogation.

> Hilde *(looks at him with an enigmatic expression)*: And yet you are building all these nurseries?
> Solness: Haven't you noticed, Hilde, that the impossible—beckons and calls to us?
> Hilde *(thinks)*: The impossible? *(Excitedly.)* Why, yes! Is it like that with you as well?
> Solness: It is.
> Hilde: Then you have something of the troll in you, too. (*MB*, 331)

In Aristotelian plays *unwitting* pursuit of the impossible unexpectedly makes the possible disastrously real. At the end of this self-canceling logic, advanced by agents' hamartia, the fallibility by which they confuse possible and impossible ends, those agents either die or are delivered from the contradictory matching of cause and effect in their lives by the intervention of a superior human force or a god. Ibsen transforms the dramatic and ethical force of contradictory praxis by enlarging the role of divine cause in action, a force Aristotle denigrated and all but omitted from *Poetics*. Even when gods do intervene in classical drama, they operate inside the natural order, magically resolving contradictions between origins and ends in human action, but never enabling, commanding, or inspiring people to do the impossible. Building uninhabitable nurseries, Solness at once reenacts and defies the original hamartia that gave him imperfectly transcendent power to enact happiness. As he will soon relate to Hilde, the trolls have made him preserver of others' happiness, and destroyer of his, in the human realm. Whether they can also mystically transport him, through Hilde's provocation, from the contradictory human realm to a transcendent happiness—the impossible willfully, not pragmatically, achieved—will occupy the master builder for the rest of the play.

Solness's narration of his career once more discloses the contradictory activity of messianic liberation, which Ibsen returned to again and again in his career. The builder's narrative of his worldly self-creation once more blends Protestant Christianity's salvational concentration on ordinary life and a mixed Enlightenment/romantic aspiration to deliver humanity from oppression into Scandinavian superstition about the ambiguous force of supranatural agency in human creativity.[2] Solness's rendition of himself as a martyred aesthetic savior, his ambition to spread the gospel of the joy of life in opposition to the authority of the church, and his anxiety over the tragic mix of innocence and guilt in his purpose recall Oswald and Mrs. Alving from *Ghosts* and Rebecca West and John Rosmer from *Rosmersholm*. He differs from them in his deliberate pursuit of the impossible, and that difference, provoked and sustained by Hilde, signals the crucial shift Ibsen made in this play in his understanding of the reality of change. Essentially, the shift involves a new concentration on the internal logic of subjectivity, a diminished relation of the subject to social orders, and an increased reliance on the subject's grounding in natural power mystically conceived and invoked. This move against humanism, and its inherited expression in Aristotelian poetics that favor realistic mimesis of the subject's ethical activity, emerges primarily through Hilde, especially in her association of impossible action with trolls. They increasingly dominate Solness's conversation with Hilde and eventually present themselves as the symbolic agents of the Nietzschean mode of action that dominates this play and the final phase of Ibsen's career.

In their final appearance the trolls lead Solness away from any ambition to act in the world as builder, husband, or lover. They start out less forcefully here, introduced ambiguously as supranatural agents of worldly idealism and corruption. That ambiguity gives a metaphysical origin to the contradictory power, which Solness complains has made his artistic accomplishment a sacrifice. Casting himself as a scapegoat benefactor, who establishes the possibility of domestic happiness by impoverishing himself, Solness silently invokes both Faust and Jesus as comparison cases to his—Faust to present his guilt, Jesus to present his innocence. Later Ibsen will make both analogies more explicit frames for action conceived metaphysically; here they are subtly evoked by Solness to account for the moral purpose guiding his building of houses.

Throughout his career Ibsen explicitly invests the theatrical convention of domestic realism with the moral force of the biblical analogy between spiritual well-being and prudent creation of houses. *The Master Builder* culminates that investment by invoking and transforming Europe's traditional grounding of familial life in monotheistic fideism, replacing religious metaphysics with a species of Nietzschean voluntarism associated with popular superstition. A brief précis of the European religious inheritance should make clear the spiritual transpositions Solness and Hilde work into the builder's crisis-ridden account of his tragically messianic professional and personal self-creation. In Judaism the analogy of home to heaven primarily asserts the coherence of the moral universe and presents instructions for ordered, "righteous," maintenance by creatures of the Creator's plan. The ark of the covenant and the Temple at Jerusalem that houses it provide an earthly home in which God mystically transmits to humanity some portion of the joy and power of His celestial dwelling. That integrating architecture receives incessant symbolical elaboration throughout the Old Testament, as the principle of historical and national identity for "the house of Israel," as the spiritual ground of moral life, most notably in the Psalms and the Song of Songs.

Christianity transforms the analogy, maintaining the sanctity of the Temple, and its historical complement, by which the Jewish nation is named a "house," but adding a concept of transcendence into spiritual life, an injunction to complete and improve an unfinished moral order. The imperative to transcend corrupt worldly life clearly plays an essential role in Judaism, in which it animates the prophetic tradition that emerged in contrast to theocratic corruptions and in response to historical reversals in Jewish history. The distinct element in Christ's prophecy comes in his repeated assertion that even virtuous domestic life corrupts or, at the very least, dangerously diminishes spiritual achievement. In Jesus' preaching the sanctity of physical houses, even of the Temple, must not be violated, but also must be superseded. Under the right conditions spiritual identification with God requires departure from home. The parable of the prodigal son (Luke 15:11-32) presents both an account of imprudent worldly disregard for the values of domestic life and a symbolic account of the soul's errant departure from spiritual to earthly values, followed by the soul's delivering recovery of its transcendent home.

Jesus presents the ambiguous value of the soul's worldly habitat continually in the Gospels. In Matthew 21:13 he drives the moneylenders out of the temple, complaining of their profanation of the place's material sanctity. But in John 4:23-24 he tells the Samaritan woman that no physical structure contains innate spiritual value and denigrates all worldly religious observance, asserting that it must be superseded for union with God: "But the hour cometh, and now is, when the true worshipers shall worship the Father in spirit and in truth: for the Father seeketh such to worship him. God is a Spirit: and they that worship him must worship him in spirit and in truth."

While he continually preaches the sanctity of domestic life —performing his first miracle at a wedding, circumscribing divorce, praising the spiritual insight of children, restoring dead children to desolated widows and fathers, restoring dead Lazarus to his sisters Martha and Mary, favoring that family with his company—Jesus also harshly denigrates familial life as an impediment to spiritual progress. Disavowing his own mother as an example, Christ promises a superior domestic unity in the transcendent realm: "Verily I say unto you, There is no man that hath left house, or brethren, or sisters, or father, or mother, or wife, or children, or lands, for my sake and the gospel's, But he shall receive an hundredfold now in the time, houses, and brethren, and sisters, and mothers, and children, and lands, with persecutions; and in the world to come eternal life" (Mark 10: 29-30).

Jesus announces the cost to himself, and others, for such transcendence explicitly and often. Scorned at Nazareth, in Mark 6:4 Jesus tells his neighbors and relatives, "A prophet is not without honour, but in his own country, and among his own kin, and in his own house." In Luke 9:57-62 he turns back all candidates for discipleship who would settle familial responsibilities before joining him, telling a man who wants to bury his father, "Let the dead bury their dead: but go thou and preach the kingdom of God," warning another that to follow him is literally to become homeless: "Foxes have holes, and birds of the air have nests; but the Son of man hath not where to lay his head." The warning of worldly desolation prepares for the superior bliss of transcendent dwelling, most famously presented in the building metaphor in John's Last Supper scene (elements of which Ibsen used in his depiction of the ruin of Rosmersholm): "Let not your heart be troubled: ye believe in God, believe also in me. In my Father's house are many mansions: if it were not so, I would have told you. I go to prepare a place for you. And if I go and prepare a place for you, I will come again, and receive you unto myself; that where I am, there ye may be also" (John 14:1-3).

While Solness has abandoned church building, he has preserved religion's ambiguous relation of domestic and metaphysical order in his thinking and in his work, especially the ambiguity in Jesus' prophecy over transcending or sanctifying familial domesticity. The houses he builds all have steeples, including the new one he has built to cancel Aline's loss of her ancestral home. Indeed, mounting that new house's steeple, and so canceling a long-term debt to Hilde incurred when he mounted the steeple of a church he built in her town ten years ago, Solness will finally resolve the ambiguities that have tormented and nurtured him. That apocalyptic transposition of guilt into self-overcoming, which ends the play, begins in Solness's attempts in this act to reclaim, through confessional narration, the vanished power that for so long granted him professional success. The reclamation requires first that Solness explain why that success has brought him misery instead of happiness. Inchoately hoping to invent a new future by telling Hilde his past, Solness inevitably colors his narration with those habitual confusions and anxieties that at once make the narrative's objective—deliverance from false to real happiness—so necessary and so hard to achieve.

In her inciting questions, Hilde guides Solness, as Virgil did Dante in the *Commedia*, through the self-accusing and self-exculpating maze of guilty autobiography. Whereas Virgil's moral authority was imperfect, because non-Christian, it was not ambiguous, but, rather, a preparatory phase of Dante's guaranteed spiritual deliverance from misery to happiness. Hilde's moral authority, especially as displayed in her identification of herself and Solness with trolls, is radically ambiguous and offers no spiritual guarantees, only challenges and risks. The modernism of Ibsen's career lies primarily in that distinction between certain and ambiguous moral authority governing action. Ibsen's modernist ambiguity puts humanistic pragmatism and Nietzschean voluntarism into an unstable competition for authority over all Solness's actions—his professional behavior and his narrative self-creation. At this point in the play the compounded ambiguities of those historically antagonistic cultural orders display themselves in Solness's alienated, self-aggrandizing, and self-victimizing return to the religious values he has rejected, but as yet cannot do without.

Little of the Old Testament prophetic call to restore social and domestic order, which Ibsen treated so extensively throughout his prose cycle, survives in Solness's self-conception. His opposition to religious authority and his costly, ambiguous success in promulgating the value of secular life through building houses for the wealthy professional class have none of the generalized political or social resonance that make *An Enemy of the People* or, to a lesser extent *Rosmersholm* jeremiads that ambivalently call for renewed cultural vitality. The corruption in Solness's house stems from a metaphysical problem that plagues his self-creation. While that problem has realistic psychological and social manifestations in Solness's life, he will not solve it by revising the codes that govern marriage and professional life. He needs to change his orientation toward the world, and that requires disengagement from ethical struggle, followed by reorganization of the internally conflicting forces by which he resists and masters creative activity.

Rather than excoriating its audience for inadequate pursuit of worldly justice, this play constantly urges the spectators to contemplate how radical pursuit of life's values requires transcendent disengagement from the world. Christ's ambiguous evaluation of the world and his complex strategies for alienated moral attention to it, ironically transposed into Solness's guilty machinations and his conflicted desire to enact a transforming, delivering impossibility, do much more to set the terms for this play's critique of action than those of Amos, Isaiah, or Moses. While Jesus carries over the thinking of those three prophets, especially their emphasis on deliverance from misery through strict adherence to principles of rational loving-kindness, he changes their thinking by insisting that virtuous worldly experience counts only as qualifying preparation for deliverance to the superior, imminent kingdom of heaven. While Old Testament prophets insist on recovery of an immanent order of value, Jesus constantly preaches that God's kingdom is elsewhere, has not yet flourished on earth, and, in its full manifestation, will not.

Some portion of that kingdom belongs incipiently to worldly life, made up of those who love and worship Jesus, acknowledging him as the incarnate God. This new saving remnant differs from Isaiah's primarily in its objective, which seeks not primarily to bring God's kingdom to the world, but to make that dignified exit from the world that will allow for delivering entrance into God's transcendent realm. Jesus advises two strategies for this transforming retreat, both functions of the kingdom's imminence. One strategy sets forth the protocol for waiting in this world to be delivered to the next one and involves distinguishing between what must be rendered unto Caesar during life and what unto God (Matt. 22: 21). In this strategy Christians, born in the spirit after their fleshly birth, live amphibiously in human society, in the world but not of the world, sheep in the midst of wolves who must be wise as serpents and harmless as doves as they carry out their inferior duty to mammon and their superior duty to God (John 3:3,6; Matt. 10:16; Luke 16:1-13). Patiently, scrupulously, tending to inferior mundane responsibilities with cheerful, scrupulous indifference, Christians bestow the highest value on earthly life and make themselves "the salt of the earth" and "the light of the world" (Matt. 5:13, 14).

The second strategy sets forth a more radical protocol for those who will not wait, but, instead, jump the life to come. It replaces distancing appraisal of the world's inferior goods with joyous disavowal and, in its most radical form, with sacrificial repudiation. In this mode the kingdom is not so much imminent as immanent, already achieved in the lives of the most faithful. When, in Luke 17:20-21, the Pharisees ask Jesus for signs of the kingdom's arrival, he answers with the text that Protestant Christianity especially made the ground for a theology of God's immanence in the lives of the faithful: "The kingdom of God cometh not with observation: Neither shall they say, Lo here! or lo there! for, behold, the kingdom of God is within you." For those already dwelling in the kingdom, any attention to worldly goods counts as nothing more than vanity and distraction. "Take no thought for your life," Jesus tells those who seek to dwell at once in the kingdom; God has already made sufficient transient provision for the transient physical realm (Luke 12:22-31). The joy in this disavowal comes from knowing that the prudential appraisal of the world's good has already been made by God, inestimably to the benefit of mankind. Again, Luke 12:6-7: "Are not five sparrows sold for two farthings, and not one of them is forgotten before God? But even the very hairs of your head are all numbered. Fear not therefore: ye are of more value than many sparrows." Here the metaphor of stewardship, which counted so much in the protocol of waiting, switches from a description of man's responsibility to the world God has made to a description of the bountiful occasions for transcendence God's immanence has introduced into worldly life.

But that bounty doesn't guarantee only gleeful rapture. Those sparrows are sold for sacrifice in the temple, and, while taking no thought for your life can express confident joy in life's secured continuance, it can also command sacrificial death for inclusion in the kingdom. Christ's passion establishes the paradigm of literally dying to be born, and he enjoins a similar sacrifice on those who seek, or already intuit, God's immanence in their earthly lives. In John 12:24, at the Last Supper, Jesus tells his disciples: "Verily, verily, I say unto you, Except a corn of wheat fall into the ground and die, it abideth alone: but if it die, it bringeth forth much fruit." In Mark 8:35-36 a more explicit injunction to die in the world and to it occurs: "Whosoever will come after me, let him deny himself, and take up his cross, and follow me. For whosoever will save his life shall lose it; but whosoever shall lose his life for my sake and the gospel's, the same shall save it. For what shall it profit a man, if he shall gain the whole world, and lose his own soul? Or what shall a man give in exchange for his soul?"

Prudential disengagement from rationally appraised and employed worldly goods follows from a view of the kingdom of heaven as imminent, a view preserved in the pragmatic, even domestic metaphors in which Jesus presents progression to the kingdom: sowing of seeds, harvest, the burgeoning increase of a mustard seed, of leaven (Mark 4:3-9, Luke 10:2, 13:19, 21). The ambiguous joyful and painful separation from the world that follows from viewing the kingdom as immanent also carries over into Jesus' description of the second, radical mode of disengagement. To those living rapturously in the world without being of it, the interior kingdom is light shining in darkness, a wedding feast, new wine in old bottles, a treasure hidden in a field, a pearl surpassing all others in value, a treasury from which a householder can withdraw new and old valuables (John 1:5, Mark 2:19, 22, Matt.

13:44-47, 52). To those sacrificially repudiating the preparatory worldly phase of sanctification, the kingdom's immanence demands at the least flight from home and family, as well as impoverishment; at the most it demands dismemberment and finally, death (Matt. 10:34-36; Mark 10:21; Mark 9:43, 47; Mark 10:39). With the exception of bearing one's cross, Jesus rarely uses metaphor when describing this sacrificial mode of disengagement. While the admonition to cut off offending limbs seems especially offensive, and has hence steadfastly been rendered metaphoric by church commentary, the context of that instruction, in that temporal suffering is trivialized in comparison to the eternal perdition that the offending limbs earn a believer, argues powerfully for radically literal intention on Jesus' part.

The diverse calls for conversion in Christ's prophecy—his metaphoric instruction for attentive disengagement from worldly experience, his metaphoric description of gleeful ignoring of the world, and his revolutionary instructions for negation and violent repudiation of worldly life—display one constant conviction: reality is elsewhere and changeless; entering it comes only through paradoxically self-creating self-denial, through active inactivity in the unreal world. While that conviction seems conceptually antithetical both to Aristotelian humanism and Nietzschean voluntarism, history, which has more than conceptual work to do, aligned classical ethics and romantic psychology with Christianity, and that alignment occupied Ibsen incessantly. In his self-creation Solness struggles with that same confluence; indeed, his self-creation consists largely in his struggle to master its mastery of him. The initial stages of his self-revelation show him replicating, in the story of his life, the historical merger of these foundational accounts of change, transforming the ideational tension that binds them now into the familiar ambiguity of guilty compromise, now into the fresh hope that new effect can come from old cause. To the guilty compromise first.

Distinguishing various goods in worldly experience and pursuing them with a balanced sense of their different relations to a standard of well-being not immediately given in experience, but discerned by an inner vision applied to experience—that procedure for happiness describes Christian waiting and Aristotelian humanism equally. Although opposed standards for evaluation divide the systems, Christianity insisting on transcendence and Aristotle insisting on the sufficiency and necessity of worldly life, their compatible tricks of balancing divergent desires and needs made these systems cooperating norms in European culture, especially after the Protestant emphasis on the sanctity of ordinary life took hold. Solness has turned active waiting to paralysis and made necessary, sufficiently happy self-creation in the mundane sphere doomed confinement in eroding machinations. The realistic, Aristotelian dimension of *The Master Builder* turns the most serviceable devices of nineteenth-century problem plays and melodrama into narrative revelations of the builder's failure to manage humanistic cause-and-effect logic.

The imminent happiness Solness wants to bring into life has always been earthbound: he builds houses where the happiness no longer possible in churches can flourish. His mistake has been misjudging the value and nature of those interior and mundane resources through which he pursued his objective. Confining Ragnar through vain seduction of Kaja to preserve his career, Solness does not diminish Ragnar's power to exceed him professionally, nor does he banish his guilt over forging his career out of an offense against Aline. The suppression enhances both Ragnar's strength and Solness's guilt by putting them constantly before him, where, in combined force, they present themselves as the power of retribution that has frightened him into stopping his career. Telling his story to Hilde, Solness presents it as sacrificial disengagement from worldly happiness and suppresses any account of himself as failing properly to discern or enact prudent connections between mundane ends and means.

Presented as a sacrifice, Solness's self-creation has two symbolic dimensions. Insofar as Solness has deprived his own domestic life of happiness to build happiness for strangers, he sees himself as Christlike, especially in his relation to Aline, in which he suffers dishonor, rejection of his salvational efforts on her behalf, and false accusation. Joyous entry into the kingdom, which follows such transcendental repudiation of personal welfare in the mundane sphere for Christians, has failed Solness. Instead of satisfaction, he complains that he has received mockery from a troll, who commands him to pursue the impossible and who, harpy-like, exacts expiation for his professional success in incessant torture of remorse.

Insofar as he complains of the remorse and sees the sacrifice as an unfair price, rather than a delivering repudiation of the distractions of personal worldly life, Solness presents himself as Faust, as a man who gained the world at the cost of his soul. Faust, of course, eventually tricks the demonic trickster who persuaded him to make the bad bargain proscribed by Christ. In part 2 (1832), through his exertions to enact a transcendent vision of the possibilities of happiness in human life—which result at one point in failed reclamation of land from the sea to establish an ideal society—Faust cancels the nihilistic effect of Mephistopheles over him. The transcendent redemption comes about largely through the protecting and transforming inspiration that "the eternal feminine" provides Faust. While Solness in act 2 clearly has the tragic first part of Faust on his mind, Ibsen has both parts on his. Hilde's mystical allure in some way presents the uplifting, progressive power of the eternal feminine to Solness, but her association with the demonic trolls, the sexual danger she poses to Solness, and her invasion of his nurseries clearly invoke the damning feminine magic that Goethe presents in Faust's vision of Helen of Troy more than they invoke the delivering purity of the Virgin Mary, which ushers Faust into salvation at the end of his struggle.

The irony in Solness's Christian identification of himself as redeeming scapegoat—unlike Christ, the builder did not deliberately repudiate domestic happiness to fulfill his destiny, but unwittingly lost it—carries over to his Faustian identification. Unlike Faust, Solness did not deliberately bargain away his soul, but lost it unawares. A magnified resonance from the Faust parallel enters the play in the next scene, when Solness describes what part his half-conscious invocation of the trolls had in the fire, but even then ambiguities about Solness's exertion of will render the symbolic grasping after transcendence ironic. These ironies, culminating in Hilde's ambiguously pagan, Christian presentation to Solness of the transposing virtue of "the eternal feminine," cut at least two ways.

They demonstrate the fraudulent lengths to which guilt extends in the self-presentation of a compromised soul. Faust and Jesus magnify Solness's introjection of inherited morality. Invoking them, Solness ironically validates the realistic account of his life in which he is not a troll-tormented genius, but a lucky seducer, too cowardly and vain to acknowledge the naturalistic force of accident in his life or the licentious opportunism by which he made accident look like destiny. Strong enough to make good in worldly terms, his will is too weak to acknowledge truthfully his offense against the moral norms governing that success and too weak to dismiss or submit to them manfully. But the sick will belongs to Nietzsche's thinking as much as it does to humanism's, more so, and in the Nietzschean realm of the play Solness's invocation of Faustian and Christian transcendence indicates more than introjection of inherited morality.

In the sphere in which action means doing the impossible—willing the past, invoking the eternal return of identical and identifying accident, progressively destroying subjective integration to recreate it in new strength—Solness's inappropriately grandiose invocation of Jesus and Faust and Hilde's ambiguous conflation of the female presences in the opposed models of transcendence show the builder striving to break out of introjected morality, trying to create himself freely and joyously. For all his hatred of the idealistic ontology of metaphysics, which always locates happiness somewhere outside the present time and place, Nietzsche analytically demands transcendence constantly. He departs from idealism by insisting that transcendence occurs in an eternally changing present, transforming a subject's integrity, not transporting the subject to another time or place.

Christ's first mode of transcendent disengagement, prudent balancing of different goods, which fit well enough in Aristotelian humanism, meets nothing but scorn in Nietzsche's work. But the second two modes, in which the will detaches itself in gleeful or violent power from the corrupting inadequacies of mundane life, proved rich sources for Nietzsche's vision of the laughing, dancing superman, on the one hand, and the eagle, on the other. In fact, Ibsen gives Hilde symbolic identity as a falcon later in this act and immediately adds one of Nietzsche's titles as well, in Solness's description of her as dawn. Invoking Christ's sacrificial mode of immanent transcendence, however ineptly, Solness takes steps that, with Hilde's encouragement, might turn him into a Nietzschean dancer. In their mutual identification with the troll who commands impossibility, Solness and Hilde come closest to that dance, but he falls back quickly into guilt, as the sick will does until it heals. At this point Ibsen has not resolved the ambiguity binding Aristotelian and Nietzschean thinking into Solness's self-creating confession, but presents them, instead, as oscillating visions in the builder. Throughout this transitional second act, however, the movement is toward Nietzsche's gleeful and violent disengagement.

Solness's aspiring reference to the inspiring troll spills over immediately into complaint about a mocking troll who makes him pay for success not only through sacrifice of his own personal happiness but also through remorse for ruining that of others. Here Ibsen adds the humanistic action of retribution to the Nietzschean self-overcoming originally derived from the troll world and shows the confused inversion of power that makes the builder's allegiance to both systems tormenting. Solness explains to Hilde that he offended Aline not only by building his career out of the ruination of her home, but, more disastrously, by destroying her chance to build the souls of children. When Hilde tries to understand why he feels guilty for the fire's effect on Aline, Solness collapses into enigmatic protestations of absolute guilt and innocence, provoking her discouraged observation that such disorientation suggests at the very least a severe illness. He fearfully enlarges the remark, telling her the malaise has no cure.

This return to the morbid guilt that Solness fell prey to at the end of his first conversation about the fire with Aline works ambiguously. In the humanistic domain it gives Solness tragic stature; in the Nietzschean one it diminishes him, displaying his will's weakness. When Solness's identification with Christ's sacrificial pursuit of immanent and imminent spiritual reality is read against his relation to Aline, the Nietzschean account of guilt's recurrence, ironically enough, weighs more heavily than the humanistic one. Aline's dress, demeanor, barrenness, and perpetual mourning all identify her as one of the dead burying their dead. Attaching himself in confusedly innocent penance to that confining familial loyalty Jesus dismissed as an impediment to joyful, righteous self-creation, Solness enacts the division Christ made between the inferior value of mundane duty, however affectionate, and the superior value of transcendence and enacts it wrongly.

For the most part European civilization diminished that division, elaborating Christ's sanctification of familial life at great and often repressive expense to his command for sacrificial conversion from earthly love. Ibsen grappled early with that social mollification of Christ's radical spirituality in *Brand*, in which humanist ethics and Christian absolutism both come up short as sources for happiness. He continued paying attention to the problem, transposing it in his later work into an opposition between expedient and principled worldly action. In *The Master Builder* he transposes the problem again, circling back to the religious issue of family-breaking transcendence that Brand experienced as a problem of adequate loving, but that Solness experiences as an existential problem besetting willful self-creation.

In Solness's life the cooperation between Aristotelian prudence and Christian waiting that draws the builder to Sisyphean familial duty appears primarily as expedient, oppressive corruption of artistic accomplishment. The radical advocacy of violent or naive alienation from social reality in the New Testament survived in Europe in variously marginal religious sects and in revolutionary political and intellectual forces. Those revolutionaries or philosophers who did not preserve religious authority for alienation gave it various pragmatic or conceptual validations. Ibsen's plays display a significant affinity for the Nietzschean innovation, which grounds hope for disengaged happiness in an aesthetic psychology centered on a self-creating, self-overcoming will to power. For all his fulminations against Christ, Nietzsche's theory of action as will to power preserves much of the formal logic of the radical prophecy of Jesus, especially the insistence on repudiation of worldly norms of value. Taking up humanism's explicit assimilation of Christ in his guilty, oppressive allegiance to Aline's death-in-life, Solness negatively demonstrates how clearly his chances for happiness lie in some pursuit of Nietzsche's transcendent theory of the will, which silently assimilates Christian radicalism while explicitly desecrating Jesus, his churches, and all their works.

Ragnar's entrance at Solness's second surrender to guilt shifts the ambiguous forces in Solness, moving him from damaging humanism to a confused, damaging exertion of will. With his father on the point of death Ragnar has come to ask some approval of his work from Solness, some commendation that he can carry back to soothe Brovik's death. When Solness violently puts him off with a command to leave off inquiry about his professional future, Ragnar forces the builder to confess that he has looked at the drawings. Solness makes no comment on their quality, and Ragnar dares him, with rhetorical questions, to pronounce explicitly the drawings and their author talentless. Evasive again, Solness advises Ragnar to keep working for him, offering him anything he wants, including marriage to Kaja and financial security, in exchange for the young man's abandoning any pursuit of an independent career. When Ragnar asks if he should report that bargain as comfort to his father, Solness wavers, guiltily telling him to say what he likes to Brovik then advising silence. This wavering gives way to Solness violently requiring Ragnar's compliance and imploring his forgiveness. In a paradoxical account of his adamant willfulness Halvard tells his apprentice: "I can't help it, Ragnar. I have no choice" (*MB*, 333).

Ragnar moves to take the drawings home, but Hilde stops him, saying she wants to see them. Solness allows the interference and sends Ragnar away with a second desperate, self-exculpating and fearful defense of his inability to act on the young man's behalf. Again, the defense comes in a command, which now displays more weakness than authority: "(*as though desperate*): Ragnar—you mustn't ask of me something I cannot do! Do you hear, Ragnar? You mustn't do that!" (*MB*, 334). Enigmatically polite, Ragnar agrees not to ask it, and exits with an ambiguous "I'm sorry," which neutrally acknowledges Solness's authority, tactfully and generously notes the master's suffering, and patiently expresses the young man's grief at being prevented by that sorrow from advancing his own career and so honoring and comforting his dying father.

In effect Solness commands Ragnar to follow him. Blocking Ragnar's professional advance and, consequently, diminishing Ragnar's power to comfort his dying father, the builder carries on that stalled confusion of familial and professional duty by which he feels he must live. Solness vindictively forestalls Ragnar's successful combination of those duties out of fear that the apprentice's success will prove the master's failure and stand, therefore, as an accusatory counterexample, as retribution. In all this confusion of Ragnar's predicament with his own, this refusal to allow familial duty any happy part in creative self-fulfillment, Solness dismally transfigures that liberating advocacy of transcendent sacrifice that Christ presents to the gospel's bereaved son: let the dead bury their dead (Luke 9: 59-60). Indeed, after Ragnar ignores Solness's offer, the builder reverses Christ's instruction and tells the aspiring son to go home to his father.

Christ's command promises joyous self-fulfillment for acceptance of its harsh distinction between duty to primary and secondary goods. Solness's weakly disguised plea that his apprentice deny his father, and himself, and take up perpetually subordinate worldliness as a means to happiness proffers a compound error as deliverance. First, no worldly life that constrains creativity, as Solness well knows, could possibly bring joy to Ragnar. Second, married love cannot compensate for such constraint, indeed only exacerbates it, as Solness also knows well. The builder's treacherous bargain would have Ragnar sell his artist's soul to gain an incommensurate worldly prize. And so Solness's diabolical reversal of Jesus' advocacy of sacrificial disengagement from the world also reenacts the nihilistic stratagem by which Mephistopheles seeks to wreck Faust's advance toward joy. Marring Jesus' action by reversing its moral logic and by transmuting it into Mephistopheles' ruinous fraud, Solness acts out that corrosive inversion of power against itself that Nietzsche found at the heart of Christian humanism. That inversion appears most clearly in Solness's repeated presentation of himself here not as active, but as powerless to carry out Ragnar's request. In this second appearance of the paired comparisons of Solness to Jesus and Faust, the builder's role changes from martyred victim to damaging authority. He acts toward Ragnar as the commanding savior, not the repudiated scapegoat, as the trickster instead of the tricked—all the while presenting himself as besieged by an offensive power. Ibsen keeps Solness unaware of the symbolic depiction of his power to act. With rare exceptions in Shakespeare, dramatic characters normally remain unaware of the formal properties depicting them, until Beckett's theater. Ibsen here uses that fact of theatrical representation— the stage's built-in split reality—to make a dramatic point about the problem in Solness's self-creation. Just as he doesn't know or control the formal conditions creating him in the theater, so he remains unaware, inside the play, of how to act positively. Trapped in humanistic morality, in which power appears only punitive to him, Solness cannot recognize the willful agency in his repression of Ragnar. While Solness disguises his will to power as penance and remorse, he cannot enact whatever transcendence from worldliness that blinded willfulness could make possible were it illumined.

Precisely such illumination waits for him, in fact begins as soon as Ragnar leaves. Hilde succeeds where Ragnar fails. Accomplishing the apprentice's wish for him and getting Solness to praise the drawings for Brovik's sake, she makes the builder do what he thinks he can't. That compulsion, ironically enough, inverts the inversion in the builder's will, turning him away from humanism's stasis, toward Nietzschean transcendence. The opposition of Hilde's and Ragnar's persuasive power over Solness in this act discloses many dimensions of the instability making Solness's self-creation an ongoing crisis of possible and impossible action. To put the matter philosophically, that crisis involves the problematic relation of identity and difference.[3] Ibsen presents that relation in psychologically realistic terms over which he superimposes a metaphysical opposition.[4] That complex superimposition makes for all the difficulty in staging, or understanding, this play. Much of the difficulty abates once the psychological terms come clear.

A professionally self-made man makes his will a preeminent worldly force and so generates out of himself the worldly resources and opportunities that advance his craft or enterprise. That creative action necessarily entails an opposite reaction, which the self-made man experiences internally as well as in relation to the existing worldly order. In the world, as in himself, the self-advancing agent progressively eliminates or nullifies reactive opposition, transforming it into the occasion for success. Relative to the world, the creative agent's self-advancement happily enacts self-preservations, as each successive projection of the agent's will masterfully establishes the agent as both means and end in any action undertaken. Identifying himself with a world he wills into being, the self-made agent closes what would otherwise be a ruinous gap between his projecting and projected will, his private and public life.

Considered internally, however—apart from the agent's public acts—self-advancement and self-preservation are more painfully at odds for the self-made man, and this interior gap proves more dangerous and more difficult to close. To make the world over in his image the self-made man must remake himself, must change an already accomplished identity into a projective one. The remaking involves reflexive unmaking, a simultaneous doing and undoing. The self-creating agent must either discover some hitherto unknown constituent force in himself or introduce a new one or combine the innovative actions. In any case the existing self will resist imposition of the new force. The already functioning self will likewise resist reconstruction, especially disruptive reconstruction through projection by an alien principle of identity into the alien, hostile worldly realm. It will resist defensively with anguish and paralysis. It will resist offensively with assaults on the self-creating agent's powers of discovery and invention. Ultimately, it will resist with chaotic disintegration.

While the self-creator's will may increase or diminish in the face of worldly resistance, it does not disintegrate, since such resistance does not constitute the will, but invokes it. When the creative agent wills a change in himself, in his psychic economy, he risks disintegration not only of his will but of his whole being, since he sets himself against himself. To overcome that resistance, to eliminate, nullify, or transmute any of the self's constituent forces, especially once they have been put on reactive alert, the new constituent force must exceed and compensate for the forces it displaces. To close the division in the self that it opens, to change from a principle of difference to a principle of unity, the new force must either contain an irresistible principle of developmental unity itself or be governed by some external one.

When the developmental unity belongs to the changing self, the willed change, however turbulent, enacts the creative agent's power alone. Operating continuously, that power turns division in the self from disintegration to growth, a process that subsumes self-preservation in self-advancement. When the developmental unity belongs to a force outside the self, when the self-creator wills transformation through invocation or submission to an external force, self advancement requires some disintegration. This case, continuous self-preservation, gives way to the apocalyptic renewal of conversion. The former inadequate or impeding composition of the self is not subsumed in the newly developed identity, as it was when change was growth, but erased, burned off by the refining fire of conversion, to put the matter biblically. Jesus' advocacy of rebirth and sacrificial repudiation of the natural man, "take no thought of your life," presents the apocalyptic continuity of this second kind of self-creation clearly. If you would act, identify yourself with a principle of developmental unity outside your present capacity to act; die to be born.

Successful self-creation requires that the agent overcome the world's resistance to his willed change and the reciprocal, internally nested resistance that this worldly willing arouses in the agent's psyche. Self-making can be balked, or undone, when the world exceeds the agent's force and stunts the agent's psychic growth or banishes the new developmental unity grafted to the agent in conversion. Conversely, the failure can emanate from within, if the agent cannot regulate his growth or maintain his new, grafted identity powerfully and coherently enough to make his self-advancing will a worldly force. In complex cases the failure can be reciprocally brought about by composite external and internal disequilibrium, which the agent experiences as weakness in himself. This last composite collapse can, like successful willing, occur gradually or can stall at any point of weakening strength, leaving the agent imperfectly powerful, unable to capitulate or revive.

Solness is so stalled when Hilde arrives. Telling his story to her, this self-made man discovers how worldly force has stunted his growth, how he has failed internally to manage the suprapsychic developmental identity ambiguously provided by the trolls, and how the externally and internally induced failures have trapped him in a stalemate. Hilde sees that divided psychic composition as offering the chance for resurgence of power; Solness, responding from the divided state, both believes and disbelieves her confident hopes for him. While Hilde hopes to make weakness strength, Ragnar hopes to diminish the builder's power. Consequently, Solness displays the authoritarian dimension of his weakness to the apprentice. Shifting to reactive self-assertion with this man, Solness coils the spring of resurgent self-creation that Hilde flicks into action as soon as Ragnar leaves. The creation of identity out of difference involves some time of division for the psyche. In this scene Ibsen shows how that division tends toward self-negation when the different identities forced into composition are both male, and how the division moves toward positive self-creation when the different identities in the composition are opposite genders. That sexual distinction bears metaphysical weight in *The Master Builder*, which should emerge clearly after analysis of Solness's fearful, world-bound identification with Ragnar.

For 13 years Solness has lived divided against himself, ambivalently and ambiguously balancing creative self-preservation and self-advancement through guilt. Criminal and judge in one, Solness uses guilt to stay alive. He has split himself into acceptable and unacceptable parts whose tense relation makes his life a disease. Approving Ragnar's creativity, Solness would be finally condemning and approving his own, breaking the stalemate of guilt, ending the disease, and so relinquishing his psychic integrity. That death, more than the professional fear of competition, prevents Solness's approval. While acknowledgment of the apprentice's talent implies endorsement of his professional future, Solness never complains that Ragnar will displace him financially or artistically. The young man's success threatens moral ruin, retribution, as Solness makes fearfully clear throughout the first two acts of this play. By act 3 the divine element of that retribution comes clear. At this point the psychological dimension is in play.

Creativity, as far as Solness is concerned, comes from the world of the trolls, who bestow it deceitfully, promising innocent glory in its achievement and exacting remorse and self-denial once it is achieved. Solness has weakly managed to control that remorse and self-denial through professional and marital machinations that keep success alive as self-imposed anguish. If he approves Ragnar's drawings, the builder not only wrecks the professional and marital machinations by which he remains prominent in a worldly way, and which he has been so busy preserving in the realistic dimension of the plot, but also relinquishes the weakness by which he controls his self-denying and self-preserving remorse. As long as he can punish himself with worldly machinations that preserve his success, Solness has not submitted utterly to the destructive power of the trolls. Once he gives those machinations up he relinquishes the role of judge and so wrecks the guilty compromise by which he has kept himself alive privately.

Approving Ragnar's drawings, Solness would be acknowledging that another man has become successfully creative without paying the troll's criminal price. That acknowledgment would stand as a final condemnation of his own self-creation. In it Solness would approve energetic self-advancement, which he has had to disapprove in himself. Judging Ragnar, Solness would also finally judge himself, this time by reference to the external, alien, opposed, and unassimilable standard of youth, rather than from within. No promise of self-advancement, however ambiguous, lies in judging Ragnar fit, as far as Solness is concerned. No second birth or reinvigoration lies in identification or endorsement of a new builder, only annihilation. If Solness heard music when he looked at Ragnar asking for approval, it would surely be Handel's retributive phrase from *The Messiah*, "and who shall stand when he appeareth."

In his fear that Ragnar will condemn him Solness has reversed one crucial dynamic in the normal sexual and professional competition between older and younger men. Like any older man, Solness does not want his authority exceeded or diminished by a youth's challenge. The difference here lies in what constitutes Solness's authority: not directly enacted power, but power turned against itself and so etiolated into something worse than weakness, into corrosive and life-denying stasis. Instead of maintaining a developmental relation between his needs and resources and the world's, Solness confines the interplay of needs and resources to a holding pattern in which neither he, nor anyone else, can advance through creativity or any other means. Perverse or proper, humanist praxis makes a ratio between an agent's possible action and the world's actual state. Rational orientation toward the world's goods, the hallmark of classical and Christian humanism, has devolved in Solness into machinations that sustain guilty self-presentation and eliminate any chance for happiness. Self-correcting action in the world has yielded to self-defeating defense against the world. That perversion of humanist praxis stands threatened by Ragnar's need to act happily, and, since Solness stays alive by means of that perversion, he cannot, as he desperately complains to Ragnar, help the young man.

Just as he cannot match his need for self-creation to the world's occasions for that event except through stifling penance, Solness cannot remain himself in the presence of another man except by stifling him. Development that comes through self-preserving and self-advancing adjustment to difference has ceased in Solness. Thus, he can only respond to the difference in Ragnar's masculine aspiration, its innocence and incipient mastery, by erasing it, turning it into balked submission identical to his own and controlled by him. The identification bears traces of the Oedipal crisis, especially in its mix of destruction and self-creation, but Ibsen doesn't stop at the familial psychology of the intergenerational conflict posed by Ragnar. Instead, he extrapolates and extends the apprentice's challenge into a test of the builder's adherence to humanist construction of his power to live creatively. That construction has led Solness to believe creative action requires destruction of others and therefore, according to the ethical and ontological law of balance that governs rational humanism, eventually requires destruction of the creator's power to act, ultimately of the creator himself.

Opposed to the Aristotelian and Christian humanism that makes Solness's creativity doomed error stands Nietzsche's voluntarism, in which the extravagant difference is Solness's power to create figures as transcendence from the humanist norm and not criminal destruction. Hilde urges Solness to identify himself by embracing the active difference that the trolls offer him, the extraordinary power to create ex nihilo as far as worldly opportunity goes. Her sexual allure, while it has a crucial role to play in the criminal familial tragedy Solness enacts in the Aristotelian dimension of the drama, also transposes the realistic ethical and psychological story into a spiritual, philosophical, and cultural struggle. In this second dimension, which overtakes the realistic one steadily as the play progresses, the artist's struggle to be reborn perpetually through exerting the indwelling and external power of creative activity presents Ibsen's modernist hope that the theater might not only represent reality, as Aristotle required, but transform it, as Nietzschean aesthetics urged. Hilde's different gender beckons Solness to a different kind of being from any he has yet enacted. At the realistic level Ibsen signals that call to "the impossible," the transcendent order, by having Hilde interfere with Solness's oppression of Ragnar. In the next scene she temporarily succeeds in breaking Solness's allegiance to humanist guilt, and its strategic subsuming of radical change and difference under the punitive law of retribution, by seducing him into approving Ragnar's drawings. The motion forward comes through her revision of his justification for suppressing Ragnar, a revision that focuses directly on the relation of creativity, conscience, and desire.

When Hilde calls Solness cruel, vicious, and beastly for suppressing Ragnar, Solness defends himself by saying he paid dearly for the professional position that allows and requires him to keep Ragnar from working independently. She thinks he refers only to the domestic happiness whose loss he has already explained to her, but Solness tells her he has paid with peace of mind and now reveals the active role he believes he played in destroying Aline's house. Before the fire Solness regularly and hopefully imagined it would occur, internally picturing the cause and scene of the blaze repeatedly and in great detail. The fantasy consistently included Aline's comfort as efficient cause of the fire and consistently included her witnessing the event with him. Assuming Solness attributes the blaze to his powers of telekinesis, which the two of them have confirmed in this act and the first one, Hilde asks if the hoped-for cause, a cracked chimney, in fact brought about the disaster. When Solness tells her the fire started across the house from that chimney, in a linen room, Hilde demands that the builder make sense of his guilt over the fantasy. He does so with this account of telekinesis and the will's power to invoke paranormal forces of change:

> Solness(confidentially): Don't you think, Hilde, that there are people singled out by fate who have been endowed with grace and power to wish for something, desire it so passionately, *will* it so inexorably that, ultimately, they must be granted it? Don't you think so?
>
> Hilde (*with an enigmatic expression in her eyes*): If that is so, the time will come when we shall see if I am one of them.
>
> Solness: No man can achieve such things alone. Oh, no. There are—helpers and servers—who must be at our side if we are to succeed. But they never come of their own accord. One must call on them with all one's strength. Silently, you understand. (*MB*, 336)

Clearly, Solness regards his fantasies of the fire as the fatalistic call of his creative destiny to those helpers. The heroic, religious terms ascribed to his will balanced against the necessity for strenuous supplication of the demanding helpers display an ambiguity in Solness's understanding of creative power, an ambivalent pride and remorse that recombine in every dimension of his self-creating narrative. Only he was gifted, strong, persistent, and humble enough to deserve and compel the helpers to start his career. Deserving special dispensation for his admirable desire to enact the extraordinary grace and power of his artistic vision, Solness simultaneously merits special punishment for summoning murderous assistance for his advance. The builder concludes his account of the guilty expiation exacted for his courageous pursuit of innocently bestowed creativity with the following remark: "(*In increasing turmoil*): This is what people call being lucky. But I'll tell you how it feels to be lucky! It feels as though the skin had been flayed from my breast. And the helpers and servers go round taking the skin from other people's bodies to cover the wound. But it can't be healed. Never, never! Oh, if you only knew how it burns sometimes" (*MB*, 337).

This metaphor condenses psychological, ethical, and ontological varieties of that negating relation of identity and difference that keeps self-creation an unsatisfactory, incomplete action for Solness. The skin he has lost is humanist praxis, rationally lawful matching of his power to the world's. Instead of glorying in that sacrificial repudiation of the world's norms, one possible response to the metaphoric martyrdom implied in the flaying image, Solness shuns his new birth. He concentrates only on the unhealing wound, the negative difference between the disruptive Nietzschean action of aesthetic self-creation and the integrating Aristotelian action, in which power advances not apocalyptically but through balanced interchange of potency and act. Failure of nerve has stalled him, has turned his power away from creativity and delivered him into the longing weakness of recrimination.

Solness's nostalgia for Aristotelian interchange stems from and magnifies his remorse for calling on the Nietzschean helpers. Under that compulsion he can only experience the organically developmental relation of identity and difference that governs humanistic praxis as gruesome and unsuccessful grafting of other people's skin onto his wound. He cannot live with others and help them achieve happiness, only draw their chance for happiness into his guilty machinations to stay impotently powerful. Aline, Brovik, Kaja, and Ragnar have all been flayed by the helpers for his sake, and none of the sacrifices have closed the gap in his identity, none have integrated the opposed humanist and Nietzschean principles of change according to which he paralytically enacts himself. Of course, Solness has done the flaying, as the realistic dimension of the play indicates. His refusal to acknowledge that, which surfaced so clearly in the previous scene with Ragnar, displays clearly the self-denying strategy by which guilt perversely enacts the Aristotelian law of self-preservation.

Given that Nietzschean self-creation involves projection of the existing self, and summoning of an imagined one, it makes sense for Solness to reverse that projection when he thinks of himself in the guilty Aristotelian mode, to project the agency and destructiveness of his creativity onto the helpers, as he does in the flaying metaphor. When he lapses from the logic of free power to the logic of power inverted against itself that this metaphor displays, Solness enacts his role as tragic humanist hero, simultaneously exonerating and chastising his self-creation, making hamartia the ruinous divider and unifier of possible and actual ends in his life. Conscience rules in the inversion of power against itself, and it is Solness's conscience that Hilde assails in order to free the builder, Ragnar, and herself from the anguish that blocks them all from the joyful experience of free creative power. Acting under the law of conscience, of moral obligation, means dividing power into good and evil, and Hilde has to confront Solness on that issue to free him. For the remainder of the scene she counters his ambivalent analysis of trolls and helpers as ambiguous moral agents with a steady insistence, sexually presented, on the supramoral obligation he has to her and himself joyfully to exceed the confining logic of humanism and pursue the apocalyptic necessity of transcendence.

She begins by telling Solness that his suffering does not display madness, as the world and he presume, but, rather, a weak conscience. This diagnosis acknowledges guilt and dismisses it at once by eliminating virtue as an evaluative principle in conscience and substituting strength. The proper functioning of conscience, she argues, should be willful acknowledgment and affirmation of self-creation's difficult choices and the pain they may bring. When Solness asks if Hilde has such a "robust conscience," she tells him that she came to him in pursuit of his decade-old promise, despite the pain of departing from the father she is "frightfully fond of" (MB, 338). Solness ignores the courage and sanity displayed in Hilde's successful separation from father love. He will not acknowledge that she has joyfully distinguished competing goods and chosen the higher without grumbling at the cost or destroying the lesser good. Just as he could not allow Ragnar to integrate successfully loving devotion to his father with self-creation, he cannot allow that Hilde has happily separated those actions.

Mired in a continued, and largely imagined, creative offense against his own paternity, Solness cannot contemplate the woman's father rightfully abandoned or allow the apprentice's father to be honored properly by his son's professional success. Embedded in the opposed psychosexual prohibitions he feels against taking on the symbolic role of surpassed father vis à vis the young woman and the young man is the more fundamental opposition of power directly enacted and inverted against itself, the divisive unity of identity and difference in his self-creation that keeps Solness moribund. To acknowledge either of the youths' paternal relations requires him to abandon that division, to father himself in a way he refuses, preferring weakness. Such fathering is precisely what Hilde gets him to accomplish by the end of this scene, in which she turns Ragnar's presentation of youth as retribution into a re-presentation of Solness's youth to him, this time as a new chance for self-creation. For that change to occur Solness must first make the sexual identification with Hilde, which he could not make with Ragnar. When she first mentions her father, however, Solness cannot take up the sexual dimension of her sacrifice of family life. It takes her direct presentation of the willfulness of that sacrifice to bring Solness into the confessional sequence that will end in his turn toward freedom with her.

She makes that direct presentation only when Solness obtusely tries to graft her situation onto his, as he did with Ragnar, only when he tries to take some skin from her to cover his wound. Continuing his guilty projective elimination of the saving difference distinguishing her familial story from his, he asks if something wrong at home prompted her exile. Hilde forgoes insisting on the courage of her familial sacrifice and answers that she was driven and tempted to seek out Solness by an irresistible internal force. The ambiguity of her response lies in its formal relation to Solness's question. Hilde does not say she was wrong to heed the internal force, but she does not say she was right to either. She ignores the moral dimension altogether, offering her zeal as proof of the quest's unimpeachable necessity. Solness, however, imposes the moral dimension on her response immediately. He elides his attempted identification with her through the presumption of familial conflict, which Hilde has dismissed, into a new statement of their true, tragically exalted identity as self-creators. And he transposes the denied domestic "wrong" into a spiritual one that plagues such self-advancement. Repeating his analysis of the mixed humanist/voluntarist nature of self-creation, he further enhances his moral confinement by adding ethical and ontological ambiguity to his description of the helpers.

> Hilde (*earnestly*): This thing inside me drove me to come here. Tempted and drove me.
> Solness (*eagerly*): That's it! That's it, Hilde! There's a troll in you, too; the same as in me. And it's the troll, you see, that calls to the powers outside! And we have to submit whether we like it or not.
> Hilde: I begin to think you're right, master builder.
> Solness: (*paces the floor*): Oh, there are so many invisible demons in the world, Hilde. (*Stops.*) Good demons and evil demons. Fair demons and dark. If only one always knew whether it was the fair that had hold of one, or the dark! (*Starts walking again.*) Ha, ha! It would all be so simple.
> Hilde (*watches him as he walks*): Or if only one had a really brash and hearty conscience! So that one dared to do what one wanted. (*MB*, 338)

Hilde concedes here to Solness's description of self-creation as irresistibly projective, as conversion rather than growth, but she resists his moral analysis of the external principle at work in that projection. The concession and resistance both show the play's Nietzschean logic overtaking humanism. Solness believes the personal and professional charisma and authority of his activity as maestro derive from occult forces that duplicate the moral opposition governing action in the mundane sphere. Success means aligning personal power with the virtuous demons, who transfer generative power, through the creator, from one realm to the other. Failure comes from submitting personal power to the evil demons, who transfer destructive power through the creative maestro to his mundane sphere. In either case this view of creative activity, even though it exceeds the known orders governing the balanced interchange of resources and needs, rests on the Aristotelian concept of energeia, according to which action brings about systematic, lawful change. When he calls his drive to exceed the self given by nature and culture an indwelling "troll," Solness expresses a Nietzschean conception of the will as transcendent. So long as he describes that transcendent impulse as directed to and by external powers superior to the self calling on them, Hilde agrees with the master builder. As soon as Solness lapses from that Nietzschean view into humanist reduction of the constitutive external power, into morally divisive inversion of creative will into good and evil kinds, she immediately asserts the Nietzschean position that will justifies itself. That position eventually wins the builder over, but he resists for a while longer.

The scenario of creativity Solness delineates for Hilde recalls the humanistic, Aristotelian worldview that governs Prospero's charismatic status as magus, master knower, in Shakespeare's *The Tempest*. In both plays a partially defeated maestro strives, largely for the sake of a nubile woman, to turn his ambiguous mastery of the occult realm into a means for restoring generative praxis in the mundane one. One telling difference lies in how Shakespeare and Ibsen conceive and present the maestro's power to control and move between the two realms. Shakespeare presents Prospero as possessing an indwelling rationality sufficient for distinguishing between successful and ruinous alignment of his power with the laws governing and binding the two realms. Ibsen presents Solness in search of such internal coherence. Lacking the unimpeded expression that Prospero's wisdom gives to power, Solness remains stymied. He confronts Hilde fearfully divided between the voluntarist conviction that a creator's transcendent willing governs occult and mundane creativity and the rationalist conviction that these realms govern the creative agent's will and sometimes do so without the authority of his informed consent.

Whereas Shakespeare's action displays copious coherence, with Prospero restoring political, familial, natural, and supernatural orders to lawful *prosperity*, Ibsen's displays multiple crises, with Solness caught in the ambiguous stasis of resisting and requiring change in all his relationships and circumstances. When Hilde tells him creativity would be simple if he abandoned moral analysis of projected and indwelling power and trusted desire to be its own authority and guarantor of happiness, she offers him the Nietzschean way out of his humanist confinement in conscience. As Miranda provides the occasion for Prospero's active undoing of his confining power, Hilde provides the opportunity for Ibsen's maestro to relinquish power that maintains half-life. The different sexual dynamics in these calls for transformation display radical differences in the two play's conceptions and presentations of action, differences that make comparing them instructive.

Miranda never asks her father to carry out the benevolent magical violence by which he manages simultaneously to marry her and restore himself to his appropriate ruling office in distant Milan. Nature and wisdom urge him to the deed. Acting under the correctly understood rule of both, Prospero virtuously enacts the generative order that his daughter's dawning sexuality innocently and unconsciously manifests. The convulsion in nature he makes through calling on occult forces subsumes the existing order into a higher one, develops rather than destroys. His paternal creativity bestows life a second time, and more abundantly on all those dependents, resistant and compliant, under its control and on him. Desire has much more ambiguous effects in Ibsen's world. Instead of innocently allowing for an integrating action from this play's maestro, a young woman's desire explicitly urges Solness to transcend worldly norms, not to subsume them, but to exceed them through resuming the cast-off Nietzschean will to power and aesthetic self-creation that she embodies. Ibsen presents the offense of that challenge to the Aristotelian norms by which Solness maintains his natural and cultural identity as the double crime of incest and adultery.

Solness is grievously convinced that his willful creativity is a crime of and against paternity, one that he builds empty nurseries to expiate. In addition to her realistic presence as a discrete dramatic person, the play repeatedly presents Hilde as a telepathically generated embodiment of Solness's criminal willfulness, a nordic Athena supranaturally born from the ruined creativity of this will-sick Jove. That transcendent, mythically familial identity with Solness, read against her claim that she, like the builder, feels compelled to leave her natural father behind to enact irresistible transcendence called for by an indwelling troll, indicate that Ibsen has embedded an account of metaphysical transgression in the complex transformation of *Oedipus Rex, Theogony,* and the melodramatic nineteenth-century adultery intrigue that Hilde and Solness gingerly carry out in this play.

When he makes his magical masterpiece by accomplishing Miranda's marriage, Prospero perfects his knowledge and power by aligning them exhaustively and beneficially with the given order lawfully binding disparate realms of reality. Marrying his daughter to a prince, he marries himself to his previous cultural station. He subsequently relinquishes his magic because it has nothing substantial left to do anywhere in the natural or supernatural world. Solness cannot enact such harmony because he has put himself on the wrong side of Aristotelian praxis by imperfectly mixing it with transgressive, voluntarist self-creation. Hilde calls on him not to bind disparate orders of reality lawfully but, rather, to cast off the inferior realm of nature and culture and take up the superior good of self-justifying will to creative power. The transposition of Solness's wounded desire to resume that creative power into forbidden sexual desire in the play's realistic marital and professional intrigues displays his mixed commitment to voluntarism and humanism. The displaced spur to incest she presents in the marriage plot makes sexually symbolic the prohibition Solness maintains against the self-justifying, and self-generating, creativity of Nietzschean will to power. The threat of adultery in her call to action gives symbolic sexual presentation to the fact that Solness, who has maintained himself by an adulterous corrupting submission of desire to obligation, cannot conceive a clean break from that stasis, can only imagine partial, negative defection from it.

From her Nietzschean perspective the transgression Hilde calls for is neither incestuous nor adulterous but a spiritually virgin new birth. To father himself and her, Solness has to break that unity symbolically presented in the taboo on incest and adultery; he has to exceed the limits of Aristotelian obligation to balanced, rational matching of resources and needs in creativity and return to the previous freedom of self-governing, self-creating will to artistic power. The sexual dynamic of Hilde's filial authority over Solness's power inverts the metaphysics embedded in Shakespeare's philosophical marriage plot. She does not innocently occasion the father's subsuming alignment of his power to reality, as Miranda did. Instead, she seductively requires the father to will the real creatively for her sake and for his, with no integrating principle other than desire for authority. For Hilde and Solness that desire remains a motive without a deed or, more exactly, a motive sublimated into her call for a deed from him: that he carry out the promise, sexually engendered a decade ago, to give her a kingdom.

That Miranda receives a kingdom because her father sees reality calling to him in her unvoiced need and that Hilde must variously seduce, cajole, and demand her kingdom from a resistant symbolic father fearfully, imperfectly, longing for the real shows the crucial difference between the convulsive actions of Shakespeare's metaphysical romance and Ibsen's. While the change sex calls for requires disruption in Prospero's world, it can be enacted with benevolent intelligence that never requires violation of natural, cultural, or metaphysical law. The change sexually called for in Solness's world cannot be enacted through the builder's benevolent intelligence until he violates his negative submission to anachronistic natural, cultural, and metaphysical law. Solness takes his first step toward embracing violence as deliverance by asking if Hilde has read Norway's romantic, nationalist Viking sagas. When she says she has, in a past life when reading mattered to her, Solness suggestively recounts his admiration for those amoral ancestral men of action, who created joyful lives by conquest instead of wisdom, by rape, plunder, burning, and killing.

He aims to discover how much robustness of conscience Hilde expects from him and discovers, when she eagerly adds sexual conquests to the Viking accomplishments he lists, that her hopes are not timid. He tests her sexual bravado twice, telling her that the Vikings were trolls to their captive women, which Hilde, with eyes half-closed, calls exciting, and asking her directly whether she could live happily with such a brutal man. She responds she could if she grew fond of the man. Solness carries out this allusive, literary seduction somewhat gingerly, unsure throughout of how much of Hilde's passion this coded reference to the Viking sagas accurately identifies. She settles the matter decisively in the following exchange, in which she grafts the metaphysical problem of self-creation, which Solness has reintroduced by mentioning the trolls, into the builder's irresolute performance as seducer in a melodramatic adultery intrigue.

> *Solness:* Could you grow fond of a man like that?
> *Hilde:* Oh, God, one can't help whom one grows fond of, can one?
> *Solness (looks at her thoughtfully):* No, no—I suppose it's the troll in us that decides that.
> *Hilde (with a little laugh):* And all these blessed demons you know so much about. The fair and the dark.
> *Solness (warmly and quietly):* I hope the demons choose kindly for you, Hilde.
> *Hilde:* They have chosen for me. Once and for all. (*MB*, 339-40)

Until her last line Solness can, and in a good performance should, maintain a tone of fatherly admonition and instruction while he engages Hilde in this coy, sexually charged analysis of their response to romantic, nationalistic literary celebration of robust conscience. Fascinated by the innocent familial happiness of the Vikings—"When they came home, they ate and drank, and were as merry as children" (*MB*, 339)—he never forgets that they rape and murder to establish their kingdoms. When he asks if Hilde would willingly live with such a man, the question should simultaneously display his rejection of and longing for such masculine force in his own life, should proclaim his warning that she shun any man who would offer that and his urging that she encourage it in him and shun him as long as he cannot offer it. The climax of this ambivalence comes when Solness retreats from the sexual field with the strongly paternal wish that the demons will act benevolently when they choose Hilde a mate.

His transposition of moral value—"kindness"—into Hilde's assertion that sexual joy is an amoral destiny and his refusal to choose that destiny, after teasing her with it, are the most refined corruption of the joy of life Solness has made so far. In the moment he makes it Hilde transposes the builder's refined denial of transcendence into rapturous affirmation and turns the play toward its resolution. When she tells him that the demons have already, irrevocably, chosen for her, she dismisses the father who prefers the compromised conscience of civilized moral life and commandingly isolates the self-creating suitor, the spiritual Viking. Seizing the sexual initiative from Solness, eliminating his moralistic resistance, Hilde transgressively and transcendently takes up the conventionally masculine prerogatives of adulterous seducer and virtuous suitor to encourage Solness to exceed cultural convention in the same way himself.

In this double inversion the young woman's demanding assertion of masculine force symbolically renders the builder female, seduced as well as seducing, self-creator. That Solness must pass through such psychic conversion, such doubling, in order to retrieve his manly creativity joyously, shows Ibsen shifting the play's balance from Aristotle's ideas of systematic natural and cultural praxis toward Nietzschean action, in which apocalyptic power gives birth to itself for itself. That shift recurs more drastically in the final moments of the scene, in which Hilde explicitly reverses the terms of her arrival and presence in Solness's life and presents herself as munificently bestowing creative power on him, instead of seductively requiring it of him. This last inversion vitiates the Aristotelian logic of tragic recognition, according to which Solness has identified youth with retribution, and enhances the builder's Nietzschean will to power. In that logic Solness identifies youth with Hilde's unwavering creative purpose and sees her demand for a kingdom as the return of his lost power to create with no resources except his will's—to do, once more, what the humanist order destructively calls the "impossible."

The following dialogue follows Hilde's direct assertion that the demons controlling creativity have chosen Solness as her destiny:

> Solness (looks deep into her eyes): Hilde—you are like a wild bird of the forest.
> Hilde: Far from it. I'm not shy.
> Solness: No, no. There's more of the falcon in you.
> Hilde: Yes—perhaps. (Violently.) And why not a falcon? Why shouldn't I go hunting, too? Get the prey I want? If only I can get my claws into it! Bring it to the ground!

Solness: Hilde—do you know what you are?

Hilde: Yes, I'm a strange kind of bird.

Solness: No. You are like a new dawn. When I look at you, it is as though I were watching the sunrise.

Hilde: Tell me, master builder—are you sure you've never called to me? Silently?

Solness (quietly): I think I must have done.

Hilde: What do you want from me?

Solness: Your youth, Hilde.

Hilde (smiles): Youth, which you are so frightened of?

Solness (nods slowly): And which, in my heart, I long for. (*MB*, 340)

The subject here remains "robust conscience." Solness drops the evasive camouflage of literary self-presentation and switches from imagining himself as a Viking to imagining Hilde first as *an* animate and then as *the* animate force of nature. In his first metaphoric rendition of her as a wild forest bird Solness continues the romantic, magical idealization of will that he hesitantly approached in the Viking analogy, dropping all the violence, assigning Hilde only delicate inspirational mystery. When, under her correction, Solness adds some measure of destructive violence to her inspired sense of purpose, Hilde magnifies the violence immediately. Her remark that she has every prerogative to seek her goal as a falcon seeks prey, to achieve her end by clawing Solness's creative will to the ground, prefigures the violent death she eventually brings to Solness by requiring him to climb the spire of his new house and inadvertently causing him to fall from it.

But at this point neither of the enraptured pair knows that willing, even violently willing, is anything but all-powerful joy. As if shy of the implication of fatal savagery in the falcon metaphor, Solness switches figures once he hears Hilde proclaim herself a hunter. He turns robust conscience from a raptor plummeting greedily to the ground into the life-giving sun rising at dawn from the earth's horizon. This metaphor transposes her inspirational force out of the occult world of demons and trolls and renders it the preeminent active force in nature. Hilde restores the occult dimension of her power when she stops Solness's projective identification with her through nature metaphors and forces him to acknowledge his telepathic summoning of her. The last time Solness acknowledged his use of this occult power to cause change at a distance (the burning of Aline's house), he portrayed the act as a crime against nature and civilization. The vengeance of those orders against his magical summoning of the demons, he fears, will be retributive professional supplanting of him by a virtuously successful, civilized youth.

Hence, his suppression of Ragnar. Under the authority of his sublimated sexual adoration for Hilde, Solness acknowledges that, summoning her youth, he willed an opposed consequence for artistic self-creation via the occult powers: a chance to regain the robust conscience that they previously enhanced, and which he has mortified. After too long a sacrifice of his happiness through guilty, weak submission to the humanistic order of rationally managed cause and effect, the stony heart that has made life anguish for Solness, which he provocatively displayed to Ragnar in Hilde's disapproving presence, now calls out to her for new life.

Having finally overcome all the strategies of evasion and resistance in Solness's ambiguously confining and delivering narration of his self-creation and mastered the builder's conception of power through sexual arousal of it, Hilde now forces Solness to enact that power. She moves from the table where they have been conversing to retrieve Ragnar's portfolio and requires Solness to approve the drawings. Solness lapses immediately into his old resistance, repeating his fear that Ragnar's rise will mean his retributive fall, again associating his rise with crimes against paternity, this time against the elder Brovik's career and hopes for his son. Additionally, he now fears that the occult powers will not lend their force to him to create again, this in direct contradiction of his rapturous hope expressed moments before. When she tells him that he will have to manage without them, if it comes to that, Hilde presents Solness the supreme Nietzschean model of transcendence— that power apocalyptically overcomes each of its successive configurations— and hopes the builder will enact it. He does not. Instead, he reinstates his fearful, passive view of the occult, which was so recently joyous confidence, in a doomed retreat to his habitually confining association of creativity with tragic offense against civilization. He replaces the sun metaphor, by which he hopefully identified Hilde's magical youth as an irresistibly natural force that would bring new effect out of old cause, with another natural figure, the turning of the tide of his life. This image changes the self-governing regeneration of his sunlike self-creation into oscillating purposeless reaction, into passive, mechanical transition from high to low, into submission to unwilled, unopposable law.

The builder's lapse provokes the following reaction from Hilde:

> Solness: Hopeless, Hilde. The tide will turn. Sooner or later. Retribution will come.
> Hilde (frightened, puts her hands over her ears): Don't talk like that! Do you want to take away from me what I value more than my life?
> Solness: And what's that?

Hilde: To see you great! See you with a wreath in your hand! High, high up
   on a church tower! (*Calm again.*) Well, at least you must have a pencil.
   Give it to me.
Solness: (*takes out his notebook*): Yes, I've got one here. (*MB,* 341-342)

Born great, having achieved and corrupted greatness, Solness here has
greatness thrust upon him. Rather than joyfully willing his deliverance from
the guilty view that murder gave birth to and compromised his greatness,
Solness sacrifices that view to avoid a second kind of murder, a transposed
spiritual destruction of Hilde's transcendent longing for his magnanimous
self-creation. He releases Ragnar to preserve Hilde.

Acting under obligation to another person, or even under obligation to
oneself projectively identified with another person, is not acting from
unimpeded, self-justifying desire and power—the Nietzschean cause and end
of happiness—but reactive submission to the divisive moral law by which
humanist praxis diminishes power and engenders misery. When she asks if
Solness *wants* to destroy her spiritual life by relinquishing his greatness, Hilde
turns the builder's reactive submission away from moralism and puts it under
the sway of transcendent willing. Once she has converted his weakness to
her cause Hilde must make it strength; she must transform the power binding
her to Solness from an obligating command into liberating inspiration. She
inverts her inversion of the builder's reversed will to power, to speak in
Nietzschean terms, by repeating her memory of his ascent of the church spire
at the end of the act. Ibsen has presented the eternal return of the same
negatively throughout this act, as Solness's constant and ever-abating justification of his past under the pressure of Hilde's interrogation. Once Solness
lets the justification go, Ibsen presents the positive potential of Nietzsche's
unfailing opportunity for affirmative self-creation positively by changing the
builder's fearful praxis into promissory assent to Hilde's joyful willing that
the past become the future. Her demand that he free Ragnar for her sake
correctively isolates and exhausts Solness's moralism; her dangerous vision
of him high atop a church tower, like his vision of Aline's burning house,
telepathically generates his self-creation.

While he approves Ragnar's drawings, Solness asks Hilde once more
what she wants to follow from that action, and she answers, "I want my
kingdom" (*MB,* 343). The amoral self-generating power of the Vikings, the
transcendently robust conscience of Christian identification with imminent
and immanent reality, and the dangerous force of sexual abandon aroused by
creativity all make up Hilde's kingdom. To bestow that realm on Hilde,
Solness must realign himself with those forces. In act 3 this artist's projective

recreation of identity, the disruptive, dangerous combination of imminent and immanent power that makes up his aesthetic willing, makes its final assault on the systematic developmental change of rationalist praxis, whose ordered and intelligible serenity Solness has converted to paralysis. Act 2 closes with a split account of Solness's first, failed rebellion against praxis: the church spire ascent at Lysanger, which culminated in his telepathic seduction of Hilde ten years ago. Hilde wills an affirmative reenactment of the ascent and seduction when she suggests Solness should hoist the wreath on his new house himself. Solness submits to the inspiring suggestion, as he submitted to the transforming command to free Ragnar, with more affirmation than he expressed under the command but still expressing residual, weak obedience to the logic of obligation. Act 2 has proceeded by transposing the inversion in Solness's will over and over again, upward to transcendent Nietzschean willing. It ends masterfully in this mixed affirmation of his originally imperfect transcendence at Lysanger.

As Solness adds his approbation to Ragnar's portfolio, Aline returns. Solness asks Aline to take the portfolio out to Kaja, but Hilde intervenes, eager to keep control of her project. In Aline's presence Solness dismisses Kaja, telling her she must leave his service to look after her future husband's new professional and personal needs. Aline assumes immediately that Solness will replace one adulterous servant with another, and the builder and Hilde ambiguously toy with the offended wife's habitual reproach. With Ragnar dismissed the only guilty machination, the only invocation of retribution left to Solness, is the misleading adultery intrigue that he and Aline have substituted for sexual life between them. In the following exchange Hilde wraps the builder's adultery masquerade into the authentically delivering challenge her unanswered desire presents. With that reversal, Ibsen starts the third act's culminating transformation of Solness's guilty action into dangerous Nietzschean self-overcoming.

> Mrs. Solness: But how can you manage without her? Oh, I see. You've something else up your sleeve, haven't you, Halvard?
>
> Hilde (gaily): Well, I'm no good for standing at desks, anyway.
>
> Solness: I shall manage somehow, Aline. You must make arrangements for moving into our new home as soon as possible. This evening we shall hoist the wreath—(turns to Hilde)—to the top of the spire. What do you say to that, Miss Hilde?
>
> Hilde (looks at him excitedly): It'll be so marvelous to see you standing high up there again!
>
> Solness: Me!

Mrs. Solness: Oh God, Miss Wangel, you mustn't think of it! My husband gets
   dizzy. He has no head for heights.
Hilde: Dizzy? I don't believe it.
Mrs. Solness: Oh, yes, he's always been like that.
Hilde: But I've seen him myself high up on the top of a church steeple.
Mrs. Solness: Yes, I've heard people talk about that. But it's impossible.
Solness (violently): Impossible, yes! But nevertheless, I stood up there!
Mrs. Solness: How can you say that, Halvard? You hardly even dare to go out
   on to the balcony on the second floor. You've always been like that.
Solness: You may think otherwise this evening. (*MB*, 344-45)

For all its diminishing confinement the fantasized and falsely projected
role of seducer has kept Solness mysteriously attractive. Neither Aline nor
Solness want that vestige of sexual energy to vanish from their marriage, and
so both move immediately to reinstate it once Kaja, who helped sustain the
fantasy, is dismissed. Aline has only masochistic reasons for casting Hilde as
the new sexual offender. Solness has ambiguous damage in mind when he
boldly encourages his wife's suspicion by officiously dismissing it. He wants
to go on hurting her for making him feel guilty; he wants to go on innocently
hurting himself, and so continue expiating his offense against her. That
complex damage maintains his Aristotelian action. He also wants to pursue
the freedom Hilde's frank desire has led him to, and so he allows the
insinuation of adultery to stand as a promise to Hilde that he will finally do
the liberating damage to his ethical confinement that she has called for, and
which he has partially enacted by freeing Ragnar and Kaja. Hilde intends
unambiguous damage to the guilty sexual machination the spouses variously
enact and to the paralytic moralism that supports it. She carries out that
damage by invoking more of the builder's power than he puts at her disposal
in his magisterial, recklessly coy request for her approval.

That Solness boldly requires Hilde to encourage and admire his command that Aline prepare for immediate removal to the compensatory new
house, that he fully expects gratitude as well as praise from Hilde, indicates
that the builder remains divided against himself, that his will to power is not
yet self-generating. The sexual scenario that his ambiguous command and
offer creates around the two women clearly displays his will's division
between self-negating and self-creative identification with duty and desire.
Hilde immediately takes charge of the ambiguity, as she has done all along,
and turns it from devious maintenance of guilt into dangerous inspiration to
defy the moribund safety of his falsely criminal marriage. When she deliberately or mistakenly revises Solness's plan for consecrating his changed life by

assuming aloud that he has announced his intention to climb his new home's spire and hoist a wreath there himself, Hilde changes the imagined thrill of moral danger tingling in the builder's coded, promissory boast into the most drastic thrill of all: the threat of death.

That reversal provokes Aline's prudential response that Solness cannot and never has lived that way, that he has no "head for heights." What began for Solness as a would-be roué's preening has lapsed into a struggle between an emasculating wife and a provocative child-bride for control of the builder's sexual will. The division in his will has reproduced itself as a Scylla and Charybdis choice in the physical, social realm. Traduced, delivered to that choice by power enacted in fantasy, by vanity and sexual bravado, Solness decides to risk death and so try for immediate mastery of life, power's most highly developed action. Inspired by Hilde's Nietzschean will, he affirms his power to ascend the full height of his own spire, even though he fears doing so. He violently repudiates the emasculating wife and her prudence, reminding Aline that he has already accomplished the dangerous climb she calls impossible once before and implying that he will do so again that evening. Vowing that God and the doctor, the alpha and omega of religious and rational authority for prudence, will help her prevent Solness from carrying out his dangerous action, Aline exits. In the last moments of the act Solness and Hilde associate his imminent impossible action with affirmative willing of the past. Identifying the new spire with the church tower at Lysanger, associating both ascents with unimpeded desire for sublimely dangerous aesthetic self-creation, they clearly oppose Nietzschean power to Aristotelian praxis.

But the lingering division in Solness's will shows up even in these last moments. Hilde refuses to acknowledge that Solness suffers from the physical limitations Aline fearfully describes, and Solness, committed by self-esteem to bravado and to its higher expression, courage, will not acknowledge them. When Hilde casts his physical weakness as defective will, the builder, instead of remonstrating with her, says, "I begin to think there is nothing in me that is safe from you" (MB, p. 346). The remark balances reluctance and longing to accede to Hilde in equal measure. Hilde annuls the reluctance by ignoring it and turns to look longingly through a window (as Mrs. Alving and Rebecca West also did) onto the site of transcendent liberation from domestic confinement. Looking from one house to another with her, Solness changes the emphasis from his climbing the new tower to Hilde living in its nursery. This hoped-for domestic arrangement continues his adultery plan, ensures that his youthful inspiration will stay nearby, symbolically resolves his ambivalent guilt and glory over artistic crimes of and against paternity, and is a means to distract her from her dangerous demand as one would distract an overeager child, by switching toys, giving her a room to avoid his climb.

Childlike thinking—specifically resistance against acknowledging moral or physical impediments to willed desire, resistance that takes the shape of stubbornness, cheerfully ingenious scheming, self-conscious deviousness, obsessive perseverance, and rapturous creative fantasy—presents Hilde's Nietzschean willing in realistic psychological terms here. A modern Greek proverb advises that promises to God and children must never be broken. In the next act Solness makes clear what his broken promise to himself, made atop the Lysanger tower ten years ago, had to do with God and children. In this exchange Hilde prevents him from fearfully breaking the promise he made to her when she was a child. For the curtain of act 2 Ibsen casts the delirium of Nietzschean willing as a childish game that Hilde won't allow Solness not to play, which Solness cannot fully enter. The ambiguity and resistance in familial identification across generations and the analogous ambiguity and resistance in sexual identification across generations, superimposed one on the other in the symbolic and realistic action of this finale, present the last stages of the struggle anachronistic rationalism makes against fledgling voluntarism in Solness.

> Solness (*goes closer*): You could live up there, Hilde. In the highest room in the tower. You could live there like a princess.
> Hilde (*enigmatically, half-seriously, half-jesting*): Yes, that's what you promised me.
> Solness: Did I?
> Hilde: For shame, master builder! You said you'd make me a princess, and that you would give me a kingdom. And then you took me and—Well?
> Solness (*gently*): Are you quite sure it wasn't a dream? Something you just imagined?
> Hilde (*sharply*): You think you didn't do it?
> Solness: I hardly know myself—(*More quietly.*) But I know one thing—that I—
> Hilde: That you—? Say it!
> Solness: That I should have done it.
> Hilde: (*suddenly laughs*): You dizzy! (*MB*, 346)

Solness's evasions of his promise and the seduction that sealed it display his prudential fear of the dangerous willing that Hilde requires from him for transcendent fulfillment of the promise. That he fears living dangerously without shunning it once and for all indicates the builder's continued backward progress toward voluntarist, away from rational, action. Solness began

that progress when he evasively rendered Hilde's first retrospective arrangement of the conjoined spur to love and work ambiguous. His renewed doubt
about the status of the obligating exploits at Lysanger—were they conjoined
deeds, an Aristotelian dramatic praxis that he did or did not perform in
physical time and space; were they telepathic projections of aesthetic will to
power that transposed him up and out of the intelligible realm of cause and
effect?—subversively makes whatever action Solness might pursue somehow
Nietzschean.

The problem of willing transcendent change cannot occur in a strictly
Aristotelian plot, in which reality remains stable while agents' apprehensions
of it change. When the problem does occur in Ibsen's plays, Aristotelian
praxis changes from a structure generating events into an embattled motive
or contested thought, a more or less lost action. By this point Solness has
understood and explicitly embraced the Nietzschean thinking his doubt
silently advanced, without fully abandoning the opportunity for paralytic
retreat from freely creative will to power that his habitual rationalism
provides. The continuing ambiguity in Solness's action vis à vis Hilde now
explicitly involves his capacity to change reality by willing power freely,
instead of pursuing dutiful observation of unchanging laws. Both characters
know that the builder's fear of consummating the sexual promise to Hilde
puts that capacity for free willing of power at risk, and both act now to escape
that fear, to resolve the confusion it makes between care and desire, between
death and life.

His halfhearted fatherly attempts through corrective questioning of
Hilde to make her renounce the exploit—"Did I?" "Are you quite sure it wasn't
a dream? Something you just imagined"—are lapses from joyful acceptance
of will to power's creative danger into sad, temporizing submission to
rationalist praxis, according to which no obligation attaches to the promise
or seduction if they were merely the child's imaginative projections. Hilde
immediately counters the regression and defies its weakly projected, confining rationalist authority, by challenging Solness to deny the deeds himself.
She will not simply accede to his pragmatic dismissal of the conjoined events
and so release him from the free, creative willing that her Nietzschean
reenactment of them offers. Her question "You think you didn't do it?" dares
him to relinquish the deeds' transcendent power explicitly, to confine himself
willingly, by means of a fraudulent denial of the deeds' origin in power and
praxis, to static reality.

When Hilde first presented the event to Solness in act 1 he responded
with denial, accounting for it as telekinetic projection. Soon after, he
ambiguously admitted its status as praxis, ironically indicating to her that his

confession might simply be exasperated tolerance of her insistent fantasy. This time, after a long tutelage in willing, when directly challenged—"You think you didn't do it?"—Solness admits his confusion about the deeds' status: "I hardly know myself." The growing authority of Nietzschean action in the play governs Solness's reversal of the skeptical dodge, which he hoped would contain her demand, but has, instead, heightened its power. Instead of destructively eliminating the ambiguity of the deed's status by submitting to her willed insistence that it did in fact occur, and so abandoning the free affirmation her will calls for, Solness preserves the ambiguity affirmatively: "I should have done it."

That transition to the subjunctive mode makes the exploits subjective and hypothetical and so attenuates Solness's prudence and magnifies his willing assent to living dangerously. With this inversion upward of the builder's inverted will, Ibsen lifts the play to its culminating action; Solness's third-act decision to create himself again. This time the father's rebirth will not come, as it first did, at the cost of unknowingly willing his male children's accidental death. This time, inspired by the will-born female child of his genius, the father joyfully takes up self-overcoming by risking his own accidental death. When he climbs his own spire Solness confronts danger's eternally creative recurrence more willfully detached from humanist logic than he is at the end of this exchange with Hilde. But "I should have" mixes retrospective affirmation of the past's eternal recurrence with regret and so taints the Nietzschean tragic joy of amor fati with the rationalist impulse to manage and correct power.

Transposed from fear to nostalgia, the division in Solness's willingness to confront creativity's danger now sorts out as follows: I should have sung on the tower and promised you a kingdom and revealed my desire ten years ago at Lysanger, because now I am about to face death because you say I did all that, and I would be happier knowing my risk fulfills real ethical cause and effect instead of suspecting that I am vainly facing death for the sake of your manipulative, stubbornly childish fantasy. Thus, the voice of the bamboozled weak father, the resentfully prudent humanist who negates himself into and out of existence. This voice tells danger's thrilling story from the Aristotelian perspective. The opposed voice says: whether or not I did all that you said I did ten years ago doesn't matter, because I hereby declare you worthy of all those deeds, and, declaring you worthy, I retroactively will the exploit, I bestow rather than suffer its authority over me. With the bold praise of "I should have" I enact now the freedom and power I might have enacted then. To magnify that free power I will risk death and so honorably deliver us both to the long-ago-promised kingdom. Thus, the voice of the enlightened, enraptured lover, the visionary artist who joyfully wills himself and reality out of and into existence. This voice tells danger's thrilling story from Nietzsche's perspective.

Whoever plays Solness should speak with both voices when he plays this scene so that Hilde's laughing response—"*You* dizzy!" —can resolve the builder's ambivalence ambiguously and so notch up the tension that moves the play into its closing catastrophe. Commending the second voice negatively, by explicitly dismissing the first, Hilde triumphantly preserves her subversive, gaming authority as child warrior of the will. She will not command, even at this point, but strategically maneuvers her opponent, partly for his sake, partly to enhance the contest. Whether Solness is humoring the child or saluting the warrior when he exits, promising "Princess Hilde" that they will hoist the wreath that night, matters less than her solitary summation of the impending climb as "frightfully exciting" (*MB*, 346). That curtain line presents the unambiguous factor around which all the subtle reversals, transpositions, and divisions of this scene move: physical danger. Under the imaginative lure of this most precise, inerrant indicator of action, the symbolic father and child enact the ultimate opposition of praxis and power. In that conflict's result Ibsen presents his most complex resolution of the struggle between classical and modern ideas and experience of change.

That the opposition happens in childish terms, in verbal tilting over the significance of fairytale language, at once reduces and magnifies Solness's struggle. Insofar as Hilde is an overgrown adolescent regressing to kittenish posturing to seduce a hesitantly goatish old man, the scene satirically endorses the conventional ethical and dramatic codes of Ibsen's audience. Insofar as Hilde is a mystic changeling, by turns comically and sternly requiring that the old man exchange his state for hers, the scene offers Solness the magnificent chance for rebirth into free, ascendently creative power and offers Ibsen's audience deliverance to a new ethical and dramatic kingdom. The analogy of Hilde's fairytale kingdom to Christ's religious one, announced by the site of Solness's imminent climb—the church spire he added, as an eccentric signature, to his house—weights the scene toward transcendent, not mundane, danger. Indeed, humbling conversion to childhood consciousness is so crucially required for transcendent entry into Christ's kingdom that Jesus symbolically identifies himself with children, names them agents of his salvation, and guarantees punishment worse than death to anyone who offends them (Matt. 18:1-6). How danger might establish an imminent or immanent kingdom for Solness, whether he damns or saves himself through adult repetition of an erstwhile delivering or offensive romantic identification with a child, occupies the play's last act.

The Master Builder, Act 3:
"Then, like Him, I did the impossible."

Act 2 begins early in the morning and ends sometime before noon. Act 3 which takes place that evening, shows the various strands in the play's sexual intrigue unraveling under the pressure of Solness's abrupt decision to confront danger. The revelations Aline makes in the marriage plot and those Ragnar makes about the sham adultery's effect on his career force Hilde and Solness to a culminating pair of scenes that drastically refine and resolve the builder's divided action: ambiguous pursuit of praxis and power as sources for renewed self-creation. The sublimating inversions in those scenes—Hilde's call for the construction of a castle in the air, Solness's promise to build it on a solid foundation, and the pair's projective recapitulation of the Lysanger seduction, in which they reverse their past roles—all constitute Solness's second delivering, impossible self-creation. Doing the impossible ends in accidental death in this play, and that *accidental* death makes the resolution of Solness's recurrent self-creating action a contested catharsis: has death proved the intelligible and ineluctable authority of praxis in this struggle, or has it demonstrated the sublime authority of transcendent power; has it enacted constantly changeless or constantly changing reality?

Act 3 begins with the play's only scene between Aline and Hilde. Throughout Ibsen has made the social and sexual antagonism that binds these women in the adultery plot an ironic device for subversively displaying the drama's metaphysical conflict. In this scene he transforms the women's already defamiliarized conventional antagonism into eerie empathy. That reversal produces a recognition by which Hilde advances the play's metaphysical action. Paradoxically, this Aristotelian dramatic structure enhances Nietzsche's authority over the play's central action by revealing the longstanding inversion of power against itself that Aline has carried out and that

Solness has unwittingly made the ruinous occasion for his confinement to
humanist ethics. That Solness has grafted an Aristotelian action onto his
wife's perverted Nietzschean one, that the mistake has everything to do with
divided and disguised resentment about imaginary and real children's death,
ushers the play's matching of artistic self-creation with criminal violence
against nature and culture into a new order of dramatic and ideational
complexity. That new order induces the metaphysical action's climax:
Solness's last scene with Hilde, in which the builder makes his completely
transformative revelation of the conversion he underwent at Lysanger.

During final evening preparations at the old house for Solness's imminent ascent of the new house's spire, Hilde enters, wearing flowers she's
plucked in the garden, and finds Aline resting on the veranda. Enhancing the
setting's symbolic, ambiguous rendering of transcendence (the new house
can be glimpsed from the veranda), Aline initiates a conversation with Hilde
about the garden, explaining that she can no longer appreciate its beauty,
has not enjoyed its flowers (beauty continually reborn) from the time Solness
surrounded them with other people's houses. Surprised by Aline's oppressed
alienation in her old house, Hilde asks if she feels happy about moving to
the new one, trying to extend her cheerfulness to Aline. This instance of the
young woman's vivifying, generous joy—the primary active value of her
Nietzschean willfulness, symbolically presented here by her adornment with
flowers—evokes a morbid response from Aline, who calls happiness a duty
she cannot live up to: "I should be happy. That's what Halvard wants . . .
That's my duty, don't you see, to do what he wants. But it's often so difficult
to force oneself to be obedient" (MB, 349). Embedded in this opposition of
will and duty, in which strong weakness resists obliged content, is Nietzsche's
analysis of resentment, the inversion by which morality separates happiness
from free, self-creating power. Ibsen has already presented that inversion as
the primary dynamic in the Solness marriage. At this point, when that union
faces the positive crisis of eternal recurrence of the same in the husband's
climb, which Hilde has urged, Ibsen presents negative eternal recurrence by
restaging the wife's second-act vindictive nostalgia, this time revealing its
previously undisclosed authority over the play's action.

The revelation comes under Hilde's questions about the fire, as Solness's
reversals and recognitions concerning willed action did. The wife's story
differs drastically from the husband's, and that formal relation of identity and
difference—one catechism, two imperfectly opposed faiths—advances the
play's metaphysical argument significantly. Aline calls her failure to please
Solness weakness of character; Hilde calls it blameless sorrow induced by
extraordinary suffering. Unwilling at first to clearly accept or oppose this

kindly exonerating revision of her self-accusation, Aline challenges Hilde's authority to make it with the ambiguous question "How do you know that?" Hilde responds that Solness has told her the family history, and, after expressing suppressed indignation about her husband's disclosure of their private life to a stranger, a rival at that—"He so seldom speaks to me about these things"—Aline confirms that she has suffered unjustly: "Yes, I've had more than my share of suffering in my lifetime, Miss Wangel" (*MB*, 349).

Hilde ignores the wife's jealous insinuations about invaded privacy and continues narrating Aline's life, sympathetically citing the fire as an anguish succeeded by even worse grief. When Aline asks what that worst thing was and Hilde answers, "You lost your little boys," Aline responds: "Oh them, yes. Well, that was different. That was an Act of God. One must resign oneself to such things. And be thankful" (*MB*, p. 349). As the conversation proceeds, it becomes clear that Aline's pious view of the deaths is not curt, noble hiding of a private grief indecorously tapped at by a naively sympathetic sexual rival nor stoically, instructively affirmed religious virtue, but defensive indifference. Probing this unnatural abdication of familial love, Hilde uncovers the corrosive Nietzschean self-creation by which Aline has balked her husband's joyful one.

When Hilde asks if Aline feels thankful and resigned about the deaths, the wife puts her obligation to be content with heaven's wishes under the same description that governs her imperfect assent to Solness's wishes: "Not always, I'm afraid. I know so well that it's my duty. But I can't . . . Time and again I have to remind myself that I've been justly punished . . . because I wasn't resolute enough in the face of adversity" (*MB*, 350). In both divine and human projects Aline affirms happiness as a duty that her weak will cannot enact. Hilde's continued scrutiny reveals that Aline has turned this guilty paralysis into vengeance on the ethical norms that induced and maintain it. That Nietzschean corruption of humanistic praxis has everything to do with Aline's corrupted maternal feeling and emerges under Hilde's persistent probing of the contradiction in Aline's view of the suffering her sons' deaths caused.

Aline believes the extraordinary adversity she suffered— the destruction of her house by fire—proved her inadequately courageous, revealed her irresolute will. She further believes this twin weakness earned her the "just punishment" God dealt out after the fire. And, finally, she believes that, by keeping her from affirming God's justice, or Solness's restitution, her inadequate will condemns her to shameful and perpetual sorrow over the losses she incurred in the fire. Appalled that Aline views her sons' deaths as "just punishment" for cowardice, Hilde tries to argue Aline's self-accusation away. Her humane remonstrance provokes the following revelatory outburst:

"No, no, Miss Wangel—don't talk to me anymore about the two little boys. We should be happy for them. They're so much, much better off where they are. No, it's the little losses which leave the deepest wound. Things which other people would regard as unimportant" (MB, 350).

Aline now explains that she has remained disconsolate over the loss of her family heirlooms—lace, dresses, jewels—and especially her nine dolls. The heirlooms made up her feminine domestic identity, the historically accumulated social and cultural resources for womanly self-creation that she ceded to the low-born Solness when he took possession of her house. The dolls made up her imaginative and emotional self-creation, a more crucial action that she preserved by keeping it secret from her husband: "I didn't just keep them. They lived with me . . . As long as he didn't see them" (MB, 350). Mourning that lost resource secretly for 13 years, Aline has buried her husband's hopes for familial happiness not, as he believes, in their sons' graves, but in her dolls'. As she puts it, tearfully: "But then they were burned, poor dears. No one thought of saving them. Oh, it makes me so sad to think about it . . . They were alive, too, in a way, you see. I carried them under my heart. Like little unborn children" (MB, 350-51).

Hilde's baffled queries about Aline's suffering, provoked by this mother's contradictory account of her children's death—their loss was an act of God performed with no moral reference to her, for which she feels pious gratitude; their loss was just punishment for her cowardly, vain attachment to mundane goods, a divine imposition of dutiful penance that she cannot enact—end after this eerie lament over the dolls. Before Hilde can ask for clarification of Aline's revealed anguish, Dr. Herdal enters to confer with Aline about Solness's dangerous decision to climb the spire. In the brief conversation between the wife and doctor that precedes Solness's entrance and the prudent pair's exit, Ibsen allows time for Hilde and the audience to clarify for themselves what bearing Aline's divided consciousness has on the impending action that she so desperately wants to stop: Solness's conclusive performance of the impossible.

Aline has transposed the objects of her grief—doll's for children—and that transposition advances the protean contest in which classical and modern forms of action, both dramatic and metaphysical, vie for control of this play. In classical terms Aline's confession of suffering over the dolls makes for simultaneous reversal and recognition in the marriage/adultery plot and thereby tragically advances the erotic action Hilde and Solness mutually undertake. In modern terms revelation of the nihilism in Aline's inverted will to power leads Hilde, after an initial faltering, to enhance transcendent willing in Solness. That Aline's inverted will to power should advance

Solness's creative struggle toward freedom this way shows how thoroughly Nietzschean conceptions of action have interpenetrated Aristotle's in this play. Making reversal/recognition logic in the naturalist plot the occasion for transcendent inversion of aesthetic will to power in the metaphysical story, Ibsen submits praxis to power and so tilts the argument about action in this play heavily to Nietzsche's side. Aline's resentment, disguised as grief over the dolls, makes a travesty of the ethical norms that she guiltily strives to obey and of the perverse willfulness by which her striving subverts those norms. She remains unaware of the complex burlesque effects of her morbidity, however, insisting always that her defiant mourning for the dolls is simple weakness. That she cannot acknowledge the power of her weakness is Aline's triumph and ruin and this play's most painful and bizarre transfiguration of classical into modern tragic form.

Like Solness, Aline is imperfectly committed to the ethical norms that imposed her grief and so can no more bring compassionate healing out of that grief than he can. Unlike him, she rejects the conversional norm that Hilde offers as deliverance from regarding imaginative self-creation as criminal. For Solness guilt over the boys' death maintains an internal battle between two fully articulated principles of action, humanistic and Nietzschean. For Aline guilt over the boy's death is a doubly negative device that inverts both humanistic praxis and imaginative will to power. The forces driving her complex negation of both modes of action converge in Aline's contradictory claim that the boys' deaths result from and bear no relation to her moral weakness. From that incoherent assertion of guilt and innocence in which Aline confuses mourning for born and unborn children, and so sabotages humanism by secretly inverting Nietzschean will to power, Ibsen unpacks the subversion of thought and feeling by which Aline has secretly compelled and invalidated Solness's perversely sacrificial repudiation of domestic and professional joy. Uncovering the secret of the marriage plot in this scene, Ibsen makes resolution of the metaphysical contest between praxis and power that has governed the professional and philosophical plots more urgently necessary and more difficult. The addition of that difficulty, especially, makes Ibsen modern.

Aline's implacable presentation of herself as weak amounts to self-assertion through self-denial. Her action is not the transcendent self-denial of joyous Christian or Nietzschean aspiration, which both aim at recreation of the self through sacrificial submission of praxis to an imminent, conversional principle of identity mystically ascertained. Instead, her guilty promotion of weakness as the identifying failure of her life enacts Nietzsche's argument that Christian humanism, especially its morality, is not an autonomous force opposing will to power, but, rather, a diseased adaptation of that ineluctable will, one that vindictively sanctifies fear of power, corrosively turns reason into a strategy for evading creative change, and in the process evacuates life of all value. Aline's weakness holds both Christian humanism, together with its Aristotelian basis, and Nietzschean will to power in nullifying contempt: she will not defy God (who did and did not punish her by taking her children) or dismiss Him, nor will she assert the subjective autonomy of her imaginative self-creation with the dolls or dismiss it. Instead, she vindictively submits her power for self-creation to divine judgment, making God the unjust murderer of her unborn children. With that compromise she commits her life to nihilistic egotism—resentment—instead of creative self-overcoming.

As much as Hilde's rebellious joy, Aline's unacknowledged nihilism works as a fulcrum turning subversion of the conventionally sexist marriage/adultery plot into forward motion in the play's metaphysical action. Theatrical and social convention required that marriage plots depict the preservation of domestic life as the primary mode for human happiness, for harmonious discovery of identity in difference. Normally, the factor disrupting that identity is some deed, usually adultery, and the unifying power is renunciation of that deed. *The Master Builder* reverses that convention. Here the disrupting factor, adultery, is merely feigned or sublimated, a pretext that falsely but tenaciously binds the husband and wife in conjoined recrimination over mutually undisclosed, opposed guilts. Solness's anguish in the marriage arises from knowledge of the bad faith by which he maintains guilt-inducing adultery charades and, more importantly, from confused paternal and spousal guilt over his sons' deaths. Caught in an ambiguous conviction of his criminal innocence where the deaths are concerned, ambivalently loyal to self-justifying violence in creativity and to humanism's condemnation of that violence, Solness displays his secret guilt with displaced clarity in his sham philandering.

As is conventional, Solness struggles in this marriage plot to renounce the offense alienating him from his wife. Ibsen's subversion of the convention comes in rendering the offense— transcendent aesthetic willing—its domestic consequences, and Solness's renunciation of both in Nietzschean as well as Aristotelian terms. Renouncing his joyous self-expression and taking up humanism's punitive attitude toward transcendent willing, Solness only increases the fraudulent misery of his marriage, a consequence indicated by Aline's repudiation of the new chance for conventional domestic happiness Solness builds for her. Renouncing the humanist ethos and the cowardice by which he submitted transcendent willing to it, Solness renounces his guilt, the offense that gave rise to it, the sham adultery that maintained it, the repression of Ragnar's career that adultery achieved, and, most significantly, his marriage to Aline, by which all the displaced confinements arising from his cowardice are most powerfully enforced. That all this delivering renunciation, which wrecks instead of preserves marriage, comes about in Solness under the tutelage of an ambiguously real and hypothetical adulteress, Hilde, snaps dizzying irony through the play's conventional domestic plot, through its illusionistic realism, and through the humanistic morality and ontology that authorizes them. The fastest spin in that irony comes in this first scene of the third act, when the putative adulteress sympathetically uncovers the unwittingly perverse renunciation by which the resentfully virtuous wife has simultaneously invoked and nullified her husband's imperfectly virtuous renunciation.

That Aline remains unaware of the sad strategy in her "weakness" is an innovation in Ibsen's career-long critique of sexist views of women as "the weaker vessel." Maternal and romantic love prove the strong weaknesses that confound Mrs. Alving's liberating action in *Ghosts* and Rebecca West's in *Rosmersholm*. In both cases Ibsen explicitly presents these women as tragic heroines destroyed by their experimental reformation of the conventional idealization of feminine consciousness. Struggling to bring the new effect of life's joy out of the old cause of maternal instinct and feminine chastity, virtues assigned to them by and for the benefit of patriarchal authority, Helene and Rebecca actively indict that authority and explicitly call those virtues into question. Withholding any cathartic resolution from these women's ultimate capitulation to convention, Ibsen subverts both the dramatic and ethical norms that call for women to sacrifice themselves to men, and ironically enhances the value of Nietzschean willing that his heroines could only partially enact.

To speak in Nietzschean terms, the will to power acts weakly but directly against a diseased articulation of itself (humanistic patriarchy) in Helene's and Rebecca's cases. Their defeat displays some admirable measure of health and joy, since it follows from power's struggle to heal itself, to make resistance—power's self-created and self-creating occasion—generative instead of corrosive. In Aline's case will to power does not directly oppose patriarchal humanism, but turns back against itself, making resistance the end of power instead of a means for generating more. Hence, her strong weakness displays no oppositional measure of health or joy, only ever more etiolated and miserable negation. Perfecting itself, that negation also undoes the diseased articulation of power it ostensibly serves: pleading weakness, Aline formally acknowledges the authority of duty only to leave it unaccomplished. This portrayal of Aline's negative willing as unconsciously successful resistance to convention marks a new point of sophistication in Ibsen's Nietzschean critique of humanist action.

In *Ghosts* and *Rosmersholm* Ibsen presents an unexplored and a repudiated opportunity for liberating revision of male cultural authority. The road not taken by Mrs. Alving and forsaken by Rebecca West twists off from the conventional path assigned to women—sacrificial maternity and chastity, the dramatic and ethical idealization of strong feminine weakness. Transposing Aline's sacrificial maternity and chastity into Nietzschean resentment in *The Master Builder*, Ibsen shows the unlooked-for and inevitable self-immolation (for men and women) latent in conventional idealization of women's subservient sustenance of men. Adding Hilde to this plot, Ibsen breaks the deadlock of divided, subjugated willing that wrecked Mrs. Alving and Rebecca West. Hilde's call for Solness to do the impossible—to survive deliberate enactment of the self-immolation latent in masculine idealization of women—perfects Ibsen's subversion of the conventional feminine virtues of domestic fidelity and transgression. This liberating woman is neither sacrificial mother nor chaste, lover but sublimated erotic consort, whose strong weakness, juvenile enthusiasm, Ibsen experimentally idealizes in Nietzschean, not humanistic, terms. Hilde's purpose is transcendent willing, joyous assent to danger's creative violation of stasis. The self-denial required for Solness and Hilde to accomplish such action is precisely opposite to Aline's and makes masculine self-immolation a willed achievement of personal and cultural regeneration, a Dionysian joy instead of an Aristotelian hamartia ruinously revealed through conventional action.

The first scene of act 3 fully exposes the competing pragmatic and metaphysical actions required of Solness by the two women in his life. Hilde's refusal to reveal Aline's secret anguish to Solness once he enters in the next scene shifts the play's central contest—duty contra happiness—to its final ground. For the rest of the act Ibsen transposes realistic resolution of that contest into Solness's symbolic performance of the impossible. Hilde initiates this final modulation from praxis into aesthetic will to power by persuading Solness in the act's second scene that his ascent of the new house's spire will be construction of the kingdom he promised her long ago. In this logic the house Solness built to restore spousal happiness to his wife, the house Aline refashions as a tomb for her resentment, becomes a new site of Nietzschean joy, an anti-Christian spiritual house not made with hands, to speak biblically (2 Cor. 5:1.). Now Solness's ascent on that indecorously revisionist spire will not be toward the spiritual domesticity that inspired its invention and construction. Under Hilde's inspiration the ascent will be a return, through retrospective willing of the past, to the Promethean joy Solness sang out on the Lysanger church tower ten years ago, a return that consummates the promised joy she has come to claim.

Hilde's inversion of the spire's meaning follows directly from her subversive resolution of the adultery intrigue. When Solness enters he immediately asks why Hilde appears so cold and solemnly downcast. He receives the metaphorical answer that she has just emerged from a tomb and correctly understands her veiled reference to Aline. Hilde keeps the full chill of the reference secret from Solness. Instead of carrying out the recognition scene Aline has just begun, Hilde strengthens Solness's mistaken isolation from his wife. Through pointed questions she elicits his confession that separation from Aline mitigates the remorse that observation of her unfinished mourning for the dead twins causes him. Hilde remains silent in response to three direct questions from Solness about her conversation with Aline. When he presumes that Aline disclosed the long anguish of her maternal mourning, Hilde misleadingly confirms his ignorance of Aline's resentment with two rapid nods. Immediately after completing the fraud that confines him to vain remorse, immobile and remote—like a statue, Solness says—Hilde announces her desire to leave. When Solness asks her to stay, she responds, "What can I do here now?" (*MB*, 353)

Now that she knows, that is, as he doesn't, that Solness's guilt has been wasted, that her adultery would not end but enhance the unavailingly punitive union of both spouses and uselessly harm Aline in the process. If Hilde reveals that Aline's confession has shown Solness's repudiation of self-creation to be an absurd folly instead of sacrificial praxis, she reveals that Aline, who has protested weakness all her married life, in fact has the power to free Solness from guilt. Since Hilde has abrogated that power to herself with the saving demand that Solness deliver her promised kingdom, it is not in her interest to give Solness a full explanation of her reasons for leaving. If Hilde reveals Aline's secret, she reveals Aline's power and thus diminishes her own. If Solness responds to the news by seeking reconciliation with Aline, Hilde loses; if he despairs of his future on learning of the absurdity of his past, Hilde also loses. If he acts out the promised adultery with her, the transcendent receipt of her delivering kingdom becomes merely conventional moral offense against a sad, violated woman—the worst loss for Hilde. Ironically parried in a power play for authority over a weak husband by the resentfully virtuous wife, Hilde finds herself in a variant of the situation Rebecca West suffered in *Rosmersholm*. With this difference: Hilde's self-advancing, amoral ardor aims at spiritual, not political or social, liberation and involves no pragmatic ethical reformation of sexual morality. Both in motive and deed, Hilde's project—advancing her will to power by bringing Solness's back to life—slips the bonds of humanist obligation that ensnare Rebecca.

Enacting a modernist poetic justice by ironically binding social convention and natural law, Ibsen resolves Rebecca's adultery plot by having the imperfectly chaste violator pay the wages of murderously lustful sin. In *The Master Builder* Ibsen goes farther in his ironic disengagement from humanist dramatic structure and resolves Hilde's adultery plot by transposing the ambiguous sexual memory of her Lysanger seduction into a muse's liberating reminder of the prerogatives and costs of aesthetic will to power. The transformation starts with Hilde's rejection of Solness's first explicit assent to adultery, made immediately after she announces her departure. When Solness impulsively commends the inevitable sexual crime that Hilde predicts will result if she stays—"So much the better!"—Hilde violently rejects his hope: "I can't hurt someone I *know*. I can't take what belongs to her . . . someone I've got close to—! No! No! Ugh! (*MB*, 353)

Moral restriction of self-creation that does violence to others moves from principled restraint to personal repugnance here. With that transposition Hilde naively and ambiguously clarifies and advances the essential struggle of aesthetic will to power against ethics that she has sought to free Solness from throughout the play. Hilde's emotional yielding to ethics matches Solness's ten-year marital yielding. In her case, as in his, will to power falters when it confronts the resistant force of Aline's sorrow. Ironically, their identity through weakness allows Hilde to reenact the strong willing she urged on Solness in her role as demanding, liberating muse. Their mutual recognition and reversal in strong weakness has two stages: Hilde switches from baffled amoral to self-protective moral response to the Solness's marriage; through consequent provocation of and encouragement from Solness, Hilde quickly turns self-protective morality into amoral willing that simultaneously compels the deliverance of her kingdom and the elimination of the adultery intrigue. Her descending emotional ascent, staged in an Aristotelian reversal, ends in Nietzschean self-overcoming. Once again modernist metaphysics governs classical dramatic and ethical action.

Joyous emotional energy aims at self-enhancement, whether offered by ethics or will to power. When the actions that promote such happiness clash, as they do now for Hilde under Aline's authority, the logic of reversal requires that one action prevail over another or that both combine in a compromise that corrupts or advances happiness. The sick will advances corrupt compromise; the healthy will passes the weaker force through direct confrontation of it. Confronted with the clash of ethics and will in his marriage, Solness makes a corrupt compromise. When the same clash ensnares Hilde in the adultery plot, she confronts the weaker ethical force directly; she takes it on as an action to govern emotional self-enhancement. This adoption is the first reversal. The next one, which follows immediately, is her shedding of ethics as an opportunity for happy action. She begins this second spin by enjoining ethics on Solness, who protests that he can imagine no purpose for living if she leaves.

> Solness: And what's to become of me when you've gone? What shall I have to
> live for? Afterwards?
> Hilde (*with the enigmatic expression in her eyes*): It's easy for you. You have your
> duty to her. You must live for that duty. (*MB*, 353)

The builder's panicked question acquiesces to her rejection of the role of adulteress and desperately announces dependence on her function as muse. The enigmatic expression, and the derisive insouciance of "It's easy for you," belong to the affronted, demanding muse in Hilde. Reinstated by Solness's life-threatened invocation, the transcending Hilde ironically advocates those obligations of duty she militantly approved of and submitted herself to when Solness fashioned her an adulteress. Solness understands that her riddling moralism reimposes the familiar choice between duty and the happiness of aesthetic willing. He responds first with the habitual despairing account of his paralyzing doublebind: because his aesthetic self-overcoming emerged from and foundered in violence that wrecked Aline, he can no longer take up aesthetic or dutiful action toward her. "(*Laughs desperately.*) It was done for my happiness. (*Heavily.*) And for my sake she died. And I am chained to the corpse. (*In anguish.*) I—I, who cannot live without joy!" (*MB*, 354).

Pressed to imagine life without Hilde, Solness regresses to the state he was in when Hilde first appeared. Searching for a way to bring the possibility of joy back to him, to turn this eternal return of the same into an occasion for transcendence, Hilde moves to the stool where she talked with Aline in the previous scene, props her head on her elbows, and fixes a steady, silent gaze on Solness for a moment. Testing his commitment to joy, teaching him to know what he might do once she leaves, Hilde repeats the vivifying tactic she used in act 2 when she confronted his creative funk: she asks what he will build next. Solness quietly abandons the plan to build for the sake of familial happiness that he announced to Hilde in the second act, announcing his defeat with the remark "God knows whether people will want that kind of thing any more" (*MB*, 354). What God has to do with Solness's building for domestic happiness will emerge prominently in his final conversation with Hilde. At this point Ibsen plants the association as a conversational grace note.

As she did with Aline, Hilde shows compassion for Solness's self-defeating withdrawal from a ten-year struggle to enact happiness, with this difference: where she acquiesced to the wife's withdrawal she impetuously protests against the husband's.

> *Hilde (bursts out)*: Oh, I think it's all so wrong, so wrong!
> *Solness*: What?
> *Hilde*: That one should be afraid to seize happiness! To seize hold of life! Just because someone stands in the way. Someone one knows.
> *Solness*: Someone one has no right to pass by.
> *Hilde*: Haven't we that right, I wonder? But even so—Oh, if one could only sleep and forget it all! (*MB*, 354)

These first two exchanges work by ambiguous implication. The outburst comes from the frustrated young girl, the principled impersonal reasoning about personal prerogative from the muse of aesthetic willing. Is she berating herself to provoke his approving permission to act out her right to will; is she goading him to seek her approving permission for his enacted right—or both? Unwilling to clarify the floating agency, Solness extends the ambiguity with his implicit moral identification of Aline as victim of their single or mutual advocacy of criminal self-creation. Psychological realism and metaphysical tension play off each other in this challenge to action, which, in a conventional drama, would come in direct charge and countercharge. The slant, unresolved dares leave the consummating action unnamed as well as undone. Writing significance off the page and stage this way, Ibsen created a modernist idiom for dialogue, a dramatic language for representing the absent presence that Samuel Beckett and Harold Pinter, to name two illustrious benefactors, put to masterful use.

The absent presence in this case is joy, construed by Ibsen as Nietzschean aesthetic willing. Keeping it absent but discernable in this ambiguous exchange, Ibsen not only invents a new mode of identification, by requiring the audience to fill in the resolution of the characters' conflict, but also stages an important moment in Nietzschean transcendence out of humanism: the uncertain glimpse of a new life, powerless to be born, from the edge of an old life, powerless to die. This Edwardian problem that in various ways afflicted Nietzsche, Tennyson (*see Tithonus*), early Yeats, Arnold, and Ibsen often led to literary studies in evasive despair, a strategy that Hilde invokes with the wish for amnesiac sleep. In this play evasive despair always conjures a provocation to joy. That coiled action—the lapse that springs forward—occurs here as Solness takes on Hilde's cast-off role as condoling liberator of the sorrowful will to power.

In a physical signal of the psychological and metaphysical inversion this scene makes of the first, Solness moves to the armchair from which Aline took resentful charge of the play's action, sits in it, and steers Hilde past the emotional impediment of ethical sympathy for Aline with the apparent non sequitur "Did you have a happy home with your father?" (*MB*, 354). The same logic of acting by not acting present in their ambiguous complaining about Aline's woe works in Solness's implicit juxtaposition of Hilde's familial struggle against his. The apparent non sequitur, in fact, continues the tense approach to and withdrawal from criminal self-assertion, focusing the question of powerful willing on Hilde now, since she has most recently lapsed from it. That the artist should invigorate the muse to preserve her power over him is a modernist innovation in the ancient idea of poet as divinely authorized creator and revealer of values, one that follows directly from Nietzsche's atheistic conception of the aesthetic will's advance through continual self-overcoming. The Nietzschean signature in this passage appears in the symbolic language that makes Hilde a wild bird of prey who broke from a cage when she left her family and in the culminating return to Solness's second-act fascination with robust conscience.

To Solness's biographical question Hilde responds as follows:

> Hilde (*without moving, replies as though half asleep*): I only had a cage.
>
> Solness: And you don't want to go back into it?
>
> Hilde (*as before*): Wild birds don't fly into cages.
>
> Solness: They want to chase the free air—
>
> Hilde (*still in the same tone*): Eagles love the chase.
>
> Solness (*resting his eyes on her*): If only one were a viking. They had hunting in their blood.
>
> Hilde (*opens her eyes, but does not move, and says in her natural voice*): What else did they have? Tell me!
>
> Solness: A robust conscience. (*MB*, 354-55)

In act 2 when Solness reveals his fear that the murderous violence his self-creation did to Aline's maternity may have cost him his sanity, Hilde consoles and encourages the builder by diagnosing his anguish as an instinctual rather than mental problem. In an innocent variation of Lady Macbeth's sexual daring of hesitant male action, Hilde suggests that a native physiological deficit halts Solness: "I'm wondering if you weren't born with an underdeveloped conscience." Protecting himself from that part of the speculation that diminishes him, implicitly submitting himself to the therapeutic promise in her wondering, Solness reenacts the Thane's indirect self-assertion and challenges her to prove that she has the "robust conscience" he lacks.

He asks if she has ever had to test her conscience, and she proves her courage by responding that leaving her father forever, whom she was "frightfully fond of," to return to Solness and demand her promised kingdom was difficult (MB, 337—38). He explicitly asks if she was unhappy at home, and she evasively answers that an irresistible impulse drove her out. Solness identifies that impulse as the troll of aesthetic willing who calls them together to unavoidably criminal self-creation. Referring to the Vikings as sexual exemplars of robust conscience, he escalates the adultery intrigue by asking Hilde if she could "grow fond" of such robust violation. Hilde says yes, cancels his ethical and personal qualms about criminal passion with the exonerating assertion that sexual feeling is involuntary, and agrees when Solness concludes that the forces controlling ineluctable aesthetic willing also control sexual attraction. Having successfully transferred her paternal "fondness" to putative adultery, Solness closes the scene with Nietzschean symbols of Hilde as a bird of prey, as an incarnation created from and delivering him to his own desire for rebirth, his dormant robust conscience.

The adulterous goal of that desire now canceled, only aesthetic willing, the ineluctable command of the trolls who have chained him to Aline's corpse, remains for Solness and Hilde to deliver each other with. Replaying the Viking seduction scene with sex denied and with a psychological reversal for Hilde and Solness, Ibsen writes out the eternal return of the same as an occasion for increased will to power. Solness plays the first Viking scene as a sexual corruption of Hilde's call that he enact the impossible. When reversal and recognition in the adultery plot uncouple sex from performance of the impossible, Ibsen makes the putative lovers' psychological disappointment an opportunity for spiritual transcendence. This much is conventional humanistic moralizing. The innovation comes in Ibsen's realistic presentation of the psychological sublimation as a radical, transgressive metaphysical event. When Verdi's Aida and Radames sing "Oh terra addio" they stage sentimental confidence in a heavenly reward for fatal ethical transgression, a happy resolution that the composer despaired of and that like-minded radicals in his audience are meant to regard as a tragic repudiation of worldly power, a triumph ironically emerging out of conventional piety. The rebirth of Solness and Hilde through sublimation claims the higher ground of antipragmatic realism. Ibsen brings his audience to that new ground by the path of incandescent psychological portraiture, by supra-Aristotelian fusion of plot and character.

Solness's condoling scrutiny of Hilde's past uncovers the weakness in her strong emotional resistance to ethical restraint on self-assertion. In the first Viking scene Hilde presented her fondness for her father as a good whose sacrifice validated her own self-creation and should inspire Solness's own liberation from loveless domestic duty. With that self-creation balked by ethically compelling emotional entanglement in Solness's familial obligation, Hilde reverses her original filial self-presentation. The enigmatic expression she has worn throughout the play when she has challenged Solness to chose between duty and happiness has always been a provocation to overcome the emotionally weak, resentful perception of duty as confinement and to take up the emotionally strong perception of duty as a sacrificed good that validates willing. She wore that enigmatic expression in this scene until Solness revealed that her departure means the end of his artistic career.

Advance in that artistic career is the only vestige of her longed-for kingdom that Hilde can hope for from the builder now, the only action left in their now alienating, once mutual project of self-assertion. When Solness annuls that career, he annuls her power over them both and spins Hilde into her only moment of hopeless complaint in the play. This despair reverses the balance of strength and weakness in her own emotional resistance to ethics. The so recently enigmatic, ironic encouragement to create a new kingdom falters now into her half-conscious, withdrawn brooding on a vacant future that has followed a vacant attempt to flee a vacant past. With closed eyes, entranced by her grief, she responds three times to Solness's questions about her home life by calling her filial fondness a wild bird's confinement and sadly opposing it to the free chase she now despairs of. Solness offers a hypothetical hope for resumption of the chase when he wistfully turns her natural metaphor into a literary invocation of the hunting instinct of the Vikings, and that invocation suffices to stir Hilde out of her brooding resentment over familial life's pervasive restriction of willing.

His inquiry's metaphoric ascent from animal to human willing, to heroic masculine willing, signals an increase in Solness's daring, and that impulse rouses the strong part of Hilde's ambiguous, resentful semiconsciousness. Fully awake, in her normal voice, but not moving, Hilde takes up the transcending challenge she made in the first Viking scene again, pressing Solness to name the consciousness that governs "hunting" blood. When he answers, "A robust conscience," she responds as follows: *"Hilde sits up, alive. Her eyes are again excited and aflame . . . (nodding):* I know what you're going to build next!" (*MB*, 355). For the rest of the scene Hilde imparts a modernist muse's wisdom to Solness, teaching him how "a robust conscience" is both the form and matter of his next building, the design and erected dwelling of their mutually delivering transcendence. Subsuming the physical activity of building into affirmation of mental force, Hilde and Solness pass Aline by without sexually offending her. Enacting purely aesthetic willing, they reverse the reversal Aline's resentment made in the action and avoid criminal violence against her by eluding the ethical realm altogether, by asserting themselves only in the metaphysical one.

Hilde makes all this known to Solness by converting his conditional recourse to powerful willing—"If only one were a Viking"—from a compensatory, evasive hypothesis, a fantasy symptom of resentful psychology, into a creative, visionary hypothesis, a "let there be" performed in and for aesthetic will to power. Just as his conversion of her weakness involved an inverting replay of the discovery of "robust conscience" in the act 2 Viking scene, her transfigured recuperation of his desire to build involves an inverting replay of the finale of act 2. Her call for Solness to build her "a castle in the air" reverses the builder's second-act curtain project to have her live in the new house's tower. Bringing him to accept the inspired command to spiritual action, Hilde also inverts the childlike diction and psychology of their sexual teasing in that scene. Most significantly, she changes his ambiguously hypothetical affirmation of criminally erotic self-creation at Lysanger—"I should have done it"—from a weak willing of the past into a positive promise for future action: "From now on we two shall build together, Hilde" (MB, 346, 357).

The exchange begins comically, as Solness protests ignorance of the future project Hilde has hit on. With a blunt impatience, part mirth and part provocation, she tells him, "Master builders are very stupid people," and then explains that he must deliver her kingdom within the hour by building that long-promised realm's governing castle. The demand stays an exhilarating game for Solness until he responds to the construction deadline with deflating pragmatism and pitches Hilde into commanding, childlike sublimity.

> Solness: It's no joke to have you as a creditor, Hilde.
> Hilde: You should have thought of that before. Now it's too late. Now then!
>   (Thumps on the table.) Where's my castle! It's my castle! (MB, 355)

Leaning closer to her with his arms on the table, Solness hesitantly enters her vision, asking her to describe the castle. She answers that it must be built high up, with a panoramic, clear view for miles. Solness quickly sees that Hilde has conflated the promised kingdom delivered in this castle fantasy and the promised kingdom to be supplied by his dangerous climb of the new house that she called for at the second-act curtain and nervously signals as much with a rhetorical question about the imagined castle: "It's got a tower, I suppose?" (*MB*, 356). Giving no quarter to his fear or weakness, Hilde calls the projected tower "frightfully high" and then elaborates the symbolic link of climbing and building by picturing herself installed in a balcony that symbolically tops the real tower he has promised to ascend. Hilde's image transforms Solness's hopeful second-act curtain promise that she might live in the tower's highest room like a princess into a fact accomplished by her will, not his, a fact preceding his climb and inspiring it instead of a benefit following his ascent as a reward for it. Together with the switch in willed power, Hilde's tower vision ousts Aline from dominance, even from residence in Solness's new building, changing what Solness imagined would be the adultress's hidden chamber in the wife's material house into the muse's lookout in the artist's spiritual house of joy. Thus, Aline is passed by, and Solness is successfully called to the delivering power Hilde alone can will for them both. The builder, as ever, fearfully resists this latest subsuming, transcendent call to unity with the muse: "(*involuntarily clutches his head*): How can you want to stand so high? Doesn't it make you giddy—?" Hilde has already made all her arguments, disregards his resistance altogether, and, fully confident that she can overcome him, finally makes her transcendent purpose for them both perfectly plain: "I want to stand up there and look down at the others—the ones who build churches. And homes for mothers and fathers and children. And you can come up there and look down too" (*MB*, 356).

She will not be looking down with benevolent approval on the subjects of her kingdom nor with a longing to be restored to them by the hero who climbs to her. The gaze down joyfully measures her liberated distance from humanist praxis, celebrates the resistance that brought about increased will to self-creating power, and sublimely enacts the retrospective willing of the past that advances and rewards Nietzschean self-overcoming. This backward look inverts the paralyzing remorse over self-creation that Solness has enacted for a decade, subsuming the crabbed force of ethical compromise into the serene mastery of self-generated aesthetic freedom. That subsumption is the ascent Hilde invites Solness to make, guarantees he will achieve, when he joins her in the tower: a converting effort that suspends his will between the two strengths it has served weakly—humanism and will to power—in order to annihilate the first and recreate him, under her liberating authority, in the second.

With the symbolic petition of a knight-errant rescuing a princess in a fairy tale, Solness humbly asks if he has leave to climb. In this resumption

of the children's game that ended act 2 Solness assents to Hilde's revised
visionary assertion that climbing the spire is building a house not made with
hands, that by braving death through the creative force of robust conscience
he acts out their deliverance from the world. When she answers that the
leave is granted by his wishing to climb, Solness takes up her now courteous
invitation to will his own self-assertion with the humble, whispered promise:
"Then—I think the master builder will come" (MB, 356). He follows this
advance immediately with the by now familiar lapse that attends all his
transcendent willing, observing that once he has climbed up to the princess
he will never build again. Either Solness expects to die in the physical climb,
or he expects to exhaust self-overcoming by one willed enactment of robust
conscience. In either case he has not fully grasped the promise of new life
offered by her Nietzschean challenge, does not yet understand or credit the
creative force of hypothetical willing symbolically presented to him in her
castle vision.

For the rest of the exchange Hilde inverts the dragging balance of strong
weakness in Solness's will. His final reversal upward comes when she forces
him to understand the distinction between weak and strong hypothetical
stances toward reality, to disavow the safe paralysis of evasive fantasy and
take up the dangerous, subsuming self-advancement of creative willing. Like
Dante's Beatrice, Hilde rescues Solness by symbolically representing the
salvational dimension of his craft to a spiritually and emotionally confused
but still aspiring artist. With alternating comic and severe encouragement
and reproof she secures his advance by requiring an intellectual affirmation
of aesthetic will to power from the builder, a commitment in the language
of his craft to the subsuming authority of ungrounded building.

All this begins with Hilde's correction of Solness's relieved, self-pitying
assent to the climb as a final act. His observation that once ensconced in the
tower's balcony with Hilde "he will never build again. Poor master builder"
provokes the following epiphanic tutelage from her:

> Hilde (alive): Oh, yes he will! We'll do it together! And we'll build the most
>   beautiful thing—the most beautiful thing in the world!
> Solness: Hilde—tell me. What is that?
> Hilde (looks at him with a smile, gives a little shake of her head, pouts and says, as though
>   to a child): Master builders—they are very-very stupid people.
> Solness: Yes, they're stupid, I know. But tell me—what is the most beautiful
>   thing in the world? The thing we two are going to build together?
> Hilde (is silent for a moment, then says, with the enigmatic expression in her eyes): A castle
>   in the air.

Solness: A castle in the air.

Hilde (nods): A castle in the air, yes. Do you know what a castle in the air is?

Solness: It's the most beautiful thing in the world, you say.

Hilde (jumps up angrily and makes a contemptuous gesture with her hand): Yes, of course!
    Castles in the air are so safe to hide in. And easy to build. (*Looks at him
    scornfully.*) Especially for master builders with a—a giddy conscience.

Solness (gets up): From now on we two shall build together, Hilde.

Hilde (with a doubting smile): A real castle in the air?

Solness: Yes. Built on a true foundation. (*MB*, 356-57)

This last exchange tips the balance in Solness's will through chiasmic
pairing—*ABBA*—of exhortation and instruction. The stronger action, exhortation, begins and ends the exchange; instruction goes on in the middle, when
exhortation has temporarily failed. In the opening outside movement of this
miniature quartet Hilde proclaims Solness's necessary act, and the builder
responds by doubting the act's power. In the closing outside movement the
reverse occurs, as Hilde doubts the builder's readiness for the necessary act,
but finally ends assured, by his courageous assent to her proclamation, that
he can and will perform it. The inner movements containing that instruction
that restores her exhortation work with the same doubling reversal as the
outside movements. In the first she makes an assertion that he repeats as a
question, which she answers with a definition that he repeats. In the second
she twice makes his repetition of the definition a question, which he answers
twice, first repeating elements of her opening assertion and finally validating
the term distributed in their dispute—the mutually demanded, constructed
gift, the castle in the air.

The internal reversal in chiasmic structure, *ABBA*, stages the endgame
strategy by which Hilde and Solness finally bring joyful identity out of their
competing psychosexual and metaphysical differences with eloquent, concise force that requires perfect attention from the audience and consummate
expressive command of ideational and emotional nuance from the actors. The
essential event comes dead center in the scene, in the inner movements that
turn on the couple's fourfold repetition of "castle in the air." Each iteration
of that epiphanic phrase inverts and so advances the contesting wills and
understandings of the protagonists. This antiphonal irony—part child's
game, part sublimated lover's struggle—discloses and then unites opposed
meanings in the repeated phrase, makes a dramatic as well as semantic
chiasmus out of the airy castle's recurrence. The source of all power and
resistance, all action in the play, Hilde's incessant demand that Solness bring
dangerous life out of dangerous death is finally satisfied when she wins the

symbolic argument staged in their chiasmic repetition of words he disparages as clichéd and she pronounces as a magic incantation.

The play of difference and identity that separates and unites both sides of the inverting repetition in a chiasmus makes that rhetorical figure a richly ambiguous structure, one whose pivotal inversion at the center can equivocally emphasize continuity or discontinuity between the transposed elements. Both Aristotelian praxis and Nietzschean will to power operate with the logic of internally generated sundering and reconciliation that a chiasmus displays, and both orders bear on the struggle to define Hilde's airy castle. The inferential nuances of this dialogue, its cumulative references backward to Hilde's previous demands that Solness deliver on his promise to act—to build—for her, culminate in a final sundering of will to power from praxis. The pivotal reversal Hilde enforces here irreconcilably moves Solness out from the possible/actual dynamic of Aristotelian action and turns him fully toward Nietzschean performance of the impossible, more precisely the suprapossible. That inverting reversal occurs in the last three sentences of the exchange, when he cedes his Aristotelian definition of *castle in the air* to Hilde's Nietzschean one, when the muse's taunts of the creator's stupidity and giddiness turn the weakness by which he differs from her into strong assertion of their unified creative purpose.

For both the airy castle symbolically unites willing and doing and so converts reality from material substance enacted and masterfully known through pragmatic control into subsuming will to power enacted and masterfully known through hypothetical invention. The difference comes in their estimation of the value of that hypothetical invention. Hilde epiphanically proposes it, with her customary enigmatic tone, as salvational ascent to imminent beauty. Her enigmatic expression at once probes and challenges his belief in this transcendence. True to form, Solness first seeks the comforting strength of his unbelief, which her enigmatic tone exposes and makes bold, implicitly expressing doubt about this higher reality in his flat repetition of the subject and predicate of her proposition: "a castle in the air . . . It's the most beautiful thing in the world, you say." He only ambivalently acknowledged the obligating Lysanger seduction in act 1 by thinking of it hypothetically, only ambivalently endorsed it with the same strategy in act 2. Now, at the apex of self-creation, he again asserts and evades his criminally aesthetic will to power by taking up the weak meaning of a hypothetical claim. The Aristotelian humanism controlling his previous equivocations has been ethical; here it is ontological. He implies, in his querulous repetition of her assertion, that a castle in the air may not be the eidolon she beholds, but only a chimera, a delusion accomplishing no transcendence from nature's all-limiting, fixed reality, but merely etiolating that realm's power, casting its insubstantial shadow into weak imaginations.

When she tells Solness that, having climbed up to the castle, he will then build it, Hilde symbolically shows him what inventive as well as what liberating transcendence waits to be enacted in his renewed advocacy of robust conscience. This ontological claim for aesthetic willing is the last sticking point for Solness, whose creativity—building—goes on, after all, in and for the natural, material realm. Confronted with defensive skepticism and mimicry more than a touch snide, Hilde does not prevail by arguing ontology with Solness. She turns his strategic jibes offensively back on him, resharpened, provoking and instructing him by angrily mocking the fear, the constitutionally strong weakness, that stalls his final hypothetical approach to her transcendent realm. The rebarbative mockery works. He assents to the reality and foundational truth of her airy castle and to the paradoxical notion that he will build it after scaling its tower. With this assent Solness makes the spatial and temporal absurdities of Hilde's envisioned building encouraging symbols for his own Nietzschean self-overcoming and aesthetic willing.

Climbing the castle and then constructing it is literally preposterous, a reversed conflation of cause and effect. Absurd in the order of praxis, such sublimation of doing into willing amounts to creative performance of the impossible in the order of will to power. For ten years fear has confused Solness's longing for the impossible inventive action with longing for successful performance of the possible happiness worldly building offers. After fighting that fear for two days, Hilde knows its nature well enough to successfully exacerbate and extinguish it with her emphatically irrational, mystic insistence on the strong hypothetical meaning of her airy castle. Solness's fear presents his strength to her weakly. Retreating from the robust conscience he hypothetically aspired to in the middle of this scene, seeking refuge in the negative power of doubt—intellectual giddiness—Solness ambivalently proffers the unstable mix of stalled mystic and rational power in his creative life to Hilde's enthusiastic will: partly to defeat her strength with his weakness, partly to surrender that weakness to the uplifting reversal into strength promised in Hilde's symbolic eidolon. Staging Hilde's inverting transcendence of the builder's will obliquely here, in dense symbolic inference, Ibsen enacts that blank psychological moment when a subsuming inversion in personal identity advances self-creation. The suspension in psychological realism subsumes Aristotelian teleology in Nietzsche's mystic aesthetic will to power and so makes *The Master Builder* a paradigmatic instance of the transmuting loss of action sustained in modernist drama.

Solness's struggle to act takes place in the cluster of dramatic topics
that Ibsen reconfigured throughout his career: identity psychology, sexual
and familial ethics, social and cultural reformation, and metaphysical speculation. Ibsen began and ended the last phase of his career by subsuming all
these topics into symbolic treatment of artistic creativity. In both *The Master
Builder* (1892) and *When We Dead Awaken* (1899) symbolic actions depict
artists willfully transforming creativity, loosening it from the bonds of
ethically responsible representation of social and material reality, exalting
it into the invention of a new, transnatural order of being. Ibsen focuses
emphatically on ontological transformation in these late dramatic experi-
ments by having both plays' artists work transcendently in dense material
modes, architecture and sculpture.

Combining contemplative and pragmatic ends, architecture puts the
argument about reality in terms of social action. Sculpture, which normally
represents human figures, can exalt social norms but more often takes up
psychological reality, especially erotic and religious awareness, when it
depicts bodily forms. Rubek, the sculptor in *When We Dead Awaken*, starts and
ends his mystically sexual action at the extreme verge of normal human
affairs, abandoning an alienated wife to pursue erotic sublimity with a former
model encountered at a seaside vacation spa and a neighboring mountain
sanitorium. The scene, the domestic situation, and the artistic career Solness
acts in all present an earlier phase of Rubek's transcendence, a moment when
spiritual power still struggles to free itself from multiple, interlocked modes
of material consciousness. An avalanche presents Brovik's descending ascent. Solness's comes not on a natural but on a domestic architectural height,
one he has built himself, one he is willfully refashioning as a supernatural
plateau when Hilde's praise turns his newly robust artistic conscience into
fatal giddiness.

The ontological crisis of artistic action staged in that fall is symbolically
advanced by Solness's willed ascent to Hilde's airy castle. Where earlier
symbols—the burning orphanage in *Ghosts*, the white horses in *Rosmersholm*—
are omens characters observe and analyze, the airy castle is a symbolic
predication of the future that characters do not analytically observe but
mystically will in private imagination. How this innovation in symbolic
writing presents Ibsen's final construction of modernist action—creative
will's conflicted release of power from reason—comes clear through a quick
tracing of the psychology and metaphysics built into the fairytale image
Hilde and Solness use to generate artistic inspiration.

The forms of architecture reconfigure substance, in the Aristotelian
order, in accordance with free, self-governing rational agency, they don't

invent or ontologically transpose it. The Aristotelian order also asserts that such self-governing rational intervention in material reality as architects practice will bring about personal and social well-being, happiness. When this second assertion proved false in Solness's case, the builder resolved the discrepancy by fearfully consigning his self-governing power for creative intervention in the material realm to suprarational forces in it—to trolls—. Unable to distinguish the mystical trolls' service to his career from their mastery over it, Solness has confused the rational and irrational relations of cause and effect in creativity. That confusion—moral and intellectual giddiness—has confined him to ambivalence and guilt, to remorse's negative, punitive reversal of creativity's power to bring new effect out of old cause, to change substantially spiritual or physical reality.

Throughout her two-day stay Hilde treats Solness's crippling, long-standing ambivalence as an opportunity to achieve joy herself by reviving it in him. To accomplish that, she needs to exterminate his allegiance to the Aristotelian humanistic order. She also needs to preserve his belief in that order's confident assertion that self-governing creativity brings about happiness. She seeks such preservation by cajoling, berating, seducing, and inspiring Solness into daring affirmation of the new mystical order of creative power that her demand for a long-ago promised kingdom presents to him. The new mystical order, which she symbolically calls a castle in the air in this scene, is a Nietzschean one in which the transcendent force of aesthetic will to power supplants the morally vindictive force of demons and trolls.

Under Hilde's various styles of command Solness has ambivalently retreated from his ambivalence. He affirms the new order, pays the old debt that should free him, with weak belief in a weakened creativity—hypothetical recasting of reality. His sentimental, fantasized conjectures, the "suppose I did" or "I wish I had" indulgences of Hilde in acts 1 and 2 abate his ambivalent guilt, but the reversals that follow from Aline's interventions in acts 2 and 3 turn that fragile ease back into confining remorse. When Hilde finally ousts Aline from the builder's life, and hers, by withdrawing from the adultery plot, she at once magnifies and reduces Solness's confusion over creativity. When Solness concedes that climbing the physical tower he built for Aline is building a metaphysical tower for himself and for Hilde, he finally transmutes that confusion into transcendent inversion out of the Aristotelian account of action.

Adopting the ontologically strong meaning of hypothetical invention— let there be a castle in the air—Solness eliminates the humanistic idea that creation is rational intervention in a fixed material order bound by cause and effect. With art's rational intervention in nature and culture banished, the trolls' supernatural control of that intervention also vanishes from Solness's life. Their negative affirmation of humanism—the remorse that access to their power cost him—gives way to the self-governing spiritual authority by which creativity exceeds and measures the natural world, to the joyful, exalting view downward on the world of churches and houses from Hilde's airy balcony. This happy displacement of the trolls ironically brings Solness face to face with a supernaturally creative authority already reigning in the kingdom of airy castles, one whose power over the humanistic ordering of nature far exceeds the trolls' demonic force, namely God.

According to that late stage in the Christian compromise with Aristotle that governs sanctioned metaphysics in Solness's epoch, God made nature a system of interlocked, ontologically ascending and descending ratios of His own creative power, a fixed dynamic relation of possible and actual being that culminates in conscious human agency, whose proper activity is sustaining its ascendancy in the fixed dynamic and thereby discovering God.[1] The airy castle ousts God from ontology and re-presents Solness's own will to power to him as a symbolic ratio that creates and reveals reality as an unfixed dynamic ascent apocalyptically reenacted in every moment of artistic consciousness. Solness has hypothetically upheld and then renounced the secular rationalism impeding his assent to the airy castle's competing ontology already in this scene. The divine authority for that rationalism still remains, however. It takes his strongest hypothetical projection of will to power in the play—the final projective/retrospective affirmation of the Lysanger climb in his last words with Hilde—for the builder to master that forbidding authority and perform the impossible. Ibsen stages that symbolically transcendent artistic achievement by resuming psychologically realistic depiction of the play's conjoined professional and sexual intrigues; at the verge of transforming recognition, he moves down to move up, as the inverting advance of Nietzschean will and Aristotelian dramatic action require.

Solness's fear has moved the action forward by stalling it throughout this play. Aline, Ragnar, and Hilde have all variously struggled with Solness's fear, and their competing interests in it, especially Hilde's and Ragnar's, peak as that fear resurges, abates, and then triumphs in the rapid closing scenes. The reappearance of the violated apprentice starts that culminating retrospective rearrangement of strength and weakness in Solness's will to artistic power. For the finale Ibsen uses stock-in-trade plot devices—the amassing of a crowd on-and offstage, a falsely delivered message, the aborted intervention of a friendly medical authority—to give Solness's impossible action the magnifying urgency of ironically conventional suspense. The subversion lies in making a familiar theatrical treat provide an unfamiliar theatrical pleasure, in turning melodramatic apprehension of Solness's impending fall from the material house into metaphysical longing for his impending climb into the spiritual castle. Ibsen works that switch at the end as he has throughout the play, by forcing Solness toward strong hypothetical exertions of will. Ragnar helps exert this final pressure on the builder's creativity when he returns to the action as soon as Solness has agreed to erect Hilde's airy kingdom.

Hilde and Ragnar are paired figures of youthful liberation and retribution governing Solness's ambivalent second-act repudiation of sexually repressive professional stasis. Now that Hilde has transposed Solness's lingering professional struggle against repression into a mystically erotic ascent to her, Ragnar enters and reveals that the damage Solness's repression did to this apprentice's filial and sexual life has outlived the builder's professional withdrawal from the mundane sphere. Ibsen emphasizes the ominous, retributive irony of Ragnar's bitter judgment that Solness cannot free himself or anyone else by having the apprentice interrupt the long transcendence scene with Hilde. At the moment Solness confidently promises to build creativity's immaterially "true foundation," Ragnar delivers the ceremonious wreath that will be raised to celebrate the builder's latest material achievement. The character and his prop return Solness to the order of humanist praxis which he has just promised to repudiate, and dare him to pass actively through the possible world in order to hypothetically will the impossible. Ragnar's career, and his father's, has always involved Solness in conflicted struggle against the conjoined metaphysical and mundane authorities for artistic action. In the final moments of the play Ibsen stages that struggle as an eternal return of the same, the ultimate challenge to the Nietzschean willing the builder has affirmed with Hilde. Throughout their last scene together Solness and Ragnar replay, for the final time, their unending Oedipal contest of artistic wills, explicitly assigning rapidly shifting and opposed implicit meanings to their shared wreath.

The maestro hesitated to free Ragnar to build in act 2 because he feared that those demonic forces that had uncannily, criminally advanced his career would exact retribution for his telepathic summons of them by transferring their service, and consequently the builder's mastery, to the newly authorized, younger, innocent creator. At that young man's first appearance after his liberation, Solness fears the demonic retribution may have come. Hilde makes a joyful exclamation when Ragnar brings on the dangerous tower's decoration, convinced that it promises transcendence. Solness is amazed when he sees Ragnar, who has not heard the builder's promise to hoist the wreath, bearing it. The surprise harbors presumptive fear about the bearer's intention. To discover if Ragnar expects him to climb, to discover if that expectation is retributive demonic urging of fatal boldness in him, a negative variant of the telepathic willing by which he summoned the criminally liberating Hilde, Solness makes an insinuating question out of the feared rival's appearance; "Have you brought the wreath, Ragnar?" (MB, 357).

In performance the actor should utter the personal pronoun and the word *wreath* ambivalently affronted and so reveal how panicked Solness is by the uncanny insolence of this upstart's apparent challenge. Ragnar ignores the builder's startled insinuation and responds with polite, pragmatic neutrality that the foreman sent for the wreath. The subordinate's courteous disclosure of his menially professional service to another subordinate relieves Solness in two ways: it eliminates unexpected, unwanted, and uncanny pressure on him to act bravely, and it presents an alternative climber (the foreman) to Hilde, one the community at large expects to see. The relief, explicitly required by Ibsen's stage direction, gives Solness renewed power to command and evade action, power the builder immediately expresses as noblesse oblige when, to exonerate and aggrandize himself, he asks if Ragnar's fetching means that his ailing, offended father, Brovik, has recovered enough to be left alone.

Solness is fishing with this inquiry for appreciation of the restitution he made for ruining Brovik's career. Earlier that day, under Hilde's influence, he sent Kaja to deliver Ragnar's praised, and so professionally enfranchised, drawings to the broken father ambitious for his son. For many conflicted reasons Solness is eager, at this point of psychological and ontological crisis, to learn the outcome of his liberating praise of Ragnar. The play starts with Solness withholding that corrective boon when the failing Brovik begs it. The builder all but admits that his own tormented self-creation requires the oppressive refusal when he justifies it by telling Brovik that he cannot change himself to make the old man happy (see MB, 3-6). The play's reversals that follow that initial refusal show Solness trying to change himself to make himself happy. That change comes primarily in repudiating the worldly career that he maintained by repressing the Brovik line, repudiating the sexual imbroglio with Kaja that reinforced the professional tyranny, repudiating the charismatic creative and professional power bestowed on him by the super-natural trolls, and gradually committing his will to transcendent spiritual creation with and for Hilde. As it unfolds, Ibsen casts that progressive renunciation of punitive magical power over worldly love and work in symbolic terms that ironically refer Solness's action to Faust's and to Prospero's in *The Tempest*.

In both cases the irony emphasizes the modernist difficulty and neces-sity of making exile from the world of praxis a transfiguring entry to an airy kingdom. When Ragnar balks Solness's aspiring will to transcendent power and redirects that will to worldly affairs by frightening him with the wreath, the ambivalently grandiose builder tries immediately to make his cowardly regression from airy happiness an advance by indirectly compelling worldly submission—a filial expression of gratitude for kindness to a weak father— from the young mundane challenger. Psychologically, Ragnar's thanks would submissively confirm the older man's regressive assertion of power; ontologically, it would allow Solness to accomplish successfully his compensatory, habitually weak switch from longed-for transcendent self-creation back to pragmatic humanist ethics. In both cases the strategy can only fail, since it makes Solness's autonomy a function of Ragnar's will.

Nor is the heavy hint to Ragnar a successful moral reentry to the realm of praxis, one that matches Faust's social striving or Prospero's just reconciliations. Whatever Christian kindness Solness feels at this moment, his masterly generosity fails the Christian test for virtuous action; it is not what Wordsworth called a soul-making "nameless, unremembered act of kindness," but, rather, a desperately self-infatuated, pharisaical vanity.[2] If Ragnar exonerates Solness's first criminal confusion of strength and weakness with Brovik, the builder can recoup some of the self-esteem that his most recent confusion of strength and weakness—flight from the airy castle, flight instigated by Brovik's avenging son—has annulled. So the tender search for thanks is more significantly an exploitative plea for revitalizing forgiveness, a weak raid by a once-more giddy conscience on the worldly resources for self-creation that Solness long ago stole from the father and that he has so recently, and in his mind bounteously, restored to the violated son.

Robust or giddy, however, conscientious humanist action cannot do the work of transcendent self-creation in Ibsen's plays; it can only take and then lose that other action's name. Mrs. Alving and Rebecca West both come to grief when they try to invent a new future by managing or undoing a criminal past. Solness comes to the same grief. Ragnar stalls the reformed villain's tenuous self-creation as liberator when he tells Solness that the newly praised drawings were delivered after Brovik had been rendered unconscious by a stroke that will momentarily claim his life. Ibsen points the conventional tragic irony in this defeated action by having Ragnar and Solness antiphonally lament that the builder's kindness came "too late." Solness responds strategically to the disappointment, ambiguously advising Ragnar to return to Brovik and bear conventionally symbolic witness to his father's passing authority. The builder's honest, sympathetic urging of conventional domestic piety, against which his whole life has been an ambivalently willed offense, conveys the following implicit instruction to Ragnar: I grieve with

you that death has forestalled my will to liberate your father; vindicate him
and me by ceremoniously honoring the paternal love whose aims I have
enabled you to enact. This self-protective advocacy of the dying father's
prerogative, by which Solness covers his offense against Brovik's house,
repeats that corruption of Christ's belittling of filial responsibility to paternal
death that symbolically governed Solness's previous suppressive encounter
with the aggrieved son. A device of melodramatic intrigue—schemers never
exhaust the modes of fraud—the repetition of this symbolically magnified
moment in the play's domestic, professional intrigue also does modernist
thematic work here. Solness's *habitual* confusion of strength and weakness
bears witness not only to an Aristotelian hamartia in him, but also to the
power over him of the Nietzschean action that constantly brings will,
strength, and weakness about—the eternal return of the same.

"Let the dead bury their dead: but go thou and preach the kingdom of
God" (Luke 9:60) sounds ironically throughout the scene in act 2 when
Ragnar bootlessly pleads a disappointed father's hope for the advancement
of a talented son to the defensively adamant Solness. In that scene Solness
corruptly urges Ragnar's prudent performance of domestic filial piety to keep
the confined youth from working independently and so bringing the kingdom of God retributively upon his oppressor. In this scene Solness urges the
respectable death vigil on Ragnar for the same reason: to prevent the young
man from bringing him face to face with the kingdom of God. But Solness's
power to protect himself by confining Ragnar to the mundane sphere is
greatly reduced here. The death vigil and Ragnar's thanks are the only
humanist expressions of power Solness can command now to evade his
promised rebellious entry into God's kingdom. And, unlike the professional
oppression that Solness has now lifted, these controls hold only sentimental
sway over Ragnar.

For a long time Solness has indirectly ruled Ragnar by exerting uncanny
psychosexual force over his fiancée Kaja, fraudulently inducing her erotic
collusion in his oppression of the younger man. Face to face with the newly
empowered, belligerently bereaved son, however, the builder's charisma, his
uncanny sympathetic charm, fails. And how could it not? By publicly humiliating his father and privately alienating the affections of his promised
spouse, Solness has not only forestalled but also compelled Ragnar's hostile,
oedipal emergence into self-assertion. He can no more claim emotional
allegiance from the now resurgent Ragnar than he can claim thanks from the
unconscious Brovik. Nonetheless, summoning the resources of an astonishing
audacity, Solness undertakes the impossible social and psychological action
here and makes an extorting, insinuating claim on Ragnar's unavailable

sympathy. Trusting his charismatic personal authority, he turns hubristic in this avuncular cajoling of exonerating obedience from a scornful rival.

The audacity and hubris ironically stage an ambivalent weakness, a giddiness at the core of Solness's strategic bravado. The weakness involves, as usual, the builder's split commitment to sanctioned and criminal willing. And, as usual, when reversal makes that ambiguity plain to Solness, he reenacts it, with higher metaphysical stakes attached, with giddiness turned toward more dangerously robust conscience. The second duel with Ragnar comes very late in the play, reversing and transposing the builder's concatenated long-term evasions rapidly and decisively. The crucial inversion here sends him flickering back toward the metaphysical action that his social bravado stalls but does not annul. The self-justifying, arrogating performance of social authority with Ragnar requires a weak variety of hypothetical self-creation from Solness. Even were it noble or honest—strong—such transformational willing could not count or succeed as action in the sanctioned order of praxis, since there self-creation, indeed all agency, starts and ends in identity with the limiting fixity of natural and social facts. Nothing but a strong variety of hypothetical self-creation counts or succeeds as action in the criminal Nietzschean order, since there any limiting concession to fixed natural or social facts annuls the will's power to generate and then surpass reality.

Solness's attempt to make a weak Nietzschean action govern retreat to the pragmatic realm turns out to be what Joyce's Stephen Dedalus in *Ulysses* calls a "portal of discovery"—the volitional error by which a man of genius advances his creative life.[3] Absolute power is the promise and prerogative of Solness's genius; contingent willing of that power is his volitional error. The play's action moves Solness back and forth through weak and strong varieties of hypothetical self-creation—"I would be thus" and "I will me thus"—and in the process incrementally disentangles absolute from contingent willing. These last scenes with Ragnar dissolve the contingent intrigue, the realistic and melodramatic plot presenting Solness's negatively impossible performance of the absolute. That dissolution opens the way for his positively impossible action, the joyful construction of Hilde's castle in the air atop Aline's new house of old, mournful marriage. Ragnar, whose appearance unwittingly provoked Solness's compensatory, pragmatic aversion to transcendent willing, ironically, and again unwittingly, turns Solness back to that willing when he refuses the builder's instruction to leave the veranda and behave respectably at home. The inversion upward of Solness's inverted will, the rival's reversal of the builder's flight from Hilde's airy castle, emerges in the following exchange which is brief, but not so brief that Ibsen cannot load it with subversive poetic justice and transmuting symbolic allusion to Christ's demand for sacrificial repudiation of worldly virtue.

> Ragnar: He doesn't need me any more.
>
> Solness: But surely you ought to be with him?
>
> Ragnar: She's sitting with him.
>
> Solness (a little uncertainly): Kaja?
>
> Ragnar (looks darkly at him): Yes. Kaja.
>
> Ragnar: Go home, Ragnar. Go home to them. Give me the wreath.
>
> Ragnar (represses a scornful smile): Surely you're not going to—?
>
> Solness: I'll take it down there myself. (He takes the wreath from him.) Go home now, we won't need you today.
>
> Ragnar: I know you won't. But today, I'm staying.
>
> Solness: Oh, stay—stay, by all means. (MB, 357-58)

Previously, Solness has kept the criminal demands and power of his genius at bay by infatuating Kaja in order to keep Ragnar near him. Now that Ragnar's presence no longer checks but magnifies the criminal threat that genius poses to Solness, the builder wants him gone. At this point Ibsen brings Kaja back into the plot to work a quick, complex turn on poetic justice. Her part in the oppressive erotic triangle has not changed along with the shift in her suitors' rivalry: she still keeps Ragnar near Solness, but now she does so innocently, by taking Ragnar's place at his father's deathbed. Doing virtuous familial service to a man whom Solness has made sure she can never love, Kaja unwittingly hoists the builder on his own petard—ambiguous adherence to domestic duty—and so enacts that simple form of poetic justice in which vice and virtue are rewarded, however ironically, in the time, place, and terms in which they are performed. Solness and Ragnar both give conventional histrionic signals that Kaja's deed has justly reversed the builder's ambivalent social ploy: the older man elicits the surprising disclosure with "a little uncertainty"; the younger man offers it with a menacing, dark look.

In more complex poetic justice actions in one sphere are rewarded in another. The splitting of retributive effect from incriminating cause can happen across time, as in the Old Testament visitation of fathers' sins on subsequent generations (recall Ghosts), or in different dimensions of reality, as is the case in Oscar Wilde's The Picture of Dorian Gray, published in 1891, one year before The Master Builder was written in Norway and two years before it was first performed in Berlin. In the English novel vice's effects on their agent are supernaturally transposed back and forth from his immutably strong, young, beautiful life to his ever-aging, increasingly hideous portrait.

Displaying poetic justice in the unchecked criminal's aesthetic image, finally giving that painting power over the protagonist's life, Wilde toys with the traditional moral dynamic in art's mimetic function.[4] Ibsen subverts the traditional moralism governing art's creative function and displays his complex poetic justice by magically transforming his checked builder's criminally productive energy. Solness has committed that energy to opposed sources, rationalist humanism and Nietzschean voluntarism. That dual commitment amounts to vice in both systems; hence, poetic justice is especially complex in Ibsen's play. There retribution resolves an ontological crisis suggested but finally suppressed in Wilde's witty, fantastic association of life, art, and transgression.

Solness's ambiguous passage between absolute and contingent willing and his failed attempts to enact both powers at once always require the service of women. Without exception Solness ambivalently enlists that aid through charismatic emotional corruption of their domestic erotic lives. To varying degrees the conquered wife, mother, daughter, and fiancée all advance Solness's metaphysical crisis by subverting the builder's uncanny sexual hold over their pragmatic lives. It is fitting, therefore, that Solness's last, weakest attempt to pass between contingent and absolute willing, which is also his last and most tenuous suspension of both powers, should be rewarded with simple and complex poetic justice meted out accidentally by the thoroughly victimized Kaja, that foolishly, innocently, simple accomplice in the maestro's complex treason against domesticity and genius.

The simple poetic justice she works in the realistic intrigue—thwarting Solness's latest corruption of familial loyalty—not only impedes but also helps reverse the builder's treasonous flight from genius, since her absence keeps Ragnar onstage taunting the builder, shaming him into a metaphysical act of robust conscience. That ambiguous result blends complexity into the simple poetic justice, makes retribution in one sphere a chance for exoneration in another. The giddy builder can, after all, annul the familial and professional crimes if he wills his life-threatening climb of the domestic church spire to be immaterial construction of a rewarding airy castle. Solness and Hilde both know that, Ragnar does not, and that difference supplies the heady tension in this ostensibly social struggle over Ragnar's eviction from the veranda.

For Solness salvation now lies in sacrificial repudiation of the worldly good, especially the familial ethics, of building. In this scene Ragnar unwittingly advances that salvation by presenting himself as the mute avenger of Solness's offense against male and female familial life. Murderous father, philandering husband, molester of a nubile child, cynically licentious intruder in his dependents' engagement—Solness has played out all the melodramatically villainous roles that the popular Aristotelian stage offered in Ibsen's time. To say he out-Herods Herod is anachronistic, but only slightly: he does scheme to repress youthful successors to his kingdom; two male infants have died to guarantee his mastery. Of all the damage Solness has done to female life, Ragnar knows and cares only about the crime against his own impending marriage. For reasons that come clear in the next scene, he reveals the full measure of his vindictive anguish to Hilde only after Solness leaves the stage.

About Solness's offense against male life, familial and professional, Ragnar knows and cares more, as befits his young, and conventionally self-regarding, virility. The builder has violated women by subverting their conventional function as accessories to male achievement. He has violated the Broviks, father and son, by subsuming their achievements, by making them accessories to his career, and so undoing their manly function and identity. But the Broviks' offended manly labor and loyalty—their negated action—ultimately work redemptive, complex poetic justice on Solness, as does his ethically mixed victimization of Kaja, Aline, and Hilde. And that deliverance comes ironically, as Solness and Ragnar grapple, once the builder has freed his apprentice, for control of how, why, and for whom this young man's action, his loyal attendance, is necessary.

That disputed necessity's ethical and psychosexual complexities wrap conventionally realistic professional and romantic intrigue up into modernist, metaphysical conflict between worldly and transcendent action, between contingent and absolute willing. Ibsen signals this ontological transposition by twice presenting the struggle between Solness and Ragnar in terms of Christ's advocacy of sacrificial, transcendent repudiation of familial loyalty. In its second appearance the ironic distortion of Christ's injunction to the orphaned son —"let the dead bury their dead: but go thou and preach the kingdom of God" (Luke 9:60)—occurs in Ragnar's lines to Solness. In its first appearance in act 2 the distortion occurs in Solness's lines to Ragnar. This inversion in the play's allusive design marks a crucial reversal and recognition for the builder and prepares the audience for his final transforming account to Hilde of past and future building and climbing as defiant, transcendent repudiation of service in and to God's kingdom.

When Ragnar declares that his dying father doesn't need him anymore, he unwittingly and symbolically attaches New Testament transcendence to his thwarting evasion of the builder's weak, confining advocacy of respectable worldly action. Two distortions make the allusion an ironic advance in the play's metaphysical action. First, Ragnar doesn't forgo respectable filial duty, but fulfills it through Kaja's proxy service and tells the builder so. Hence, no sacrificial pursuit of transcendent virtue makes his attendance on Solness necessary. Rather, he stays to expose Solness's cowardice and so avenge the father whom that cowardice ruined. Pursuing humiliation as worldly retribution for the builder's professional and sexual crimes against the male Broviks, Ragnar goes about his earthly father's business, despite his mute invocation of transcendent indifference to the worldly service due paternal death. That first distortion of the allusion gives rise to the second. Solness feared Ragnar had come to enact divine retribution. When he discovers that the young man wants worldly vengeance, Solness finesses the assault with equivocation that turns Ragnar's taunts of cowardice into the call of robust conscience. Heeding that call, even hesitantly, Solness revives the sacrificial repudiation of worldly virtuous action that Ragnar abortively invokes. The turn is doubly complex, since Solness contemplates an ascent directly, criminally opposed to the Christian transcendence that Ragnar has transformed into vengeance. This distorted, elevating retrieval of a lost action—the negation of a negation—once more twists Aristotelian praxis into Nietzschean willing and so subtly advances the play's radical, experimental staging of the impossible.

The second, richly ambiguous distortion of Ragnar's mute biblical citation, which turns his vindictiveness into complex poetic justice, escapes him completely, as the first did, but its substance, if not its form, registers on Solness and Hilde. Instead of urging Solness to advocacy of God's immanent kingdom, Ragnar finishes his ironic evocation of "let the dead bury their dead" with an unintended provocation of the builder's Promethean defiance of divine power. Bested in his social intrigue by the news of Kaja's proxy devotion, Solness answers the apprentice's complex oedipal denial and defense of his dying father with a direct command that acknowledges and eliminates Ragnar's need to stay on the veranda: "Go home, Ragnar. Go home to *them*. Give me the wreath" (my italics). Ragnar ignores the apologetic acknowledgment of sexual rivalry and the anxious advocacy of domestic loyalty in Solness's addition of Kaja to the needy home scene and presses his vengeful jeering, withholding the wreath with a scornful implication that the famously acrophobic older man is too cowardly to climb with it: "Surely *you're* not going to . . . ?"

The builder dodges the finally explicit insult and challenge with his first action in this scene: "I'll take it down there myself," he says, physically depriving Ragnar of any further reason to stay by taking the wreath from him. In possession of the talismanic prop Solness tries once more to transform Ragnar's metaphysical challenge into an easily reproved breach of professional and social courtesy with the dismissive line "We won't need you today." When Ragnar recalcitrantly defies this fourth, strongest admonition to return home—"I know you won't. But today, I'm staying"—Solness trumps the youth's rudeness with an astonishing reversal that mixes noblesse oblige, cowardice, and audacity in inseparable measures: "Oh stay—stay, by all means." Hilde takes the invitation to be a gloating promise on Solness's part that he will prove his robust conscience and humiliate Ragnar by making the ascent: "It'll be frightfully exciting." But Solness curtails hope for that resolution with a subdued evasion—"We'll—talk about that later, Hilde," and exits through the garden from which she first entered to start this act's assaultive reversals of his weak will to power.

For Solness, metaphysics are at stake in the fight over Brovik's deathbed; for Ragnar the concern is purely worldly. Solness ironically preserves that distinction with an exit that ambiguously switches the terms of victory governing the social contest. Stay, his departure tells Ragnar, I am magnanimous enough to disregard your ethical reproof; stay, the departure mutely promises, and you may see me surpass that reproof. Ibsen frames the ontological divergence binding the two builders here by beginning and ending their struggle for ethical and psychosexual dominance with antiphonally ironic assertions, first from the apprentice then the master, that Ragnar's conventionally dutiful manly action, his filial staying power, is dispensable, not necessary, to his domestic or professional father. The antiphonal inversion that turns Ragnar's ironic abandonment of Brovik and punitive cleaving to Solness, "He doesn't need me any more," into the builder's self-liberating dismissal of Ragnar, "We won't need you today," culminates in Solness's ironic abandonment of Ragnar, the defensive exit by which he preserves himself and deftly stymies the hectoring young man. Ambiguously resolving their conflict with an exit that suspends the scene's complex power negotiations to Solness's advantage, Ibsen makes the simplest element of stagecraft—who comes and goes—do extraordinarily sophisticated thematic work. Briefly: multiply opposed, interlocked father-son relations are enforced and dissolved in Solness's confiscation of Ragnar's ominously delivered wreath. Stalled advance in the play's realistic intrigue once again invokes a discharging Nietzschean reversal here, as Ragnar's balked filial challenge speeds the end of Solness's ambivalent struggle with cosmological patriarchy, an end ironically crowned by the reclaimed wreath raised in Solness's sexually and metaphysically symbolic climb.

The relation of fathers and sons, symbolically and conceptually rendered, is a controlling topic in Western literary, religious, philosophical, and psychological accounts of how people strive for a stable place in a changing world. Until recently women have usually figured in this cultural inheritance as powers existing almost exclusively in relation to male force, as ancillary, expedient, or functionally opposed instances and symbols of originally and finally male reality. In theorizing about pragmatic affairs—ethics, politics, familial and social psychology—and in metaphysical inquiry, especially philosophical and religious puzzling over being, time, and truth, the reciprocity between fathers and sons has consistently established or clarified arguments that show how identity comes out of difference, unity out of multiplicity, and permanence out of loss. Aesthetics, the practice and theory of art, has normally held an intermediary place between pragmatic and metaphysical activity and inquiry, now integrating, now separating, action and contemplation.[5]

In that fluid, middle realm the controlling value and authority is beauty, whose creative and expressive origin and end, from Homer's Muses forward to Dante's Beatrice, and Joyce's Molly Bloom, has been consistently symbolized as female. Indeed, pragmatic and metaphysical opposition to art's malleable authority and value in human affairs, again from Plato forward, has consistently argued that aesthetics depraves action and reality by yielding both to some species of inconstant feminine domination. Defenses of art have construed service to the feminine power of beauty as some species of intermediate, enhancing service to masculine authority, a retrieval, illumination, and glorification of it. This feminine enhancement normally allows for male integration of pragmatic and metaphysical concerns. For all the differences in their ontologies and ethics, Dante and Wallace Stevens, for instance, both present the significant coherence their poetry makes of active and contemplative experience—mystic illumination in one case, imaginative sensation in the other—as an achievement of and from feminine powers.[6]

In *The Master Builder* Ibsen forces the conventional topics and aesthetic of his theater—familial, erotic, and professional conflicts rendered in illusionistic realism—past their familiar conceptual and imaginative limits in two ways. He makes the pragmatic relations between fathers and sons and feminine mediation in those relations terms for contemplation of metaphysical conflict and so gives the Victorian stage a dramatic grandeur comparable to Sophocles' theater and to Racine's. More significantly, his neoclassical realism paradoxically undoes the metaphysical tradition it revives. *The Master Builder* recasts the coherence aesthetics makes between action and contemplation in many different ways. Driving and unifying them all is a radical change in woman's pragmatic and conceptual part in male action: feminine power now supersedes the father-son relation instead of mediating it.

Begetting and begotten, visiting muse and psychogenic child-bride, Hilde
annuls the heavenly and worldly patriarchal order that has enmeshed the
three builders when she resolves the mundane creation intrigue binding
Ragnar to Brovik and Solness, his physical and ghostly fathers.

Hilde's resolution of the professional intrigue—her forcing of Ragnar's
enfranchisement by Solness in act 2—devalues Ragnar's worldly building and
ends Solness's. Requiring Solness to build her airy castle, and so recreate
himself and her, Hilde makes her negation of praxis a potential sublimation
of it. Her imminent summoning of an immanent action operates with the
same logic governing Christ's patriarchal call for sacrificial repudiation of
worldly ethics, in fact employs the same aggrandizing symbolism—strong
hypothetical urging that "the heavenly kingdom" come to be—but the
convergence is competitive, not harmonious. Ibsen stages the competition
between Nietzsche's transcendent willing and Christ's brilliantly by having
Ragnar enter to interrupt Hilde's demand for the airy castle with a distorted
allusion to Christ's upward inversion of right action. That distortion continues Ibsen's strategic casting of Ragnar as Hilde's double, a retributive youth
called forth by Solness's strong weakness. At this moment, as in act 2 the
opposed genders and philosophies that identify this elected son and daughter
coalesce to form an objective (as well as symbolic) correlative to the builder's
internal dilemma. The unified opposition staged by these two children of
conscience repeats and disentangles the criminal conflation Solness has
made, and under their compulsion must undo, between contingent and
absolute willing.

The resolution Ragnar offers—punitive transfer of worldly power—
casts all willing as male generational conflict, casts intelligible change as
ousting of one state by another. This Aristotelian model for action, which
moralizes and rationalizes the power of annihilating selection, is metaphysically grounded, from the Greek Titans through to the Christian Trinity, in
divine filial or paternal killing. Hence, this son's resentful indifference to a
dying father and his murderous taunting of a weakly living one, both
ironically made in famously Christian definitions of filial duty. The resolution
Hilde offers—majestic, exonerating sublimation of earthly powers through
aesthetic self-assertion—surpasses Ragnar's, replaces male conflict's annihilating end with beauty's transformative female prize: free, creative sover-
eignty over reality, Nietzsche's "great health," what Solness and Hilde think
of as a "robust conscience." Hence, this telepathic child-bride's longing for
mental erection of an airy love palace. That Ibsen weighs Hilde's resolution
more heavily in the dramatic order is obvious from her central position in
the action, her power to control Ragnar's fate. That Ragnar presents

Christianity's transcendent action mute and distorted makes for complex competition between the philosophical tradition and rebellion embedded in the play's dramatic order.

With this opposition of sacrificial obedience to ennobling self-determination as modes and goals for Solness's absolute willing, Ibsen repeats the religious opposition of privative duty against prodigal happiness that stalled action in *Ghosts* and *Rosmersholm* and moves Hilde and Solness past the ethical conflicts staged in those plays. Whereas Mrs. Alving and Rebecca West struggle to revise the symbolically and pragmatically male law of God's created world, Hilde urges Solness, an alternately murderous and liberating father, to supplant the murderous and liberating sky god's creative power per se. Shifting the female mediation in male action from ethics to aesthetic ontology in *The Master Builder*, Ibsen subverts drama's preservation of the Christian humanist tradition more radically than anyone before or since. He works this apocalyptic transformation by having Ragnar and Hilde require identical but opposed performance of the impossible from Solness.

That mirrored opposition uniting these characters, and uniting Solness to them, gets played out in unprecedentedly dense but basically familiar psychological realism, from which the play's cosmological argument extends. The central, all too familiar, psychological action is self-creation through mixed- and same-gender identification, from which Ibsen works out the negative and positive consequences of conforming to or creating the real. Solness, Ragnar, and Hilde all view his climb as the impossible action, and they all attach gendered meanings to the deed's impossibility, but only Solness and Hilde see the nature of reality itself at stake in the climb; only they know the ontologically positive meaning of doing the impossible.

In Aristotelian praxis instances of reality supplant one another developmentally, but reality remains unchanged throughout the process. In Nietzschean willing power supplants itself creatively instead of developmentally. In this logic, in which reality is nothing but power's atelic self-aggrandizement achieved through resistance generated and overcome internally, the changes brought about in power's sublimating inversions change reality itself, continuously moving it through the difference of increase to more potent self-expression, more active identity. That at least is the noble mind's experience of Nietzsche's hypothetical insight into being, the joyous, aesthetic response to and evocation of the eternal return of the same. From the Aristotelian perspective creative evocation of the real through burgeoning sublimation of difference and identity in will to power is an impossible action. From the Nietzschean height, or depth, confinement of the will to rationality's zero-sum transposition of developing and decaying instances of the fixedly real is more unworthy than impossible an action, since it annuls joy, health, and their active source, power.

Ibsen makes this philosophical contest about how identity and difference in changing combination preserve or transform the real concrete onstage by assigning both views to Solness, by assigning the Aristotelian one to Ragnar and the Nietzschean one to Hilde. He makes the assignation dramatic by embedding the abstract conflict in conventional sexual and professional intrigue in which ontological conflict between identity and difference can be presented as psychological conflict between men and men and between men and women. The plot device that shows all the conflicts at once, and moves them to their final resolution, is Solness's final confrontation with Ragnar, hence the long attention it has received here, despite the brevity of their staged dispute.

The fulcrum in that dispute, dramatically and conceptually, is the relation between earthly contingent and heavenly absolute power, between physical and ghostly fathers and sons. The mediating factor, conceptually, is transcendence. Its dramatic agents are female—secondarily Kaja, who frees Ragnar domestically to confront Solness, and primarily Hilde, whose professional freeing of Ragnar and whose urging of the airy castle require that Solness confront what Ragnar does: the oppressive ghostly father, God in the older builder's case, who punitively, defensively hobbles the insurgent artist's vital will to joyous self-determination. Ragnar's case is easier; his ghostly father has freed him. The defiance he expresses of Solness in this scene does not establish him as a creator but as a scourge of the older creator's worldly crimes. Ironically, his retributive, symbolic reversal of the Christian call for transcendent negligence of worldly filial duty provokes the older builder into an exonerating transcendence, a repudiation of all worldly and heavenly patriarchal power.

Scourge to Solness, Ragnar makes Solness a scourge to God, with this difference: the older builder has not been freed by his ghostly father when he defies the celestial masterbuilder's moral and creative power, but must wrest the power for defiant self-determination from Jehovah himself, largely encouraged by Hilde's demanding admiration. Ragnar's strong weakness, vindictiveness, reverses Solness's strong weakness, guilt. Identity and difference coalesce here in characters who enact opposed social and psychological functions of the same profession and gender, and the merger comes about because of and for the sake of a character from the opposite gender who has no worldly profession, but an implacable project to restore action's vitality, the robust conscience dissipated and dispersed in the mundane sphere. Once more the Aristotelian reversals in the intrigue plot have led to Nietzschean inversions upward in the metaphysical contest.

Solness exits this scene wavering between Ragnar's mode of action and Hilde's. Ibsen underscores that tension by giving the two youths their only scene alone together, during which they discuss, appropriately enough, Solness's fear. Hilde, eager to magnify Solness, chastises Ragnar for rudeness and ingratitude toward his professional benefactor. Ragnar continues to ignore his new creative freedom, complaining instead of the emotional damage Solness has inflicted on him. He rehearses the professional and adultery intrigue with erroneous accusations that lead to a reversing recognition that once more amplifies and advances the metaphysical action. His first error is factual, his second interpretive. Mistakenly, Ragnar believes his father lost faith in him, as he did in himself, while Solness oppressed him. The reverse, of course, is true, as the play's first scene, in which Brovik pleads for his talented son's liberation, demonstrates. Revealing Ragnar's ignorance of his father's esteem for him, Ibsen gives further psychological grounding to the argument about transcendence carried out symbolically in the son's refusal to heed Solness's command that he return to his father's deathbed.

This backward clarification of the realistic action, a conventionally tragic and melodramatic device, moves forward with a familiar strategy of suspense—questioning interruption from an uninformed antagonist, Hilde in this case—to present Ragnar's interpretive error, his conviction that Solness wrecked the male Brovik line to keep Kaja infatuated and sexually available. Hilde, provoked to violent jealousy by this allegation, accuses Ragnar of lying and so elicits his revelation of Kaja's confession that Solness has taken possession of her mind, that she cannot and will not leave him. Hilde enters the sexual contest fully at this point, promising to oust Kaja, insinuating that Solness will abet that deed. Ragnar's response—"Oh yes. I see. Now she'd only be a nuisance to him" threatens to mire Hilde's desire in conventionally immoral sexual intrigue. To evade that, and to vanquish the rival she will not acknowledge before Ragnar, Hilde transposes their dispute over the builder's telepathic action and sublimated erotic domination up to the plane of Nietzschean transcendence in the following exchange.

> *Hilde:* You don't understand anything, if you talk like that. No, I'll tell you
>   why he kept her on.
> *Ragnar:* Why?
> *Hilde:* To keep you.
> *Ragnar:* Did he tell you that?

Hilde: No, but it's true! It *must* be! (*Wildly.*) It is, it is, I want it to be! (*MB*, 359)

Rationally unfolded knowledge of a protagonist's secret cause for action, strategically distributed cumulative inference and deduction via confessions, confrontations, overheard conversations, intercepted letters, and the like, has always organized the plot of realistic drama. Irrational access to such knowledge, through divine revelation or mystic intuition, often competes ambiguously with reasoned discovery for control of the plot. Indeed, that competition often makes drama metaphysically challenging, as Sophocles, Racine, and Shakespeare all indicate. Such competition drives this scene, indeed the whole play. The modernist, Nietzschean signature here comes in Hilde's willing the secret action herself instead of learning it irrationally. Her wild assertion that desire's necessity is the origin and end of truth—"You don't *understand* anything if you talk like that"—is as clear an instance of psychological cause at a distance, an especially mysterious power of anti-humanist voluntarism, as the play offers.

The ferocity in her outburst ironically displays fearful attachment to the world of praxis more than confident knowledge of how willfully to surpass it. Ragnar, as his subsequent behavior indicates, remains oblivious to this struggle in her, a fact that further demonstrates the metaphysical distinction in their modes and objects of "understanding." Hilde frantically exerts this absolute strength against him to overcome the contingent weakness of her position, which he has revealed to her. The unexpected emergence of Kaja as Hilde's rival once again extends Solness's primary conflict—the incoherent aim of simultaneously controlling and surpassing worldly power—to Hilde, who has throughout the play guided him out of that struggle. Once more sexual feeling gathers conventional dramatic and worldly action into a metaphysical crisis. For the rest of the play's finale Ibsen will symbolically elaborate that bond. At this point he stages it to Hilde's advantage, to increase the dramatic and conceptual tension over Solness's impossible rescue of them both from the world of praxis.

In addition to all these thematic ambiguities, dramatic irony qualifies this intuitive piece of voluntarism, since the audience knows that Hilde's judgment of Solness here is correct, irrespective of her desire toward him. For the rest of the scene that irony, which should diminish the wild authority of Hilde's *must*, bolsters it instead. Hilde not only preserves her desired truth but prevails with it by compelling this conventionally outraged suitor to adopt her interpretation of Solness's relation to Kaja. Ragnar, true to form, hears only sexual anxiety in Hilde's childish/Nietzschean outburst—"It is, it is, I want it to be!"—and immediately turns that feeling back on her as

incriminating refutation of her chaste, high-minded understanding of Solness: "And the moment *you* came he let her go." Hilde responds to the
debasing characterization of Solness as merely licentious not by disproving
it, but by eliminating Ragnar's resentful motive for making it, by implicitly
restoring the self-esteem, the robust conscience, that Ragnar has forfeited by
complaining of Kaja's betrayal: "*Hilde:* It was *you* he let go! What do you think
he cares about girls like her?" (*MB*, 359). Ragnar takes the bait—"(*thoughtfully*):
You mean he's been afraid of me all these years?—" and they play out the
short remainder of the scene on Hilde's terms.

Hilde switches the topic from adultery to building by exploiting the
ambiguity in oedipal antagonism. The gambit puts her directly in touch with
skittish, and therefore dangerous, male force, which shakes her even as she
shapes it to her own transcendent end. Making her arrival the cause of
Ragnar's liberation instead of Kaja's banishment from Solness, she cancels
the hostility of the bested son. Ragnar replaces it immediately with the
vaunting hostility of the besting son, a self-determining ferocity Hilde
cannot entirely master. Trivializing the professional and emotional violence
Solness cowardly practiced on the Broviks, damage that moments ago educed
the son's inflamed resentment, Ragnar now extravagantly magnifies the
accidental victory he has just won by delivering the wreath and exposing the
builder's humiliating fear to climb. Hilde responds to Ragnar's audacious,
callow insistence that Solness cannot summon the courage to climb with five
repeated and equally audacious assertions that her witnessing of the builder's
previously glorious climb at Lysanger proves he will make the ascent now.
Her first four responses are serenely aspiring and confident, but Ragnar's
repeatedly blunt, contemptuous instructions not to believe that her remem-
bered vision will move Solness to do the impossible finally unnerve Hilde.
Provoked and frightened, she bursts forth in a second, fiercer spasm of
strongly hypothetical assertion to counter the corrupting rationalist weakness his oedipal vindictiveness has induced in her: "*Hilde (violently, uncontrolla-
bly*): It will! I will!—I *must* see it!" (*MB*, 360).

Having brought her Nietzschean inversion of Ragnar's revelation about
Kaja to an impasse, Ibsen extends the tension with some stage business that
allows Hilde to advance her metaphysical project by working another switch
in the realistic action. The change involves Ragnar again, but this time he is
the unwitting agent of Hilde's equivocal ruse, instead of a sexual, conceptual
force of resistance that tests and magnifies her will to power. Throughout
this next scene Ibsen uses entrances and exits of Aline, Ragnar, and Dr. Herdal
to further leaven the realistic dimension of the play with symbolic and
conceptual material that will exalt Solness and Hilde in their duet that follows

and in the final scene, in which they interact across symbolically and theatrically distinct realms. The first significant exit is Ragnar's. Just as he caps Hilde's outburst with his culminating declaration of Solness's weakness, "He's got this yellow streak—the great master builder!"(*MB*, 360), Mrs. Solness, the primary object of the builder's hobbled will, enters.

When she left at the end of the first scene of this act, Solness was approaching the veranda, and Aline is concerned to find him absent now. Ragnar tells her that Solness has joined the workmen at the new house, and, significantly, Hilde tells her that he has taken the wreath there. Aline immediately understands Hilde's implication that Solness will climb the spire and, in an ironic reversal of the contest that ensued when Ragnar entered with the wreath, sends the young man off to bring Solness back to the veranda, away from the climb. Innocently obedient to the wife of the man he rudely defied, Ragnar asks if he should retrieve Solness by saying she asked for him. Relieved at his courtesy (no one else in the play ever does what she asks without challenging her), Aline accepts Ragnar's suggestion, but quickly remembers that Solness always avoids her and instructs the messenger to say only that he must come at once to see "someone" at the house. Ragnar willingly agrees to carry the vague summons and exits.

When Ragnar goes his certainty about Solness's cowardice is replaced by Aline's contrary apprehension that Halvard will climb the spire for unfathomable, possibly insane reasons. Alone with Aline for a brief moment, Hilde joins in her apprehension, with contrary anxiety about Solness's will that makes her apparently sympathetic questions to Aline, "(*tensely*): Do you think he will?" and "Oh, so you, too, think he's a bit—er—?" sharp instances of the dramatic irony Ibsen has saturated this play with. Their discussion of the builder's medical condition, which has metaphysical meanings for Hilde and only empirical ones for Aline, summons the wife's professional male ally, a benevolent authority and guardian of Solness's praxis, Dr. Herdal, to the door of the house. He, too, is anxious over Halvard's absence, but has come, as it turns out, not to seek his patient but to bring Aline back into the house she has left in search of its negligent master.

Herdal never actually enters the veranda but delivers his recalling summons from the bereft home's threshold. Ibsen makes this piece of stage business an ironically symbolic as well as objective correlative of Aline's conflicted, doomed action, a signal in the play's spectacle of the central thematic ambiguity in its plot. Unable to do, not do, or undo the social duty that inhibits her natural desire for happiness, Aline has made her marriage a Sisyphean performance of inhibiting social forms. Eager now to preserve Solness as the guarantor of that domestic deadlock, she is thwarted by her spousal responsibility to act as hostess to an intruding group of her husband's feminine admirers. In the last scene Ibsen stages this female chorus's identity with the more dangerously intrusive Hilde. At this moment he silently establishes the analogy, as Herdal interrupts Aline's spousal retrieval with the news that ladies from the town have come to watch the ceremonious hoisting of the wreath. Significantly, Hilde responds to Aline's despairing surrender to dutifully receiving them by asking, as she did in the act's first scene, if the wife can't dismiss her social responsibility. Aline declares that self-assertion impossible and passes on the responsibility of retrieving Solness from the climb to Hilde, asking her to speak to the builder when he returns. Herdal adds his voice to the request, and Aline repeats it with the innocently ominous phrase "Keep him as long as you can." Giving Aline one more chance to maintain her ruined life, as she did in her long argument with Solness earlier in the act, Hilde answers: "Hadn't you better do it yourself?" Ibsen's staging of the wife's answer seals Aline's doom and opens up the imminent transformation of Solness. In the following dialogue Aeschylan ironies move the social players, doctor and wife, offstage, clearing it for the impossible action of the metaphysical agents.

> *Mrs. Solness:* Oh dear, yes—it's my duty, really. But one has so many duties—
> *Herdal (looking towards the garden):* Here he is.
> *Mrs. Solness:* Oh dear, just as I have to go inside!
> *Herdal (to Hilde):* Don't tell him I'm here.
> *Hilde:* Oh, no. I'll find other things to talk about with the master builder.
> *Mrs. Solness:* And keep him here. I think you can do that better than anyone.
>   (*MB*, 361-62)

The structural rhythms at work in this exit once again make psychological realism a polyvalent fulcrum that concentrates and advances the play's metaphysical conflict. Ibsen builds this third act around three scenes dominated by Hilde and Solness; their two conversations alone, which call for the impossible climb, and the last scene, in which Hilde, onstage with Ragnar, Herdal, Aline, and the lady visitors, exultantly, telepathically, wills the climb Solness makes offstage. The lovers' duets, which provoke and confirm the builder's impossible act, do so by disengaging contingent from absolute willing. The three scenes intervening between Hilde's repeated reversals of Solness's guilty conscience and her double revelations of his robust aesthetic will to power all return Hilde to the professional and domestic intrigue plot. This large-scale oscillation from one pole of the play's action to the other opposes the concatenated resistance of mundane power, contingency, against the strongly and hypothetically creative, absolute claims of Hilde's transforming airy kingdom.

Ibsen advances the play's dynamically inverting passage from Nietzschean through Aristotelian back to revived Nietzschean action first through the builder's and next through Hilde's equivocal evasions or reversals of the contingent aims of their opponents. Confronted with Ragnar, Aline, and Herdal, Solness, and especially Hilde, ironically enact Christ's strategy for transforming earth into the heavenly kingdom, behaving wisely as serpents and innocently as doves toward the socially demanding, conventionally scheming son, wife, and doctor. Ibsen stages the play's summary equivocal transformation of contingent intrigue into absolute aesthetic willing in the next scene. There Solness, once again compelled and inspired by Hilde, fully reveals and finally transforms the controlling cause of his stalled worldly action: creative competition with God that originated in Hilde's presence at Lysanger ten years ago and that has since lapsed into irresolute fear of divine retribution.

The reversing recognition starts, appropriately enough, with Hilde and Solness equivocally carrying out the forestalling of his climb required by Aline and Herdal. Entering through the garden, that offstage symbol of renewal that Ragnar and Hilde, but not Aline, all pass through repeatedly in this act, Halvard announces that he has arrived to answer someone's summons, and Hilde responds with the prevarication that she wants to speak to him. When he hits on the disguised truth accidentally—"Oh, it's you, Hilde. I was afraid it might be Aline and the doctor" (MB, 362), she exploits an ambiguity in his self-description to dismiss those mundane agents from the conversation, commenting that he scares easily. He takes up the challenge, asking if she thinks he's fearful. When she reports his reputation for acrophobia, he confesses it, but says that the object of his fear of heights is not the fatal danger they pose but, rather, a moral one: retribution. Consternated by that distinction, Hilde shakes her head and tells Solness she doesn't understand him.

At this point the builder ends his equivocal sparring with her, drops his desire to know who summoned him and why, and starts his culminating exposition of the play's heretofore secret metaphysical action. In previous scenes Hilde has to work long and hard to bring Solness to this point. Here the reversing progress from criticism of his worldly life to invigorating scrutiny of his private one requires only three quick exchanges, whose brevity Ibsen underscores by having Hilde start the scrutiny with the terse command "Out with it" (MB, 362). Telescoping their familiar conflict this way, Ibsen increases dramatic tension over the practical outcome of Solness's fear. More significantly, he accelerates the play's conceptual conflict, indicating how close to the final Nietzschean assertion of the absolute self Solness and Hilde have come. Opening that approach with their mutually equivocal reversals of the mundane contingencies that have brought the builder back onstage, Ibsen once more makes conventional dramatic structure, and the humanistic logic it stages, an ambiguous matter ripe for radically modernist dramatic and philosophical transformation.

Throughout the play Solness has said that he fears retribution for the criminal violation his career made against his and Aline's domestic life. True to classically tragic form, the great reversal of this scene comes in a recognition derived from exposition of his past, in this case his originating artistic triumph ten years ago at Lysanger. His conventionally revelatory retrospective redefines the familial violation he narrated in his long second-act duet with Hilde and makes the twins' deaths, which Solness has all along called his crime, God's intolerable summons of the builder's undistracted service. Pivoting on a conversion in understanding of familial violence, this conventional dramatic crisis subsumes humanistic praxis in exonerating Nietzschean willing. It does so largely by transforming the value of affectionate desire, moving Solness out of familial confines into Hilde's visionary companionship. The nineteenth-century audience responded, with a frisson lost on contemporary viewers or readers, by naming that switch "adultery" with their censorious, conventional voice and "free love" with their radical one. Attention to Hilde's interrogatory timing of the builder's exposition indicates how their sublimated sexual intrigue changes the retrospective closure of classical catharsis into the open aspiration of Ibsen's modernist dramatic project.

Solness starts by telling Hilde that he took up a career building churches under the influence of his parents' humble rural piety. Devotedly erecting the divine houses that sanctified human ones, Solness expected God to show His pleasure by rewarding him with a normally accomplished working life providing normal familial happiness. When Hilde asks why Solness believed God was not pleased with his work, Solness answers that he viewed God's visitation of the demonically inspiring trolls on him, and their burning of his house and murdering of his children, as proof of God's dissatisfaction. When she asks what more these messages indicated God required of him, Solness gives the following complex answer: God required his paternally distracted artistic genius to be exclusively devoted to the creation of divine houses and, therefore, simultaneously disencumbered and tested that genius by sacrificing the builder's impeding children to it.

At this point Ibsen adds Hilde's role as an original player in Solness's crisis to her contemporary role as adjudicating, educing auditor of his retrospection of that crisis. She asks precisely when Solness understood the action binding him to God and hears the answer she tells him she expected—one September when he built a tower at Lysanger. She then asks what action his understanding led to and hears how he broke with God atop the tower. That break occurred on 19 September, the very day whose ten-year anniversary Hilde has observed and has forced Solness to observe, by returning to him the morning before this conversation. For the rest of this scene she and Solness revive and revise that original defiance and so move the play to its imminent end. By requiring him to *will* more than simply acknowledge that past whose eternal return she personally enacts, Hilde subsumes the classical tragic logic inducing Solness's professional retrospective, transposes it upward to the Dionysian tragic action Nietzsche endorses: abandonment of the contingent self, recuperation of the absolute one in untrammeled aesthetic self-affirmation. Hilde's subsuming willing requires that Solness somehow consummate the promising sexual dare he made with the 13-year-old girl who has now returned to him as a young woman. That dare crowned Solness's professional, religious one at Lysanger, and to make the first good he must account to Hilde for the lapsed outcome of the second. He cannot recuperate his strength until he abandons the weakness mixed in it, and in the following excerpt he begins to do just that:

> *Solness:* You see, Hilde, up there, where I was a stranger, I spent so much time
> by myself, brooding and puzzling. Then I saw so clearly why He had
> taken my little children from me. It was so that I should have nothing
> to bind me. No love or happiness or anything, you see. I was to be a
> master builder—nothing else. And all my life was to be spent building
> for Him. (*Laughs.*) But that wasn't the way it worked out.
>
> *Hilde:* What did you do?
>
> *Solness:* First, I examined and tried myself—
>
> *Hilde:* And then—?
>
> *Solness:* Then, like Him, I did the impossible.
>
> *Hilde:* The impossible?
>
> *Solness:* I could never bear to climb up high before. But that day, I did it.
>
> *Hilde (jumps up):* Yes, yes, you did!
>
> *Solness:* And as I stood high up there, right at the top, and placed the wreath
> over the weathercock, I said to Him: "Listen to me, mighty One!
> Henceforth I, too, want to be a free master builder. Free in my field,
> as You are in Yours. I never want to build churches for You again. Only
> homes, for people to live in."
>
> *Hilde (her eyes wide and glittering):* That was the song I heard in the air. (*MB*,
> 363-64)

Ibsen's by now perfected technique of silent structural allusion to biblical and classical references brings highly significant actions from the humanist tradition to bear on this modern builder's account of his definitive action. Alienated, struggling with death's part in guilty and innocent sacrificial obedience to an unsatisfied, demanding heavenly Father, Solness unwittingly presents himself as a modern Cain, Abraham, and Jesus (who was himself a filial builder by worldly and heavenly origin and trade). After a trying self-examination, Solness, unlike those beleaguered biblical favorites of God, moved out of the struggle of righteous obedience into the struggle of self-affirming defiance: "Listen to me, mighty One! Henceforth I, too, want to be a free master builder. Free in my field, as You are in Yours." Here Solness silently invokes as fused precedents the criminally arrogant builders of Babel from Genesis and the Greek Titan Prometheus, a prime competitor to his world governing, fatherly cousin Zeus and, variously, the divine artisan and criminal benefactor of man.

That symbolic conflation marks a crucial ambiguity in defiance—its equivocal potential to end in foolish, fatal moral lapse or tortured, but finally triumphant, moral achievement. This irresolutely split potential in revolt magnifies the ambiguity binding contingent and absolute willing in Solness and, finally, governs Ibsen's complex staging of his death. This excerpt stresses the triumphant, Promethean half of Solness's ambiguously criminal defiance atop the Lysanger tower, especially in his definition of the "impossible action" as the physically courageous climb that enables and initiates his free, masterful creation of domestic sites of human happiness. (To restore fire to mankind, which Zeus had forbade them after Prometheus impishly offended the Olympian father with a guileful sacrifice, the Titanic human benefactor, with Athena's help, scaled heaven, stole fire from the chariot of the sun, and brought it, on a fennel stalk, to earth to sustain mankind's domestic life.) The exchanges immediately following this excerpt symbolically move the scene to Prometheus' torture (which followed his ascent to the heavenly theft) and to the contrarily negative biblical end of defiance at Babel's tower, as the builder cryptically asserts that his Lysanger rebellion ended in punitive despair: "But He took His revenge later" (*MB*, 364). Hilde induces the crucial shift with her exuberant memory of the builder's tower speech as song. Brief elucidation of Hilde's repeated experiences of that song helps catch the Nietzschean element in Halvard's inversion into and out of failure that Ibsen stages here, at the center of the couple's final affirmation of robust conscience.

When Hilde recalls her telepathic intuition of Halvard's defiant self-assertion—"That was the song I heard in the air"—Ibsen ironically adds

Nietzsche's model for transcendent willing, the annihilating music of Dionysus, to the builder's original heavenly revolt. In the first act, during her initial meeting with Solness, Ibsen stages the first exposition of this event from Hilde's point of view. Before she recalls his seduction of her after the Lysanger climb, Hilde describes the builder's tower song as having sounded like "harps in the air" (*MB*, 308). Scoring a new Babel/Promethean climb with conventionally angelic music, Ibsen turns his career-long poetic impulse to ironic conceptual purpose. This dissonant pairing of Jehovah's airy praise and Dionysus' at the first climb sounds in Hilde's memory again when Solness presents his exposition of the event in this, their last, conversation and sounds for the third time when he fatally ascends his house's church spire in the play's final scene. At that point the song and harps, which once more only Hilde hears, resound at their most dissonant as they announce the final strain of Aristotle's logic yielding to Nietzsche's. Hilde's second mention of music, and Solness's response here, remind and promise the audience that an ontological transformation moves in the incrementally repeating aesthetic symbolism.

In act 1 when Hilde first mentioned hearing the builder's song at Lysanger, he resisted but finally accepted her mystical account, thoughtfully calling it "most extraordinary" (*MB*, 308). Now, when she recalls it again, Solness resists her telepathic command of his will for a different reason. In act 1 she was demanding his forgotten allegiance; now he is trying to offer it freely and insists on doing so on his own terms. Her "wide and glittering" look when she remembers the song in this scene, instead of inspiring, interrupts him. Older than Hilde, he has more instances of the eternal return of the past to affirm, more failure to acknowledge and more psychic cost to pay than her youth can know. He understands that the ontological transformation that her willed music calls for has a negative as well as positive vanishing point, that these points converge, and that his advance to the robust life can come only through an inverting passage through his accumulated weakness. To that end he overrides her naively encouraging memory of his "song" with the following saturnine account of God's revenge:

> *Solness (looks at her dejectedly)*: Building homes for people isn't worth twopence, Hilde.
>
> *Hilde*: How can you say that now?
>
> *Solness*: Because I realize now that people have no use for the homes they live in. They can't be happy in them. And a home wouldn't have been any use to me—even if I'd had one. (*Laughs quietly and savagely.*) So when all

> the accounts are closed, I have built nothing really. And sacrificed
> nothing. It all adds up to nothing. Nothing. Nothing. (*MB*, 364)

In Genesis the Babel punishment symbolically alluded to here immediately follows the preservation of Noah's family from the punitive flood.
Chapter 10 presents the lineages of Noah's sons, the new divinely favored
human family preserved by God to replace the drowned heathen. Chapter
11 presents the favored remnant's attempt to build a city and protective tower
on the plains of Shinar and so preserve the unified identity that their single
language gives them. Unlike Zeus, the offended biblical God descends to the
ascending artisans, resolved to ruin their project because the united civilization they plan will annul and supersede their righteous bond to Him—"now
nothing will be restrained from them, which they have imagined to do" (Gen.
11:6). He confounds their speech; divided, they scatter "abroad upon the
face of all the earth," and so radical, ungovernable contingency becomes the
end and means enabling and defeating any future human struggle to compete
with univocal God's absolute creative will.

Collation of the two chapters implies that the civilizing project originated with Ham's people, since the ruined city is named Babel in 11:9 and
since Ham's grandson, Nimrod, is credited with beginning four kingdoms on
the plain of Shinar, one of which is named Babel, in 10:6-10. Of Noah's three
sons Ham offends against paternal dignity by seeing his drunken father's
nakedness and, more severely, by relating the event to his brothers. For this
Noah damns Ham's lineage, cursing his son Canaan, promising Ham's people
will serve the more righteous descendants of his two brothers (Gen. 9:18-27).
In sum the arrogant artisanal offense collectively practiced against the
universal father at Babel descends from, repeats, and magnifies a diminishing
filial offense against that father's bibulous, earth-tilling favorite. Civilization—univocal, unrestrained creative imagination—is invented by and forbidden to those tainted with unrestrained knowledge of weakness in
masculine authority over sexual and appetitive domestic life.[7]

At least that is the reading of the Babel story that corresponds most
suggestively to Solness's life and to the cause of his dejection here. At Babel
God's revenge aborted a physical project by turning unified, aspiring human
creativity into intellectual and social chaos. Revenge for Solness's lack of
restraint involves a more subtle and protracted divine interference with his
civilizing project. Solness is a descendant of Ham who, ironically, has
mastered building through uncannily strategic professional exploitation of
strong sexual weaknesses in his domestic world: at first chthonic

appropriation of his estranged wife's ancestral home; more recently, the punitively compensatory construction of her new house and his mystically compelled, cynically sublimated infatuation of Ragnar's Kaja.

That he has brought his absolutely willed vision of domestic happiness about through such diminishing, violating immersion in barren erotic contingency; that his innocent courage to do "the impossible" lapsed into corrosive fear of retribution as soon as he did it, as soon as he submitted to his freely allowed, cruelly tempting power to compel sacrificial obedience through telepathic willing; that such omnipotently mystical charisma has ended as rearguard vanity and brittle, irksome posturing—these compounded ironies seethe in Solness's sardonic observation to Hilde that God took a cold, late revenge for the bereaved father's rebellious emulation of Him initiated so long ago on the Lysanger tower. The biblical Hamites, whom God viewed as ambitious but not competitive, suffered when divinely imposed confusion forced them to abandon unrealized aspirations for absolute creative control of worldly life and value. Their modern, explicitly rivalrous descendant suffers a worse fate: to vary the biblical text nothing that he imagined to do has been restrained from him, yet nothing he has done has brought happiness about. Hence, the builder's dejected, retrospective certainty that he has built and sacrificed "nothing," that "people have no use for the homes they live in," that a home, even if he'd had it, would have been no use to him.

When he declares that people can't be happy in homes, Solness symbolically repudiates the Aristotelian idea of right living, which, added to the Judeo-Christian sanctification of domesticity, establishes the value of humanist, especially of modern bourgeois, culture. Part of the revenge Solness complains of in this scene is his divinely abetted disillusionment with secular domestic life, a domain whose contours and laws Ibsen presents as modified Aristotelian praxis throughout this play. Restraining the creative aspiration of civilized life by scrupulously observing the lawful authority that engenders that creativity and aspiration amounts to righteousness in Judaism and Christianity. When the lawful authority is reason instead of God and the restraint is logic instead of worship, civilization displays Aristotle's concept of the happy life. *Eudaemonia*, his principle for ethical self-realization, advises an actively rational disposition that pleasantly matches the resources and needs of people to those of the natural and social world.[8] As Solness declares to God at Lysanger: "I never want to build churches for You again. Only homes, for people to live in" Ibsen ironically condenses those Enlightenment and romantic revisions of eudaemonism that he searchingly extended in *Rosmersholm* and so many earlier plays.

Probably by accident, that compression recalls Aristotle's own accounts of ethical and other modes of self-realization. Throughout his work building houses occurs frequently as an instance and metaphor illustrating the rational and practical actions by which people take their places in the world and by which the world maintains itself as a place hospitable to people's efforts.[9] Failure or success in such universally substantial and substantiating praxis can be edifyingly experienced onstage as well as in life, Aristotle argues in *Poetics*. The theater's moral authority initiated in that text survived in an aesthetic and philosophical humanist tradition that Ibsen inherited and transposed throughout his career. The bourgeois audience, whose members saw their homes and the lives they lived in them represented in unprecedentedly realistic detail on Ibsen's stage, might not have recognized the Aristotelian ethos at work in that representation. But none of them could miss the assault Ibsen makes at this moment in *The Master Builder* on their confident, if unwitting, inheritance of that ethos. When Solness repudiates the outcome of his symbolically Promethean decision to make building serve man's contingent domestic good, instead of God's heavenly one, he names the wishes, tastes, deliberations, values, and deeds that make up daily-life vanity. When he calls that vanity God's revenge, his judgment sunders humanism. Both elements of the long-lived collaboration between classical rationality and Christian faith, symbolically invoked by the sacrifices and projects Solness adds up to zero here, are now, to borrow a phrase from Beckett's Clov in *Endgame*, "corpsed."[10]

The sundering of Promethean exertion and Aristotelian balance from the Enlightenment God of natural theology occurs under a late species of romantic compulsion to pursue absolute creative willing through passionate self-affirmation. Hilde, who embodies that compulsion and governs the builder's increasingly robust pursuit of it, advances the pursuit now. Satisfied that his fear of retribution presents a disappointed but not abandoned aspiration to do the impossible, Hilde, again in a question, offers Solness the chance to recoup that ambition: "And are you never going to build again?" (*MB*, 364). The question itself reverses Solness's self-description, since he has just told her he has built nothing and therefore can hardly build again. The rhetorical ploy subtly returns him to the metaphysical meaning of building. On that plane Hilde has always been able to draw Solness into courage, because he has always willed that she should, especially when, as has been true throughout this professional theodicy, he has urgently sought to justify and dignify his fear to her. Hilde's quick, catechistic turn on this ambivalence is a wonderful instance of Ibsen's talent for making realistic psychological dialogue, especially sublimating dialogue, advance a play's abstract action.

When Solness answers "Yes, now I shall begin!" Hilde's exalting authority as the builder's Nietzschean muse is once more confirmed. Most important, her ontological competition, in that role, against the divine artificer, to whom Solness has surrendered himself throughout this scene, is restored at a higher level than ever before in the play. God's partnership in humanism may be corpsed, but His biblical function as absolute creative willer still occupies Solness. Hilde moves quickly here to end that occupation.

Solness yields the contingent realm to God as not worth the leave-taking when he renounces free-thinking humanism's social project. With her next question Hilde makes sure the concession has only disencumbered, and not sacrificed, the builder's absolute creative will: "What will you build? What? Tell me! Quickly!" In the exchange that follows Ibsen inverts the Babel analogy that until now has symbolically displayed the weakness in Solness's artistic will to power. Planning to transpose his competitive creation directly to the biblical God's airy ground, the modern builder wills primal revolt as the transcendent eternal return of the same in his own creative life and, by virtue of the ironic biblical allusion, in all humanity's.

> *Solness:* Now I shall build the only place where I believe that happiness can
> exist.
> *Hilde (looks at him):* Master builder—you mean our castles in the air.
> *Solness:* Yes. Castles in the air. (*MB*, 364)

The Babel offense posits unlawful sexual knowledge of intoxication as the tainted origin of the aspiration to build. Hilde's castle in the air, first promised after a banquet to an infatuated, licentiously violated child at Lysanger, carries that offense forward into the builder's projected transcendence. Having transposed building from the contingent to the mystic realm in this last assertion, Solness also needs to transpose the spiritually intoxicated sexual violation of Hilde, which capped his first Promethean rebellion. Before he can do that the builder must sever his connection to Kaja, whose ongoing infatuation with Solness, initiated by his transcendent, telepathic will, binds that will to earthbound building and so impedes his ascent with Hilde to her airy castle. Throughout the play Ibsen stages unconsummated sexual intrigue as the fulcrum transposing conventional action into modernist revolt.[11] Now that Solness is about to enact that revolt, Hilde, who has all along dominated the sexual intrigue, brings it to a surprising conclusion.

Ibsen writes more stage directions for the rest of this scene than he does anywhere else in the play, and they all add the dynamic of sexual consummation to Solness's renewal. A list makes the point: "angrily," "heavily," "passionately," "pleadingly," "looks deeply into her eyes," "with mounting excitement," "flings her arms wide," "looks at her with bowed head," "curtly, decisively," and finally, appropriately enough, for Hilde, "jubilant, clasps her hands" (*MB*, 365-66). As was true in the Viking allusion in act 2 the sexual language probes and tests the measure of robust conscience, of Nietzschean great health Solness must display, or acquire, if he would simultaneously build, climb into, and inhabit his castle with Hilde. She starts the test with an insinuating reference to his weakness, provocatively saying she fears giddiness will overcome him halfway through their climb. He counters with courtly flattery, promising that, hand in hand with her, he will evince prowess equal to his aspiration.

Solness has only touched Hilde once in the play, in act 1 and that was a chaste, paternal touch on the arm to persuade her, when she narrates her childhood encounter with him, that he did not kiss her at Lysanger. His promise here of a future touch to renew the Lysanger revolt ironically brings Hilde's rivals into the scene. At this point, when the eternal return of the same generates a sexual crisis, Ibsen stages a complex modulation in the builder's manly self-assertion that finally brings the sexual plot fully in line with that aspiration that his first touch of Hilde denied: the founding of her kingdom. The following dialogue ensues once the builder imagines held hands as the first, gentle avowal of the visionary couple's physical love.

> *Hilde:* Just with me? Won't there be others?
> *Solness:* What others? What do you mean?
> *Hilde:* Oh —that Kaja at the desk. Poor thing, aren't you going to take her along too?
> *Solness:* Oh. So that's what Aline and you were sitting here talking about!
> *Hilde:* Is it true or isn't it?
> *Solness (angrily):* I won't answer that. You must believe in me unquestioningly.
> *Hilde:* I have believed in you for ten years. Unquestioningly.
> *Solness:* You must go on believing in me.
> *Hilde:* Then let me see you stand up there, high and free! (*MB*, 365)

Hilde flirts for very high stakes here, and she wants to make sure that Halvard can't lower them, that he can't make construction of her airy castle another instance of the artistically expedient, sad sexual game he played with Kaja. When Ragnar exposed her beloved's philandering, just moments ago, Hilde willfully, but correctly, discounted Kaja's value to Solness. The sympathetic hauteur by which she brings Kaja into the discussion shows that Hilde has had time to transform her anxiety about Solness's devotion into

friendly and admiring sexual mockery. With the exonerating banter of sly
worldly wisdom she invites Solness to discount the girl without embarrassing
himself by denying, admitting, or explaining the conquest. But he is not
insouciant. Instead, he defensively concludes that Aline had passed on the
accusing information about Kaja in the conversation with Hilde that he
interrupted earlier in the evening. He is wrong about that but not wrong
about the fact that Hilde hid the real topic of her talk with his wife. When
he tells her, "Oh. So that's what Aline and you were sitting here talking
about!" Solness deflects Hilde's suspicion about Kaja with a just, if imprecise,
complaint about her own recent disloyalty. There is enough tit-for-tat
incrimination here to indicate that Solness has not yet disentangled absolute
and contingent willing.

Hilde takes the builder's fantasy of entrapment in an inculpating female
conspiracy for what it is: a failure of nerve that has more to do with Aline
than with her or Kaja. Withholding the news that Kaja herself has exposed
Solness, and her own understanding of that news, Hilde uses the fantasy to
reverse the familiar weak conscience it proclaims. She evades his just accusation that she deceived him about Aline not only because he cannot prove
it, but, more important, because her prevarication then was essential to the
task she is still about now: preserving him from sexual bad faith. Ignoring,
and so allowing, his belief that Aline made the accusation, Hilde gives Solness
a new chance to cut loose from guilty attachment to the paralyzing recrimination he and Aline, with Kaja as a premier occasion, have made of their
domestic life. She calls forth his nascent, delivering strength and her own
power to make the elevating summons, as she has always done, with a direct
question that will bear no equivocation. Stated simply—"Is it true or isn't
it?"—the question is nonetheless complex enough to bear some scrutiny.

The conventional question of sexual intrigue plots—Do I have a rival?—
is normally a moral as well as appetitive one. Ibsen transposes the moral,
appetitive conflict into an ontological one when Hilde asks the conventional
question here. Solness's adultery with Kaja, as with Hilde, is, after all, a
thought and not a deed. Hilde takes that thought, as she takes all thoughts,
for a deed, and her question to Solness forces him to adopt the same logic.
Where adultery is concerned, Jesus also took the impulse to be equivalent to
the deed (Matt. 5:27-28). But Hilde, of course, does not share Jesus' reasons
for making impulses acts, and she is more interested in sexual impulse's
physical expression than Jesus was—hence, the irony of her New Testament
inquiry into Solness's infidelity. In order to create her airy castle Solness must
respond to her New Testament question by adopting Hilde's Nietzschean
conviction that impulses amount to deeds. In that ironic fusing of sanctioned

and insurgent radical thinking, Ibsen perfects his career-long subversion of the conventional adultery plot and stages a definitive modernist defection from the Christian norms that plot invariably enforced on the nineteenth-century stage.

Jesus and Nietzsche both call impulse an active principle of self-realization but differ on how and to what end the principle operates. Jesus preaches that impulse has a moral dynamic that grounds life in God and a historical end that makes that grounding fully manifest at the imminent arrival of God's immanent earthly kingdom. Nietzsche argues that impulse is its own ground, that its dynamic is self-affirmation, and that its atelic end is ceaseless creative transfiguration of its own power to be. When Hilde puts the Christian test to Solness, she does so not only to ensure the exclusive primacy of her sexual claim on him, but also to bring about his conversion to her Nietzschean view of impulse as transcendent action, as self-affirming, world-making play. It is not enough that the builder has defied God by putting a church spire on his new house. He must make that symbol's vestigial Christian meaning explicitly heretical. The imminent kingdom Jesus promised must be made the imminent kingdom Solness promised to Princess Hilde, and for that to happen Solness must yield to her inspiration and command of his most secret life of feeling.

And yield he does, but not without the resistance that ambiguously makes him worth commanding, sexually and spiritually. That he handles her suspicions about Kaja as he handled Aline's—"*Solness (angrily):* I won't answer that. You must believe in me unquestioningly"—at first seems only like a failure of nerve, a frantic and disappointed dismissal of Hilde as no more understanding than his wife, especially given the fact that he has just, for the first time, imagined them as allies (*MB*, 365). But some unpacking of his refusal shows that the loyalty it enjoins on Hilde is not the same loyalty he requires of Aline. Nor is the authority by which he resists their questions the same in each case. These contrasts amount to a critique of conventionally virtuous feminine action—self-abnegating, trusting care of men—and an ironic subversion of that action's conventionally edifying force.

Aline's questions about Kaja accuse him of physical adultery. Solness alternately denies and disallows them to preserve her conviction that he callously asserts his conventional masculine prerogative of free gratification with servants. Once more Ibsen works an elevating turn on melodramatic plot devices with this version of the master who ruins the maid. Solness's contrivance is vanity, but not delusion, since it displays, however weakly, the important truth that charismatic virility persists in the aging Solness. More important, the masquerade of spousal infidelity is a convenient domestic

pretext ensuring that Solness can feel justly punished for what he regards as
his real violation of Aline: his part in their children's death, which he has
always kept secret from her. This martyring adaptation of false to real guilt
does double duty for Solness. The private, paternal penance stifles his
creative will, sacrifices it as atonement for the real violence that will did to
his familial life. Contrarily, as a pose equivocally denying and protecting the
truth about his charismatic virility, the contrived spousal penance resuscitates
his creative will, keeps that will's professionally expedient infatuation of Kaja
intact. Stalling with both penances, Solness never completely smothers or
revives his will, but, instead, suspends it. This timid builder's adultery of the
heart goes Jesus one better and annuls impulse as well as act. With that ironic
excess of virtue Solness enacts Nietzsche's critique of Christian morality as
nihilism. The command of loyalty from Aline, which Solness overtly cites as
her duty to regard him with conventionally honorific spousal respect, is in
fact a plea for her continuing partnership in a nihilistic equilibrium by which,
after a fashion, he keeps himself alive.

He ambiguously requires an opposite fidelity from Hilde, on whom he
relies for revitalizing deliverance from that mortifying equilibrium. In part,
as he does with Aline, he disallows Hilde's question to defend his manly
prerogative and prowess. The vanity that flecks his anger at her is as much
an offensive as defensive ploy to keep her an enthralled contestant in the
charismatic sexual game that they play to revive his creative genius. In part
he disallows her question out of shame that he has debased his telepathic
allure by summoning Kaja to an expedient project. That he has renounced
the project under Hilde's compulsion is proof enough, from his point of
view, of the builder's capacity and intention to requite this superior muse.
His acknowledgment of prior defections, which she calls for, would, at this
point, diminish the authority they exert together, would expose it as
conditional rather than absolute. That absolute power to will the real
creatively makes up the "unquestioning" loyalty, the subversively "edifying"
feminine action, Solness demands from Hilde. Exerting and extorting absolute aspiration here, Solness renounces the conditional equilibrium he
contingently willed with Aline. Thus, ironically, his refusal to act on the
dare Hilde includes in her question—can you be faithful to your best
self—clears the ground for erection of Hilde's air-anchored castle, the
impossible deed that meets her dare.

Hilde understands all this and responds accordingly by calling for his
constructive climb to that castle. Solness, for all his longing after unconditional inspiration from Hilde, has submitted that inspiration to a condition:
his sexual weakness with Kaja must remain secret. Hilde, characteristically,

inverts that vestigial weakness as soon as Solness defensively exposes it. Rolfe Fjelde's translation lacks the sexual charge of Michael Meyer's but gives a clearer sense of how Hilde changes her conditional function into an absolute one at this moment.

> *Hilde:* Is it true, or isn't it?
>
> *Solness (hotly):* I wouldn't answer a question like that! You'll have to trust me, absolutely!
>
> *Hilde:* For ten years I've trusted you utterly—utterly—
>
> *Solness:* You'll have to keep on trusting me.
>
> *Hilde:* Then let me see you high and free, up there![12]

Aiming, as always, at transcendence, Hilda draws a second, more potent challenge to Solness from his evasion of her first one. To his demand for completely faithful trust, she responds, "Then let me see your free ascent." Part bargain and part affirmation, the exchange equivocally transposes his plea and her challenge concerning Kaja into a mutual offering. She meets and rescinds the condition he imposes on their absolute willing by strategically fusing *if/then* and correlative logic in her subjunctive declaration "Then let me see you stand up there, high and free." If you climb, she tells him, then I will reward you by continuing my faithful willing of your best self. Conversely, and simultaneously, she tells him: I will always remain as faithful as I have always been. Climb then, reciprocate my already long-willed creation of your best self. Presenting the climb as an agon and a ceremony, Hilde ambiguously condenses Aristotle's idea of action as deliberate pursuit of an absent good and Nietzsche's idea of action as spontaneous, transfiguring celebration of an eternally present and recurring joy—the will to power.

Fear has kept Solness from performing either action. Urged to perform both here, fear overcomes him once more: "*Solness (heavily):* Oh, Hilde. One can't do things like that every day" (*MB*, 365). Making repetition an impediment rather than a call to action, Solness ambiguously concedes that the climb is more a ceremonious revival of strength than an agonistic striving. He resists what he concedes, shielding himself from the absolute's claim on him by striking a pose that mixes offended dignity and panicked shame. With the long-suffering authority of old age, whose wisdom must and cannot be communicated to uncomprehending youth, Solness pragmatically instructs Hilde that the past cannot be retrieved. But, even as his gravity counsels, it supplicates, pleading defensively that he be excused from the climb on account of the weakness of age. Following immediately on his insistently virile self-presentation, the plea of infirmity obviously begs to be denied. His ambivalence here ironically shows Solness, as usual, advancing toward Nietzschean self-affirmation through weakness, and, as usual, Hilde converts that weakness into strength. She urged the agon by announcing her power to reward him for taking it up. Now that he has submerged the agon in disguised longing for the reviving ceremony, she stops rationally proposing and turns again to exhorting, the irrational persuasion that suits Nietzschean self-creators. "Hilde (passionately): But I want you to! I want you to! (Pleadingly.) Just once more, master builder! Do the impossible again!" (MB, 365). Showing him that her desire mixes need and strength, as his does, Hilde no longer tests but finally establishes their mutual erotic identity. That challenging concession turns the scene.

Adding the voice of the naively expectant child-princess to the voice of the all-knowing consort and muse, Hilde offers Solness the chance to act as bestower and beneficiary of her absolute will and his. With this complex doubling, which presents erotic reciprocity as enhancing repetition of the builder's self-affirmation, Ibsen finally turns sexual psychology fully away from contingent gratification and fully toward Nietzsche's absolute joy: willing the eternal return of aesthetically transfiguring self-overcoming. This strong hypothetical self-creation belongs to the Nietzschean super-man, not the Aristotelian agent. Envisioning his own strong hypothetical satisfaction of Hilde's promising desire, Solness finally transforms conven-tional action into the superman's destiny. "Solness (looks deeply into her eyes): If I try it, Hilde, I shall stand up there and speak to Him the way I spoke to Him before" (MB, 365).

What Solness and Hilde don't say about Kaja in this scene moves them through a stall in their consummating rehearsal of his gloriously impossible action. Hilde's second exhorting dare tests whether their silence has indeed converted the builder's stalling weakness into strength sufficient for his impossible self-assertion. Solness takes up her dare by rehearsing what he will say about Hilde's love and his building if he repeats the Lysanger defiance atop Aline's house. This presentation of the effects of silence and speech on action enacts the two reversals that make up Nietzschean change: self-overcoming and self-transfiguration. The sublimating inversion of old into new identity that occurs in self-overcoming involves an ex nihilo generation of the new self from the old one. Ibsen stages that potent void and the couple's passage through it, in their silence over the builder's defective infatuation of Kaja.

Repudiating her with silence, the couple move to the second Nietzschean change, self-transfiguration, in which the potent void empties itself positively, through physical creation in God's case, through defiant spiritual emulation of it in the builder's. God said let there be light, Solness says let there be the Lysanger Babel again, on Aline's domestic church spire. That speech's power to generate the hypothetically real is both the form and content of Solness's renewal here makes his action much more a matter of aesthetic will than praxis, and makes Ibsen's play theatrically as well as conceptually Nietzschean. Nietzsche concentrated on decadence and nihilism, personal and cultural, so persistently because he viewed them both as both the negative and positive vanishing points through which reality manifested itself as the will to power. Portraying an artist's recovery from personal and cultural decadence and nihilism by staging the negative and positive power of speech, Ibsen takes up the same transfiguring view of reality and action.[13]

Solness now turns out of the vanishing point of silence over Kaja's infatuation upward to the vanishing point of announcing his love for Hilde to God. The speech he promises to make atop Aline's spire repeats his Lysanger dare but moves the seduction of Hilde, which originally followed that dare, onto center stage. In act 1 Hilde reminds Solness that in Lysanger he kissed her "many, many times" after the feast and supper that celebrated his carrying a crowning wreath to the top of his new built church spire (*MB*, 309). Here Solness promises to tell God that he will now build happiness in airy castles with the princess he loves who stands below watching his defiance. He also promises to tell God that he is descending to take the princess in his arms and kiss her, at which point Hilde interrupts the vision to edit it. She insists that he repeat her earlier description of their first defiant, intoxicated kisses: "Many times! Tell Him that!" (*MB*, 365). Solness complies. Adding an enhancing repetition of Hilde's retrospective account of the prestaged and staged past to Solness's defiant projection of that past into the future, Ibsen makes the eternal return of the same the means as well as the end of this builder's action. Finally acknowledging and affirming the sexual dimension of his once and future Babel defiance, Solness at last grasps how aesthetic will to power ceaselessly makes Hilde's ever-imminent kingdom an immanent one.

That impossible action is celebrated and willed at a higher order in the following exchange, which, appropriately, opens and closes with significant repetitions of earlier dialogue from this scene and act.

> Hilde (*flings her arms wide*): Now I see you again as you were when I heard that song in the air!
> Solness (*looks at her with bowed head*): How have you come to be what you are, Hilde?

Hilde: How did you make me what I am?

Solness (curtly, decisively): The princess shall have her castle.

Hilde (jubilant, clasps her hands): Oh, master builder! My beautiful, beautiful
  castle! Our castle in the air!

Solness: Built on a true foundation. (*MB*, 366)

Ibsen's rendition of metaphysical struggle in psychosexual terms has
been almost inextricably complex throughout this play. Questioning each
other relentlessly, this couple has snaked the plot forward through concatenated reversals and incrementally transcendant inversions. Their mutual
scrutiny—aggressive, evasive, creative, and destructive—leaves little that
can happen between men and women unjudged. Seen entire, their judgments
amount to subversive revision of a standard action for men and women in
nineteenth-century drama: edification. In this coda Ibsen stages their summary revision of edification with a direct and very simple question: how does
it happen?

In conventional, humanistic terms edification involves refining submission of creative masculine energy to idealized feminine objectives. Physical
origin and civilized end of male life, women educe, confirm, and enjoy men's
achievements in this model. Female identity stands as exemplary being to
emulative male becoming in this system: women always already are what they
can be; through inspired service to women's confirming self-possession men
become what they can be. By the nineteenth century the primary scene for this
female development of male action had become domestic. The primary mode
remained what it had always been, sexual. Under the restraint of naturally
decent spousal and maternal care, men's impulse to preserve and extend life by
rapaciously gratifying appetite gains the enhancing, adaptive benefit of conscience, the moral and emotional awareness of appetitive decorum.[14]

In some forms this awareness has a sanctioned supernatural dimension
in the nineteenth century, in some it has only earthly dignity, but in all forms
conscience adds a governing, consummating perception of value to male
action.[15] That value had been known before, of course, and had not always
been bestowed by women. In Aristotle's eudaemonistic theory of action, for
instance, conscience is a function of rationality. As such, it belongs to men
and is presumed by them to be normally out of women's reach. Although
power over conscience had shifted by the nineteenth century, the worldly
work of conscience had not. Through their loving revelation to men of that
sublimating balance that makes action pleasantly consonant with virtue,
women presided over latter-day European men's civilized pursuit of
Aristotle's pragmatic well-being, especially on the stage.

Adultery made up the plot of so much nineteenth-century theater largely because the presentation of infidelity's damaging allure reinforced the high value bourgeois Europe placed on familial life's power to generate and sustain civilized happiness. Hilde's praise of Solness's retrieved defiance, her joy at seeing him a revived Dionysian singer, flouts cultural and theatrical convention by making adultery's defection from familial decorum a competing, superior edification, one that exceeds the limits of family, civilization, and sanctioned metaphysics altogether. Solness's humble response to her praise acknowledges the radical novelty of her edifying function with a reverent question about its origin: *"(looks at her with bowed head):* How have you come to be what you are, Hilde?" Educating, as she always has, with a question, Hilde replies: "How did you make me what I am?"

Solness's question inadvertently puts new wine into old wineskins. He wants to know how she became someone who could give him a second, spiritual birth. Naming himself her creature, Solness once again gets the self-generating action of will to power slightly wrong, imagining that it is conditionally derived, earned, rewarded from an external source. Feminine edification of male striving works that way in the contingent, Aristotelian order. In her corrective responding question Hilde reminds Solness that, together, they have left that order. The question he should be asking, she implies, is what native power does he have that brought her to his aid, that made her his maker. Her question recalls the long Nietzschean conversations about Solness's telepathic willing, and its charismatic summoning of demons and infatuated girls to the builder's criminally creative ends, that made up so much of the first two acts of the play. You have conjured your conjurer; you have delivered your deliverer, she tells him. Reverencing me should only mean reverencing your best self. The reciprocity Hilde announces transforms the vestigial dependence Solness feels. Recalling his telepathic Dionysian singing atop the Lysanger tower, Hilde finally convinces the builder that his creativity is not service but expression, not reasoned but willed, not duty but joy. She requires her imminent kingdom from him to reveal that it has long since been immanent in him as an impulse. An adulteress of the heart offers this edifying definition of impulse as action to requite a worshiping adulterer of the heart. That irony, which inverts inherited and insurgent metaphysical orders by switching the gendered roles and objectives of conventional edification, is Ibsen's grandest subversion yet of the religion, ethics, and theater of his culture.

Solness enacts Hilde's lesson about inspiration by immediately renewing the pledge to build her castle that she elicited from him in their first duet in this act. In that scene Hilde fears that Solness regards the castle only as an evasive fantasy and says so, when she responds to his promise to build it for her with the following smiling doubt: "A real castle in the air?" His courage to will the absolute is at issue there, and Solness symbolically asserts that courage when he assures Hilde that the castle will be "built on a true foundation" (MB, 357). The question of his courage has been settled here. Now when he tells her she will have her castle, Hilde has no doubts, but only exclamations about its beauty. Solness exalts those exalting exclamations when he tells her that the beauty will be "built on a true foundation." Where the first architectural image presented the self-overcoming paradoxically enacted by a robust conscience, this repetition presents the impossibly air-anchored foundation as an image of the second paradoxical change in Nietzschean willing: self-transfiguration.

In that change the active creator discovers that the imminent kingdom is immanent in him, that his impulses are deeds, that his power to make beauty by making himself ex nihilo is grounded in the potent void, "the true foundation," of ever-increasing aesthetic will to power. Both self-overcoming and self-transfiguration are eternal returns of the same apocalyptic moment of change in Nietzsche's theory of action. To will one is to will both and also to will perpetual magnification of their transformative power. Through reprising the foundation promise to Hilde, Solness has finally wrapped himself into that Nietzschean spiral and left his linear striving to master contingency, left it for good. The promise to Hilde repeats his impossible action and commits him to repeating it again, at a higher order of power, by climbing the spire. This Nietzschean action establishes a new kind of suspense in the theater. One doesn't wait to see if the action will happen; one waits to see how it will happen again, what enhanced self-expression it will engender. This logic accounts for the random variation of singular and plural castles in the air that marks the couples' two duets in this act. Like the kisses that erect and promise it, the airy castle is one aspiration with many transfiguring satisfactions.

At this point the Aristotelian world returns to the veranda. From behind the new house distant music of an offstage brass band floats onstage as Ragnar, Dr. Herdal, Mrs. Solness, and the chorus of neighboring ladies enter to watch the wreath ceremony. Their arrival starts the play's rapid final scene, a three-part sequence that ambiguously presents Solness's climb as an Aristotelian and Nietzschean action. The ambiguity begins immediately, with an ironic change from symbolically willed mystic harps to amateurly sounded tubas and cornets as music for the ceremony. Hilde may expect a Dionysian song from Solness, but the opening exchange here between Mrs. Solness and Ragnar indicates that the offstage music, which stops the couple's castle making, comes from musical members of the Builder's Association, who have come to celebrate their star member's latest worldly achievement. The ambiguity continues in Solness's exit line, the last words he speaks in the play.

Ragnar, reprising his earlier challenge to the builder's courage, tells Solness the foreman has sent word he is ready to climb the spire. Solness, ignoring the dare because he has already taken it up with Hilde, says he will go down to the house himself. Aline picks up the bravado in Solness's declaration and anxiously asks what he plans to do there. Solness hears Aline's unvoiced fear that he will replace the foreman and climb the spire himself and responds to her panic as follows:

> *Solness* (curtly): I must be down below with the men.
> Mrs. *Solness:* Yes—down below, of course. Down below.
> *Solness:* I always do it. It's my everyday custom. (*He goes down the steps and out through the garden.*) (MB, 366)

Two kinds of complexity work in this exit. The first is dramatic irony, which promises that the climb will and will not happen. However much Solness expects Aline to believe he goes to observe the foreman, the builder, and the audience, understand that his going down is the first part of his ascent. The dramatic irony also works against Solness as well, since Aline, and the audience, understand that his ascent will be the first part of his fall. Doubling the edge of dramatic irony this way, Ibsen turns conventional prediction of action into oracular, enigmatic interpretation of it: Solness will and will not climb and fall. A conceptual irony is thus embedded in the dramatic one, and suspense becomes angst. The question now is not what will happen but what does *happen* mean. The riddling term that makes a puzzle of action here is *down below*. The triple appearance of this abasement in the spouses' exchange once again presents metaphysical struggle over action as an ambiguous psychosexual contest. But this time the contest is resolved instead of stalled, and that change signals a shift in the metaphysical struggle. The question is no longer whether either competing action can occur, but, rather, which one will, to put the matter in Aristotle's terms, which one already has, to use Nietzsche's.

In Aristotelian terms, Solness's "going down" is a pragmatic event, an error that proves will cannot successfully supplant reason or obliterate contingency's power over agents. In Nietzschean terms his going down is a sublimating mental event, a symbolic assertion, rather than a proof, that reason and contingency hobble life. Self-overcoming and self-transfiguration always require the superman to will his own annihilation perpetually, to "go under," as Nietzsche repeatedly puts it.[16] Since such absolute willing is always its own outcome, any physical contingencies that may accompany it, even fatal ones, do so not as results, but as sideeffects, negative proofs of the positive glory of living dangerously. When he makes dramatic irony oracular in Solness's exit, Ibsen raises the question of which of these down-goings will occur without settling it. The competing actions both claim absolute authority over agency and brook no compromise. Compromise has been Solness's primary action. Its obliteration now in the conceptual symbolism governing him signals that the builder has come to his moment of truth. The way Solness plays that moment with Aline ironically indicates which truth he has chosen.

Throughout the play Solness has not "gone down" either in Aristotle's or Nietzsche's sense. Instead, he has negated both actions by submerging rational and willful agency in a stalling, prudent compromise that gives him fragile control over increasingly unmanageable contingency. His final line, "I always do it. It's my everyday custom," confesses as much, but does so ironically. He does go to inspect the men's work daily. Up until now he has done so to preserve his professional status. But this day's repetition of the everyday custom is done to annul the custom, to repudiate the professional status, to bring a prodigal, joyful "always" out of his formerly prudent one. He knows the ceremonious climb threatens death, but bravery ironically makes death's danger irrelevant, makes the envisioned amorous joy with Hilde a present bliss. Hence, his certainty that going down to the men is guaranteed and permanent exaltation. Solness savors that courageous irony alone.

When Aline threatens his transfiguring resolve, he reverses another everyday custom and prevaricates, as he has habitually to preserve their deadlocked, punishing marriage. Instead of opposing her confining, accusing fear, he evades it with a misleading display of masculine authority and put-upon rationality. I'm only going to exercise the mastery that daily maintains our life, he tells her, so possess your soul in patience. But in this prevarication Solness provides himself an escape hatch instead of a snare. On first sight the ruse seems another cowardly submission to contingency, a weak way to subvert conditionally his wife's competing weakness. A second, harder look can discern that his curt comforting of Aline is also an opportunity for him to will self-overcoming and so permanently dismiss her fear's damaging control of him. Disposing of the preserving action of his marriage by performing that action to affirm nonmarital love instead of spousal guilt, Solness finally does with Aline what he has just done with Hilde: he converts his domestic weakness into strength, makes contingency irrelevant to absolute willing, and frees impulse to be its own deed.

Solness exits with his truth a secret. Herdal and Aline, the male and female agents of humanist well-being, are taken in by his prevarication. Their confidence that Solness will not climb amounts almost comically to causal proof that he will. To indicate as much, Ibsen closes this ambiguous overture to the ceremony with another dramatic irony, this time centering it on the play's other Nietzschean agent. Hilde has not spoken or been spoken to since the crowd entered. Convinced that Solness cured himself of the passing mad desire to climb while Hilde, as they earlier requested, kept him away from the new house, the doctor and Aline approach her now to acknowledge her incidental aid to Solness and to them.

> *Mrs. Solness (Turns to Hilde)*: Thank you so much for holding on to him. I'd
> never have been able to budge him.
> *Herdal*: Yes, yes, Miss Wangel, I'm sure you know how to hold on to someone
> when you really want to. (*MB*, 367)

This dramatic irony is simpler than Solness's prevarication and has more focused narrative and conceptual effect. Hilde returns silence for the wife's and doctor's thanks. The moment presents rich opportunities to a director, who must decide if they are to notice her response or not when they leave her standing center stage, at the railing in front of Solness's old house, and cross backstage to join the ladies at the garden steps. Hilde's silence displays much: perfect, proud confidence in the builder's bravery; an unwillingness to reveal and so defile love; confirmation of and allegiance to the superior order she and Solness move in; exalted, bemused surprise at her opponents' presumptive credulity; patience; and cunning. Withholding the truth from them, she prevents their sullying interference in Solness's action. Their cross from her to the garden unwittingly denies what their thanks to her at the railing magnanimously confirmed: that she is of them. Giving a false victory to the Aristotelian interpretation of Solness's action, magnifying the Nietzschean one, Hilde's silence moves the conceptual contest unstably forward. Dramatic irony's conventional pleasure—suspense stoked by inside knowledge—now promises that Solness's climb will be a reversal inducing the recognition that Aristotelian logic cannot account for action. Clearly, Ibsen knows how to hold onto conventional drama the way Hilde knows how to hold onto Aline's husband and Herdal's patient.

He tightens that hold in the next exchange, which begins the second section of this closing sequence. Ragnar crosses to the railing where Aline and the doctor have just left Hilde and utters his version of their confidence that the climb will not happen. Ironically, his scorn opens the question their relief ambiguously closed. Upstage from the garden where the ladies are gathered Ibsen has set a street, which Ragnar now directs Hilde's gaze to. With barely suppressed glee he identifies the young men gathering there as apprentices whom he has brought to watch the master. Hilde asks what special interest they have in him, and Ragnar tells her they have come to watch Solness keep himself down as he has for so long kept them down: "They want to see him not dare to climb up his own house" (MB, 367). Hilde is content to let Solness's climb speak for itself to Aline and Herdal. No longer willing it to occur or not occur, those two take no active part in the event. Ragnar, however, has amassed a throng of maliciously participant observers willing the builder's failure and said so. Hilde must therefore once more act so that her independent creator can.

Aristotelian witness to Solness's climb, Ragnar is also, unwittingly, a Nietzschean agent of it and, as such, an active antagonist to Hilde. Ibsen plays that ambiguity by having Hilde and Ragnar contrarily announce the power of intention. With the avenging certainty of anticipated hindsight, Hilde tells Ragnar his intentions will be thwarted by Solness's revived intention to climb to the spire's top during this customary civic and professional celebration of his craft. She has trumped Ragnar's Nietzschean willing here, and he counters with the Aristotelian authority she has left him. Arguing from precedent observation of the builder's cowardice during this ceremony, Ragnar asserts that intention is not outcome in Solness's case, that habitual moral and physical fear will corrupt his revived strength and send him crawling backward on hands and knees before he's climbed halfway. Their standoff repeats the last conversation they had in this act, in which he discredited her belief in Solness by reminding her of the builder's fear, and raises the dispute to a higher order of antagonistic conviction. Linear development and cyclical enhancement of the play's action, this exchange, which ambiguously submits praxis to willing, once more makes dramatic structure conceptually as well as aesthetically subversive.

By this point three different accounts of action's relation to impulse have repeatedly struggled for control in this scene's structure and content. Hilde's silence advances the Nietzschean account past the Aristotelian prudence of Aline and Herdal. Her debate with Ragnar over cause and effect and the relation of character to action ironically advances Aristotle's logic, makes it once more a contender against Nietzsche's. Only *Hamlet*'s conceptual structure does and undoes itself with such exasperating, exhilarating regularity. And, like Hamlet's, the deed by which Solness ends, or at least stops, the simultaneously linear and cyclical incremental repetition of coward-making, hero-making conscience comes swiftly, in the midst of error, and has as much accidental chaos in it as cathartic necessity. At the moment Ragnar asserts, against Hilde's faith, that Solness will be defeated by fear, Herdal announces that the foreman is climbing, and Aline adds that he is carrying the wreath.

For a moment Ibsen seems to have aborted the Lysanger revival altogether. Appropriately enough, Ragnar and Hilde revive it immediately.

> Ragnar (*stares incredulously, then shouts*): But that's not!—
> Hilde (*cries ecstatically*): It's the master builder himself!.

The confusion is not resolved until Aline, taking her cue from Hilde, identifies the climber: "*Mrs. Solness: (screams in terror*): Yes, it's Halvard! Oh, my God, my God! Halvard! Halvard!" Giving, rescinding, and then restoring knowledge, the reversal yet once more reclarifies and escalates the scene's ever-converging narrative and conceptual tensions. From this point on fear and bravery contend on the ground as they do on the spire for control of Solness's climb. Aline and Herdal contrarily act out the fearful overthrow of prudence—she with hysterical, vertigo-inducing shrieks and a run to stop Solness, he with desperately preservative restraint of her dangerous motion and noise. In opposition Hilde and Ragnar contrarily act out the brave triumph of absolute will—she joyfully announcing each grade of Solness's ascent, he counterfactually commanding retreat at each new rise. The climactic ascent, appropriately enough, comes through exchanges between Hilde and Ragnar. When Hilde announces that Solness has hung the wreath, Ragnar responds with incredulity, calling the event "impossible." Hilde answers; "Yes! That's what he's doing now! The impossible!" (*MB*, 368).

Echoing Ragnar's description of the builder's ascent as impossible, Hilde spins the logic of praxis up into the power of willing, in which *impossible* means "joyfully necessary" instead of "unreal." Having announced the conversion of contingent reality into absolute reality with a philosophical pun, Hilde turns to another equivocation to celebrate Solness's immanent transcendence. "*With the enigmatic expression in her eyes,*" she asks if Ragnar doesn't see anyone arguing with Solness on the spire or doesn't hear a song in the air. Ragnar, of course, sees only Solness and hears only the wind and tells Hilde as much. Hilde hears and sees the repetition of Solness's Lysanger revolt, which she has for so long been expecting, but only tells Ragnar that she sees Solness arguing with someone on the spire and hears a mighty song. Their different accounts of the climb—his rationalist, her's visionary—mark off very clearly the divergent Aristotelian and Nietzschean accounts of action at work in this play. The dramatic irony of Hilde's questions, the innocence of Ragnar's

replies, raise each account to its highest power. While Solness is still on top
of the spire, Nietzsche's account prevails.

Whenever Ibsen indicates that Hilde has an "enigmatic expression in her
eyes," he instructs the actress and director to play the scene so that the other
characters onstage, and the audience, know that Hilde is clairvoyantly discerning some secret reality hidden in theirs. Normally, the insight comes with
dangerous authority attached, which authority Hilde variously expresses as
contempt or compassion for those who cannot see. Now her questions to
Ragnar are neither contemptuous nor compassionate, nor do they seek information about the builder's achievement or enhancing confirmation of it. They
are, rather, like Christ's riddling parables about his imminent kingdom, put to
separate those in whom the kingdom is already immanent from those who do
not already possess it and can therefore never receive or enter it.[17] Hilde and
Ragnar both know they have just witnessed the second coming of Solness's
ceremonious physical bravery, first displayed at Lysanger. For Ragnar the
repeated bravery is only colloquially impossible, a psychologically and morally
unlikely fulfillment of Solness in time, but by no means a defeat or transformation of that medium. For Hilde the builder's second coming perversely transfigures the omnipotent creator-judge's Second Coming, which delivers the
faithful from time to eternity. Her Christ returns as Babel's self-divinized
Nimrod, a rival titanic creator who scorns the celestial judge's authority and
realm, who establishes for and with her, on God's ground—the will—an
unending kingdom of exalting, world-making, sexual joy.

When Hilde announces her knowledge and Ragnar's ignorance of
Solness's eternally creative will, she only incidently puts the retributive
youth's will in its dead place in dead time. Her primary purpose is to declare,
heretically, that on this domestic churchspire Solness has visibly fulfilled her
willed faith in things once seen, long unseen, and now seen again—has made
things hoped for transcendentally substantial. When it defined faith as "the
evidence of things not seen" and "the substance of things hoped for,"
Christianity cannibalized classical Greek logic and ontology to make a
modernist reform of second-century humanist civilization (Heb. xi:1). When
he made his modernist reform of nineteenth-century humanism Nietzsche
cannibalized Christianity's appropriation of classical Greek logic and ontology to undo what he regarded as the decadent traditional continuity of both
ancient metaphysical authorities in Europe.[18] Nietzsche's theory of action,
which presents self-grounded willing as the atheistic evidence of things not
seen and the chaotic substance of things fatalistically hoped for, is both
anti-Christian and anti-Aristotelian. And it is, as Nietzsche insists repeatedly,
dangerous.

So far Hilde has successfully brought Solness from the wrong to the right side of living dangerously, from fear to bravery. Now that she hears Solness's Dionysian song again she discovers that bravery has a wrong side as well. When Hilde equivocally affirms Solness's impossible power to Ragnar, Ibsen allows a joyous victory for Hilde and the builder. When she turns directly to Solness to celebrate the absolute, Ibsen stages their joy as conventionally tragic hubris, the hamartia that proves contingency's authority over action. That reversal takes the play to its final resolution of the conflict between praxis and willing.

> *Hilde:* I hear a song. A mighty song! (*Cries in jubilant ecstasy*) Look, look! Now he's waving his hat! He's waving to us down here! Oh, wave back to him! He's done it at last, he's done it! (*She tears the white shawl from the Dr., waves it and cries up*) Hurrah for Solness! Hurrah for the master builder!(*MB*, 369)

That shawl is Aline's. When Hilde waves it, Mrs. Solness's peers, the town's edifying ladies standing at the garden, wave their handkerchiefs, and Ragnar's male cohort, who came to the street to jeer at their oppressor, now shouts his praise there. Ragnar, significantly, remains silent. The doctor tries to quiet the dangerous clamor, but fails, and this second segment of the final scene ends with Mrs. Solness and the ladies simultaneously shouting: "He's falling! He's falling! (*MB*, 369).

Solness falls because women, following his lead, unwittingly call forth his weakness when they incontinently celebrate his strength. The sequence, props, and symbolism by which Ibsen stages the fall ambiguously present the builder's sexually induced catastrophe as an accidentally and necessarily premature consummation of his sexually induced "impossible" action. At the end, as throughout, Ibsen stages this play's metaphysical contest on the body's equivocally physical/mental ground: erotic impulse. And, as usual, the impulse is sublimated and symbolically depicted. The final question is what to make of the impulse that brought Solness's body so disastrously down to earth and what to make of the symbolic depiction. Is the reversal in impulsive strength an Aristotelian or Nietzschean change, or both? The logic of praxis sorts things out as follows.

Solness waves his hat exuberantly, secure of his male triumph. Civic sign of masculine dignity, that male garb is normally ceremoniously removed to express courteous social deference to masculine superiors or courteous emotional deference to the exalting weakness of the "fairer" sex. Hats also came off, in Ibsen's day, in banks, professional offices, and churches, as conventionally reverent observation of the power of social institutions and of God.

At Solness's ceremony his hat comes off in defiance of all worldly and celestial power. Part overthrow of mundane dignity, part exalting salutation of his renewed strength, and its earthbound observers, Solness's hatwaving, on the spire that is equivocally his wife's and his consort's, is a manly undoing of the old civic, marital self, a ceremonial disrobing by which the newly potent man summons his consort to bliss.

The consort responds by tearing the wife's shawl from the doctor's grip and waving the matronly, marital garment to celebrate the builder's transgressive departure from civic and domestic order. The social symbol is clear enough. The frightened wife has prudently ceded her domestic authority over Solness to the doctor; the triumphant adulteress ironically spares the wife, usurps her place indirectly. Seizing authority over the marriage from the doctor, whose courteous, prudent intelligence has received but cannot preserve power over Solness's household, Hilde acts as accomplice on the ground to the builder's airy crime. For a moment these compounded ironies work in Hilde's favor, as the ladies witlessly enhance them, waving their diminutive signs of conventional feminine delicacy to celebrate what they believe is a moment of civic and domestic pride for Solness and Aline.

But adultery, like murder, will out. The cranial flag of Solness's rebellious disposition, the ambiguously respectable banners of feminine domesticity, together with the apprentices' civic shouts, all spin the builder's rapture into vertigo, and he plummets. To make good the hat's dangerous provocation of the shawl and handkerchiefs' dizzying acclamation, Ibsen has offstage voices report the builder's death as follows: "His head was crushed. He fell into the stone-pit" (*MB*, 370). In classical Greek theater, and in its later imitators—Racine's *Phaedra*, for instance—the tragic protagonist's death occurs offstage and is reported in a messenger speech, normally a set piece in which the playwright can wax lyrical or moralistic as the case demands. Ibsen shades that convention deftly into this play's finale. From Solness's exit forward the whole last scene is a messenger speech that reports the offstage disaster while it happens. The lyric moralism of the conventional report presents the ascending half of the disaster. The fall is half-staged, accompanied by shrieks of terror from the far upstage crowd: "A human body and some planks and poles can be indistinctly glimpsed falling through the trees" (*MB*, 369). The death does occur offstage, as convention requires, but its florid report is reduced to blunt empirical narration of one somatic and one occasioning fatal fact.

Ibsen's ambiguous revival of a classical technique for staging catharsis brings Aristotle's account of action full center stage at the end of the play but poses it there aslant. Writing contradictory summary commentary for the tragic deed while that deed is in progress, only minimally accounting for the deed's outcome, Ibsen turns one more loop through the curving line that brings Nietzschean will to power and Aristotelian praxis together in *The Master Builder*. The traditional, humanist line curves as follows. The builder's brave willing that his past return as his future is imprudent, delusional, and impious. When the brave deed by which he ceremoniously enacts that impossible aspiration accidentally ends in his death, that death discredits the aspiration and makes its living and dead agents, Hilde and Solness, objects of pity and fear. That the accidental end comes in the shawl and hat reversal is a plausible surprise, an unlooked-for but entirely convincing instance of poetic justice. Summoned to offend marital life by an adulteress, Solness is properly recompensed when, brandishing his offended wife's garb, that adulteress inadvertently induces a crowd of respectable ladies to praise of the builder that is unwittingly inappropriate and inadvertently fatal. For those in the audience religiously minded, the poetic justice enacted by the ladies is easily seen as a punishment sent by a God angered at the builder's transgression of natural and domestic law. Whether the avenger is nature, marriage, rational humanism, or God, or all these at once, the mode of vindication—reversal worked by weakness emerging from misused strength—seems finally to have established an Aristotelian pedigree for the action of this play.

Until, ironically enough, one gives further consideration to the classical Greek theater's association of other-worldly danger, violently retributive or sacrificial death, and exultant crowds of ecstatic women. Insofar as they are civic matrons, the women induce an Aristotelian change in Solness's impulsive action. Insofar as they are Bacchantes, the change they induce is Nietzschean, not a reversal but an intensification of the chronic struggle between weakness and strength. Brief attention to Dionysus' legendary and theatrical attributes and to Ibsen's use of them during the period he was writing *The Master Builder* should make the philosophical distinction between reversal and intensification of action clear.

Aristotle's rationalist account of tragedy pays no direct attention to the Dionysian ethos of the form. Indeed, one objective of his aesthetic treatise is to rescue drama from the opprobrium that Plato cast on that art when he complained of its Dionysian pleasures—irrational outbursts, counterfeit shape-shifting identities, licentious enhancement of violence and chaos. At least one Greek playwright, Euripides, did pay direct attention to the Dionysian ethos of tragedy, obviously admiring attention. His play *The Bacchae* presents the temporary possession of civilized wives and mothers by Dionysus and their ecstatic overthrow, during that possession, of Pentheus, who has made praxis itself a hamartia. Euripides' play stages much of the

cultic and legendary worship of Dionysus. *The Bacchae* pays scant attention
to the god's habit of inducing ecstatic frenzy in humanity by providing wine
and concentrates, instead, on his infatuation of female worshipers.

In the cult and legends Euripides drew on, Dionysus has divine and
human female devotees. The divine females, Maenads, were nymphs who
nurtured Dionysus during a period in his childhood when his father, Zeus,
had turned him into a baby goat and hidden him in the forest to protect him
from the jealous vengeance of Hera. The nymphs' reward from Dionysus,
once he regained his divine form, was to be possessed by the god, who sent
them roaming through the countryside, drinking water from springs and
thinking it milk and honey. In their more violent frenzies he inspired them
to dismember animals and so commemorate their god's deliverance from an
animal form. Dionysus' human female worshipers, the Bacchantes, were
priestesses who, naked or clad scantily with a veil, imitated the Maenads. In
some cases they ecstatically devoured wild animals they had first mystically
infatuated; in others, garlanded with ivy, they worshiped with ceremonious,
symbolic sacrifices on altars and with wild, frantic utterances, gestures, and
dances. In its most refined form their ecstatic identification with Dionysus
was a subject for ornamental and ceremonial visual art, which often depicted
the Bacchantes riding panthers and holding wolfcubs.

Ibsen used the Dionysus legend and cult as part of his modernist staging
of tragic inspiration and disastrous cultural, social, professional, and domestic
conflict in *Hedda Gabler*, the play he wrote in 1890, immediately before
composing *The Master Builder*. Frantically dissatisfied with civilized life but
unwilling to realize the ecstatic deliverance from it that lies at hand, Hedda
is a crippled Maenad. Her Dionysus, the reformed alcoholic and Promethean
intellectual Eilert Lovborg, praised throughout the play by the visionary
Hedda as a man with vine leaves in his hair, returns from her past with an
adultery proposal to reward and secure her inspiring worship. The proposal
hinges on Lovborg publishing his new manuscript. After destroying the
manuscript in a monstrous parody of ritual sacrifice—"I'm burning it! I'm
burning your child!"—Hedda sends Lovborg off to commit what she hopes
will be a Dionysian suicide.[19] When she finds out that his death may not have
been suicide at all and was only parodically Dionysian, she takes up the
Bacchic end herself. Rushing to an out-of-sight upstage piano, she plays a
frantic dance and then shoots herself.

Throughout *The Master Builder* Ibsen has staged Hilde's inspired deliverance of Solness from professional and domestic entrapment as a Maenad's
worship of Dionysus. The builder's description of her as a predatory, natural
force of ecstatic revival, an eagle at dawn; her constant enigmatic outbursts,

which discern a spiritual order trapped in the mundane one; and finally, her culminating praise of the builder's artistic power—"How did you make me what I am?"—all indicate that Ibsen has reversed *Hedda Gabler* in *The Master Builder*. Where earlier, in *Ghosts* and *Rosmersholm* as well as in *Hedda Gabler*, Ibsen stages change as a self-canceling reversal in Dionysian action, in *The Master Builder* he seems prepared to stage change as an unimpeded intensification in Dionysian action. Through such intensification the impossible Dionysian achievement, absolute willing rather than conditional managing of impulse, becomes transcendently possible.

To speak philosophically, Nietzsche's critique of rationalist humanism seems finally to have taken hold in the conceptually and aesthetically subversive adultery/professional intrigue binding Solness to Hilde. Solness's death, however, staged as a contingent reversal, apparently silences the Nietzschean critique of rational humanism. Clearly a matter of mismanaged impulse, the death returns action to the realm of mundane possibility, and that turn obviously enhances the explanatory force Aristotelian aesthetics and philosophy have over this play. But Ibsen stages Solness's contingent death as an event ecstatically governed by Dionysian Bacchantes, agents famous for absolutely impulsive willing. And Nietzsche, the theoretician par excellence of ever-increasingly dangerous and absolute willing—the self-enhancing, climactic action Solness lives and dies for—calls such willing Dionysian explicitly and repeatedly in his books. Those ironies require that Solness's fall be seen as an intensifying change and a self-canceling change, a Nietzschean continuity and an Aristotelian outcome, simultaneously. And so it seems Ibsen has killed Solness to ensure that the dramatic and philosophical questions concerning his action will stay bafflingly alive. But he has not killed the Maenad Hilde, and that is a clear indication that, if answers are to be found for this play's enigmatic ironies, the questions must be put to her.

In the Dionysian reading, Hilde's vision of the Lysanger revolt atop Aline's spire is an ecstatic frenzy sent her by her shape-shifting god, as he revives an old incarnation to begin a new life. When Hilde waves Aline's shawl she symbolically affirms that new life by turning the shroud of Solness's marriage into a Bacchante's veil. Waving the veil, this divine worshiper symbolically disrobes to indicate her new incarnation as the airy castle's princess. Exciting the town's ladies with her jubilant gesture and cry, Hilde acts the part of a Maenad and temporarily extends the builder's Dionysian frenzy to the ladies, makes them unwitting Bacchantes who shout a joy they only partially understand. Dramatic chorus, attendant priestesses, they also follow the chorus leader's and celebrant's gesture and wave their handkerchiefs without understanding that their mundane cloths are turned to so

many cast-off sacred veils under the sympathetic magic of Hilde's transformation of Aline's shawl. But the magic has transforming power that exceeds
Hilde's control as soon as she exerts it. Those veils bring Solness down, and,
when they do, the ladies forget their ecstasy immediately. Ignoring Hilde,
they rush to the aid of the violated wife, who has fainted to see her shawl,
still in Hilde's hand, kill her husband.

When Bacchantes kill they either kill their god's enemy, as they do in
The Bacchae, or sacrifice an animal to reenact their god's shape-shifting
deliverance from Hera, the protector and avenger of wives. Here they
unwittingly dole out destructive punishment all around. Praising the god,
they kill the husband at the moment he escapes his wife. Abetting the
Maenad, they vindicate the wife with a sacrifice lost on the adulteress and
probably fatal to the wife. Aline falls back unconscious when Solness plummets, presumably the victim of a fatal, or soon-to-be fatal, apoplexy.[20] Ibsen
leaves her in that condition at the end of the play, ironically surrounding her
with the vain succor of the now unpossessed Bacchantes. As if that were not
enough poetic justice for the living death Aline made of her life, Ibsen adds
the almost snide ironic insult of having her medical ally, Herdal, ignore the
wife's injury and rush off to heal her obviously dead husband.

That supererogatory touch of absurdity in the multiply accidental deaths
once again recalls the confusion in which action is suspended when *Hamlet* ends.
It appears at this point that Hilde was no more successful a Maenad than Hedda
Gabler and that her prized object of idealizing zeal, Solness, was no more fit
for transformation than Eilert Lovborg. Is Hilde's inadequate mastery of the
Dionysian moment of truth with Solness a reversing change that discredits her,
Solness, Nietzschean action itself? Or is her increase of danger, at its most
chaotic moment, an intensifying change in which danger's creative, exalting
force is once more summoned and governed by will? If the second is true, then
Hilde has not mismanaged Dionysian ecstasy at all, but has evoked its greatest
force: the power to keep impulse joyously living beyond reason and beyond
reason's perishable realm, the body.

That Solness perishes, in the Nietzschean account of change, no more
discredits his ecstasy than a flaccid penis discredits orgasm. Clearly, male
sexual anxiety about women's power to dash the male height they raise has
much to do with the ambiguities and ironies surrounding the builder's death.
And, while Ibsen is less floridly neurotic on this account than his contemporary and rival, Strindberg, a Freudian reading that accounts for the Bacchic
symbolism in *The Master Builder* as an expression of that anxiety has much to
commend it.[21] But sex is a stage for metaphysics as well as psychology, in
Ibsen's work. And, while the builder clearly has not ascended from his

descent, not gone on to any Christian or even pagan afterlife in this play, his summoning of the "robust conscience" required to answer Hilde's challenge has amounted to defiant resurrection of his joy in this life.

Joy's measure, like that of defiance, is intensity, not duration. And with duration gone, praxis yields full authority to willing. To ask, therefore, about the outcome of joy or defiance is to misunderstand both fundamentally: they are their own outcome. Indeed, to will them at all, singly or in union, is to make death irrelevant, whenever and however it comes. At least that is so in Nietzsche's, and in Hilde's, ontology. As a playwright, an artist who had to show something happen, Ibsen had much at stake in preserving a transitive relation between will, reason, duration, and outcome. As a radical thinker at war with himself, his art, his culture, and his culture's demand on his art, Ibsen also had much, perhaps more, at stake in preserving the nontransitive experience of defiant joy as an action for his stage. Throughout, this play has been shifting the balance of those divergent aesthetic and philosophical aims. The coda that follows Solness's death, in which Hilde and Ragnar respond to that death, shifts the balance of transitive and nontransitive action for the last time.

Ibsen closes the second segment of this death scene and opens the third by scripting a "short pause" between the ladies' response to the fall and Hilde's (*MB*, 369). There are only two other short pauses scripted in this play. The first takes place in the opening scene. The mortally ill Brovik interrupts his work in Solness's office and, against the protestations of his son and future daughter-in-law, announces that he must force the moment to its crisis and request his son's retributive enfranchisement from Solness. Kaja hears Solness arriving, they all return to work, and the short pause separates the stalled rebellion from the oppressor's entrance. The second short pause also occurs in the first act. Hilde has just finished reminding Solness that ten years ago, exultant after crowning his latest church steeple in the wreath ceremony, he kissed her "many, many times" to seal his promise that he would return in ten years to deliver her a fairytale kingdom. Solness denies the kisses; Hilde scorns his denial and crosses from him with her back turned. After a short pause Solness tries to pass the kisses off as a telepathically induced hallucination. When Hilde won't acknowledge that explanation, Solness ironically, equivocally, allows that he did kiss her, at which point she tells him she has returned to require her kingdom from him. Both these short pauses signal undoings of Solness's oppressive confusion of weakness and strength. The pauses both come at moments when he is required to relinquish a constituent element of his worldly life: with Brovik, his profession; with Hilde, his marriage. Now that he has sacrificially repudiated his worldly life more drastically than he, Brovik, Ragnar, or Hilde expected or required, the change wrought by Solness's willed transformation is again punctuated with a dead space of time onstage.

Hilde fills up that charged void with Solness's artistic name. She and Ragnar are still centerstage, side by side at the railing in front of Solness's old house. The coda begins as she stands, shawl unwittingly in hand, *"still staring upwards, as though turned to stone,"* says "My master builder!" (*MB*, 369). Unlike the ladies, Hilde does not report his fall. Given that she narrated every moment of his ascent, this is a significant omission. In place of the impossible deed's outcome Hilde reports only her relation to the impossible deed's agent. The substitution of his creative name, with her possessive modifier, for his finished deed ambiguously condenses both Aristotle's and Nietzsche's ideas that identity exists only in action, that being is doing. The creative name itself contains the same ambiguity. *Master builder* describes Solness's worldly function as a civic craftsman who expertly organizes the domestic foundations of civilized life; *master builder* describes Solness's unworldly function as a renegade self-creator who ecstatically wills that his uncreated joy should raze the foundations of his civilized life.

Hilde's possessive pronoun *my* settles that ambiguity, and Ibsen italicizes it in the script, thus making it very difficult for actors and directors to miss the point. Throughout the play, after her first conversation with him in act 1, Hilde never refers to Solness by his Christian or married name. Most often she uses the intimate instead of courteous form of the second personal pronoun when she addresses him. The audacious breach of etiquette, given her age and social status and his, establishes their sexual crime and their spiritual affinity. Ibsen's Lutheran audience would have recognized that her metaphysical aspirations for their love were always expressed with the intimate, familiar pronoun Protestant Christians used to petition or to praise their personally attentive God. When Hilde challenges or praises his will to joy she invariably calls him "master builder," usually to move him from the civic to the self-creating meaning of that title. And, when she speaks of him to others, she invariably uses either this title or a pronoun, except for one moment, in the dollscene with Aline that begins act 3, in which, in a rare moment of generosity, she describes him as a husband.

The possessive pronoun establishes another ambiguity inside Hilde's Nietzschean claim on Solness's creative will. She belongs to him as adult child-bride, as petitioner and worshiper of his power to deliver her a kingdom, much as a Lutheran, or any Christian soul, belongs to their father, their heavenly bridegroom and once and future celestial king, the mastering creator God. And he belongs to her as supplicant of her muse's gift, as errant and penitent fugitive from and builder of her promised kingdom, as reborn, elderly lover shunning the wrong aged form of desire for the right youthful one, again much as a Lutheran soul belongs to its infant, parent, spousal celestial source, the joyous, beckoning, forgiving creator God. Lutherans act toward their God exclusively by willing faith; their worldly deeds count only as ceremonies of faith. Staging the builder's climb of Aline's house as a mundane ceremony that confesses a heretical, transmundane faith, Ibsen radically subverts his religion's metaphysical definition of action and its idea of God.

When she calls out, "*My* master builder," Hilde settles the ambiguous identification of power with itself that characterizes her Dionysian willing with Solness. She affirms a new divine death and resurrection, a joyous, Nietzschean eternity of impulsive willing that ousts the rational, Aristotelian pursuit of moderate happiness and the Christian hope of personal afterlife. Ironically, her first affirmation has the pall of Golgotha on it, witnessing, as it does, the negative point at which her God's mastery is apparently vanquished by his service. Her stillness also depicts the moment when the Maenad has lost but not yet recovered from her possession by the God. And, finally, it depicts the baffled, suspended pleasure of a woman whose lover has just preceded her to bliss. A quick glance from Yeats's Nietzschean/Christian perspective should make the startled joy Hilde utters here clearer. In *Byzantium* death, sexual consummation, and willed artistic transfiguring of the mundane realm all converge when the speaker sees an epiphanic eidolon in the streets of Christianity's first imperial city: "I hail the superhuman;/ I call it death-in-life and life-in-death."[22] At this moment in *The Master Builder* Hilde has seen Solness become the same kind of eidolon.

Ragnar has seen something entirely different. Where she is immobily transfixed, he is trembling, holding himself up on the railing, aghast at the violent outcome of the fall: "He must have been smashed to pieces. Killed outright" (*MB*, 369). And so the two orders of change, intensification and reversal, stand forth in their final strength, paired at the border between Solness's old and new creations. One of the ladies around Mrs. Solness calls upon Ragnar to act, to run down to the new house and get information about Solness from the doctor. Ragnar says he can't move a step, and, when another lady tells him to call down for the news, he tries to shout across to the new house: "How is he? Is he alive?" (*MB*, 369). His voice doesn't carry, though, and he is answered by disembodied voices from the far upstage garden, and nearer, who already have the news that the master builder is dead, that his head was crushed by the fall into the stonepit.

That anonymous voices deliver the news Ragnar cannot acquire himself is a subtle but telling piece of poetic justice aimed against the retributive youth. Ragnar's bravery toward Solness has been, throughout the play,

vicarious, negatively expressed as scornful mockery of the builder's cowardice, usually behind the builder's back. Playing the conventionally Aristotelian
spectator of tragic death, Ragnar is now too frightened to witness the results
of Solness's bravery. And, true to his oedipal antagonism, he submerges that
bravery in a self-serving performance of the other half of conventionally
cathartic spectatorship: pity. Hilde does not indicate whether she has heard
the news or what she makes of it if she has. She preempts Ragnar's response
to the voices, though, and supplants their report with her own: "(turns to
Ragnar, and says quietly): Now I can't see him up there any longer" (MB, 370).

Ragnar makes no direct response to her overture. Instead, he utters an
implicit "I told you so," with the solemn sagacity of a chorus member who
proffers small understanding for great events: "This is terrible. He hadn't the
strength after all" (MB, 370). His pity for Solness announces that the fatal
outcome of the climb settles the question of the builder's bravery that the
climb posed. This is textbook Poetics and displays the same error that
Aristotle's reading of tragedy does: it ignores the superhuman dimension of
the extraordinary ordinary agents' action. Ragnar's error is a necessary
expression of his oedipal stance toward the builder. Justifiably aggrieved by
the frightened builder's exploitative vanity, Ragnar has nonetheless not been
able to assert himself directly against the builder's undiminished genius.
Consequently, the admiring/resentful youth consistently reduces Solness's
obviously superhuman power, depicts it as mere chicanery and an instance
of the insolence of office.

Like Hilde, Ragnar knows Solness's genius is only dormant, not dead,
but, unlike Hilde, he is ambivalent about seeing that genius revived, since he
lacks the sexual or social resources to make good on his sexual and social
desire to supplant the builder. The ambivalence expresses itself in the wreath
delivery, in which he picks unnecessary fights obliquely with Solness and
directly with Hilde, and in his fascinated negative affirmation of the climax
of the builder's climb: "I can't believe this! This is impossible!" (MB, 369).
When Ragnar cancels the climb with fearful pity of its outcome, he gives
final, full expression to his oedipal ambivalence. It is terrible that Solness
wasn't brave, Ragnar feels without saying so, not even to himself, because his
normal cowardice exposes mine. It is terrible that Solness is dead, Ragnar
inchoately feels, because I cannot use my unwanted knowledge of his normal
weakness, I cannot finish proving myself against him. Mundanely canceling
the builder's Dionysian willing, Ragnar's pity cancels his own mundane action
as well. And so Ibsen closes off the male side of this metaphysical sexual
action with a depiction of praxis permanently stalled by its deliberate
ignorance of superhumanly impossible willing.

That Ragnar cannot act, that his paralysis is poetic justice, that the poetic justice is meted out by his unwittingly ironic performance of classical tragic response to annihilating reversal, clears the way for Hilde's final Nietzschean affirmation of her Dionysian god. Oblivious to him since the fall, Hilde responds to Ragnar's oblique claim to victory in their argument over Solness's courage. In the last spin on Aristotelian logic in the play she refers to precedent and physical evidence to refute Ragnar and then immediately turns the realistic scene atop Aline's steeple into a mystic revival of the Lysanger revolt and, as such, an establishment of her airy-castled kingdom. "Hilde *(in quiet, crazed triumph)*: But he climbed right to the top! And I heard harps in the air! *(She waves her shawl upwards and cries wildly and ecstatically)* My—my master-builder!" (*MB*, 370).

From her arrival in this play Hilde has been dressed in mountain-climbing costume, a constant reminder of her alien status in the provincial town where Solness lives. In act 1 she arrives unexpected at Solness's door, with no luggage, and makes the necessity of cleaning her clothes the pretext by which she gains entry into the builder's home. In act 2 she responds gleefully to Aline's offer to bring her new clothes from town, until Aline repudiates her cheerful affection by describing the offer as merely formally dutiful. At that point Hilde not only poutily rejects Aline's offer but piques the wife by expressing a fanciful desire to go to town in her mountain cloths. Aline advises her that people might disparage her, Hilde looks forward to the pleasure of piquing the sophisticates, and Solness warns her that such tweaking of the social norms will earn her a reputation for madness equal to his.

The sexual aggression in Solness's disclosing his, and his wife's, fears for his sanity to their surrogate daughter (she is sleeping in the unused nursery) is primarily a psychological action here, one by which Ibsen deliberately establishes a comparison between this play and Strindberg's *The Father*. While Strindberg keeps the issue of madness a domestic and professional one, Ibsen makes it a metaphysical problem. Asserting that distinction is perhaps the primary purpose of this allusion to his dramatic rival. At this point clothes drop out of the play's metaphysical inquiry into what Solness sometimes fears are signs of madness in him: his telepathic willing; his religious fear of creative power; his prodigious, strangely displaced sexual energy. Hilde conducts that inquiry and leads him through it to understand those symptoms as signs of his absolute will, his "robust conscience," struggling to free itself from his confining, time-serving prudence. When clothes show up again as part of metaphysical understanding of his "madness," it is to signal the final separation in Solness of "robust" from "giddy" conscience.

The first time Hilde waves Aline's shawl in this scene, that separation happens more radically than Hilde or Solness had ever expected. Hilde has responded to that surprise by affirming it, by regarding the bravery of the climb as its own outcome and the fall as therefore irrelevant. Her realization that the airy castle would always be what it had always been—a visionary construction of memory and desire—is solemn. During the "short pause" that precedes her affirmation, she discovers that living dangerously does not allow for stasis, that it requires unending self-overcoming and self-transfiguration, especially when defiant joy seems consummate. While she lauds and summons Solness's vanished strength, Hilde's posture—stony fixity—depicts the Nietzschean beginning and end of stasis: will's internal resistance to further intensification and will's self-enhancing mastery of that resistance, mastery that ushers in a higher order of defiant joy.

Ragnar's pragmatic denial of the builder's bravery, his confusion of it with the fall's outcome, instead of vanquishing Hilde's recurrent willing of the impossible, turns out to be the resistance that enhances her final mastering joy. Refuting him, she wills that the past happened exactly as it happened and wills that it happen that way again every time she celebrates the ascent and the airy harps. This fusion of reversing and intensifying change, the final alignment of Aristotelian and Nietzschean action, takes place when she once again waves the ambiguously marital/adulterous, ruinous/delivering shawl, when she makes that domestic and civic garment a Maenad's pagan veil and cries out the creative name of that natural spiritual force that gives her mastery of the cloth's transfiguring magic: "My—my master builder!"

Ibsen has constructed this final scene so that no one can doubt that Solness *is* Hilde's master builder. Whether that means he is her creator god or the all-too-human victim of her mischievous, unbridled, adolescent fancy is a question this play has required the audience to consider from the moment Hilde first appeared. To settle the question Ibsen finishes the play with a classically rational *and* a classically irrational catharsis, testing the power of both to provide an adequate rationale for the change Hilde has wrought in Solness's life. While she has incidentally wrought a change in the builder's fortune, reported by Ragnar's pity and fear, the operative change is clearly her separation of the builder's absolute will from fortune altogether. Insofar as such a change can have any rationale, it has joy's and defiance's—transfiguring intensification of the private self, or, to speak biblically, the raising of the celestial kingdom on natural impulse. From *Brand* (1866) forward, that rationale vexes all the Ibsen protagonists who seek to apply it as a rational principle for life in the world. In *The Master Builder*, for the first time in Ibsen's career, the world disappears for joy's sake, and impulse makes its own kingdom in the newly opened void.

The dense psychological and social realism of this play, the concatenated reversals, stalls, and repetitions in the professional and adultery intrigues, the retrospective progress Solness and Hilde make through both those intrigues toward his keeping his promise—all this adjusted positioning of agency and the contingent realm to establish an intelligible, purposeful relation between them, in the end, cancels agency's pragmatic relation to the contingent realm. Agency's relation is with itself in the last moment of this play, and that is the first arrival of modernist action in the nineteenth-century theater. Action is not only moved from the contingent world into the will here; much more important, it is changed from a navigator to a creator of the real. When Solness says his airy castle will be built on a true foundation, when he tells God that he wants to be free to create in his own field as God is free to create in his, it is this transformation, from copier of the world's intelligible forms to generator of the will's ecstatic ones, that he announces.

And that change is, of course, the transvaluation of all values by which Nietzsche sought to cure what he regarded as the long European disease of rational humanism, or, to put the matter in Aristotelian terms, moderation. More demandingly abstract than any play he had written before, *The Master Builder* is also very concrete, even simple, in a way: it is the story of a promise. Opportunity, obligation, hope, and hypothetical certainty, a promise is the perfect occasion for staging the difference between possible and impossible action, between moderate and immoderate exertions of the will. And a promise kept, as this one is, is normally considered a victory of the possible over the impossible. In this play that commonsense wisdom comes out all wrong. Solness's climb converts an impossible deed into a possible one, but it also switches dramatic and moral values away from the possible world of pragmatic affairs and relocates them solidly in the positively impossible world of self-authorizing impulse.

That change radiated out from Ibsen's stage to Shaw's, Chekhov's, O'Neill's, and, in its most radical form, Beckett's. It came to rest, as so much does, in modern drama's other metaphysical inquiry into promises, *Waiting for Godot*. The pleasures of impulse are hardscrabble there, barely distinguishable from the contingencies they arise in. Instead of a shawl becoming a Bacchantes' veil, in that womanless play a rope belt becomes a disappointing noose that breaks when the desperate tramps test its strength. Contrarily, the pleasures of impulse are grand indeed in *The Master Builder*, grandest at their greatest distance from contingent expression, where they become visionary willing. Aristotle's stable praxis and Nietzsche's dangerous living mark off that distance in this modernist dramatic redemption of alienated genius. Solness's literary ancestors in that genre—Prometheus, Prospero,

Faust—all live dangerously with their divine craft, but they all, for various reasons in various ways, use their craft to enlarge rather than exceed the scope of pragmatic reality. Solness's craft has not enlarged the scope of pragmatic reality but drawn it round him like a vise. And that distinction between this magus and his classical, renaissance, and romantic counterparts is as devastating a renunciation of rational, humanist action as the nineteenth-century theater ever makes. Hilde's ecstasy is what Ibsen gives back for the loss; her witnesses must each decide separately whether that ecstasy is enough.

Afterword

In "Zarathustra's Discourses" Nietzsche's tragic hero puts a number of tests to those who would overcome themselves. One is the test of autonomy, whose rigors Zarathustra speaks of in "Of the Way of the Creator."

> Are you such a man as *ought* to escape a yoke? There are many who threw off their final worth when they threw off their bondage.
>
> Free from what? Zarathustra does not care about that! But your eye should clearly tell me: free *for* what?
>
> Can you furnish yourself with your own good and evil and hang up your own will above yourself as a law? Can you be judge of yourself and avenger of your law?
>
> It is terrible to be alone with the judge and avenger of one's own law. It is to be like a star thrown forth into empty space and into the breath of solitude. (Z, 89)

In *Ghosts*, *Rosmersholm*, and *The Master Builder* Ibsen puts these questions to his protagonists. Mrs. Alving, Rebecca West and John Rosmer, and Halvard Solness all answer differently, each of them differently stalled by the terror of willing joy. Ibsen has made death the secret condition of joy in each play and constructed each play's action as a revelation of that secret. In doing so, he has brought together the value of life presented in Aristotle's *Poetics* and the value of life presented in Nietzsche's visionary philosophy, and challenged audiences, as he has his characters, to take up one or the other.

In *Poetics*, Aristotle presents tragic death as the severest test for a rational, humanistic view of life. His aesthetic insists that good people ruining themselves by seeking good ends can be examples of the means to happiness life offers. He defines their catastrophes as error messages, proofs offered by the logical sequence of plot that reality's stable order of cause and effect always holds. Plots incite raptures of despair when they stage the bad ends of good people, but they also subsume that despair, bring it under the solemn rationality of catharsis, which sorrowfully affirms that even ruined life displays intelligible means to well-being. Tragic death, in Aristotle's world, clarifies the action that brings about happiness: moderate conformation of the rational law that governs personal will to the rational law that governs nature and society.

The standard of life's value is joy in Nietzsche's view, not happiness, and consequently his test case differs from Aristotle's. Joy is an absolute condition, while happiness is a contingent one. Being absolute, joy, unlike happiness, is a law unto itself. It does not emerge from natural or social conditions, but exceeds them entirely. In this it resembles death, and it is that connection that a Nietzschean reading of Ibsen discovers. In Aristotle's world, projects that unwittingly end in death prove that happiness does not allow will to be a law unto itself. Ibsen stages that world but changes the relation between death and autonomous will. His protagonists have all taken the way of Nietzsche's creator. Aspiring to joy, they have all made will a law unto itself. Consequently, they all bring the test of Nietzschean creativity upon themselves. They all must face the avenging justice of their newly invented conscience to discover if they *ought* to escape from the yoke of worldly duty.

Death defines the Aristotelian and Nietzschean value of the projects Ibsen's characters take up, with this distinction. From the point of view of Aristotle's rational humanism, Oswald's demand for death, Rebecca's and Rosmer's suicide, and Solness's fall all discredit autonomous willing. From the Nietzschean view these ends all define the quality of autonomous willing by rewarding its strength or punishing its weakness. The protagonists of these plays all ought to escape from their yokes because they all know the difference between duty and joy and have all taken steps to move their lives from confinement to liberation. The question for them all is whether they can escape. Their struggles display the Aristotelian conviction that life's value, and drama's, only emerges in action, in deliberate pursuit of some absent good. Ironically enough, it is their lingering attachment to Aristotle's definition of the good, to responsible maintenance of familial and social duty, that makes their Aristotelian pursuit of Nietzsche's joy so difficult. This doublebind accounts for the exhilarating tension of Ibsen's modernist action and for the confused animosity that action aroused in Ibsen's audience.[1] His characters all suffer from an anguish Zarathustra promised to those who take the creative way. "For see, it is still this same conscience that causes your grief: and the last glimmer of this conscience still glows in your affliction" (Z, 88). Action, in Ibsen's plays, brings that glow to white heat. In the stories considered here, only Solness makes a Phoenix passage through the affliction.

Death attends each stage of the aspiration toward joy in these plays. Its repeated effects show the double force in Ibsen's actions of Nietzsche's eternal return of the same and of Aristotle's progressively revealed hamartia. Mrs. Alving's self-creation flourished once her husband died and comes to its moment of truth when her son asks her to kill him. Rebecca West maneuvered Beata Rosmer's death while she was advancing free thought, and she consummates that project by atoning for that death with her own. Solness's creativity is throughout linked to his fear that he magically brought about the death of his sons. He braves death, encouraged by Hilde, in great part to finally conquer that fear.[2] In *Ghosts* and *Rosmersholm* the protagonists confuse the judgment and vengeance required by duty's law and joy's. Mrs. Alving's confusion amounts to paralysis, Rebecca West's to sacrificial assumption of the law she has sought to repeal. In both cases death does not resolve the dutiful action or fully cancel the joyous one.

In *The Master Builder* Ibsen finally resolves the action by having his protagonist meet the Nietzschean test and in the process discredit the Aristotelian one. When he climbs the new house's church spire, Solness once more asserts that the death of his children was not punishment for his creative passion, but, rather, an occasion to exert it more strongly than ever before. He goes farther along "the way of the creator" than any other Ibsen hero, by asserting explicitly what he is free from, building family dwellings, and what he is free for, the erection of will's autonomy as a spiritual dwelling, the founding of ecstasy's kingdom on the airy base of impulse's power to command and to play. In this play the question of whether death proves duty's value or joy's is passed directly to the audience in the double catharsis that Hilde and Ragnar stage. The last sentence of Zarathustra's warning to the creators is a very apt gloss on the Dionysian catharsis with which Ibsen ends the play. "I love him who wants to create beyond himself, and thus perishes" (Z, 91).

When Hamlet complains that deliberation takes away the name of action, he is deliberating over death. His action consists to a great extent of a metatheatrical contemplation of the rationale for his vengeful behavior, in experimental search for the right thought according to which he can to do the right thing—kill Claudius—in the right way. Hamlet eventually gives his great enterprise the name of action by obeying impulse instead of thought. In the midst of error and accident he makes impulse and duty consonant and shows that they both belong to the world of familial and social responsibility. Ibsen split that consonance from the start of his career. Over and over again he returns to the classical resolution of tragic action, death, to show that even that event cannot close the gap between the will and the world.[3] In place of moderation he stages ecstasy as the right thought that allows for the right, joyous deed. And the deed is not a result, as ecstasy is not a project. Dramatic action has overcome itself by the time Ibsen writes *The Master Builder*. It has undone its function as a contingent ratio ordering worldly transformation and taken up its first, Dionysian role as celebrant, not manager, of change.

Notes

Preface

1. For an excellent study of Nietzsche's place in modernist literature, see Foster, *Heirs to Dionysus*. The second chapter, "Nietzsche's Legacy to the Modernists," which takes up polaristic thinking, creative consciousness, and the relation of life and power in moments of cultural crisis, is especially helpful for understanding Ibsen's plays. And there is a lagniappe for Ibsen scholars in the book. In a footnote to chapter 5, Foster, while discussing Alexander Bely's novel *Petersburg*, mentions Bely's association of Nietzsche and Ibsen. "In an article several years earlier, Bely had linked the image of an exploding bomb and the idea of epochal cultural change with Nietzsche, saying 'To stick dynamite under history itself in the name of absolute values not yet discovered by consciousness—that is the fearful conclusion of Nietzsche's lyricism and the drama of Ibsen'" (445-46). The rest of this book is an attempt to amplify Bely's insight, to see how it works when it changes from an idea about history to an idea about Ibsen's introduction of modernist ontology and ethics to the stage.
2. For a copious, precise, and very useful history of the theories of dramatic action, and Ibsen's place in that history, see Carlson, *Theories of the Theatre*. Especially useful are chap. 1: "Aristotle and the Greeks"; chap. 9: "The Restoration and Eighteenth Century in England"; chap. 11: "Germany to Hegel"; chap. 12: "Italy and France in the Early Nineteenth Century"; and chap. 15: "The Germanic Tradition in the Late Nineteenth Century."

Chapter 1

1. Plato's most elaborate discussion of the principles governing natural change comes in *Timaeus*, especially 49-51. See also *Phaedo*, 102b-105b, for an

account of forms indwelling in nature. On the unreliability of natural flux as an object of knowledge, see *Cratylus* 402a.

2. For Plato's theory of knowledge, see *Theatetus*. See also *Republic*, 476a-480a; and the diagram of the divided line, 509d-511e; and the allegory of the cave, 514a-521b. Plato's theory of forms is developed throughout his dialogues, especially in *Republic* and *Phaedo*. Usually problems of knowledge intersect with problems treated in the theory of forms. The mature theory of forms is subjected to an acid test by Plato in *Parmenides*. "Anamnesis" is treated in *Meno*, 803-86c; and *Phaedo*, 72e-77a. *Symposium* presents the approach to reality through "eros." For *dialektike* see *Phaedo*; 101d; *Republic*, 511e; *Phaedrus*, 265c-266b; and general treatment in *Sophist*, *Philebus*, and *Politicus*. For Plato's indictment of poetry, see bks. 2, 3, and 10 of *Republic*; and *Ion*. For a more favorable view, see *Phaedrus*. These references are not exhaustive, but presented as portals of discovery, spotlights on rich entries to Plato's thinking.

3. The primary elements in Aristotle's account of change are presented in his treatise *Physics*, I, 5-7. For Aristotle's most general account of the origin and nature of knowledge and its acquisition, see *Metaphysics*, I, 1-3.

4. For elucidation of the distinction, and its sources in Aristotle, see Lear, *Aristotle*, 15.

5. The relation of form and matter is presented in many different contexts in Aristotle's thought. The definitions of both elements of the pair occur in *Physics*, II, 194b-195a; and *Metaphysics*, 1013a-1014a. These sources also present the four causes and their relations, which will be discussed later. Together with formal, and material cause, change is governed by efficient and final cause. For the derivation of sensible qualities from *stoicheia*, see *On the Heavens*, IV, 310a-312a.

6. For an excellent treatment of the activities of the four causes in change, see Lear, *Aristotle*, 26-42.

7. For an elucidation of the different explanations that Aristotle's logical works, especially *Categories*, and *Metaphysics* give of substance, see Graham, "Two Systems in Aristotle," 215-31. For another elucidation of the distinction, see Lear, *Aristotle*, 265-93.

8. Aristotle, *Metaphysics*, 1069a.

9. L.A. Kosman cites this distinction between actuality as movement and as substance as the centerpiece of his excellent analysis of Aristotle's foundational reality, "Substance, Being, and *Energeia*" (121-51). I have followed Kosman's argument about substance in its dual relation to possibility and actuality in my analysis of the matter.

10. For a synopsis of the argument of *De Anima*, see Theoharis, "Joyce and Aristotle," *Joyce's Ulysses*, 2-10. For Kosman's citation of the soul as the

energeia, substantial activity, of human beings, see "Substance, Being, and *Energeia*," 33-34.

11. See Aristotle, *Metaphysics*, 1025b-1026a.

12. See Aristotle, *De Anima*, I, 402a1-9.

13. See Aristotle, *Nicomachean Ethics*, III, 113a11-12.

14. Plato's account of happiness, and what activity leads to it, is developed throughout most of his dialogues. The most important analyses of the relation of contingency to the good life are in *Republic, Phaedo, Gorgias, Philebus*, and *Protagoras*. Aristotle takes up the same problem throughout his treatises and concentrates on it in *Nicomachean Ethics, Rhetoric*, and *Poetics*. The best contemporary treatment of the distinction between Plato and Aristotle on this point and the relevance of that distinction to classical literary theory is Nussbaum, *The Fragility of Goodness*.

15. For an excellent analysis of Aristotle's theory of tragic action, see Burke, *Grammar of Motives*. Burke's analysis of Aristotelian tragedy, made to advance his own new theory of action, "dramatism," is extravagant, but always brilliant and insightful. For specific treatment of the double logic of tragic cause and effect, see the section entitled "Dialectic of Tragedy" (38-41).

16. Halliwell, commentary, *"Poetics" of Aristotle*, 94.

17. Bywater, in *Poetics*, 1450b24-25.

18. For an account of the distinction between result and product as the ends of action and the relevance of this distinction to Aristotle's moral theory, see Charles, "Aristotle" (119-45).

19. Stanford, *Greek Tragedy and the Emotions*.

20. The bibliography of critical disputation about the meaning of *katharsis* is immense. My thinking on the matter is in line with the definition of *katharsis* offered by Martha Nussbaum in *Fragility of Goodness*, 388-90.

21. Shakespeare, *King Lear*, Act I, Scene 4, line 305.

22. For an analysis of *anagnorisis* in Aristotle's literary theory and a history of the term's meanings in narrative theory and practice from the classical to the modern periods, see Terence Cave's brilliant, copious study *Recognitions*.

23. Charles, "Aristotle," 136.

24. For essential information about Ibsen's early theatrical experience, see Williams, *Drama from Ibsen to Brecht*, chap. 1: "Henrik Ibsen," especially 26-34. For 13 years before his first major success (*Brand*, 1866), Ibsen was playwright, stagemanager, and producer in small regional theaters in Norway. During that time he produced a great number of well-made plays, the modern instances of Aristotle's unified actions. Williams presents an excellent account of the moral and intellectual vacancy of those plays, which preserved only the shape but not the spirit of Aristotle's rationalist vision.

Vacant as they were, Ibsen understood that these actions still gripped audiences, and he used them himself, subversively, to present his own account of the world's promised happiness. The rest of this book argues that Ibsen had less and less confidence in the eudaemonism and praxis that bourgeois humanism had inherited from Aristotle and that he displayed his doubts by mastering Aristotelian dramatic form and using it to repudiate Aristotelian thinking about reality and change.

Chapter 2

1. Nietzsche was the son and grandson of Lutheran pastors and thought of taking up that calling himself until his adolescence. For a picture of the religious influences on Nietzsche's childhood and adolescence, see Hayman, *Nietzsche*, 3-50.

2. One definitive encounter in this controversy has been, and remains, the challenge posed to traditional philosophy—truth-oriented, educative, logocentric discourse—by deconstruction, which shuns truth claims and, instead, ceaselessly undoes conceptual terminology (its own as well as traditional philosophy's), thereby recasting informative, definitive argument as the infinitely free play of interpretation. Martin Heidegger's four-volume *Nietzsche* makes the most powerful case that, despite his ironic subversion of the philosophical tradition, Nietzsche remains an ontologist and metaphysician. Heidegger views the will to power as a culminating reversal of Platonic idealism, a transposition of being entirely into the subject. Jacques Derrida, in *Eperons: Les Styles de Nietzsche (Spurs: Nietzsche's Styles)*, opposes Heidegger, emphasizing Nietzsche's insistence on the provisionality of all thinking, the free play of all objects and methods of inquiry, and the multiplicity of rhetorics and modes in Nietzsche's writing that conveys this provisional, sliding view of things. For an excellent summation of these opposing views and their influence in Nietzsche scholarship in the last 30 years, especially in North America, see Behler, *Confrontations*.

3. Nietzsche makes this argument continuously throughout his works. For the most focused presentations of the case, see: *BGE*, preface and pt. 1: "On the Prejudices of Philosophers"; *GS*, 359, 110, 111; and especially *TI*, "The Problem of Socrates," "'Reason' in Philosophy" and "How the 'Real World' at last Became a Myth." For excellent accounts of Nietzsche's relation to the philosophical tradition, especially to the Greeks, see Strong, *Friedrich Nietzsche and the Politics of Transfiguration*, chap. 6: "What Is Dionysian? Nietzsche and the Greeks" and Nehamas, *Nietzsche*, chap. 1: "The Most Multifarious Art of Style," and chap. 2, "Untruth as a Condition of Life."

4. Maudemarie Clark's study *Nietzsche on Truth and Philosophy* treats this problem extensively, as do Strong and Nehamas, and includes a response to Nehamas's reading of Nietzsche's truth claims as perspectival and aesthetic.

5. For an excellent account of the philosophers of the future, and how they will enact "the free spirit," see Nehamas, "Who Are 'The Philosophers of the Future'?" (46-47).

6. Nehamas, *Nietzsche*, 68-69. Nehamas' book is justly celebrated, and I have relied on its second chapter, "Untruth as a Condition of Life," for part of my argument here about *Beyond Good and Evil*. I take a slightly more "positivist" view of Nietzsche's perspectivism and aestheticism than Nehamas does, but that is more nuanced appreciation of his argument than disputation.

7. The relation of reason to reality is, of course, a constant topic in philosophy, and Nietzsche is not the first to argue that reason observes itself whenever it observes reality. The innovation in Nietzsche's argument comes in his assertion that perspectival reason generates not only terms for reality but reality itself, a permanently transformed reality. Previously, rational terminology was regarded as transparent or opaque access to some world that existed apart from the terminology and was not affected by the terminology. From Plato through Kant the vexed relation of reason to reality is a constant topic in ontological and epistemological treatments of the appearance-reality dichotomy. But nowhere in that long argument does reason claim that reality is nothing but appearance or that appearance and reality and reason are purely imaginative, hypothetical, subjective terms—strategies of a disposition and nothing more.

That is precisely what Nietzsche claims throughout his work in the 1880s. His insistence that reason is willed and unfixed in its creative capacities distinguishes Nietzsche's argument from the nativist functionalism that permeates the description of pure and practical reason that Kant made in his critiques. And, while there is an analogy between Nietzsche's case that reason is a dispositional function and Hume's empirical separation of reason's laws from nature's, little can be made of their similarity. Hume's skepticism preserves a separation between reality and reason, after all, and Nietzsche's "philosophy of the future" does not. Nietzsche's thinking most closely resembles Hegel's idea that reason is *geist* dialectically unfolding the real in and through human consciousness, but differs from Hegel's developmental ontology in at least two crucial respects: there is no telos in Nietzsche's progressive generation of the real in the subject, and there is no cumulative coherence binding the successive generations of the real in one subject or in the aggregate of subjects. There is an increase of dispositional power in Nietzsche's free spirits but not, therefore, an increased stability or fixity in whatever reality their power generates. For scholarly commentary on this matter see Nehamas, "Untruth as a Condition of Life," *Nietzsche;* Schact, "Truth and Knowledge," and "The World and Life," in *Nietzsche;* and Deleuze, "Active and Reactive" and "The Overman: Against the Dialectic," *Nietzsche and Philosophy.*

8. See Nietzsche, "'Reason' in Philosophy," and "How the 'Real World' at last Became a Myth," *TI,* 35-40.

9. For an excellent treatment of the form/content problem in Nietzsche's theorizing about music and of Nietzsche's theoretical place in the development of modern thinking about music, see Janz, "Form-Content Problem in Nietzsche's Conception of Music," 97-116.

10. For a comprehensive account of the compatible and incompatible relation *The Birth of Tragedy* bears to Aristotle's *Poetics,* see "*The Birth of Tragedy* and Aristotle's *Poetics*" in chap. 8: "Tragedy, Music and Aesthetics," in Silk and Stern, *Nietzsche on Tragedy,* 225-238.

11. The only remarks Ibsen is known to have made about Nietzsche came in the year of the philosopher's death. Ibsen was then, in 1900, a celebrated, aged, cultural authority living at home again in Norway. He granted an interview to a local newspaper, and, when he was asked to comment on Nietzsche's death, Ibsen observed that Nietzsche was "a rare talent who, because of his philosophy, could not be popular in our democratic age." He further observed that Nietzsche was by no means "a spirit of darkness, a Satan." The story of the interview is told in Meyer, *Ibsen,* 841. Nietzsche was equally distant but, characteristically, more caustic about Europe's rival scourge. In his autobiography *Ecce Homo,* written in 1888 but not published until after his death, in 1908, Nietzsche presents himself as an unequaled psychologist. In the chapter entitled "Why I Write Such Excellent Books" Nietzsche takes up the psychology of love. In section 5 of that chapter he disparages altruistic love as an invention of feminine *ressentiment.* Disparaging the whole feminist project, especially the quest for democratic enfranchisement in the power structures of the day, Nietzsche argues that women's great role in life is to wage sexual warfare, not to edify men domestically or culturally. Against this natural function the contemporary idealists, Nietzsche argues, have reared the degenerate ethos of amity and equality. And it is here that Ibsen comes in for his blow: "An entire species of the most malevolent 'idealism'— which, by the way, also occurs in men, for example in the case of Henrik Ibsen, that typical old maid—has the objective of *poisoning* the good conscience, the naturalness in sexual love" (76). This view of Ibsen as essentially a social reformer, a revolutionary moralist, is also expressed in Shaw, *The Quintessence of Ibsenism* (1891). While the view captures Ibsen's obsessive

inquiry into life's value, it reduces that inquiry's metaphysical scope drastically, and counts, consequently, as less than even a half-truth about Ibsen's project.

12. Strong, *Friedrich Nietzsche and the Politics of Transfiguration* 302.

13. For an excellent account of will to power as a cosmological principle, see chapter 4: "The World and Life," in Schact, *Nietzsche*, 187-286.

14. The discrimination of different orders of will to power in different people has obvious bearings on the traditional political, moral, and ethical philosophy that Nietzsche constantly undid in his own writing and thinking. I have concentrated in this book on the ontological and psychological aspects of this ranking. For two excellent studies that concentrate on moral and political philosophy, see Hunt, *Nietzsche and the Origin of Virtue* and Berkowitz, *Nietzsche*.

15. Nietzsche, *Will to Power*, sec. 1067, 549-550. This book was not composed by Nietzsche nor published during his lifetime, but was compiled from unpublished notes and projects left at the time of his death. That literary estate is referred to as *Nachlass* by Nietzsche scholars. Reference to the *Nachlass* material in support of any interpretation of Nietzsche's published work is common, but not uncontroversial. For an excellent account of the "multiple explanation" problem in Nietzsche scholarship and of the place this long excerpt from the *Nachlass* has in that problem, see Magnus, "The Uses and Abuses of *The Will to Power*," 218-235. Magnus characterizes readers who confidently refer to the unpublished work to make cases about the published writing as "lumpers" and observes that those who lump do so to argue that Nietzsche's concepts should be taken as arguments for "presence"—that is, as truth claims, perspectival or otherwise (221). Those readers who distinguish between the *Nachlass* and the published books Magnus calls "splitters." He characterizes them as normally convinced that Nietzsche did not wish to subvert or replace old philosophy with a new one, but that he wished to cancel philosophy altogether, that he had no ontology, epistemology, ethics, or aesthetics to offer. Magnus counts himself among the splitters and suggests that Nietzsche might best be thought of as "the first full-blooded, postmodern, nonrepresentational thinker, the fountainhead of a tradition which flows from him to Heidegger, Derrida, Foucault, Rorty, and so much recent literary theory" (222). I must confess to having lumped here, and, while I do think Nietzsche cherished his concepts of will to power, eternal return, and the superman, all concepts Magnus argues Nietzsche dropped when he abandoned the *Nachlass* material, I do not think Nietzsche regarded any of these as "truths." If these concepts are what I have called them, rational configurations of Nietzsche's visionary passion, then

characterizing them as accounts of "presence" becomes tricky. Whatever presence vision, passion, aspiration, and imagination seek or establish when Nietzsche turns them toward improvisation and free play has enough "absence" in it to make me think that, as a reader of Nietzsche, I may be, in some measure, one of Magnus's splitters as well as one of his lumpers. In either case the Magnus essay deserves careful attention for its good humor, its intelligence, and its closing dip in the nonrepresentational, full blooded, Foucaultian, postmodern fountain.

16. Nietzsche, sec. 382: "The Great Health," *Gay Science*, 346-47. For an excellent analysis of this passage in *The Gay Science* and of the metaphoric role seafaring plays in Nietzsche's visionary writing, see Harries, "The Philosopher at Sea," 21-44.

17. For other references to the concept in *The Gay Science*, see sec. 109, 233, 285.

18. Nietzsche, *Thus Spoke Zarathustra*, 176-80.

19. For an excellent version of this interpretation, see Pippin, "Irony and Affirmation in Nietzsche's *Thus Spoke Zarathustra*," 45-71.

20. For an interpretation along these lines, see Deleuze, *Nietzsche and Philosophy*, 47-49, 68-72.

21. For an interpretation of the conditionality of the eternal return, see Nehamas, *Nietzsche*, 150-62. I take Nehamas's point that the eternal return of the same is not a cosmological doctrine, as presented in *The Gay Science* and *Zarathustra*, but a principle of identity. It does not follow from this, however, that the eternal recurrence of the same cannot be a vision of will to power's worldly life at other points in Nietzsche's writing. That power renews itself ceaselessly in the same way—by subsuming all definitive commands in impulse's improvised, free play—is exactly what Nietzsche's disposition requires "the world" to be, as I have argued in my analysis of the passage from *Will to Power*. The difference between Nietzsche's vision of eternal recurrence in the world and eternal recurrence as a principle of psychology is a difference that stems from which dimension of will to power Nietzsche is affirming at any moment. When he addresses conscious life Nietzsche puts the distinction between command and improvisation in impulse in biographical terms; when he addresses preconscious life he puts the distinction in cosmological terms. In neither case is the exact repetition of every command will ever gave itself postulated as a dogma or doctrine. In the psychological case such repetition is presented ironically, as a reminder to "argonauts of the ideal" not to confuse the joy of improvisation and the joy of command. Exact, ceaseless repetition of one improvisation is one of the possible configurations power's increase can take, but not, therefore, the sole necessary configuration. It is only presented as necessary

so that the larger vision, that power is dynamic and not substantial, can be affirmed absolutely.

I also take Tracy Strong's point that the eternal return is the product of a disposition, but disagree with his argument that it is therefore not a view of power's activity in the living "world," for the same reason I disagree with Nehamas. Strong's interpretation, that the doctrine is a strategy for eliminating neurotic fear of the past, is illuminating and persuasive. I do not see that it rules out eternal return as an account of the will to power's function as the world's life. Strong's case is made in chap. 9: "The Doctrine of the Eternal Return," in his book *Friedrich Nietzsche*, 260-93. For a book-length treatment of the problems in interpretation of the eternal recurrence in Nietzsche, see Stambaugh's *Nietzsche's Thought of Eternal Return*, especially 29-61.

22. *Amor fati* appears infrequently but potently in Nietzsche's work. He mentions it in *Gay Science*, sec. 276, 223; in *Ecce Homo*, "Why I Am So Clever," sec. 10, 68; and "The Wagner Case," sec. 4, 124; and *Will to Power*, sec. 1041, 536. The idea is also developed extensively in *Thus Spoke Zarathustra*.

Chapter 3

1. The letter is cited in Fjelde, *Henrik Ibsen*, 4. To date the most ambitious and impressive critical attempt to understand Ibsen's unified dramatic project is Brian Johnston's work *The Ibsen Cycle*. Johnston's learning is extensive, and his readings of the plays are often acute. His thesis is that "the realistic plays are structured directly upon Hegel's major philosophical work, *The Phenomenology of Mind*, and that the sequence of dialectical dramas in Hegel's account of the evolution of human consciousness is paralleled in the sequence of dialectical dramas in Ibsen's Cycle" (1-2). Although a powerful case can be made that there is more distance between Hegel's procedures and Ibsen's than Johnston acknowledges, there is no doubting that Ibsen had a philosophical imagination and an unceasing fascination with spiritual transfiguration. Whatever one makes of Johnston's influence theory, his central insight—that Ibsen can be powerfully understood in the light of modern philosophy—is a boon to scholars and students not only of Ibsen but of nineteenth- and early-twentieth-century intellectual and cultural history as well. My account of Ibsen differs from Johnston's consistently in its method and its conclusions. But I take his basic point, that Ibsen's cultural accomplishment belongs with Sophocles' and Shakespeare's, and that such an achievement merits scrutiny from a philosophical point of view.

2. For a detailed history of this aspect of Ibsen's career, for the story of his cultural presence as author and his various financial dealings with his publisher, Hegel, see Meyer, *Ibsen*. Meyer's biography is a superb account of how Ibsen's life provided material for his plays.

3. Descartes, 4: "Proofs of the Existence of God and of the Human Soul," *Discourse on Method*, 26.

4. Coleridge, like most romantics, vacillates between hope and despair over people's access to reality. Indeed, "The rime of the Ancient Mariner" is the romantic epic that Wordsworth and Byron were desperate to write, precisely because such vacillation makes up the phantasmagorical journey's story.

5. Shelley, *Defense of Poetry*, 499-513.

6. Pound, "Cantico Del Sole," *Personae*, 183.

7. Croce, "Ibsen," 157.

8. Bigley, "Praxis and Stasis in Ibsen's *Bygmester Solness*, 1978.

9. See, for example, Down, *Intellectual Background of Ibsen's Plays*. For an extensive treatment of Kierkegaard's presence in Ibsen's plays, see Valency "Ibsen," *Flower and the Castle*, 118-237.

10. For an analysis of the analogues to *The Oresteia*, see Chamberlain, *Ibsen*, 87. The structural reference to *Oedipus Rex* comes in *Ghosts'* action, which makes gradual revelation of information about the past the forward motion of the plot, and its moral logic, which makes all Mrs. Alving's attempts to become innocent events in her self-incrimination. That logic holds in both the Aristotelian and Nietzschean dimensions: in the first her prudential compromises lead finally to her son's illness, disappointment with Regina, and demand that she kill him; in the second her repeated failure to will her life joyously fuels the incrementally disastrous demand that she do so, which appears most powerfully in the final scene. For another reading of analogies between *Ghosts* and *The Oresteia* and *Oedipus Rex*, see Johnston, *Ibsen Cycle*, 194-95.

11. Ibsen, *Ghosts*, 56.

12. Halliwell, commentary, *"Poetics" of Aristotle*, 46-47.

Chapter 4

1. Ibsen, *Enemy of the People*, 385.

2. For analysis of the play's connection to motifs of the supernatural drawn from Scandinavian legend, folklore, and ballads see Jacobsen and Leavy, *Ibsen's Forsaken Merman*, esp. 121-30, 173-93.

3. Ibsen, *Rosmersholm*, 232.

4. Freud, *Some Character Types Met With in Psychoanalytic Work,* esp. section entitled "Those Wrecked by Success," 14: 324-31.

5. For an excellent account of the Edwardian theater's depiction of the complex social, economic, and psychological issues raised by marriage, remarriage, and the relation of the sexes in general, see Clarke, *Edwardian Drama,* esp. chap. 2: "Jones and Pinero," 24-50, and chap. 5: "Shaw," 95-118. Clarke's analysis of the relation of dramatic form to contemporary sexual and familial mores is clear, copious, informative, and incisive. It provides very useful information for understanding the sexual and familial situations Ibsen depicts.

6. Again, for an impressive and persuasive psychological account of Rebecca's problem, see Freud's comments on Rebecca West in "Those Wrecked By Success," 14:324-31.

7. "Rosmersholm," in Fjelde, *Henrik Ibsen,* 575.

8. Dickens, *Christmas Carol,* 3:75.

9. For an excellent account of the nineteenth-century Magdalen play see Meisel, *Shaw and the Nineteenth Century Theater,* chap. 6: "Courtesans and Magdalens." Meisel's book is the single best work on the multiple genres, styles of acting, and conventions of physical production that made up the theatrical world Ibsen moved in. It is essential reading for understanding the subversion of popular forms by which Ibsen carried out his experimental career.

10. See Jacobsen and Leavy, *Ibsen's Foresaken Merman,* 121-30, 173-93.

11. Ibsen, *Peer Gynt,* 64.

Chapter 5

1. See Meyer, *Ibsen,* 26; "The Summer in Gossensass 1889," 635-55, for the story.

2. This plot detail is an allusion to Strindberg's play *The Father,* whose misogyny Ibsen had little use for and which he ironically parodies in the relation of Hilde and Solness in this play.

3. For the sources of this idea of fortune in Aristotle's *Poetics,* see Nussbaum, *Fragility of Goodness.*

Chapter 6

1. Again, Strindberg's play *The Father* is ironically evoked.

2. For the sources of this modern religious and intellectual premium on "ordinary" (i.e., domestic life), see Taylor, *Sources of the Self,* esp. "Part III: The Affirmation of Ordinary Life," 211-85.

3. For a cogent presentation of the problem, see Taylor, intro., "System . . . Structure . . . Difference . . . Other," in *Deconstruction in Context*, esp. 4-14.
4. See Johnston, *Ibsen Cycle*, for an account of the metaphysics as Hegelian.

Chapter 7

1. For this idea's importance in the tradition of rational humanism in Europe, see Lovejoy, *Great Chain of Being*.
2. Wordsworth, "Tintern Abbey," *Lyrical Ballads*.
3. Joyce, *Ulysses*, 190.
4. For an analysis of the Aristotelian and Nietzschean dimensions of tragedy and poetic justice in Oscar Wilde's novel *The Picture of Dorian Gray*, see Theoharis, "Will to Power, Poetic Justice, and Mimesis," 397-405.
5. For an excellent account of the complex relation in modern Europe of aesthetics and ontology and ethics to the father/son bond, see Rudnytsky, *Freud and Oedipus*.
6. Stevens, "Sunday Morning," *The Collected Poems of Wallace Stevens*, 66-70. In this poem godless feminine appreciation of beauty replaces the theistic paternal and filial defeat of death celebrated on Sunday morning in Christian cultures. Here death is not defeated but converted, in the feminine aesthete's monologue, into "the mother of beauty."
7. James Joyce made much of this connection in *Finnegans Wake*, whose protagonist is, among others, Noah and Nimrod. Characteristically, Joyce pays much more attention to the low comedy of drunkenness and excess than Ibsen, who had little taste for such things in life or art.
8. Aristotle, *Nicomachean Ethics*.
9. For instance, see Jonathan Lear's citation of *Physics* in *Aristotle*, 31-34.
10. Beckett, *Endgame*, 30.
11. For an excellent account of the sexual dimension of self-realization, creativity, and action in *The Master Builder*, see Brustein, "Ibsen," in *Theater of Revolt*, 35-84.
12. Ibsen, *The Master Builder*, in Fjelde, *Henrik Ibsen* 855.
13. For the complexities that make decadence and nihilism potentially progressive forces in Nietzsche's thinking see Calinescu, *Five Faces of Modernity*, esp. the section entitled "The Idea of Decadence," 178-95, and Deleuze, *Nietzsche and Philosophy*, esp. chap. 5: "The Overman: Against the Dialectic," 147-48, 171-95.
14. Edification remained an important action on the stage well into the twentieth century, in the United States as well as in Europe. The connections between civilization, appetitive decorum, male brutality, and feminine

refinement never lost their appeal for Shaw, for instance, who reconfigured them in *Candida* (1895), *Pygmalion* (1913), *Heartbreak House* (1917), *Caesar and Cleopatra* (1898), *Saint Joan* (1923) and *Man and Superman* (1901-03). Shaw took the idea seriously in all these satiric revisions of it because his culture still did. By mid-century in America, however, the edifying woman had few dramatic advocates. She counts more to Tennessee Williams than to any other twentieth-century dramatist except Shaw, but Williams can only present her as anachronistic, ineffectual, and either innocently or criminally insane. His *The Glass Menagerie* (1945), is an elegiac repudiation of women's edifying power over men, and *A Streetcar Named Desire* (1947), in the figure of Blanche Dubois, stages the edifying woman in full flamboyant decay. Her speech to Stella in the fourth scene of that play, beginning with the line "He acts like an animal," is a programmatic parody of the refined and refining woman (83). Indeed, the whole play presents Blanche's refinement more as sentimental, opportunistic fraud than tragic error, an attitude which makes Blanche's catastrophe the first post-modernist (unstably ironic) catharsis in contemporary theater.

15. For an excellent analysis of the secular defection from divine grounding for conscience see Taylor's *Sources of the Self.* Pt. 3 "The Affirmation of Ordinary Life" (211-285) presents the rise of civic humanism in the early sixteenth through eighteenth centuries; pt. 5, "Subtler Languages," esp. the section entitled "Our Victorian Contemporaries" (393-419), brings the problem into Ibsen's period.

16. For Nietzsche's treatment of "going down," "going under," and "going across" as apocalyptic self-creation see, Nietzsche, "Zarathustra's Prologue," 39-53.

17. For analysis of the paradoxical relation of imminence and immanence in Jesus' heavenly kingdom, the paradoxically alienating disclosure of that kingdom in parables, and the resolution of these paradoxes to be wrought at Jesus' apocalyptic Second Coming, see Grant, *Jesus,* chap. 1: "The Dawning of the Kingdom," 15-24.

18. Nietzsche attacked only that classical Greek logic and ontology preserved from Aristotle and Plato, the thinking that gave rise to scientific and humanistic rationalism in Europe. He, of course, admired the logic and ontology and the science of the pre-Socratics, as his short work *Philosophy in the Tragic Age of the Greeks* indicates. Indeed, Heraclitus counted for much in Nietzsche's construction of consciousness as a hypothetical willing of the eternal return of the same, as the study of that work suggests.

19. Ibsen, *Hedda Gabler,* 2:99.

20. Falling unconscious at moments of great stress, especially when the person falling is a wife or mother, is histrionic code in the nineteenth century for

sudden death. The code has a long stage life, at least as old in origin as Shakespeare's theater, in which one victim is an ancient father, Lear.

21. Strindberg's career abounds with paranoid presentations of women as man-killers. The most famous is *The Father* (1887) to which, in many ways, Ibsen's *The Master Builder* is a corrective response. For an intelligent account of the Freudian dimension of Solness's climb, again, see Brustein's chapter on Ibsen in *Theatre of Revolt*.

22. Yeats, "Byzantium," in *Collected Poems of W.B. Yeats*, 243. For an excellent account of Yeats's response to Nietzsche, see Oppel, *Mask and Tragedy*. There is an especially useful study of the reception of Nietzsche in France and England at the end of the century in her second chapter, "The Spirit of His Time" (17-27).

Afterword

1. In *Modern Drama* Raymond Williams gives the best account of tragic presentations of this double bind. He identifies the problem as a social and historical consequence of liberalism. Classical tragedy presented mutability as an impersonal force of ruin, in Williams's view; modern tragedy presents an agent's strength as the source of his defeat. His book is a masterful work of intellectual, social, and literary history, and his reading of Ibsen in "From Hero to Victim" establishes the standard by which all others should be measured (96-103). Although I have argued that in *The Master Builder* Ibsen moved past the strictures Williams sees at work in liberal tragedy, I think Williams's attention to those strictures is very insightful, appropriate, and compelling.

2. Bennett Simon's study *Tragic Drama and the Family* is an excellent psychoanalytic approach to the recurrent pattern of interfamilial murder in tragedy. Although he only mentions *The Wild Duck* and *The Master Builder*, Simon's thesis—that tragedy is as much about parents killing children as children killing parents—could very profitably be applied to *Ghosts*, *Hedda Gabler*, *Little Eyolf*, and, with some adjustment, *Rosmersholm*.

3. For an excellent account of the modern epistemological, psychological, and cultural fortunes of the idea that dramatic action integrates the self and the world see, Bennett, *Modern Drama and German Classicism*, esp. chap. 8: "Breakthrough in Theory: The Philosophical Background of Modern Drama," 229-81.

Bibliography

Alighieri, Dante. *Inferno*. Translated by Allen Mandlebaum. Berkeley: University of California, 1980.

———. *Purgatorio*. Translated by Allen Mandlebaum. Berkeley: University of California, 1982.

———. *Paradiso*. Translated by Allen Mandlebaum. Berkeley: University of California, 1984.

Aristotle. *Categories. De Anima. Metaphysics. Nicomachean Ethics. On the Heavens. Physics. Poetics. The Complete Works of Aristotle: The Revised Oxford Translation*. Edited by Jonathan Barnes. Bollingen Series 71, no.2. Princeton, N.J.: Princeton University Press, 1984.

———. *The "Poetics" of Aristotle*. Annotated and translated by Stephen Halliwell. Chapel Hill, N.C.: University of North Carolina, 1987.

Barish, Jonas. *The Anti-Theatrical Prejudice*. Berkeley: University of California Press, 1982.

Beckett, Samuel. *Endgame*. New York: Grove Press, 1958.

———. *Waiting for Godot*. New York: Grove Press, 1954.

Behler, Ernst. *Confrontations: Derrida/Heidegger/Nietzsche*. Translated by Steven Taubeneck. Stanford: Stanford University Press, 1991.

Bennett, Benjamin. *Modern Drama and German Classicism*. Ithaca, N.Y.: Cornell University Press, 1979.

Berkowitz, Peter. *Nietzsche: The Ethics of an Immoralist*. Cambridge, MA: Harvard University Press, 1995.

Bigley, Bruce. "Praxis and Stasis in Ibsen's *Bygmester Solness*—Or What Ever Happened to Plot and Character?" *Scandinavian Studies* 50, no. 2 (spring 1978).

Brustein, Robert. *The Theater of Revolt*. Boston: Little, Brown, 1962.

Burke, Kenneth. *A Grammar of Motives*. New York: Prentice-Hall, 1952.

Calinescu, Matei. *Five Faces of Modernity*. Durham, N.C.: Duke University Press, 1987.

Carlson, Marvin. *Theories of the Theatre: A Historical and Critical Survey, from the Greeks to the Present.* Ithaca, N.Y.: Cornell University Press, 1984.

Cave, Terence. *Recognitions: A Study in Poetics.* Oxford: Oxford University Press, 1988.

Chamberlain, John S. *Ibsen: The Open Vision.* London: Athlone Press, 1982.

Charles, David. *Aristotle's Philosophy of Action.* London: Duckworth, 1984.

———. "Aristotle: Ontology and Moral Reasoning." In *Oxford Studies in Ancient Philosophy.* Vol. 4. Edited by Julia Annas. Oxford: Clarendon Press, 1986.

Clarke, Ian. *Edwardian Drama.* London: Faber and Faber, 1989.

Clark, Maudemarie. *Nietzsche on Truth and Philosophy.* New York: Cambridge University Press, 1990.

Croce, Benedetto. "Ibsen." *Benedetto Croce: Essays on Literature and Literary Criticism.* Annotated and translated by M. E. Moss. Albany, N.Y.: State University of New York Press, 1990.

Deleuze, Gilles. *Nietzsche and Philosophy.* Translated by Hugh Tomlinson. New York: Columbia University Press, 1983.

Derrida, Jacques. *Spurs: Nietzsche's Styles.* Translated by Barbara Harlow. Chicago: University of Chicago Press, 1978.

Descartes, René. *Discourse on Method.* Translated by Laurence J. Lafleur. Library of Liberal Arts. New York: Bobbs-Merrill, 1960.

Dickens, Charles. *A Christmas Carol. The Works of Charles Dickens,* Vol. 3. Cleartype ed. New York: Basic Books, 1936.

Down, Brian W. *The Intellectual Background of Ibsen's Plays.* New York: Octagon Books, 1969.

Else, Gerald B. *Plato and Aristotle on Poetry.* Edited by Peter Burian. Chapel Hill, N.C.: University of North Carolina Press, 1986.

Euben, Peter, ed. *Greek Tragedy and Political Theory.* Berkeley: University of California Press, 1986.

Euripides, *The Bacchae.* Translated by C.K. Williams. New York: The Noonday Press, 1990.

Fjelde, Rolfe, trans. *Henrik Ibsen The Complete Major Prose Plays.* New York: New American Library, 1978.

Foster, John Burt, Jr. *Heirs to Dionysus: A Nietzschean Current in Literary Modernism.* Princeton, N.J.: Princeton University Press, 1981.

Freud, Sigmund. *Some Character Types Met With in Psychoanalytic Work. The Standard Edition of the Complete Psychological Works of Sigmund Freud.* Vol. 14. Edited and translated by James Strachey. London: Hogarth Press, 1957.

Goethe, Johann. *Goethe's Faust/Part 1.* Translated by Randall Jarrell. New York: Farrar, Straus and Giroux, 1976.

Graham, Daniel W. "Two Systems in Aristotle." In *Oxford Studies in Ancient Philosophy.* Vol. 3. Edited by Julia Annas. Oxford: Clarendon Press, 1989.

Grant, Michael. *Jesus: An Historian's Review of the Gospels.* New York: Collier Books, 1977.

Halliwell, Stephen. Commentary. *The "Poetics" of Aristotle.* Chapel Hill, N.C.: University of North Carolina Press, 1987.

Harries, Karstin. "The Philosopher at Sea." In *Nietzsche's New Seas.* Edited by Michael Allen Gillespie and Tracy B. Strong. Chicago: University of Chicago Press, 1988.

Hayman, Ronald. *Nietzsche: A Critical Life.* Harmondsworth, U.K.: Penguin Books, 1980.

Heidegger, Martin. *Nietzsche.* Translated by David Farrell Krell, Joan Stambaugh, and Frank A. Capuzzi. San Francisco: Harper and Row, 1979-87.

Heller, Eric. *The Importance of Nietzsche.* Chicago: University of Chicago Press, 1988.

Hunt, Lester H. *Nietzsche and the Origins of Virtue.* London and New York: Routledge, 1991.

Ibsen, Henrik. *An Enemy of the People. The Plays of Ibsen.* Vol. 3. Translated by Michael Meyer. New York: Washington Square Press, 1986.

———. *Ghosts. The Plays of Ibsen.* Vol. 3. Translated by Michael Meyer. New York: Washington Square Press, 1986.

———. *Hedda Gabler. The Plays of Ibsen.* Vol. 2. Translated by Michael Meyer. New York: Washington Square Press, 1986.

———. *The Master Builder. The Plays of Ibsen.* Vol. 3. Translated by Michael Meyer. New York: Washington Square Press, 1986.

———. *Rosmersholm. The Plays of Ibsen.* Vol. 4. Translated by Michael Meyer. New York: Washington Square Press, 1986.

Jacobson, Per Schelde, and Barbara Fass Leavy. *Ibsen's Forsaken Merman: Folklore in the Late Plays.* New York: New York University Press, 1988.

Janz, Paul. "Form-Content Problem in Nietzsche's Conception of Music." Translated by Thomas Henke. In *Nietzsche's New Seas.* Edited by Michael Allen Gillespie and Tracy B. Strong. Chicago: University of Chicago Press, 1988.

Johnston, Brian. *The Ibsen Cycle.* Rev. ed. University Park, PA: University of Pennsylvania Press, 1992.

Jones, John. *On Aristotle and Greek Tragedy.* Stanford: Stanford University Press, 1980.

Joyce, James. *Finnegans Wake.* New York: Penguin Books, 1976.

———. *Ulysses.* New York: Random House, 1961.

Kosman, L. A. "Substance, Being, and *Energeia.*" In *Oxford Studies in Ancient Philosophy.* Vol. 2. Edited by Julia Annas. Oxford: Clarendon Press, 1984.

Lear, Jonathan. *Aristotle: The Desire To Understand.* Cambridge, MA: Cambridge University Press, 1986.

———. *Love and its place in Nature.* New York: Farrar, Straus, and Giroux, 1990.

Lovejoy, Arthur O. *The Great Chain Of Being; A Study In The History of an Idea.* Cambridge, Mass.: Harvard University Press, 1933.

McFarlane, James., ed. and trans. *The Oxford Ibsen.* Oxford: Oxford University Press, 1960-77.

———, ed. *The Cambridge Guide to Ibsen.* Cambridge: Cambridge University Press, 1994.

Magnus, Bernd. "The Uses and Abuses of *The Will to Power.*" In *Reading Nietzsche.* Edited by Robert C. Solomon and Kathleen M. Higgins. New York: Oxford University Press, 1988.

May, Keith R. *Nietzsche and Modern Literature.* New York: St. Martin's Press, 1988.

Meisel, Martin. *Shaw and the Nineteenth Century Theater.* New York: Limelight Editions, 1984.

Meyer, Michael. *Ibsen.* Harmondsworth, U.K.: Penguin Books, 1985.

Nehamas, Alexander. *Nietzsche: Life As Literature.* Cambridge, MA: Harvard University Press, 1985.

———. "Who Are 'The Philosophers of the Future?' A Reading of *Beyond Good and Evil.*" In *Reading Nietzsche.* Edited by Robert C. Solomon and Kathleen M. Higgins. New York: Oxford University Press, 1988.

Nietzsche, Friedrich. *Beyond Good and Evil.* Translated by R. J. Hollingdale. Harmondsworth, U.K.: Penguin, 1973.

———. *The Birth of Tragedy.* Translated by Walter Kaufmann. New York: Vintage Books, 1967.

———. *Ecce Homo.* Translated by R. J. Hollingdale. Harmondsworth, U.K.: Penguin, 1979.

———. *The Gay Science.* Translated by Walter Kaufmann. New York: Vintage Books, 1974.

———. *Thus Spoke Zarathustra.* Translated by R. J. Hollingdale. Harmondsworth, U.K.: Penguin, 1969.

———. *Twilight of the Idols and The Anti-Christ.* Translated by R. J. Hollingdale. Harmondsworth, U.K.: Penguin, 1968.

———. *The Will to Power.* Edited and translated by Walter Kaufmann. New York: Vintage Books, 1968.

Nussbaum, Martha. *The Fragility of Goodness: Luck and Ethics in Greek Tragedy and Philosophy.* New York: Cambridge University Press, 1986.

Oppel, Frances Nesbitt. *Mask and Tragedy: Yeats And Nietzsche 1902-10.* Charlottesville, VA: University of Virginia Press, 1987.

Plato. *Ion. Parmenides. Phaedo. Phaedrus. Philebus. Republic. Sophist. Symposium. Theatetus. The Collected Dialogues of Plato.* Edited by Edith Hamilton and Huntington Cairns. Bollingen Series 71. New York: Pantheon Books, 1966.

Pound, Ezra. *Personae.* New York: New Directions, 1926.

Rorty, Amelie. *Essays on Aristotle's Poetics*. Princeton, N.J.: Princeton University Press, 1992.

Rudnytsky, Peter L. *Freud and Oedipus*. New York: Columbia University Press, 1987.

Sallis, John. *Crossings: Nietzsche and the Space of Tragedy*. Chicago: University of Chicago Press, 1991.

Schact, Richard. *Nietzsche*. London: Routledge and Kegan Paul, 1983.

Shakespeare, William. *Hamlet. King Lear. The Tempest. The Complete Works of Shakespeare*. Rev. Ed. Glenview, IL: Scott, Foresman and Co., 1973

Shaw, George Bernard. *The Quintessence of Ibsenism* (1891). *Bernard Shaw: Major Critical Essays*. Harmondsworth, U.K.: Penguin Books, 1986 .

———. *Caesar and Cleopatra*. London: Penguin Books, 1957.

———. *Candida*. London: Penguin Books, 1952.

———. *Heartbreak House*. London: Penguin Books, 1957.

———. *Man and Superman*. London: Penguin Books, 1957.

———. *Pygmalion*. London: Penguin Books, 1957.

———. *St. Joan*. London: Penguin Books, 1957.

Shelley, Percy Bysshe. *A Defense of Poetry. Critical Theory Since Plato*. Edited by Hazard Adams. New York: Harcourt Brace Jovanovich, 1971.

Silk, M. S., and J. P. Stern. *Nietzsche on Tragedy*. Cambridge, MA: Cambridge University Press, 1981.

Simon, Bennett, M.D. *Tragic Drama and the Family: Psychoanalytic Studies from Aeschylus to Beckett*. New Haven, CT: Yale University Press, 1988.

Stambaugh, Joan. *Nietzsche's Thought of Eternal Return*. Lanham: University Press of America, 1988.

Stanford, W. B. *Greek Tragedy and the Emotions*. London: Routledge and Kegan Paul, 1983.

Stevens, Wallace. *The Collected Poems of Wallace Stevens*. New York: Vintage Books, 1982.

Strindberg, August. *The Father* (1887). *Six Plays of Strindberg*. Translated by Elizabeth Sprigge. Garden City, N.J.: Doubleday, 1955.

Strong, Tracy B. *Friedrich Nietzsche and the Politics of Transfiguration*. Expanded ed. Berkeley: University of California Press, 1985.

Taylor, Charles. *Sources of the Self*. Cambridge, MA: Harvard University Press, 1989.

Taylor, Mark C., ed. *Deconstruction in Context: Literature and Philosophy*. Chicago: University of Chicago Press, 1986.

Templeton, Joan. "The Doll House Backlash: Criticism, Feminism, and Ibsen." *PMLA* (January 1989).

Theoharis, Theoharis Constantine. *Joyce's Ulysses: An Anatomy of the Soul*. Chapel Hill, N.C.: University of North Carolina Press, 1988.

————. "Will to Power, Poetic Justice, and Mimesis in *The Picture Of Dorian Gray*." In *Rediscovering Oscar Wilde*. Edited by C. George Sandulescu. Gerrards Cross, U.K.: Colin Smythe, 1994.

Valency, Maurice. *The Flower and the Castle: An Introduction to Modern Drama*. New York: Schocken Books, 1963.

Williams, Raymond. *Drama from Ibsen to Brecht*. London: Hogarth Press, 1987.

————. *Modern Tragedy*. Stanford, CA: Stanford University Press, 1966.

Williams, Tennessee. *A Streetcar Named Desire*. New York: New Directions, 1947.

Wordsworth, William. *Wordsworth and Coleridge: Lyrical Ballads*. Sec. ed. Edited by W. J. B. Owen. Oxford: Oxford University Press, 1969.

Yeats, W. B. *The Collected Poems of W. B. Yeats*. New York: Macmillan, 1970.

Index

Aeschylus, 243
    The Oresteia, 76, 296n
Alighieri, Dante, 218, 235
    Commedia, 166
Aristotle
    catharsis, 21-23, 277-280
    compared to Nietzsche on tragedy,
        35-8, 53-7, 72-3, 91-2
    Categories, 288n
    De Anima, 289n
    Metaphysics, 9, 12, 17, 289n
    Nicomachean Ethics, 17-18, 288n, 298n
    Physics, 298n
    Poetics, 1-2, 12, 13, 14-27, 251, 278,
        283, 289n
    Rhetoric, 289n
Arnold, Matthew, 212
Aquinas, Thomas, 62, 63

Bacchantes, 272-74, 281
Beckett, Samuel, 38, 66
    Endgame, 251
    Waiting for Godot, 96, 176, 212, 281
Behler, Ernst, *Confrontations*, 290n
Bennet, Benjamin, *Modern Drama and
    German Classicism*, 300n
Berkeley, Bishop, 41, 42
Berkowitz, Peter, *Nietzsche: The Ethics of an
    Immoralist*, 293n
Bible
    Abraham, 247
    Abraham and Isaac, 75-7
    Amos, 168

Cain, 247
Isaiah, 168
Moses, 48, 168
Noah, 249
Tower of Babel, 247-9
OLD TESTAMENT
Genesis, 252
Psalms, 165
Song of Songs, 165
NEW TESTAMENT, 95
Gospels, 49
Matthew, 121, 165, 168, 169, 170,
    200, 254
Mark, 166, 169, 170
Luke, 165, 166, 168, 169, 175, 22,
    232
John, 49, 124, 165, 166, 168, 169
Romans, vii
Corinthians 2, 208
Hebrews, 268
Biely, Alexander, Nietzsche and Ibsen
    compared on new consciousness and
    absolute values, 287n
Bigley, Bruce, on *The Master Builder*, 296n
Bizet, Georges, *Carmen*, 35
Brustein, Robert, *The Theater of Revolt*,
    298n, 300n
Burke, Kenneth, *A Grammar of Motives*, 289n
Byron, George Gordon, Lord, 68, 296n
Bywater, Ian, 19

Calinescu, Mattei, *Five Faces of Decadence*,
    298n

Carlson, Marvin, *Theories of the Theatre*, 287n
Cave, Terence, *Recognitions*, 24
Cerf, Bennet, creation of the "Modern
     Library" imprint, 70
Chamberlain, John S., *Ibsen: The Open
     Vision*, 296n
Charles, David, on Aristotle, moral
     reasoning, and ontology, 289n
Chekhov, Anton, 38, 281
Clark, Ian, *Edwardian Drama*, 297n
Clark, Maudmarie, *Nietzsche on Truth and
     Philosophy*, 291n
Coleridge, Samuel Taylor, 68
     "Dejection, An Ode," 296n
     "The rime of the Ancient Mariner,"
          296n
Croce, Benedetto, "Ibsen," 71, 296n

Darwin, Charles, 52
Deleuze, Gilles, *Nietzsche and Philosophy*,
     291, 298n
Derrida, Jacques, *Spurs*, 290n, 293n
Descartes, Rene, 63-66
     Discourse on Method, 63, 296n
     Meditations, 63
Dickens, Charles, *A Christmas Carol*, 118
Down, Brian, *The Intellectual Background of
     Ibsen's Plays*, 296n

Eastern Orthodoxy, 62, 63
Euripides, *The Bacchae*, 271-72

feminism, 113
     Nietzsche on Ibsen's, 292n
Fjelde, Rolfe, *Ibsen*, 117, 122, 257, 295n
Foster, John Burt, Jr., *Heirs to Dionysus*,
     287n
Foucault, Michel, 293n, 294n
Franklin, Benjamin, 66
Freud, Sigmund, 52, 82, 106, 137, 274
     on *Rosmersholm* in *Some Character Types
          Met With in Psychoanalysis*, 297n
     "Those Wrecked by Success," 297n

Goethe, Johann Wolfgang van
     Faust, 95, 112, 123, 164, 282

compared to Christ, 171-2, 175-6
compared to *The Tempest*, 226-27
Graham, Daniel, "Two Systems in Aris-
     totle," 288n
Grant, Michael, *Jesus*, 299n

Halliwell, Stephen, *Aristotle's Poetics*, 18,
     218
Handel, George Friedrich, *The Messiah*, 180
Harries, Karstin, "The Philosopher at
     Sea," 293n
Hayman, Ronald, *Nietzsche*, 290n
Hegel, Georg Wilhelm Friedrich, 52,
     291n, 295n, 298n
Heidegger, Martin, *Nietzsche*, 290n, 293n
Heraclitus, 299n
Hesiod, *Theogony*, 187n
Homer, 1
     Odysseus, 24
Hume, David, 291n
Hunt, Lester, *Nietzsche and the Origins of
     Virtue*, 293n

Ibsen, Henrik
     Brand, vii, 59, 96, 174, 280
     A Doll House, 70, 93
     The Emperor and the Galilean, 59
     An Enemy of the People, 70, 74, 93, 167
     Ghosts, 39, 53, 55, 60, 70, 71, 72, 92,
          93, 96, 227, 230, 237, 273,
          283, 300n
     Hedda Gabler, 72, 75, 95, 272-74, 300n
     John Gabriel Borkman, 72, 74
     The Lady from the Sea, 70, 71
     Little Eyolf, 72, 300n
     The Master Builder, 39, 53, 55, 60, 70,
          72, 92, 286
     Peer Gynt, 59, 96, 127
     Pillars of Society, 60, 70, 93
     Rosmersholm, 39, 53, 55, 60, 70, 72,
          92, 167, 227, 237, 250, 273,
          283, 300n
     When We Dead Awaken, 60, 72, 222
     The Wild Duck, 71, 74, 193-94, 121-2,
          300n

Jacobsen, Per Schelde and Leavy, Barbara Fass, *Ibsen's Forsaken Mermen*, 296n, 297n

Janz, Paul, "Form-Content Problem in Nietzsche's Conception of Music," 292n

Jefferson, Thomas, 66

Jesus, 48, 49, 52, 56, 121, 123-4, 131, 164, 165, 166-70, 178, 200, 228, 232-3, 236, 243, 247, 254, 268
  and *Faust* compared, 171-72, 175-76
  and Nietzsche compared, 174-4, 205, 255-6

Johnston, Brian, *The Ibsen Cycle*, 295n, 296n, 298n

Joyce, James
  Finnegans Wake, 298n
  Ulysses, 229, 235

Judaism, 165, 170

Kant, Immanuel, 66, 291n

Kierkegaard, Soren, *Fear and Trembling*, 76, 296n

Kossman, L.A., "Substance, Being, and Energeia," 288n

Lear, Jonathan, *Aristotle: The Desire to Understand*, 288n, 298n

Lovejoy, Arthur, *The Great Chain of Being*, 298n

Luther, Martin, 30, 62, 63

Lutheranism, 276-7

Maenads, 272-4, 277, 280

Magnus, Bernd, 293n

Marx, Karl, 52

Meisel, Martin, *Shaw and the Nineteenth Century Theater*, 297n

Mencken, H.L., and Ibsen as social critic, 69-70

Meyer, Michael, *Ibsen*, 257, 292n, 296n

Nehamas, Alexander, *Nietzsche: Life as Literature*, 31-2, 290n, 291n, 294-5n, 302n

Neoplatonism, 62

Nietzsche, Friedrich
  compared to Aristotle on tragedy, 35-8, 53-7, 72-3, 91-2
  compared to Jesus, 173, 174, 205
  compared to Jesus and *Faust*, 255-6
  The Anti-Christ, 29
  Beyond Good and Evil, vii, 29, 31, 40-6, 290n
  The Birth of Tragedy, 36-7, 53-5
  Ecce Homo, 292n, 295n
  The Gay Science, 29, 33, 35, 36, 50, 294n, 295n
  The Genealogy of Morals, 29
  Philosophy in the Tragic Age of the Greeks, 299n
  Twilight of the Idols, 29, 34, 36
  The Will to Power, 46-50, 54, 293n, 294n, 295n
  Thus Spoke Zarathustra, 30, 32, 34, 36, 37, 50-1, 283-85, 295n

Nussbaum, Martha, *The Fragility of Goodness*, 287n, 289n

O'Neill, Eugene, 38, 66
  The Iceman Cometh, 99, 125, 212

Oppel, Frances Nesbitt, *Mask and Tragedy*, 300n

Pinter, Harold, 212

Pirandello, Luigi, 38

Plato, 1-5, 9, 13, 291n
  Cratylus, 288n
  Ion, 288n
  Gorgias, 289n
  Meno, 288n
  Parmenides, 288n
  Phaedo, 287n, 288n, 289n
  Phaedrus, 288n
  Philebus, 288n
  Politicus, 288n
  Protagoras, 289n
  Republic, 288n, 289n
  Sophist, 288n
  Symposium, 288n
  Theatetus, 288n

Poetic justice, 230-2, 271, 274, 277, 279, 298n

Pope, Alexander, 66
Pound, Ezra, 70
   "Cantica Del Sole," 296n
Prometheus, 247, 281
Puccini, Giacomo, *La Bohème*, 7

Racine, Jean, 235, 240
   Phaedra, 270
Roman comedy, 138
Rudnytsky, Peter, *Freud and Oedipus*, 298n

Schact, Richard, *Nietzsche*, 291n, 293n
Schopenhauer, Arthur, 41, 42
Shakespeare, William, 26, 176, 240, 295n
   and Ibsen compared, 72-3
   Hamlet, 24, 26, 73, 266, 274, 285-6
   King Lear, 24, 300n
   Macbeth, 23
   The Tempest, 135-6, 281
   and *The Master Builder* compared, 186-8
   and *The Master Builder* and *Faust* compared, 226-7
Shaw, George Bernard, 38, 69
   Candida, 299n
   Caesar and Cleopatra, 299n
   Heartbreak House, 299n
   Man and Superman, 299n
   Pygmalion, 99, 281, 299n
   Saint Joan, 299n
   "The Quintessence of Ibsenism," 69, 292n
Shelley, Percy Bysshe, "A Defense of Poesy," 69, 296n
Silk, M.S., and Stern, J.P., *Nietzsche on Tragedy*, 292n
Simon, Bennet, *Tragic Drama and the Family*, 300n
Socrates, 37
Sophocles, 39, 74, 235, 240, 295n
   Oedipus Rex, 76, 187
Stambaugh, Joan, *Nietzsche's Thought of Eternal Return*, 295n
Stanford, W.B., *Greek Tragedy and the Emotions*, 289n
Stevens, Wallace, "Sunday Morning," 235, 298n
Strindberg, August, 274
   The Father, 279, 297n, 300n
Strong, Tracey B., *Friedrich Nietzsche*, 40, 290n, 291n

Taylor, Charles, *Sources of the Self*, 297n, 299n
Taylor, Mark C., *Deconstruction in Context*, 298n
Templeton, Joan, "The Doll House Backlash," 70
Tennyson, Alfred Lord, "Tithonus," 212
Theoharis, Theoharis C., "Will to Power, Poetic Justice, and Mimesis in *The Picture of Dorian Gray*," 288n

Valency, Maurice, *The Flower and the Castle*, 296n
Verdi, Giuseppi, *Aida*, 214
Virgil, 166
Voltaire, François Marie Arouet De, 66

Wagner, Richard, 35, 115
Wilde, Oscar, *The Picture of Dorian Gray*, 230
Williams, Raymond, *Drama from Ibsen to Brecht*, 289n
Williams, Tennessee
   A Streetcar Named Desire, *The Glass Menagerie*, 299n
   tragic heroine and feminine edification of men, 299n

Wordsworth, William, 66, 227, 296n

Yeats, W.B., 99, 212
   "Byzantium," 277, 300n